SCARS OF PARTITION

SCARS OF PARTITION

POSTCOLONIAL LEGACIES IN FRENCH AND BRITISH BORDERLANDS

WILLIAM F. S. MILES

University of Nebraska Press
Lincoln & London

© 2014 by the Board of Regents of the University of Nebraska

All rights reserved

Manufactured in the United States of America

Library of Congress Cataloging-in-Publication Data

Miles, William F. S.
Scars of Partition: Postcolonial Legacies in French and British Borderlands /
William F. S. Miles.
pages cm
Includes bibliographical references and index.
ISBN 978-0-8032-4832-8 (pbk: alk. paper)
ISBN 978-0-8032-6772-5 (ePub)
ISBN 978-0-8032-6773-2 (mobi)
ISBN 978-0-8032-6771-8 (pdf)
1. Postcolonialism—English-speaking countries. 2. Postcolonialism—French-speaking countries. 3. Partition, Territorial. 4. Developing countries—Colonial influence. 5. Decolonization—Great Britain—Colonies—History—20th century. 6. Decolonization—France—Colonies—History—20th century. I. Title.
JV151.M48 2014
325'.341—dc23
2013050471

Set in Sabon by Renni Johnson.

To Dr. Andycook (*sic*),
faithful friend and correspondent over time, over boundaries,
and despite my "Wayward" ways

CONTENTS

List of Illustrations | ix
List of Tables | xi
Preface and Acknowledgments | xiii

1. Anglo-French Partition and Postcolonialism | 1
2. Classical Colonial Partition: West Africa | 21
3. Partition by Island: West Indies | 75
4. Political Arbitrariness of Archipelagoes: The South Pacific | 134
5. Soft, Sequential, and Hybridic Colonialism: French India and the Indian Ocean | 188
6. Mainland Southeast Asia and the Conundrum of Communism | 240
7. Scars of Partition in Postcolonial Borderlands and Beyond | 290

Notes | 309
Bibliography | 327
Index | 353

ILLUSTRATIONS

Figures
1. Democracy and Partition in Former Colonies | 7
2. French West Africa—Popular View | 24
3. Hausaland Boundary Marker | 32
4. New Hausaland Boundary Marker | 61
5. Nigerian Border Station | 62
6. Mauritius Francophone Commemorative Stamps | 219
7. Mekong Boundary Marker | 263

Maps
Former French and British Colonies—World | xviii
1. An Inherited Colonial Partition | 22
2. French West Africa | 23
3. Neighboring Anglophone and Francophone West African States | 26
4. Precolonial Hausa-Fulani and Adjoining Polities | 34
5. Partitioned Ethnicities of Niger-Nigeria Borderlands | 35
6. Hausaland Divided | 45
7. Local Governments of Niger-Nigeria Borderlands | 49
8. Anglophone and Francophone West Indies | 77
9. French West Indies and Anglophone Neighbors | 79
10. Vanuatu and Lesser Antilles | 135
11. Anglophone and Francophone South Pacific | 136
12. Southern Melanesia | 139

13. Indian Ocean Polities | 190
14. Mascarene Islands | 193
15. Former French India | 232
16. Pondicherry Region | 233
17. Former French and British Colonies of Southeast Asia | 241
18. Precolonial Mekong Polities | 255
19. Golden Triangle—Mekong as Lao-Burmese Borderland | 261
20. Partitioned Ethnicities of Lao-Burmese Borderlands | 273

TABLES

1. Partitioned West African Ethnic Groups | 27
2. Material Outcomes—West Africa | 47
3. Material Outcomes—West Indies | 103
4. Material Outcomes—South Pacific | 183
5. Primary Home Language in Mauritius | 205
6. Material Outcomes—Indian Ocean | 211
7. Material Outcomes—Former French India | 235
8. Material Outcomes—Southeast Asia | 243
9. Cross-Regional Typology | 294

PREFACE AND ACKNOWLEDGMENTS

"Who are we? Where do we come from? Where are we going?"
—Paul Gaughin

Who are we? Several years after commencing my career-long comparison of indigenous peoples previously partitioned into French and British colonies, a psychologically astute colleague-friend made me realize that, at heart, my subject matter was *identity*. Now, identity is a topic that transcends several intellectual disciplines and paradigms. It is also a very personal matter—which is why I had ostensibly camouflaged my personal quest for it by conducting fieldwork in remote locales and among exotic peoples throughout the developing world. And I did so as a political scientist! That tension between scholarly research agenda and subconscious preoccupation was ultimately resolved (at least on paper) with the publication of my *Zion in the Desert*, a study of American Jewish baby boomers who, in the 1970s and 1980s, opted to become Israeli *kibbutzniks* in the Negev Desert.

But every one of us has reason to ponder the randomness of being bequeathed a particular society, culture, and nation. Relatively few on this planet enjoy the luck of acquiring at birth the nationality and support system of a developed, high-income nation. That existential puzzle has nagged at me ever since a two-year Peace Corps stint revealed both the unmerited luck of having been born citizen of a "developed country" and the corresponding (and humbling) dignity, solidarity, and tenacity of the impoverished majority otherwise allotted the "third world." For allowing me to share those reflections *in extenso*, in *My African Horse Problem*, I acknowledge University of Massachusetts Press editor Bruce Wilcox.

Three questions undergird the present book: (1) How did discrete indigenous groups (e.g., Melanesian, Hausa, Tamil, Lao), respond, subvert, and adjust to the respective British and French colonial projects superimposed onto their society and culture? (2) In what ways (political, linguistic, economic) have their emergent postcolonial states differed as a consequence of their previous colonial imprints? (3) To what extent are contemporary world processes, particularly globalization and development, mediated on the national level by institutional and cultural patterns established during the colonial and early postcolonial eras?

To address these questions, I have conducted grassroots research in all regions of the world that have experienced the close-quartered impact of Anglo vs. French colonialism: West Africa, the West Indies, South and Southeast Asia, the South Pacific, the Indian Ocean, and the Middle East. In the Middle East—where colonial/mandate Anglo-French borders were those of Iraq and Jordan with Syria, and between Palestine and Lebanon—my firsthand research into colonial legacies has been restricted to Palestinian and Israeli Francophones (Miles 1995b; Miles and Sheffer 1998). Since that research is not methodologically comparable to the other cases, I do not include it in this book.

For all but one of the cases that I do present here, following local language training I spent a minimum of seven months in the field. While my level of fluency has never been the same across all the relevant languages, in the process I have become quite comfortable in French, Hausa, and Bislama, and passably conversational in Creole/Kreol, Hebrew, and (at the time) Tamil. Although my first officially sponsored research began in 1982 in Martinique, my appetite for fieldwork was whetted by a 1976 undergraduate foray to rural Québec under the supervision of Vassar College geography professor Harvey Flad, and as assistant to the late anthropologist Horace Miner, to northern Nigeria in 1980. My two years (1977–79) as a Peace Corps volunteer in a town in Niger near the border with Nigeria were also formative in honing a sensitivity to postcolonial Francophone-Anglophone differences. However one dates my status as a grassroots researcher into Anglo-French postcolonialism, it now spans over a quarter of a century.

For fear of undue academic scrutiny, I hesitate to reveal which one of the chapters is based on fieldwork falling below my standard threshold of at least half a year in the field and reasonable familiarity with the local language. But the truth is that I know only a few words of Burmese and Lao and that my three research trips to Myanmar and Laos were each of only a few weeks' duration. (A previous visit to Thailand had brought me—thanks to Kwanchewan and Witoon Buadaeng—to the border with Burma.) Accordingly, except for the few Francophones I located in Laos, in Southeast Asia I depended heavily on translators. In instances where I interviewed hill peoples who did not know their country's official language, I had to work through double layers of translation. The ensuing loss in direct access to informants was frustrating. I trust that the excellent secondary sources upon which I draw for that chapter compensate in some measure for my regional and linguistic lack of expertise there. Two of the foremost experts on Myanmar and Laos, Professor David Steinberg and Dr. Martin Stuart-Fox, respectively, graciously agreed to make improvements on my draft chapter.

I owe debts to numerous other scholars. Colleague-*landsmen* who have encouraged me in my cross-regional research include Professors Bob Charlick, Larry Diamond, Michael Horowitz, and Lenny Markovitz; Leo Villalón keeps me on my Francophone Africanist toes. Professor Tony Asiwaju of the University of Lagos has kept me anchored to the borderline perspective throughout my comparative research; Professor John Paden has kept me grounded in Nigeria throughout my supra-African peregrinations. So has Dr. Binta Audu. The "psychologically astute colleague-friend" to whom I referred earlier is David Rochefort. It was Dr. Larry Diamond, above all, who most explicitly put it to me, during a beach walk in Mauritius in 1997, that I ought to begin integrating all my separate fieldwork cases into a synthetic whole. I resisted—for about a decade. Along the way I benefited from continuous intellectual exchange, encouragement, and hospitality from former diplomat Jeffrey Liteman and Dr. Andy Cook. Professor Philip Boucher, former president of the French Colonial Historical Society, directed me to the University of Nebraska Press on account of its long-standing high-quality scholarly imprints on France's former colonies.

Various institutions have made this work possible. For travel funding, but more important, the precious grant of time off for research, I thank Northeastern University. Based at Northeastern is Terry Beadle, illustrator and map maker for this book, whose professional expertise, commitment, and camaraderie have been a boon to my entire career as scholar, author, and lecturer. Students Elvira Josifi and Heather Peltier applied themselves to rooting out bibliographic oversights in the manuscript. For the initial gift of two years in an African borderland community, I thank the Peace Corps. The Shell International Studies Research program, the Fletcher School of Law and Diplomacy, the American Institute of Indian Studies, the American Philosophical Society, the Fulbright Program, the National Endowment of the Humanities, the French Government Teaching Assistantship program, and the Ministry of International Relations and Francophonie of the Government of Québec have all provided much-appreciated grants and fellowships. Collegial and intellectual reinforcement of the value of borderlands studies has come from fellow members (and especially "chiefs") of ABORNE, the African Borderlands Research Network. To round off the fieldwork and kick-start the writing, I needed the encouragement and opportunity provided by the Earhart Foundation, whose patience and support I acknowledge with much gratitude; thanks in particular go to Earhart Fellow Research Grant director Montgomery Brown. Without Earhart, there would be no book here.

Neither would there have been this book without the interest of the University of Nebraska Press and its anonymous reviewers, who with invaluable suggestions for improvement, endorsed it. Editors Bridget Barry and Lona Dearmont worked tirelessly to improve the flow and prose of the manuscript: the remaining deficiencies remain mine alone.

In the course of my career's research, many a Frenchman has inquired into my attraction to *la Francophonie*, French colonialism, overseas France. My fascination with former French colonies has been a subconscious foil, perhaps, for my own country, culture, and history. After all, I tell my students, comparative social science enables us to better see our own society and nation for what they are. "Does America not have its own history of colonialism? Is the United States not an imperial power today?" These challenges, put to me by (otherwise friendly) Frenchmen allergic to my incessant probing of their collective colonial heritage, have forced me to confront issues otherwise too close for comfort. "Comparing empires," as Jonathan Hart (2003) puts it, "is at the same time an exercise in situating our own collective selves in imperial history."

One French national in particular has been an indispensable spur to my lifelong quest for colonial and postcolonial knowledge. Martinican by birth, ultimately American by choice, Loïza Nellec-Miles brought to our foyer prenuptial memories of colonial and postcolonial life in Niger, Senegal, French Guiana, and Tahiti. The fruit of this love, Arielle Pooshpam and Samuel Benjamin, have already, through their own journeys, begun to enrich my understanding of the world. They, too, are part of the intriguing, unpredictable, and never-ending postcolonial story.

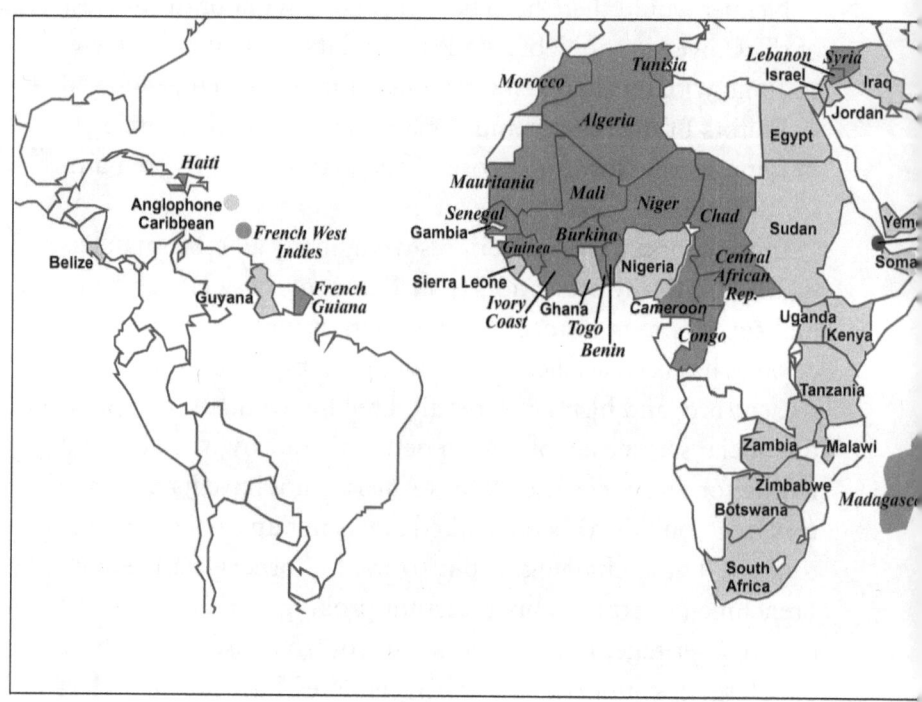

Former French and British Colonies—World

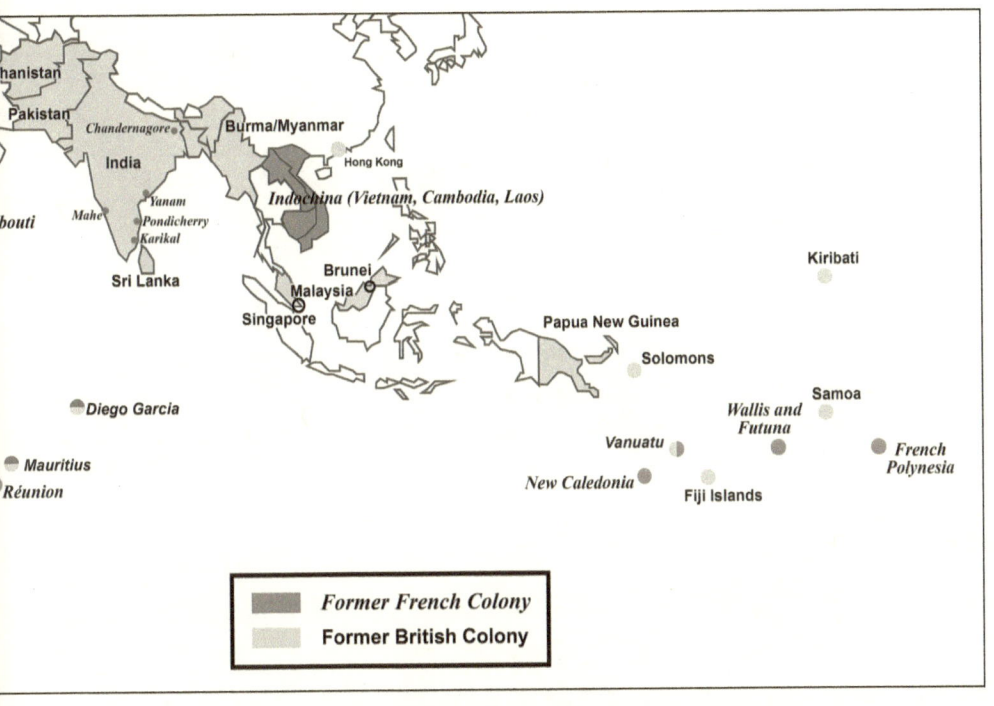

1
Anglo-French Partition and Postcolonialism

[D]ecolonization is a harlot of a word. It pleases so many needs that readers can never be sure of its real meaning.
—Karl Hack, "Theories and Approaches to British Decolonization in Southeast Asia"

There are many related words invoked in scholarly settings that, following Hack, are easily prostituted: colonialism, exploitation, superpower, discourse, narrative. How neutral, how "objective" (itself a seductive concept), can one be in describing the operation and aftermath of conquest and overrule? For sure, ideological dispositions can color one's use of such terms. But dueling meanings, I believe, stem less from bad faith than from academic discipline.

Postcolonial is the terminological bugaboo for this book. As a political scientist who borrows inordinately from history, geography, and anthropology, I use the word "merely" to describe the social and political processes following the sovereignty exercised by European powers (here, British and French) over their African, Asian, Latin American, and Oceanic colonies, protectorates, and territories. In this sense, *postcolonialism* is intimately related to *decolonization* (Hack's semantic floozy).

This comparative inquiry into the long-term implications of French vis-à-vis British colonialism and decolonization, then, is primarily about identity—that of a large swath of humanity who, through no choice of their own, find themselves in territories recently under the dominion of France and Britain, the two major superpowers from the seventeenth until the mid-twentieth centuries. These colonial powers, moreover, with little regard for the peoples soon to be under their dominion, apportioned them to French or British tutelage. What difference, in the long run, has that arbitrary apportionment made?

What deep institutional legacies (regarding governance, development, education, language policy, and religion) did French vis-à-vis British colonialism leave behind? What postcolonial commonalties link former French territories, and British ones, throughout the developing world? What accounts for the dissimilarities that have arisen? At what junctures has culture begun to trump history?

To answer these questions with a pretense of scholarly "value added," I yoke together four usually disparate clusters of literature.[1] The first is history: precolonial and colonial history, accounts of colonial explorers, diplomatic history, social history, histories of French and British imperial rule (and their respective types of administration), history of decolonization. For some of the cases, I had the opportunity to consult colonial archival sources, and with others to undertake oral history of the late colonial era.

Geography is the second cluster of literature that I invoke. Colonial borders are notoriously arbitrary even if close historical inspection uncovers some surprising contemporaneous concessions. Boundaries, those totems of political geography, condition the life prospects of the people born behind them and divided by them. Partition represents political geography at the edges of the state, giving birth to entirely new micro-societies: the borderlands. These political margins crystallize differences. "Borderline" should not be only an epithet (as in "borderline personality," "marginal," or "barely acceptable"), for it can reveal starkly different political realities. Anglo-French carving of colonial space is a significant geographical legacy: nearly

40 percent of the entire length of today's international boundaries were traced by Britain and France (Imbert-Vier 2011, 13, following Foucher 1991). Awareness of "where-ness" is critical to postcolonial understanding.

Thirdly, anthropology facilitates a focus on actual people and cultures. One of the common sins of both colonization and conventional histories of colonialism is reification of the colonized, including partitioned, peoples. For sure, great anticolonial literature has emerged from such authors as Frantz Fanon, Albert Memmi, and Aimé Césaire, to cite but a few. But only anthropology investigates ordinary life for otherwise unheralded ethnic people and peoples, both during colonialism and after. My forays into and borrowings from anthropology logically focus on those indigenous peoples most directly affected, in the long-term, by colonial partition. By zooming in on otherwise identical cultures that experienced French versus British colonialism, we can better discern the overarching effects of these two different systems on otherwise unrelated peoples. And we should gain a better appreciation of the import of this book's theme upon "real people," not just the erudite intellectuals whose writings are more widely known. I trust that whatever holes in my arguments professional historians of decolonization may feel compelled to poke are compensated for by a borderland sensitivity that conveys the contemporary perspectives of otherwise overlooked partitioned peoples.

As Emmanuel Brunet-Jailly (2005, 653) aptly observes, "each social science subfield has its own epistemology of borders." The literature and methodology of these other disciplines may be somewhat remote to students of political science. But that is indeed my home discipline, ensuring that I retain an overarching concern for the political implications (local, national, international) of my findings. While acknowledging my debts to history, geography, and anthropology, this is a career-spanning exercise, above all, in comparative politics. Through the prism of the borderlands, it refracts foundational precepts of the discipline so vividly expressed by fellow political scientist Crawford Young, as he reflects on "territorial integrity and border sanctity": "[T]he elixir of sovereignty hardened the map lines of the colonial partition into a permanent array of containers.... [T]he affirmation of the colonial partition map even sharpened the territorial lines, now an iron grid of sovereign containers" (Young 2012, 90–91, 301). The present work advances a further assertion: *Borderlands do not negate sovereignty so much as they illuminate it.*[2]

By focusing cross-culturally on ethnic groups partitioned by colonialism, this book fashions itself as the first empirically grounded comparative study of the legacies of colonialism from the combined perspectives of political anthropology and political science. It thereby resolves a problem inherent in the literature thus far. To the macro-level surveys of Anglo-French colonialism and decolonization, it advances the role of indigenous cultures in shaping the outcome of colonial policies and their postcolonial aftermaths. To the case studies that focus on ethnicity, it magnifies the scope by a cross-cultural methodology, comparing the overall impact of Anglo-French partitions in six different world regions. In this light such otherwise universal concepts as, for example, Mbembe's "postcolony" (1972) can be examined empirically, using the borderland as illuminating frame.

Why This Book—and Now?

Colonial legacies of the British and French—how archaic this phrase must sound to thinkers glued to the moment, how seemingly removed from the "relevance" of today's pressing political issues! But not to all. In a review for *Foreign Affairs* (2007, 148), Walter Russell Mead acknowledges the ongoing relevance of Anglo-French rivalry: "The interplay between these two societies has done more to shape the geopolitics, economics, and culture of the world today than the relationship between any other two societies on the face of the earth." Four other impressive books strengthen my conviction that I am indeed joining colleagues at the crossroads of critical postcolonial thought.

The first is Crawford Young's most deservedly prizewinning *The African Colonial State in Comparative Perspective* (1994). In reassessing the colonialism of Africa in light of comparable histories elsewhere, Young—who trailblazed such studies with his 1976 classic *Politics of Cultural Pluralism*—makes a strong case for the uniqueness of African postcolonial outcomes.

In a remarkable, far-reaching chapter that foreshadows the aims of the present book, Young compares colonial and postcolonial Africa with North America and Australasia, Latin America and the Caribbean, Micronesia and Korea, Malaysia and Fiji, Asian republics of the former Soviet Union, Indonesia, Indochina, Oceania, India, the Philippines, and the Middle East. From his cross-national colonial comparisons, Professor Young identifies a "singular historical personality" for Africa vis-à-vis these other regions, characterized by a "singularly difficult legacy bequeathed by the institutions of rule devised to establish and maintain alien hegemony." While sensitive to French-British colonial differences, he does not make them his overarching framework. As I intend to demonstrate, a comparative perspective that does use this lens tempers the "singular" nature of Africa in favor of a global analysis that continues to privilege, for explanatory purposes, the legacies of distinct modalities of European colonialism.

My efforts to understand the ways in which indigenous societies and former colonies throughout the developing world continue to reflect their respective colonial antecedents echoes Young's pioneering work. So do my more focused attempts to perceive the distinctive French and British stamps that continue to mark daily life for ordinary people along and behind superimposed boundaries throughout the so-called Third World.

A second signal work in comparative colonialism and decolonization also takes the end of the Soviet Union as its springboard *The End of Empire? The Transformation of the USSR in Comparative Perspective*, edited by Karen Dawisha and Bruce Parrott (1997). Several chapters focus on the British and French experiences as potential previews for what the close of the Soviet era may portend. In it, British and French colonial and postcolonial experiences figure prominently. For example, Michael Fry frames British and French decolonization as a Cold War experience that indirectly pitted the Soviet Union against the United States. Compared with the demise of the Soviet empire, Fry maintains, it unfolded in a premeditated and orderly manner.

In a subsequent, equally important edited volume *Beyond State Crisis? Postcolonial Africa and Post-Soviet Eurasia in Comparative Perspective*, Professor Young teams up with Soviet specialist Mark Beissinger to edit a cutting-edge work that again reassesses the contemporary applications of African colonial history. Shared syndromes—state breakdown and violence, economic collapse, ethnic and gender vulnerability—are identified as rooted in colonial and communist institutional patterns. Although tangential to their overarching thesis, Beissinger and Young also point out another shared legacy that is essential to our approach here: the porousness of boundaries, which reflects both their arbitrary origins and (many) states' inability to exercise meaningful control over them.

A key contribution of Beissinger and Young's volume lies in its cross-regional (as opposed to case-specific) approach. "The issues that grip Africa and post-Soviet Eurasia transcend region; they are global in scope" (Beissinger and Young 2002, 5). In like manner, many of my findings in areas where former French colonies butt up against former British ones (e.g., smuggling, human trafficking) certainly exist elsewhere, and are no less important for it.

William Easterly's critique of Western aid to the developing world, *The White Man's Burden*, might not at first blush seem relevant to a reconsideration of colonialism. Yet Easterly sees a direct relationship between the failures of today's humanitarianism and yesterday's imperialism. "The West sowed . . . mayhem with chaotic decolonization," writes Easterly in his chapter "From Colonialism to Postmodern Imperialism," "especially the arbitrary way the West drew borders." Part of the white man's burden, as he recasts Kipling's formulation, is the economic diffi-

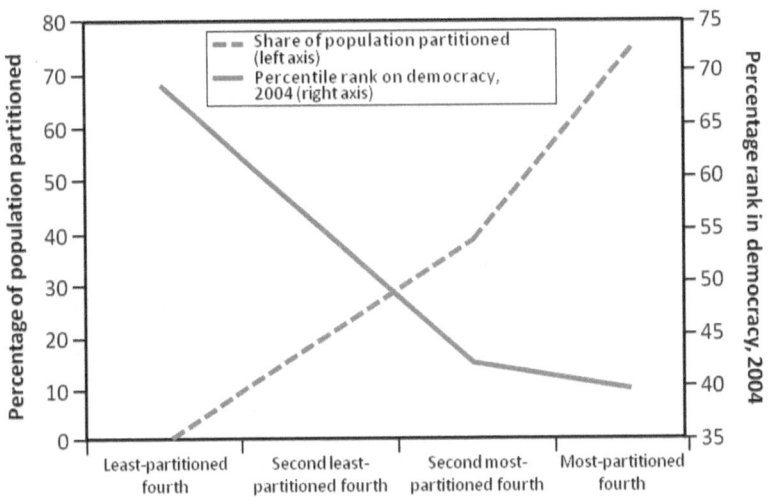

Fig. 1. Democracy and Partition in Former Colonies
From *The White Man's Burden* by William Easterly, copyright
© 2006 by William Easterly.

culty of repairing societies rent asunder by partition, even though "many will deny the relevance of colonial experience to today's allegedly more humanitarian exercises" (Easterly 2006, 272).

Easterly statistically examines the relationship between ethnic partition and economic development. Although he does not distinguish between French and British territories, he finds that globally, former colonies containing significant proportions of partitioned peoples perform relatively poorly in delivery of government services (health and education), transparency, and rule of law.

Taking literally the image of the colonial bureaucrat who, oblivious to ethnic reality on a faraway continent, draws a straight line on a map, Easterly even quantified boundaries according to their linearity or jaggedness. His intriguing finding: "artificially straight borders were statistically associated with less democracy, higher infant mortality, more illiteracy, less childhood immunization, and less access to clean water" (2006, 293) (see Fig. 1).

It is mostly in departments of language, literature, and cultural studies that *postcolonial* has become an institutionalized framework for analysis. There it is indissolubly wedded to deconstructionism and other literary devices I do not negotiate comfortably. The concept that dominates (paradoxically, given that postcolonialism postulates antidomination) is hybridization, the mixing or blending of cultures previously thought of as colonized and colonizing. Such a postcultural perspective is particularly suspicious of language as an oppressive vehicle that imposes a "master narrative."

The first journal to professionalize this paradigm, *postcoLoniaL studies*, began publishing in 1998; another manifestation is pursued by members of the Society for Francophone Postcolonial Studies, whose journal *Francophone Postcolonial Studies* first appeared in 2003. Truth in academic advertising: I do not situate my study of Anglo-French postcolonialism within that framework of analysis. This work, deliberately, is a non-Foucaultian social scientist's take on the postcolonial.[3] It intends to demonstrate that the distinctive stamps of France and Britain continue to mark daily life for ordinary people along and behind superimposed boundaries throughout the so-called Third World.

Professional historians might well disagree with this stance. With the passage of time, and the proliferation of the archival and other microlevel dissertation, there has been a tendency to cut away the forest of generality for the trees of specificity. Some have come to question the very validity of a stark difference between French direct and British indirect rule (Dulucq, Klein, and Stora 2008, 24). The debate is far from over, though, and in any event, it ought to shift location from archives to borderlands.

Framing Hypothesis

Although spurred by similar motives of national interest (foreign markets, mercantilism, competitive nationalism), Britain and France placed different emphases on the desired outcomes among their colonized subjects: technical competence for the former, cultural appropriation (even *amour propre*) for the latter. "Colonialism was as much a state of mind as it was a set of coercive practices and system of resource extraction," notes Alice Conklin (1997, 248), and the French state of mind was substantially different from the British.

Despite their formal sovereign status, former French and British colonies—which together encompass more than one-third of the world's territory—still bear the underlying imprint of their colonial pasts. Unlike the pragmatic and mercantilistic British, in their own colonial enterprise the French pursued much more culturally transformative aims. Even with respect to the pre-1789 First Colonial Empire holdings in North America, the Caribbean, and Indian Ocean, a "fusion of imagined administrative responsibility with proclaimed revolutionary purpose was the foundation of French colonial ideology" (Betts 1991, 17). This fundamental difference—embodied in the phrases *assimiliation* and *mission civilisatrice*—still assumes significant, if underappreciated, import throughout the Third World today. Whereas successor regimes to the British crown have used their juridical independence to pursue a wide array of postcolonial structures and policies, polities and nations decolonized by the French Republic have retained a comparatively formalistic, top-down, and centralized approach to governance and state-society relations.

This dichotomy holds despite basic differences in culture, geography, and political systems. And as long as it does, the process of decolonization, as opposed to formal independence, remains incomplete. But before testing this initial hypothesis on the ground, we need to acknowledge what specialists of colonial history have to say.[4]

Although covering a broad swath of time and territory—from the sixteenth to the twentieth centuries, from the New World to the Golden Triangle—the literature agrees that at least on paper, British and French policy makers marked their colonial ambitions and actions with distinctive national stamps. Both powers viewed colonies as requisites for grandeur and sources of natural and human resources. Both approached their colonized from a position of cultural (if not racial) superiority, placing greater hopes (and making more sacrifices) in settler colonies (e.g., Kenya, Algeria) than in ones without European settlers. Over time, often in response to external events, both powers did shift their official implementation strategies. But overall, whereas the French officially assumed the additional obligation of transforming the colonized into likenesses of France, with an eventual promise of *égalité*, the British rarely, if ever, harbored equivalent illusions of assimilating the colonized into their national bosom. (To take this metaphor literally, contrast the iconic symbol of the bare-breasted French revolutionary Marianne with staid British photos of the Queen; both can still be found in diplomatic outposts throughout the postcolonial world.)

The major point of colonial historicist contention is this: on the ground, did colonial policy matter? Beyond grandiose pronouncements emanating from London and Paris (or even Delhi and Dakar), in the final analysis, did it make a difference to the colonized? Did lower-level French and British colonial administrators actually implement the policies that supposedly distinguished each from the other? Did partitioned peoples experience colonialism in substantially different ways? Only if the answer is yes will we find separate legacies that continue to condition life and politics in the former colonies.

Hack, quoted at the chapter head, discusses the "software of colonialism: books, languages, customs, judicial systems, social structures, attitudes" (Hack 2003, 119). However, as with the digital age, in which there is no uncontested electronic hegemon, so with colonialism. At the risk of anachronistic analogy, we may suggest that colonial Britain may have been from Microsoft, but colonial France hailed from rival Apple. Though part of the same overarching and inescapable network, their successor states continue to filter and process the world through different operating systems.

Although Africa did not experience the earliest or longest-lasting colonialisms, it is in this continental context that the scholarly debate has been most extensive. Perhaps it is because of the legacy of Lord Frederick Lugard, who, notwithstanding his distinguished service in India, is remembered for formulating the doctrine of Indirect Rule as the "model" of British colonization in Northern Nigeria. From the heyday of colonialism in the 1920s until the wave of independence in the 1960s, the debate over Direct versus Indirect Rule dominated colonial discourse.

Since the 1970s the colonial postmortem has pitted advocates of the "similarity" versus those of the "difference" schools of Anglo-French colonialism in Africa. The former deny the overall significance, as it affected on-the-ground decisions and outcomes, of supposed differences in French and British colonial policies: colonialism was colonialism, a mere episode in the longer evolution of African history. When the similarity school measures the overall impact of French *association*, a compensatory colonial policy in the interwar years designed, in direct contrast with *assimilation*, to soften the starkly imperial and chauvinistic implications of Direct Rule, it finds it wanting.[5]

Prospects for decolonization reflected these differential pathways. Whereas the English could conceive of a trust, granting autonomy and eventual independence, the French could not (Betts 1991, 17). This is why, invoking Todd Shepard's (2006) felicitous phrase, France had such a hard time "inventing decolonization." Even France eventually had to bend to anti-imperial reality, with Algeria and Vietnam providing the most painful spurs. Still, as Shepard shows in the Algerian case, France not only resisted to the bitter end the political inevitability of a breakup, but psychologically resisted it beyond.

Achille Mbembe's provocative analysis of the African "postcolony" does not engage the Anglo-French colonial debate explicitly, but by seamlessly offering examples of abusive, excessive, and fetishist power from Kenya (formerly British), Togo (formerly French), and Cameroon (formerly French *and* British), he implicitly embraces the similarity school of postcolonial inheritance. In positing that "decentralized despotism" best characterizes the continuity between late colonialism and postcolonial administration, Mahmood Mamdani (1996) also implicitly downgrades the continuity of distinctive European influences in France's and Britain's former colonies. Longtime specialist of French colonial policy Raymond Betts seems to be of two minds on the question.[6]

Defenders of the difference school accept the traditional understanding of French-British colonial distinctions (à la Oliver and Atmore 1972, and Gann and Duigan 1969) and maintain its overall explanatory relevance for African successor states. Adu Boahen (1987) lends great authority (if debatable details) to their position.[7] Widner (1994) has demonstrated differences, based on colonial provenance, in the likelihood of sustained competition within newly democratizing political systems. Dimier (2002, 2004) plumbs the respective national interests of those who posed the question of colonial differentiation in the first place. At the level of high diplomacy, contrast the Commonwealth—an older club of independent states over which Britain exercises desultory control—with La Francophonie, in which France is still very much in the driver's seat.[8]

But how have ordinary denizens of the Third World experienced the aftermath of colonialism? Does having been colonized by France rather than Britain still make a difference to them? An economist might very well conclude that on average, former British colonies perform better than French ones in growth and development (Grier 1997), and that a more populist pedagogy (as promoted by colonial Britain) is in large measure responsible (Grier 1999). That does not, however, settle the score, especially for indigenous peoples who, finding themselves on opposite sides of artificial boundaries drawn by alien powers, were differentially colonized. There is more at stake than aggregate GDP for national societies: there is also cultural integrity, and national treatment, in postcolonial society.

The continuing relevance of the colonial paradigm is more a matter of perspective than a question of empiricism. At the macro level of change, a focus on freedom or underdevelopment or globalization may well overshadow distinctions between inherited French and British structures and mentalities of colonialism. But with respect to middle-level change—say, educational structures or traditional rulership or church/mosque-state relations—the differences still outweigh the similarities. In any event, the relevance and repercussions of the debate far transcend the shores of Africa and remain open, despite claims by some that the similarity school has triumphed. It is at the grassroots in the borderlands, I hope to show, that the national differences in colonialism have changed lives most dramatically.

Problems of Partition

Partition takes different forms. Most common is proximate territorial: either a recognizable river (as in the case of the Mekong, chosen to divide Laos from Burma) or a geometric line (drawn through the Sahelian sand to separate Nigeria from Niger). But maritime demarcations also partition. Think of the islands of the French West Indies cordoned off from the British West Indies. In the Indian Ocean and South Pacific, colonial partition has been less territorial than ethnic and psychological: in Mauritius, British supercession of French sovereignty (dichronous partition) led to institutionalized differences on the same island on the basis of race; in the New Hebrides (Vanuatu), condocolonialism[9] mentally partitioned islanders not on the basis of territory, but with respect to perceived Anglophone and Francophone varieties of religion (synchronous partition).

Those readers more used to the conventional, territorial use of partition and borders may be bothered by those cases in which I use the terms in less than literal ways. Rest assured that boundary and borderland specialists have been incorporating similarly metaphorical applications for some time. Moreover, even for those two cases that I do characterize as experiencing "lines in the mind"—Mauritius and Vanuatu—a more conventional (albeit maritime) colonial partition also persists. Thus, I shall contrast postcolonial Mauritius with its neighboring overseas French department of Réunion. Similarly, Vanuatu begs contrast with nearby New Caledonia, which also remains part of the French Republic. Beyond those familiar maritime demarcations, I still contend that undergoing British rule after French colonialism in Mauritius, and dealing with dueling colonialisms in Vanuatu, are the more interesting configurations of partition in those two island nations.

Even more than in the realm of science fiction, it may be in the colonial and postcolonial worlds that space becomes the final frontier. Colonialism entailed "respatialization," not only with respect to border lines and land use but also in deeper perceptions of place for the colonized. "In reworking the physical space of the territories into which they moved so as to ensure and justify their own domination . . . the Europeans forced drastic changes in the local geography of the mind" (Betts 2004, 90). Colonialism forced indigenous denizens to invest old places with new meanings: thus do sociologists' and geographers' formulation of social space find pertinent application in colonial and postcolonial situations.

Touching points for otherwise identical colonially separated cultures particularly excite me. It is on the periphery, on the margins of the postcolonial state—often denigrated in the term "borderline"—that one most clearly captures the long-term legacies of colonialism.[10] Rarely have I encountered confirmation of the conventional wisdom that borderlanders "ignore" the artificial colonial boundaries that divide them "only on paper."[11] Even where the border itself is invisible, I have been repeatedly impressed by the extent to which denizens of frontiers do assimilate and therefore legitimate the reality of state differences as inherited from the colonial era.[12]

Ethnic partition is not always a surgical cut of a spatially homogenous group, as with the Hausa of West Africa or the

Tamils of South India. In the case of Southeast Asia, I examine as "partitioned" into Laos and Burma (1) minority hill tribes that were already dispersed, with little preexisting territorial contiguity, and (2) contiguous lowlanders, who had a very loose sense of unity to begin with. Among some of these peoples, colonial partition immediately set into motion changes that affected the peoples so divided; among others, it merely planted the seeds for wider-reaching dynamics that have been accentuated in the postcolonial eras. In the West Indies and the South Pacific, I maintain that ethnic partition also is at work when peoples are divided not only by geometric cuts of line but by expanses of water: archipelagic societies were partitioned, too. And in the case of the Indian Ocean (Réunion, Seychelles, and Mauritius) we focus on one society, Mauritius, whose colonial partition was not spatial but temporal: a century of French colonial rule followed by a century and a half of British colonialism.

For comparative social scientists specializing either in former British or former French colonies in the developing world, the framework pursued here illuminates embedded structural constraints that continue to affect the direction and pace of development. By examining legacies of comparative colonialism from the bottom up, and paying particular attention to the mediating forces of local culture, a much more nuanced understanding of contemporary state and society in the former colonies of Britain and France emerges. For different cultures react to colonialism differently.

Borderlands crystallize the differences between the former colonies; that is why I use them as my methodological frame, despite the common criticism that I encounter, that border regions are by definition peculiar, peripheral, atypical, and otherwise unrepresentative. "Study the heartland, the urban centers, the capital," I am advised. "That is where the essence of a nation lies." Undoubtedly, borderlands *are* special, but it is precisely the extent to which they nevertheless do reflect their respective states, formally and informally, that they are instructive. One can also keep variables more constant between indigenes of the Mekong River than between the populations of Yangon/Rangoon and Vientiane, or in the case of Hausaland, between the denizens of Abuja and Niamey. Two broad questions undergird the inquiry: How did discrete indigenous groups (e.g., Melanesian, Hausa, Tamil, Lao) respond, subvert, and adjust to the respective British and French colonial projects superimposed onto their society and culture? In what ways (political, linguistic, economic) have their emergent postcolonial states differed as a consequence of their previous colonial imprints?

"A retrospective examination," writes Crawford Young within the context of the colonial state in Africa, "can illuminate some of the frailties of its postcolonial successor and perhaps even suggest avenues of escape from its more burdensome legacies" (Young 1994, 9). The following chapters aim to advance Professor Young's laudable goal by harnessing other regions' experience in comparative colonialism and decolonization. Chief among the "burdensome legacies," as we shall see, is the postcolonial inheritance of the artificial, superimposed boundary.

Plan of Book

After briefly examining several West African peoples separated by adjoining British-French colonial divisions, the second chapter focuses on the Hausa (Africa's largest ethnic group), divided into Niger and Nigeria. Distinctive colonial policies combined with characteristics of Hausa society created distinct national versions of ethnic identity. Mostly (but not completely) arbitrary territorial divisions—the classic "line in the sand"—marked the partition of West Africa into (mostly) British and French colonies.

Why do slave descendants in the French Antilles today experience a very different reality than do their counterparts in nearby Anglophone islands? This is the underlying question in chapter 3. Prior to the partitions outlined in chapter 2, Europeans were already subjecting Africans to distinct versions of imperial sovereignty: slavery scattered Africans to dozens of

West Indian islands controlled by Britain and France. In the Caribbean, France still practices decolonization without independence. Slave-based colonialism bequeathed fewer options for postcolonial transformation than in colonial lands of ethnically indigenous populations.

Chapter 4 shifts the paradigm to another partitioned ocean, the Pacific. As in the West Indies, the South Pacific was also arbitrarily parceled into French and British colonial zones. Here, however, entire clusters of islands were ruled under single administrations. In one such archipelago, the New Hebrides, France and Britain agreed to share sovereignty by establishing a condominium. Indigenous Melanesians responded by a policy of "divide though conquered." After independence, the archipelago nation of Vanuatu used language and reinvented custom to transcend inherited colonial divisions. How well has this strategy worked beyond Melanesia?

Whereas Vanuatu experienced concurrent colonialism, in the Indian Ocean (chapter 5) the islanders of Mauritius underwent consecutive colonialism: French, followed by British. So why does Francophone culture remain stronger than the one bequeathed by Britain? Lacking most of the usual preconditions for democracies—including national unity—Mauritius embraces its dual colonial heritage for the purposes of managing ethnic conflict and promoting development. No wonder the literature abounds with Mauritius as a "model." I maintain that an overlooked dimension to Mauritius's success lies in the hybridic nature of its colonial heritage, layered by South Asian immigration. The ancestral homeland of most Mauritians is India, where France remained longer than did Britain. So in chapter 5 I also examine how the Francophone Indians of Pondichéry compare, especially in their political culture, to their migrant counterparts in Mauritius. While the anomaly of French India could have been treated in a separate chapter—it is, after all a distinct case of Anglo-French rivalry with unique postcolonial outcomes—the commonality of French colonial influence over ethnic Indians, be it in the Dravidian heartland or Mauritian diaspora—provides an intriguing frame for parallel treatment.

Chapter 6 discusses how, in all of Southeast Asia, there is only one border that separates a former French colony from a former British one: the 150 miles of the Upper Mekong separating Laos from Burma (Myanmar). Dividing the Mekong River into Lao and Burmese territories affected two geocultural categories of indigenous peoples: those whose territory actually straddles the riverine boundary and those who inhabit noncontiguous communities on both sides of the international border. Postcolonial revolution greatly disturbed these spatial patterns, however, introducing a new variable into the comparative colonialism paradigm. In order to persist, colonial legacies require a critical threshold of political stability.

Until the concluding chapter, colonial policies are framed against indigenous group response patterns. In the concluding chapter, I revisit general questions of ethnicity, history, and variability in colonial policy; the overall diversity in types of postcolonial regimes and patterns of response to them; overarching regional and geocultural extrapolations; broad differentiations in material and political outcomes; long-term implications for languages (official and indigenous); and the possibility of an overarching borderland message. Despite these generalizing frameworks, my greater plea is for more empiricism within postcolonial studies, currently an overtheorized, highly abstract, field.

When I began this project, I had hoped to personalize a Rawlsian-type hypothetical: "If you did not know in advance into which culture or region of the world you would be born, but could choose between a former French or British colony, which would you choose?" Although some have used statistical models to approximate this scenario (is it a postcolonial "prisoner's dilemma"?), I realize now that the question presents a false choice. Contingencies—cultural, historical, strategic—are too multistranded to reduce the Anglo-French colonial grid into a single outcome, life choice, or number.[13] More important is the freedom to choose one's culture and society *after* achieving political consciousness.

Comparison is also complicated by time, both historical and fieldwork related. Temporal proximity to events of research focus certainly skews some cross-national generalization. On one end of the scale, thirty-five years had already lapsed between the juncture when the French West Indies opted to become *départements* of France (1946) and my first visit there. At the other end of the scale, a mere eleven years separated the independence of Vanuatu (1980) from my major block of South Pacific research.[14] So recent, so fresh was the demarcation between the colonial era and the postcolonial one that the transition still seemed fluid and the research in Vanuatu all the touchier. As time passes, some variables tend to lose their salience as others come to replace them. The long-term significance in British versus French policies of colonization is a case in point. As colonialism became supplanted by the Cold War and then globalization, the European distinction has lost much currency as an explanatory factor for postcolonial developments. My contention—tempered by the acknowledgment that decades separate the time from decolonization and my research in some polities as opposed to others—is that the Anglo-French distinction still matters a lot more to partitioned borderlanders than to students of postcolonial history.

That said, the legacies of Anglo-French partition live on in a wide array of arenas, for larger swaths of the population, in arenas I identified above: language, education, governance, religion, and so on. Francophonie remains a societal reference in former French colonies in a more penetrating way than "Anglophony" is in former British colonies. I am referring here not only to language use but to conceptualization and institutionalism. Both forms of colonization were transformative, for sure: in the long run, though, the French legacies are more constant and identifiable than the British ones. This argument holds only in the strictly comparative sense: by holding constant for similar ethnic groups who experienced both forms of colonialism.

In offering this global dichotomy of French and British colonialism and its aftermath, I hope the reader will join me in better appreciating the singularity of his or her own historicized life story. For, in our own way, are we not all postcolonials?

2
Classic Colonial Partition
West Africa

Similarity is not the same as sameness.
—Hausa proverb

Whether savanna, Sahelian, or Saharan, the topography of West Africa starkly epitomizes the seemingly arbitrary nature of colonial division and its aftermath: invisible lines in the sand crisscrossing the land and bisecting indigenous peoples into officially Anglophone and Francophone states.[1] One of those boundaries created two sets of citizens with easily confusable names, Nigerian and Nigerien, but whose natural and demographic endowments could not be more different. For if Nigeria, with its 170 million people and boundless barrels of petroleum, merits the nickname "Giant of Black Africa," what shall we call Niger, with its population of 17 million and a human development index ranking consistently at the global bottom of the United Nations' scale? It is not the Niger River, for which both colonies were named, that serves as demarcation between the two near-eponyms. The inherited colonial borderlines are geometric, not riverine or in any other way natural (see Map 1). But the distinction between being Nigerian and Nigérien[2] has become quite real. One critical geopolitical distinction: Nigerians not only have oil but seaports from which to export it; Nigériens are landlocked (Djimba 1997). The mentality, outlook, and life prospects of these two West African citizenries

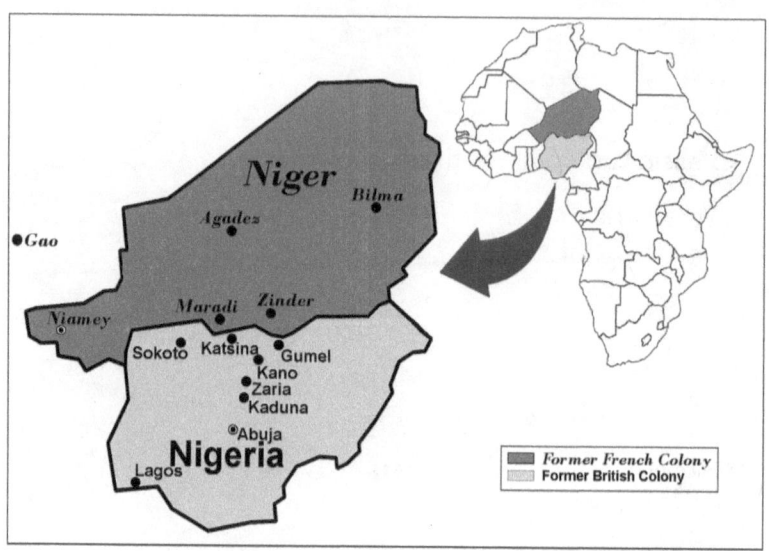

Map 1. An Inherited Colonial Partition

are truly distinct. Nowhere is this postcolonial outcome clearer than among the partitioned borderliners who otherwise share the same language, religion and ethnicity.

West African Geography, Colonialism and Decolonization

In 1884–85 the Berlin West African Conference institutionalized the parameters for the Scramble for Africa, an intra-European competition already primed by French- and British-sponsored explorers (Förster, Mommsen, and Robinson 1988). Within thirty-five years France claimed a broad swath of territory from the Atlantic coast clear across what was called the western Soudan to a gently sloping arc of territory in the center of the continent (Wesseling 1996). The latter was called French Equatorial Africa; the former, which more concerns us, was dubbed Afrique Française Occidentale (AOF), or French West Africa. On a map, AOF, governed from Dakar, looked quite impressive for its vastness and contiguity (see Map 2). French popular images romanticized West Africa, often obscuring what "belonged" to other European powers (see Fig. 2). But much of AOF lay within

Map 2. French West Africa

semi-inhabitable or outright uninhabitable zones of the northern Sahel ("edge") and the Saharan desert.

Britain, for its part, managed to create coastal toeholds that laced inland from its port cities: Banjul, Freetown, Accra, Lagos. The latter initially served as administrative headquarters for a "protectorate" under its own name before becoming capital of Southern Nigeria; in 1914 Southern Nigeria merged with Northern Nigeria, creating a single Colony of Nigeria. Partition in West Africa may well have been, as Hargreaves (1985) puts it, a matter of (European) elephants fighting and (African) grass being trampled. But when the fighting was over, the grass did spring back, albeit in a wildly new patchwork. Given the pliancy of the precolonial African boundaries (Uzoigwe 1985), the resurrected "grass" was certainly a hardier variety than that which preceded it.

Anglo-French partitions sometimes maintained the political integrity of the traditional states (Thom 1970, 1975), though often "[t]he fate of the smaller states and peoples was not dis-

Fig. 2. French West Africa—Popular View

cussed" (Barkindo 1985, 33–34). While the British and French may have *thought* that they were being sensitive to the sovereignty and geography of precolonial polities when creating colonial divisions, they inevitably overlooked the more discreet ones. Indeed, to obfuscate the ethnic surgery created by boundary demarcation, new names were often given to recognized groups that now found themselves colonially divided. For example, those of the Gude people who were sectioned off into French Cameroun from British Nigeria were called by the partitioners Djimi, and suddenly Frenchified Higis were renamed Kapsiki. Conversely, the Matakam who found themselves in British territory were renamed Wula, thereby obscuring the division from their kinsmen in Cameroun (Barkindo 1985, 38).

Germany's loss in World War I aggrandized British and French holdings in West Africa. Slivers of Kamerun were ceded to Britain, which administered them as the British Cameroons from Nigeria. France similarly inherited the bulk of Cameroun as a mandate from the League of Nations. German Togoland was also dismembered and distributed to the victors as League of Nations mandates, western Togoland eventually being incorporated within the British Gold Coast. France retained control of the rest of *le Togo*.

West Africa escaped battlefield status and territorial disfigurement in the Second World War, even though French colonies under Vichy were technically enemy territory of Britain and her Allies. The impact of Vichy rule in French West Africa did, however, have long-term consequences: it "unmasked" the racist underpinnings of French colonialism, setting an impossibly high bar for postwar French policy makers to rectify (Ginio 2006).

Administrative subdivisions within the AOF gradually matured to the point where eight constituent colonies (Mauritania, Senegal, Mali, Guinea, Ivory Coast, Upper Volta, Dahomey, and Niger) became embryonic states in the lead-up to independence between 1958 and 1960. For all intents and purposes, so did the two French mandates, Togo and Cameroon.[3] This is not to say that these ten polities were nations in the sense of a unified people with a common destiny; rather, internal French colonial boundaries were reified within and ratified without (by the international community), with Francophone African elites assuming positions of leadership.

The first West African colony to achieve independence was a British one, the Gold Coast that became Ghana in 1957. Sierra Leone became independent in 1961, Gambia in 1965. But the richest, largest (in size and population), and most promising West African colony for the British was Nigeria, which achieved sovereignty in the same year as all but one of the French colonies and mandates: 1960.

Newly independent Nigeria alone accounted for three of the eight international boundaries separating the former British and French colonies of West Africa (see Map 3).[4] To the east lay Cameroon; to the west, Dahomey (renamed Benin in 1975). To the north is the 1,497-kilometer-long border separating Nigeria

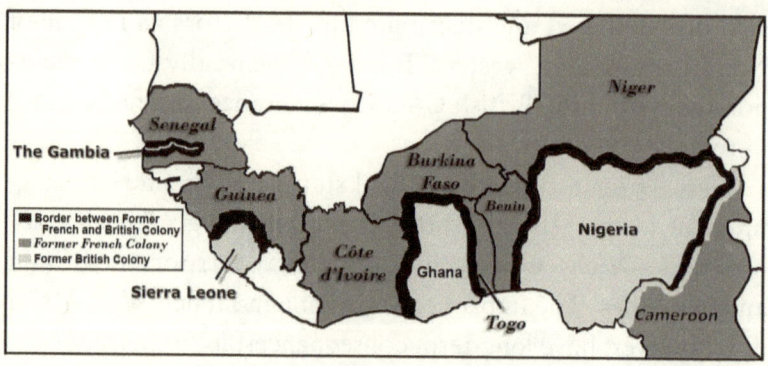

Map 3. Neighboring Anglophone and Francophone West African States

from Niger. This is the longest boundary between any former British and continuously intact French colony in all West Africa.[5]

Ghana is bounded by three Francophone neighbors: Ivory Coast, Togo, and Burkina Faso (the name taken by Upper Volta in 1984). West Africa's two other Anglophone-Francophone boundaries are Gambia-Senegal and Sierra Leone–Guinea. Boundaries separating former British and French colonies continue to divide approximately fifty ethnic groups (see Table 1). The most prominent (or at least the ones to so appear in the scholarly literature) are the Yoruba (sectioned into Benin and Nigeria), Ewe (Ghana-Togo), and Hausa (Nigeria-Niger). Of all the indigenous African peoples partitioned by colonialism, by far the most populous are the Hausa.

Colonial boundary drawing created its own indigenous dynamics. Where new colonial lines of separation divided farms from borderlanders' homes, cross-border resettlement occurred. Where colonial policies on one side of a line were adjudged relatively harsh or unfair, people moved to the other. (This usually meant moving from French into British territory). West Africans who suddenly became borderlanders did not necessarily remain passive objects of their fate. Nor was partition unidirectional; migratory responses to new colonial boundary realities meant that some African ethnic groups partitioned themselves.

Table 1. Partitioned West African Ethnic Groups

Country*	Ethnic groups
Benin-Nigeria	Adja, Yoruba, Borgu, Hausa, Fulani
Cameroon-Nigeria	Kanembu, Shuwa Arabs, Mandara, Wakura, Matakam, Gude, Veve, Adamawa, Chamba, Jibu, Ekoi, Ododop, Efik
Gambia-*Senegal*	Wolof, Pular, Serer, Mandinka, Jola, Karoninka, Manjago, Balanta
Ghana-*Togo*	Ewe, Agotime, Akposso, Konkomba, Aufo, Moba
Ghana–*Burkina Faso*	Mossi, Dagara, Sisala, Kusasi, Dyula, Birifor, Padon, Mankana, Bissa, Aculo
Ghana–*Ivory Coast*	Sanwi, Afema, Lobi
Guinea-Sierra Leone	Mende, Susu, Baga
Niger-Nigeria	Hausa, Fulani, Kanuri

*Former French colony in italics; former British colony in roman.

Source: Compiled from Asiwaju (1985).

Following independence, an almost sacrosanct principle of the Organization of African Unity was that African states would respect the territorial integrity of their fellow members as they were inherited from the colonial powers. Otherwise, it was feared, reopening questions of the injustices of colonial partition would only lead to postcolonial strife. In many instances, however, the colonial demarcation of the boundary was not as clear-cut on the ground as it appeared on paper. Binational boundary commissions have redrawn borders by mutual agreement; other disputes have gone to international arbitration, with varying degrees of acceptance.[6] As concerns borderlanders, partition is an ongoing African phenomenon, albeit at a much smaller scale than the colonial one from which it proceeds. For the borderlanders so affected, the micropartitions of independent Africa are no less significant than the macropartitions of European colonialism. Redemarcation of the boundary can have unfortunate and unforeseen consequences, particularly when borderlanders of different ethnicities continue (as did their colonized forebears) to appropriate and subvert it.

Anglo-French competition, the vagaries of partition, and internal French colonial division gave way to a notable geographical discrepancy between the five Anglophone[7] and ten Francophone postcolonial states of West Africa. Whereas all of the former are coastal, three of the latter are landlocked (Mali, Burkina Faso, and Niger). Inheriting at independence an outlet to the sea has proven a major natural advantage for postcolonial trade and economic integration. This alone constitutes a major structural difference between, say, Nigeria and Niger.

The distinction between landlocked lands and coastal countries is emblematic of another geographical problem linked to colonial conquest and state inheritance: the translatitudinal nature of the colonies. The natural and human ecology of life in West Africa is a function of bandwidth parallel to the equator. Lower latitudes are characterized by rain forest and inhabited by peoples whose precolonial religions were localist and animist. The most northern latitudes of West African colonies stretched into the desert, its inhabitants strongly influenced by (if not commingled with) the culture and peoples of the Maghreb, or North Africa. While two intermediate vegetation zones—grassland and semidesert Sahel—also lay between rain forest and Sahara, in general the most "vertical" colonies incorporated within the same polities significant proportions of two fundamentally different peoples: southern, animistic (and quasi-animistic) Bantu-language speakers; and northern, Muslim (or Islamizing) Hamito-Semitic language speakers. During colonialism, many of the animistic peoples were missionized and became Christian (or at least they integrated Christianity within traditional practices). Postcolonial states inheriting significant north-south, Muslim-Christian populations include Francophone Benin, Togo, and Ivory Coast; bilingual Cameroun/Cameroon; and Anglophone Ghana and Nigeria. All the West African states with preponderantly Muslim peoples were colonies of France: Mauritania, Mali, Senegal, Guinea, Burkina Faso, Niger.

Collectively, the population of the former AOF is today nearly 100 million; that of Britain's erstwhile West African colonies, over 200 million. If French-British colonial legacies make a difference, they will therefore do so on a very large African scale. Nigeria is surrounded by four countries, including Chad (not always classified within West Africa proper), all of them Francophone, with a total population of over 60 million. The most numerous ethnic group in Africa to have been divided into French and British colonies are the Hausa.

Hausa, Fulani, Kanuri: Nigeria and Niger

Northern Nigeria: Cradle of Indirect Rule

A century before the British and French came to carve out their respective colonies in the Sahel, an indigenous army conquered these same territories with significant implications for later European overrule. Beginning in 1804, a Fulani cleric launched a jihad, incensed at the oppression of commoners and corrupted version of Islam as practiced by the Hausa rulers in the lands fanning out from the funnel between the Niger and Benue Rivers. Within six years Usman dan Fodio had established a new caliphate, based in Sokoto, that included all of the original Habe (pre-jihadic Hausa) states.[8] But the Sokoto Caliphate also included significant non-Hausa states, including Nupe and part of Yorubaland.

Fulani leaders were dispatched to replace the Hausa ones; some of these latter went into exile, constituting rump states. This was the case, for example, of the Hausa dynasty of Katsina, which reestablished itself in nearby Maradi and was eventually to come under colonial French rule. By and large, despite a schism within their empire, the Fulani succeeded in establishing a much more coherent and centralized empire than had been created by their ruling Hausa predecessors. But if the Hausa failed in resisting the Fulani militarily, they seduced them culturally: most of the town Fulani (unlike their rural, nomadic cousins, from whom they had themselves originated) gradually melded into Hausa society, taking Hausa wives, practicing Hausa customs, and speaking the Hausa language.

When the British came to claim colonial sovereignty over this same territory for the Crown in the early twentieth century, they therefore encountered a monarchical bureaucracy that, once subjugated on the battlefield, could easily continue administering what the colonialists would dub Northern Nigeria. These Fulani, Fulani-Hausa, and Hausa chiefs and emirs (including the sultan of Sokoto) would be subject in principle to the colonial governor and his subordinates (residents, district officers, assistant district officers), but the role of the British colonials was to advise and guide the traditional rulers of Nigeria, not to rule over them or directly govern their people. And in those regions where traditional rulers did not actually exist, as was the case in smaller polities south of the traditional Hausa states, the British would appoint them. Gradually, it was believed, all these "native authorities" would incorporate British values and techniques of administration. Insofar as matters of religion and customary law did not conflict with fundamental European standards of decency, they were allowed to go their own way; indeed, the British more than tolerated indigenous culture and institutions. This, then, was the essence of Indirect Rule.[9] The spirit of this distinctively British colonial policy was conveyed to the colonized immediately after the conquest of Sokoto, in March 1903, by none other than Frederick Lugard[10] himself: "I hope that you will find our rule sympathetic and that the country will prosper and be contented. You need have no fear regarding British rule . . . for it is just and fair, and people under our King are satisfied. . . . You must not fear to tell the Resident everything and he will help and advise you. . . . It is our wish to learn your customs and fashions, just as you must learn ours" (Kirk-Greene 1965, 44). How did the newly colonized of Nigeria view such British paternalism?

Slave raiding was common in the precolonial era, so it should not be surprising that, at the grassroots, British colonial government (locally perceived as white overrule) was welcomed more than not. More than two decades after Nigerian independence, reactionary sentiments could still be heard among ordinary Hausa villagers: "When the European came, there was peace and repairing of the world. . . . The English eased problems for the peasants: they abolished raiding, fighting. . . . The British brought learning and justice. No longer could a man be evicted from his home just so the chief's son could live in it" (Miles 1994, 100, 101).

The boundaries of the Sokoto Caliphate that the British inherited were not as clear-cut as they would have desired. Warfare on its eastern outskirts (with Bornu-Kanem) and to the north (with the Tuaregs based in Agadez) had periodically destabilized the outer limits of the Hausafied Fulani empire. Intermediary city-states with ambiguous fealty and tutelage subsisted: such was the case of Damagaram (Zinder). From the lowest level of settlement (*gari*) to the highest territorial unit (*kasa*), indigenous overrule was a matter of repeated negotiation (and battle) with external claimants, necessitating navigation between overlapping claims over land and people. This was particularly the case at the fringes of competing empires, where contested sovereignty led to fragmentation and displacement of populations on account of war, looting, and slave raiding.

For the British, lines needed to be clearly drawn. But it was not the blurred zones between competing indigenous polities that called out for precise demarcation. Rather, it was the line with their home continent nemesis: France.

Le Niger: Direct Rule Exemplified

Whereas British expansion in Africa inclined to push intermittently upward from the bottom of West Africa's elbow and from its early bases in East Africa, the French systematically moved laterally from their imperial starting gate on the Sen-

Fig. 3. Hausaland Boundary Marker. Lawal Nuhu (right) stands on the outskirts of Yardaje, Nigeria, while his friend stands in Niger.
From *Hausaland Divided: Colonialism and Independence in Nigeria and Niger* by William F. S. Miles (Ithaca NY: Cornell University Press, 1994). Reprinted with permission.

egalese coast.[11] In Sudan, where this bidirectional race intersected in the famous "showdown at Fashoda" in 1898, there was almost intra-European war. In West Africa, however, intersecting Anglo-French claims were more amiably resolved. Three sets of demarcations (1890, 1898, 1904) were negotiated before settling on the one that in 1906 established the boundary that at independence in 1960 was inherited by Niger and Nigeria. Between 1904 and 1906, British and French surveyors laid 148 beacons along the 1,498 kilometers comprising the boundary. Five kinds of markers were used: palm-tree posts, dry stone pillars, cast-iron base sockets, trees with numbered plaques, and iron telegraph poles (see Fig. 3).

One can easily imagine that in the absence of regular surveillance and maintenance—conditions that were beyond the material resources available to both the colonial and postcolonial governments—several of these boundary markers would disintegrate or otherwise disappear. Indeed, it was reported in 2006 that eleven of even the sturdiest type of beacons—the telegraph poles—had disappeared entirely (*Africa News* 2006).

It would be conventional to describe the peoples on both sides of the superimposed boundary as ethnically homogenous, thereby highlighting the artificial nature of the Anglo-French partition. Songhay-speaking peoples to the west, Hausa and rural Fulani in the center, and Kanuri-speaking groups to the east: all these now found themselves split into French and British colonies, would go this narrative. Such a neat picture of partition must be nuanced, however, by three major factors: demographic, micropolitical, and post-jihadist (see Maps 4 and 5).

First, on account of the continuing conflict between rival empires (principally Damagaram-Zinder and Sokoto) much of the area that would become the Niger-Nigeria frontier had been depopulated. Paradoxically, it was the act of creating a boundary, and exercising European sovereignty on both sides, that allowed this demographic vacuum to be filled. As people returned, new colonial identities were simultaneously superimposed on and incorporated by the borderliners. There had not been greatly populated, thriving settlements along the demarcation line that suddenly found themselves split into Nigeria and Niger: partition (re)created indigenous communities. "[F]rontier

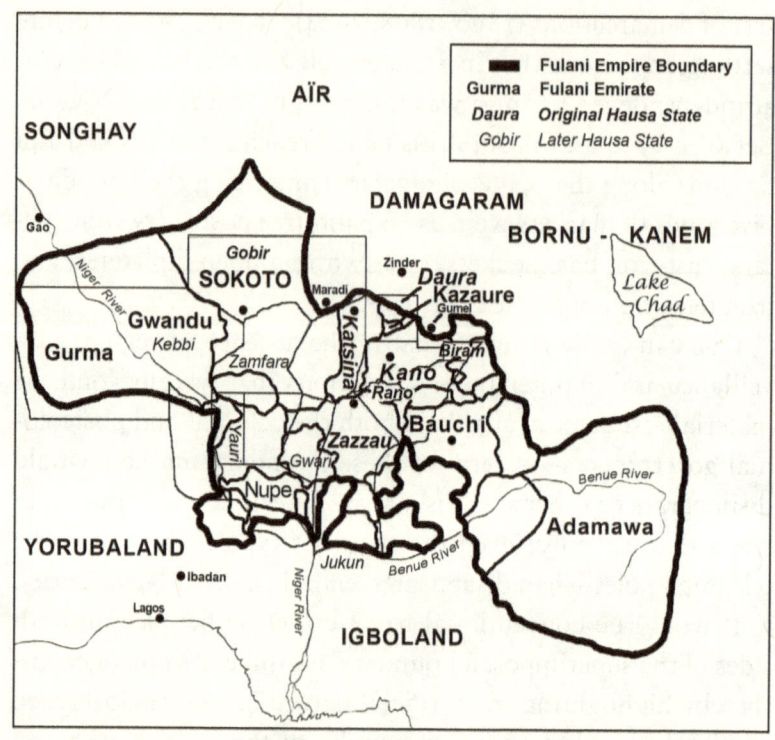

Map 4. Precolonial Hausa-Fulani and Adjoining Polities

peasants were less upset by a newly imposed border than they were enamored of the newly imposed peace" (Miles 1994b, 99).

Second, in some respects the identity of those peoples who were partitioned was more complex than they were to become under colonialism. Take the case of the Hausa. If today "Hausa" is better understood as a linguistic category than an ethnic group, this was all the more so at the turn of the twentieth century when political divisions seriously split Hausa speakers into various clans and microstates: those of Katsina, Kazaure, Gumel, Daura, Gobir, Gumel. To a lesser extent, the same can be said of the Tuareg: their internal divisions are formidable and persistent, but colonialism (and postcolonialism) has created pressures for reconciliation, if not unification. Preoccupation with partition should not allow for anachronistic ethnic

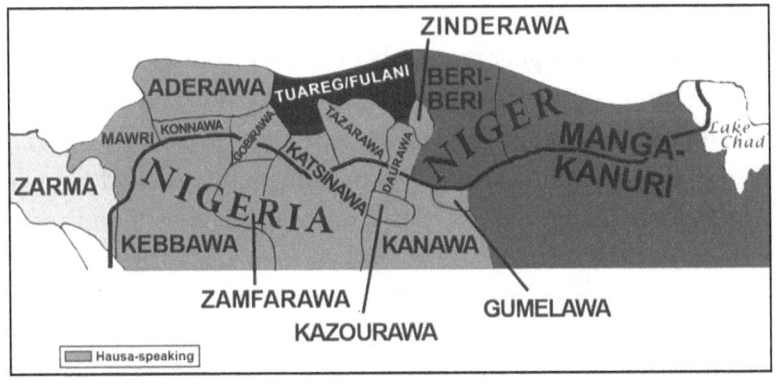

Map 5. Partitioned Ethnicities of Niger-Nigeria Borderlands

and revisionistic demographic notions to distort the real effects of colonialism.

The third factor that complexifies the partition picture of Niger-Nigeria relates back to the jihad of Usman dan Fodio. A century of Fulani-inspired Islamization meant that the Hausa of Northern Nigeria were already practicing a much more orthodox variety of the religion than those Hausa and nomadic Fulani coming under the dominion of French Niger. Greater religious fervor, as evidenced by "Muslim" dress and gender segregation, had been ingrained south of the border for a century already to a degree that had not taken hold in what would become Niger. There, the pre-jihadic tradition of syncretic Islam persisted.

Within their new territory called *le Niger* the French dealt with many fewer indigenous groups than the British did in Nigeria. Whereas the latter could number up to 250, in Niger there were only a half dozen or so. The Tuaregs, who resisted French rule until the 1920s, roamed the north, with Agadez as their capital. Despite the profits derived from their legendary caravan trade, Tuareg territory was not considered part of *le Niger utile*, the agriculturally "useful" part of the colony. This more topographically promising territory was populated in the southwest by Songhay-related Zarma (or Djerma)—to whose banks along the Niger the French moved their capital, building

Niamey—and in the central south by the more numerous Hausa speakers, both indigenous and descendants from escapees from the Fulani jihad. In the southeast, toward Lake Chad, the land was much less "useful" and sparsely populated, mostly by sedentary Kanuri and nomadic Tubu, Gourmantche, and Shuwa Arabs. Throughout the Nigérien landscape could be found rural Fulani, not the settled ones of Nigeria's northern cities. When reliable censuses were eventually conducted, the Hausa were to emerge as about half the population, with Zarma constituting about 30 percent and Tuareg and Fulani each about 10 percent.

Two tenuous ties united these Nigérien peoples. They basically (despite significant animistic exceptions, such as the Hausa-speaking Maguzawa) adhered to Islam, and they were all now subordinate to France.

French colonial policy in Niger, as throughout AOF, was premised on Direct Rule: that European *commandants* would take a proactive role in overseeing the transformation of indigenous government and society. This would bring prosperity to the French (and to their wards) and civilization to Africans. Progress could only be made, according to this theory, by extending French language, education, and administration to the colonized. To further this goal, close supervision of chiefs (whom the *commandants* did not hesitate to alternatively dismiss and appoint) was necessary. Under Direct Rule, local customs were tolerated, not preserved; local languages were neglected, not used for instruction. *Indigénat*, impressment for colonial subjects' labor, most strongly marked those who came under the colonial French regime. It was a contradictory policy, as Alice Conklin makes clear (at least for the Third Republic), but even in its contradictions, French colonial policy in West Africa distinguished itself from that of the colonially less idealistic (and less self-deluding) British. Britain may have believed in bestowing a modicum of civilization, but never strove to change identity in the way that "Africans had to learn to feel French" (Conklin 1997, 248).

Scholars of Niger (Fuglestad 1983; Charlick 1991) point out

that Direct Rule was only imperfectly implemented in Niger. In reality, the French had neither the resources nor the will to either supplant chiefs' authority or to transform society through extensive education. Fuglestad points out the changing nature of French rule and the "extremely uneven impact of that rule": revolutionary conquest up to 1908; military consolidation until 1922; classical colonialism until the end of World War II; developmentalist and democratizing up to independence in 1960. Postcolonial Niger, asserts Charlick, has been governed in a contradictory tension between personalistic rulers and bureaucratic authoritarianism. "French colonial government in Niger, as centralized and authoritarian as it was reputed to be, did not create the basis for a powerful postcolonial state" (Charlick 1991, 53).

So, Direct Rule was imperfectly implemented in Niger, but did the British, throughout Nigeria, more perfectly practice Indirect Rule? Neither European power, it is true, fully succeeded in executing its colonial policy, as crafted in Paris and London. Still, starkly differential outcomes, as recalled by ordinary denizens of the African borderlands, do not allow for such easy dismissal or minimization of Franco-British differences. It is in the borderlands, moreover, that the differences are most starkly visible.[12]

Over two decades after independence, Hausa along the border still referred to Niger as Faransa or Faranshi (France)—a telling linguistic sign of colonial continuity in its own right—and recalled Direct Rule thus: "The French squeezed the Hausa: they confiscated millet, they made men carry large, heavy trees for construction until they died." Or this: "People were forced to grow groundnuts, but were prohibited from eating them. Only in secret would one dare to eat a groundnut, burying the shell carefully so no one would know." Or this: "When the French left (unlike the British) they took everything that produced wealth."

"The French are very prone to fighting. If you anger them, they'll react very strongly" (not like the British, who "are very patient and not easily angered"). An entire folk genre of comparative colonial oppression endures, through epithets, legends, and songs. Whereas most of the local nicknames bestowed upon British colonial administrators were benign or even humorous ("Mr. Sugar Cane," "The One With White Eyebrows," "Ostrich Owner"), those that stuck to the French commandants usually evoke harsher images: "Hot Pepper," "King Stinger," "Mosquito," "Hunchback," "Woodpecker," "The Curser." Bordeaux (name of the French governor in Zinder, nicknamed "Chief Labor Maker") inspired an entire ballad recalling his mercilessness in imposing farm labor:

> Young girls selling snacks, butchers, peddlers,
> Cripples and blind men and lepers,
> Soldiers' wives, married women (What an infidel!)
> Bordeaux would not spare.
> CHORUS: Bordeaux, White Man of Labor:
> Not even an old woman selling groundnuts
> Would he spare.
> From the city, from the hamlets, from the barracks,
> People taken for labor.
> Seven days of labor, impossible to complete,
> But when Bordeaux said "Finish it!"
> They made sure they finished.
> So not to suffer even more.

Beatings, floggings, and humiliations (even of chiefs) punctuate recollections of French colonial rule in the Niger-Nigeria borderlands but are conspicuously absent in collective memories of the British. The local word for "training animals" is frequently invoked to describe French methods to get Nigériens to obey directives. A single Hausa term encapsulates the local perception of Direct Rule: *mulkin zahi*, a reign of heat or fire. One of many legendary examples of *mulkin zahi* recalled a commandant nicknamed "Hunchback" who oversaw the tax-season beating of a suspect Fulani, whose innocence was vouched for by a local chief. Hunchback's African guards nevertheless broke the hapless nomad's ribs. The soldiers and guards tied the injured

Fulani to a donkey, but he died before reaching home. Yet even the deceased man's father kept quiet, so fearful was he himself of the French "reign of fire."

World War II and Nigerian-Nigérien Nationalism

Anticolonial consciousness emerged in Nigeria long before World War II—but not so intensively in the north, where Indirect Rule buttressed the Muslim Hausa and Hausa-Fulani dynasties and mitigated against socially disruptive change. Southerners, the largest groups of which were Igbo and Yoruba, had to a much greater extent absorbed Western education and religion (mostly Protestantism) as well as Pan-African ideals. Embryonic political associations were ethnic-urban, business and professional, and student-based.

World War II, in which more than 100,000 Nigerians enlisted to fight in southern Europe, East Africa, the Middle East, and Southeast Asia, triggered questions about whose "freedom" they were defending. Many of these colonial conscripts were northerners: so much so that Hausa (along with English) served as common language for Nigerian soldiers (Coleman 1958, 254). Although easterners (particularly Igbos) proved to be the most restive of Nigerian veterans, Coleman's comment that "ex-servicemen [were] among the more militant leaders of the nationalist movement during the postwar period" may be applied across the ethnic board (254).

Still, the political parties that formed in the 1940s coalesced mainly along ethnic lines: the Action Group of the Yoruba; the National Council of Nigeria and the Cameroons (later, National Council of Nigerian Citizens), whose core membership was Igbo; and the conservative Hausa-Fulani Northern People's Congress (NPC). A more populist Hausa perspective was advanced by the Northern Elements Progressive Union (NEPU). Despite ideological disagreement over the continuing power of traditional rulers versus emancipation for the peasantry, neither NPC nor NEPU questioned the dominance of the Hausa-Fulani north in Nigerian governance. Nor did they challenge the colonial boundary that had placed millions of Hausa under French jurisdiction in Niger. NEPU might have been more eager to see an independent Nigeria than NPC; but even the NPC envisioned an independence in which traditional authority persisted within a state formed by the colonial powers. In the 1950s NPC succeeded in dominating the Nigerian political scene as the colony transitioned to statehood. The sardauna of Sokoto, Sir Ahmadu Bello, premier of the Northern Region government, was one of the most influential of the new nation's politicians.[13]

Over the border in Niger, both World War II and postwar politics affected the Hausa rather differently. For one thing, for most of the war (until June 1943) Niger was subject to the Vichy government. At the level that most concerns us, "the rural masses hardly understood the reasons for Anglo-French tensions" (quoted in Fuglestad 1983, 142–43.) Nevertheless, the presence of the "English enemy" just to the south prompted the French not only to close their border with Nigeria but to have it patrolled by "partisan units" that dug trenches. This did not prevent Hausa peasants from fleeing into *Inglishi*, especially to escape forced labor (a practice that continued even after the Gaullists eventually regained control, and obscured the difference between Vichy and republican colonialism [Ginio 2006]). Nor did local French attempts to stoke old rivalries between traditional Nigérien polities and the Sokoto Caliphate in Nigeria seem to work, either (Fuglestad 1983, 143). Nevertheless, World War II drove home to the Hausa rather dramatically the distinction between being on the French as opposed to the British side of the conflict. Actual hostilities did not occur: officially, however, their two colonies were at war.

In terms of Nigérien recruitment into the military, ethnic differentiation had been established long before World War II. Zarma (Djerma), a minority population in the colony into whose territory the French transferred their capital of Niamey from Zinder, came to occupy the center of gravity within the armed forces. They came to constitute the bulk of the officer corps; they also have come to dominate Nigérien politics (especially in its military guise) since independence.

Political party development following the end of World War II paralleled that of French West Africa as a whole. At its founding in 1946 the Parti Progressiste Nigérien (PPN) was affiliated with the leftist Rassemblement Démocratique Africaine and in 1958 with the Union pour la Communauté Franco-Africaine. The Union Démocratique Nigérienne was in succession affiliated with the French Communist Party, the French Socialist Party, and then the Mouvement Socialiste Africain. The more conservative Union Nigérienne des Indépendants et Sympathisants had the backing of France. But it was the PPN ("[f]undamentally a party of Zarma modernizers" [Charlick 1991, 43]) that prevailed from the 1952 elections until independence and beyond.

Independence and the Respective National Roles of "Anglophone" and "Francophone" Hausa

Niger achieved independence with the PPN heading the government and a Zarma, Hamani Diori, at its helm. Zarma dominance through the PPN prevailed until the coup d'état of 1974, when Diori was overthrown by another Zarma, Lieutenant-Colonel Seyni Kountché. Following Kountché's death by natural causes in 1987, his chief of staff Ali Saïbou (also a Zarma) assumed power.

Loosening of Zarma-led authoritarianism did not embolden the politically sidelined Hausa as much as it did the more frustrated Tuareg. Although their first commando action was launched in 1985 while Kountché was still alive, their action presaged the waning of military control and discipline in Niger, as well as the end of monopoly over power by the Zarma. In 1990, with the country in a flux of governance, a more widespread rebellion took hold among the Tuaregs. Despite intermittent peace agreements and treaties, it has yet to fully subside.

The advent of democratization in the early 1990s did not result in a takeover of government by members of the Hausa majority (Frère 1999; Gervais 1997; Ibrahim 1994; Ibrahim and

Niandou Souley 1998). Although civilian politics has empowered more Nigériens hailing from Hausaland than previously (most prominently Mahamane Ousmane, president from 1993 until the coup of early 1996), Nigérien political parties and politics are ethnically diverse and driven by personality, economics, foreign influence, and alliance building. Just as important, the military—never a Hausa stronghold—persists in hovering over the body politic. After backsliding into military rulership (including the 1999 assassination of the Zarma junta leader and president Barre Maïnassara), Niger reestablished democratic governance—of a sort. Colonel Mahmadou Tandja, member of the small Kanuri ethnic group, was elected president in 1999 and then reelected in 2004. Tandja's constitutionally dubious efforts to prolong his rule beyond mandated terms limit by engineering a referendum backfired when he was overthrown in 2010. Neither the original spokesman of the military junta (Col. Goukoye Karimou) nor its leader (Maj. Soulou Djibo) was Hausa; to the contrary, the earlier pattern of Zarma-led military rule seemed to be reasserting itself. Local decentralization *à la nigérienne* notwithstanding, the French colonial legacy of political centralism and directive governance—not to mention its cultivation of Zarma in the army—has perpetuated the political marginalization of the Hausa of Niger. They nevertheless remain the economic custodians of most of the country.

In Nigeria, postcolonial politics—increasingly Americanized but still institutionally molded by British regionalism—have cast the Hausa in a rather different role. In a country where southerners, and particularly Igbos, have excelled as entrepreneurs and intellectuals, the Hausa, despite their much smaller proportion (29 percent) of the overall population than in Niger, have played much more prominent roles in both government and the military.

Until his assassination in the so-called majors' coup of 1966, prime minister Tafawa Balewa steered independent Nigeria. Although the man who emerged to lead the federal forces during the violent Biafran secession campaign (1967–70) was not himself Hausa (Gowon), that civil war was largely understood as a contest between the Hausa-Fulani north and a recalcitrant (and oil-endowed) southeast, principally led by Igbos. A unified Hausa political and military hegemony was implied by the epithet "Kaduna Mafia." When the military reverted to civilian rule in 1979, it was a Hausa-Fulani—Shehu Shagari—who led the country as president.

After Shagari was ousted in a coup on New Year's Eve 1984, he was succeeded by military officers who themselves either bore distinctive Hausa (and/or Fulani) names (Muhammadu Buhari, Ibrahim Babangida) or hailed from northern, Hausa-speaking territory (Sani Abacha). Although Olusejun Obasanjo, who incarnated the return to civilian rule (and served as president between 1999 and 2006) was himself Yoruba, it is generally acknowledged that his election was at the sufferance (if not behest) of Hausa power brokers. Obasanjo's successor in 2007, Umaru Yar'Adua, was once again a Hausa; critics quickly denounced his government as "a political comeback for the 'Kaduna Mafia'" (*Africa Confidential* 2007).

For the sake of national unity, an unofficial ethnic rule in politics has been evolving in Nigeria: "rotation" of northern (understood as Hausa or Hausa-Fulani) and southern (understood as Christian) leading presidential candidates, with vice presidential running mates of the other persuasion. This helps explain much of the opposition to (Christian) Vice President Goodluck Jonathan's proactive measures as acting president during (Hausa) Yar'Adua's illness and hospitalization (much of it in Saudi Arabia) in 2009–10. Yar'Adua's death in office in 2010 stoked disquiet over which ethno-religious group's "turn" it would be to succeed the prematurely deceased president. In neighboring Niger, there is simply no equivalent to such public jockeying among the political elite over communal entitlement, no "rules" about when it is time for a Hausa to rule.

Wealth from Nigeria's mineral resources is concentrated in the south, especially the Niger Delta. National political power, though, is wielded from the north, from Nigerian Hausaland. That northern power structure, which southern Nigerians will often refer to as Hausa-Fulani, derives its legitimacy from a political culture steeped in Islam (Paden 1973). Islamic Sufi brotherhoods in northern Nigeria (principally the Tijaniyya and Qadiriyya) provide built-in national, and indeed transnational (with Senegal), networks of association. Although present in Niger, the Tijaniyya brotherhood wields much less influence than it does in Nigeria. Although beset with many fissures, the Hausa and other Hausa-speaking peoples constitute a much more unified, powerful bloc in Nigeria than they do in Niger.

Postcolonial Continuity

> It is full of trouble, this evil country:
> Faranshi is like mouse broth.
> There is fat, and there is stench.
> The chisel never gets used
> To the carpenter's hand, and
> Will slash his hand.

This epigram, still recited in the mid-1980s, reflects the perception of continuity among denizens of the Nigeria-Niger borderlands. Independence did not rupture the patterns of French and British governance: rather, "black white men" took over the reins of power on both sides of the border, basically preserving the structures and mindsets of their respective European predecessors.[14] Let us consider the arenas of identity and economics, education and language, chieftaincy and governance, and gender. Inasmuch as Islam plays a critical role in all these areas, religion is integrated into each of these discussions.

Identity and Economics

Distinctive colonial policies and legacies, interacting with core characteristics of indigenous society, give rise to discrete national

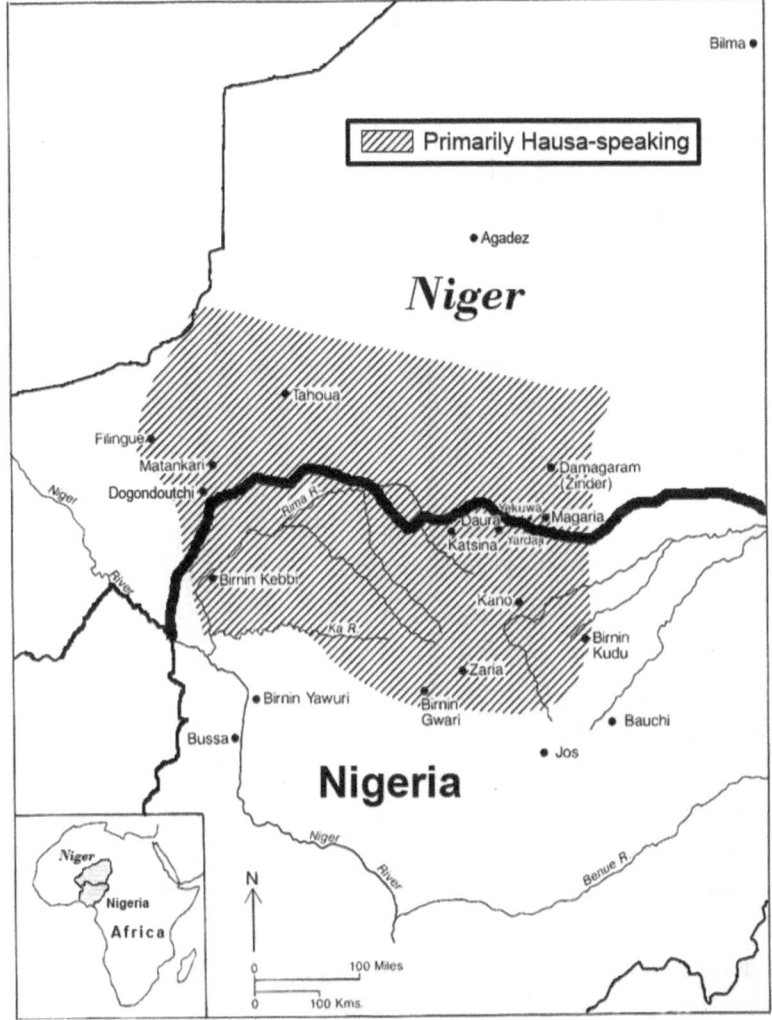

Map 6. Hausaland Divided

versions of ethnic identity. Material outcomes and expectations, which do shape national character, similarly are legatees of colonial imprints. There is no abstract human being whom we can call "Hausa," Nigerian Hausa, yes, or Nigérien Hausa, too. No Hausas are more acutely aware of the difference than those Hausas who live in the borderlands spanning historic Hausaland (see Map 6).

Few of these borderlanders are aware of statistical indicators that outside chroniclers easily invoke to make national comparisons. Even converted into Nigerian naira—used by borderland villagers in Niger instead of the CFA (or French West African franc)—they would be hard-pressed to estimate the GDP per capita of Nigeria ($1,450) in contrast to that of Niger ($354) (see Table 2). They would tell you, though, that Nigeria is a country of *arziki* (wealth, prosperity) whereas Faranshi (Niger) is one of *talauci* (poverty). And when they do so, they are not imagining differences between Niamey (which relatively few Nigériens will ever see in their lives) and Abuja, the respective capitals of Niger and Nigeria. They are referring to distinctions apparent to their own eyes, as they cross the partitioning boundary and compare neighboring communities with each other. Except for civil servants, politicians, and successful merchants described in Emmanuel Grégoire's (1992) *The Alhazai of Maradi*, to describe oneself as "Hausa" in Niger self-consciously means to be poor to an extent not so connoted by saying one is Hausa in Nigeria. Despite the widespread poverty and low life expectancy (52 years) that plagues Nigeria, its overall human development ranking is thirty-four places higher than that of Niger.[15]

To say that one is Hausa in Niger is practically synonymous with saying one is Muslim. This is a bit less so in Nigeria. Whereas the animistic or "pagan" Hausa-speaking Maguzawa have practically disappeared from both countries, there are significant pockets of Christian Hausa in the Nigerian cities of Kaduna, Jos, and Zaria. Clearly, most Nigerians associate "Hausa" with "Muslim," and in a country that is about evenly divided between Muslims and non-Muslims, "being Hausa" takes on a denominational salience that it does not in Niger, the most Islamically homogeneous nation, after Mauritania, in the entire Sahel. In Nigeria, Christian-Muslim clashes have cost thousands of lives since the return to democracy in 1999.

In surveys conducted in two neighboring Hausa villages on both side of the Niger-Nigeria border, respondents consistently

Table 2. Material Outcomes—West Africa

	GNI per capita (dollars, 2011)	Life expectancy (years)	Adult literacy (%)
Former British colonies			
Gambia (1.7)[a]	1,282	58.5	40.1
Ghana (23.4)	1,584	64.2	65.0
Sierra Leone (5.6)	737	47.8	38.1
Nigeria (151.2)	2,069	51.9	72.0
Former French colonies			
Benin (8.7)	1,364	56.1	40.5
Cameroon (19.1)	2,031	51.6	67.9
Burkina Faso (15.2)	1,141	55.4	28.7
Guinea (9.8)	863	54.1	29.5
Ivory Coast (20.6)	1,387	55.4	48.7
Mali (12.7)	1,123	51.4	26.2
Mauritania (3.2)	1,859	58.6	55.8
Niger (14.7)	641	54.7	28.7
Senegal (12.2)	1,708	59.3	41.9
Togo (6.5)	798	57.1	53.2

[a] Number in parentheses next to country refers to population, in millions.

Sources: UN Data, Country Profiles (http://data.un.org); UNDP Human Development Index 2011 (http://hdrstats.undp.org/en/indicators/89.html); CIA *World Factbook* (http://www.cia.gov).

named "being Muslim" as their most important self-identifying attribute. (More Nigerians than Nigériens did so, however, at a difference of 96 percent to 81 percent; see Miles and Rochefort 1991). As second most important identity, more Nigérien borderlanders chose "country" than Nigerian ones did; conversely, more Nigerians than Nigériens chose "being Hausa." In third place, "country" again ranked higher among Nigériens than among Nigerians.

Overall—and counterintuitively—the survey indicated a greater expressed identification with attachment to nation-station (being Nigérien, being Nigerian) than with ethnicity (being Hausa), this tendency being more pronounced among Nigériens than Nigerians. (Other identity choices were village, subethnic group, place of birth, and province/state.) Such differences in self-identity, particularly with respect to nationality and ethnicity, need to be contextualized: the surveys were conducted at a time when Niger was still (after sixteen years) subject to dirigiste, if not harsh, military rule while Nigeria was not (civilian governance having returned seven years prior). Still, it would not be surprising to find that differences in self-identity prevail in Hausa communities on opposite sides of the borders as a result of the differing colonial and postcolonial experience of Nigeria and Niger.

Although the border between Niger and Nigeria is relatively quiescent itself, borderlanders are uniformly conscious of the higher levels of violence and crime in Nigeria. Niger is understood to be a safer place to live and in which to travel. Democracy is perceived to be less problematic than in Nigeria, less subject to corruption (or at least subject to lower levels of corruption). At the same time, local governance (and the benefits that accrue from it) has always been much more advanced on the Nigerian side: elected local governments have been functioning there for decades (see Map 7) whereas elected councils for Niger's 265 rural communes were instituted only in 2006. But perhaps even more important in the identity-economics nexus is that the Hausa of Niger, by virtue of their citizenship, have been the continuous objects of state-driven and internationally funded development policies and ideologies (Charlick 1972, Horowitz et al. 1983, Lanne 1983) without equivalent in Nigeria. Though once called a "development society," Niger may be better thought of as a "development project society." In many respects the Nigérien Hausa mindset reflects a *mentalité d'assisté* (Miles 1994b, 296) at variance with Nigerian Hausa exuberance. Intra-ethnic national identity differentiation is hardly specific to Hausaland: "Ghanaians and Ivoirians are distinguished not simply by the side of a colonially created dividing line on which they happen to find

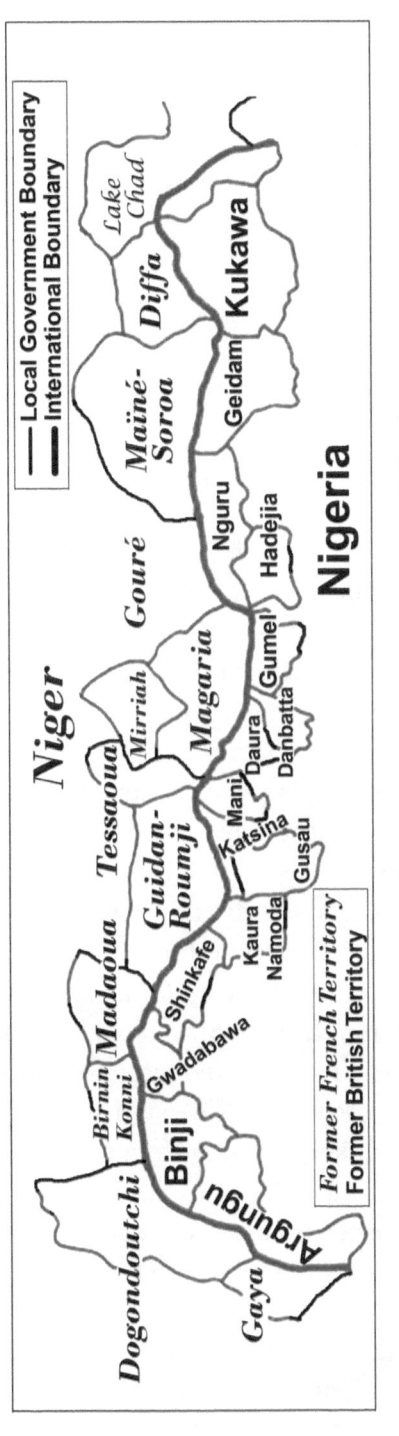

Map 7. Local Governments of Niger-Nigeria Borderlands

themselves, but by differences of historical experience and personal identity which may well deepen as they are transmitted to subsequent generations" (Clapham 1999, 62).

Education, Language, and Theater

Although there have been modifications in the educational systems inherited from Britain and France, schooling in the borderlands of Nigeria and Niger still bear the imprint of colonial pedagogy. As Michael Crowder (1968, 378–80) described it, "The French system was more concerned with persuading children of the virtues of . . . French culture. . . . The British . . . were concerned that the . . . education given be adapted to the African situation. . . . Britain sought to produce an 'African' African."

The most important difference in the two systems today remains primary language of instruction: English in schools south of the border, with many practical concessions to Hausa; French to the north, with Hausa stigmatized in the classroom. Hausa language instruction is a formal part of the regular curriculum throughout primary school in the northern states of Nigeria; in Niger, only a few pilot programs have introduced local languages for the most elementary levels, struggling against general governmental and popular disinterest in bilingual education. (Despite several efforts at reform, this is indicative of the prevailing postcolonial pattern throughout Francophone Africa [Alidou and Jung 2002; Djité 1990; Hutchison and Nguessan 1995; Parker 1996]). Islamic prayers and religious instruction (including Arabic) are integrated into the school day of Hausa children attending school in Nigeria; these have no place whatsoever in their counterpart schools in Niger. Not surprisingly, there is no equivalent in Niger to the thriving Hausa-language book and newspaper industry in Nigeria. Francophone phonetics render Nigerian Hausa literature difficult for Nigérien Hausaphones.

Parental resistance to Western education in Niger is a leitmotif of colonial and postcolonial life in rural Hausaland. Compulsory education among the Nigérien Hausa is still viewed in militaristic terms: enforced by soldiers and akin to conscription into the military. Discipline in the classroom smacks more of the barracks than the playroom.[16] Part of the resistance is economic: parents do not perceive that long-term benefits of education outweigh the immediate costs of their children not doing farm work. Part of the resistance is religious: the lack of Qur'anic education in the Nigérien schools is viewed as un-Islamic. Whereas Nigerian Hausa borderlanders may have similar opportunity cost concerns, these are more than offset by the integration of religion into their children's education. Indeed, on the Nigerian side of the border there has been more general concern with the insufficiency of educational infrastructure, particularly in rural (including border) areas: hence, the overall popularity of Universal Primary Education (UPE) policies.[17]

In Nigeria's federal system, policies, priorities, and curricula are set by individual states; in Niger, a single ministry of national education has full authority over all instruction throughout the republic. As a result, teachers may be transferred from one end of the country to the other, their knowledge of local language notwithstanding. In Nigeria, no teacher from any of the primarily Hausa states (e.g., Katsina, Kano, Zamfara) would ever be transferred to an Igbo or Yoruba school district.

As developed in colonial days, Nigerian Hausaland has a much more extensive network of government-sanctioned religious schools. In Niger, late-colonial attempts to establish Franco-Arabic schools (médersas, or madrasas) was driven more by political concerns than pedagogic ideals: it was to ensure "a controlled, a malleable, a pliable Islam that [the French] could twist and bend to serve their purposes" (Clarke 1982, 190–91). After independence, the Nigérien government (under the authority of the Ministry of the Interior) continued the madrasa schools for similar purposes. "The State is thus giving itself the means to intervene in the training of the dispensers of Koranic education—old dream of the colonial power" (Triaud 1981, 19–20). In Say,

Niger is host to an Islamic university that serves students from throughout West Africa. Here, French is not the required language. But those schooled in Arabic "feel themselves excluded from the system because of the . . . mistrust bequeathed to the administration through colonization with regard to anything Arabic or Islamic in culture" (Niandou-Souley and Alzouma 1996, 253; see also Meunier 1997, 2000).

Even informal instruments of education, such as theater, perpetuate colonial differences. Under British tutelage, popular Hausa drama in northern Nigeria developed as a literary and dramatic genre that, after independence, continued to benefit from the institutional support of local universities and the Center for Nigerian Cultural Studies. In Niger, in contrast, Hausa plays are orally improvised and only sometimes transcribed. More important, both colonial and postcolonial regimes in Niger have suborned what was once a satirical art form critical of rulers to one propagating the regime's policies (Alidou 2000, 202). A traditional art form that on one side of the border developed as autonomous entertainment has, on the other side, been an instrument of state-driven "development" (Beik 1984).

Chieftaincy and Governance

"Essentially, the French reduced the chiefs to the role of agents of the administration, a position that has not been substantially modified by the independent governments of Niger" (Charlick 1991, 21). As a carryover from colonial-era policy, traditional rulers in Nigeria continue to exercise more influence, autonomy, and prestige than their counterparts in Niger, where the central government still tends to view the chieftaincy as an administrative convenience at the service of government. This contrast is particularly manifest among the Hausa chiefs and emirs (Lund and Hesseling 1999; Miles 1987; Olivier de Sardan 1999; Sidikou and Djika 2000; Soulas de Russel 1998) and parallels what Asiwaju (1970, 1976) found with respect to Yoruba *obas* in Nigeria vis-à-vis Dahomey/Benin and Firmin-

Sellers (2001) notes regarding Bamiléké *fons* in Francophone as opposed to Anglophone Cameroon.

Formal powers of traditional rulers have diminished in Nigeria since independence, but paradoxically their actual influence and decision-making capacities have been augmented. This is the case both at the national political as well as local governance levels.

Until 1976, the colonial-era Native Authority System—a linchpin of Indirect Rule—basically maintained the supremacy of the Hausa and Hausa-Fulani emirs. Military-initiated reforms in 1976 standardized and democratized local government, ostensibly at the expense of chiefs and emirs. Local government enjoyed increased autonomy and federal revenues whereas the Northern Region's House of Chiefs was abolished and large emirates in the Hausa heartland were broken up. Two years later, the Land Use Decree stripped traditional rulers of their prerogative to determine land tenure and land-use law and practice. Within the context of Nigeria, "the 'modernising' elite, backed by the power of the state, has steadily managed . . . to erode the formal powers and influence of the strictly 'traditional' rulers" (Graf 1986, 109).

*In*formal leverage, however—especially the ability to induce masses of commoners to vote for a given political party—has bestowed upon the chiefs new kinds of power within the electoral field. So has the power to bestow honorary titles. In return, traditional rulers receive civil service pay, are appointed to public commissions and boards, and sometimes manage appointment to state executive positions.

To take one example, the outcome of Nigeria's 1979 election campaign—the country's first military-to-civilian transition—was to a large extent determined by the actions of such Hausa and Hausa-Fulani royalty as the Baraden (later Sultan) of Sokoto, the Sarkin Sudan of Wurno, and the Makaman Bida. Their influence extended beyond the campaign, thanks to the victory of their preferred National Party of Nigeria and the election of Shehu[18] Shagari. Conversely, politicians or would-be politicians, civilian and former military, benefit politically from receiving honorary Hausa and Fulani chieftaincy titles. Thus, the former military chief of staff has benefited by becoming the Tafida of Katsina, the ex-military governor of the Northern Provinces was empowered by also being the Ciroma of Katsina, and the former head of the Nigerian security services was dubbed the Marafin Sokoto. Even Shagari himself cast himself as "presidential" by virtue of his title as Turakin Sokoto. It is no wonder that a "pro-chieftaincy lobby" has thus emerged among influential Nigerians who perceive both public and private benefit in maintaining, if not boosting, the status and prestige of the heirs of the traditional rulers of the Hausa emirates. "Throughout Nigeria's political history, chieftaincy has consistently been reconstructed to reinforce the power and status of dominant classes" (Vaughan 1991, 312–13, 320, 321, 322).

During military interregna, traditional rulers also serve as "administrative-transmission links" (Graf 1986, 111), that is, intermediaries between the officers and the people. Emirate councils at the state level are still mandated to advise local government councils, assist them in taxation, and weigh in on matters of religion and traditional rulership. More contemporary language speaks of the "developmental" or "ombudsman" utility of traditional rulers (Aborisade 1985, 1986; Ayeni 1985; Nwaka 1999; Orewa 1978). For purposes old and new, historical continuity and proximity to the people confers upon traditional authorities a popular legitimacy that "modern" rulers—military and civilian alike—envy. Hausa chiefs in Nigeria have been able to avail themselves of such unofficial powers in ways unavailable to their Nigérien counterparts. They have also been able—inconceivable in Niger—to mobilize subjects against governors in mass-scale protest.[19]

The experience of Hausa chiefs vis-à-vis the independent government of Niger has been in many ways the reverse of Nigeria. In Nigeria, the First Republic (1960–66) witnessed the heyday of emir influence (especially Hausa and Hausa-Fulani) in national politics. Niger's First Republic (1960–74), in contrast, was characterized by marginalization of the chieftaincy by the secular-minded Hamani Diori and his PPN government. Under Diori, the Association des Chefs Traditionnels du Niger (ACTN), established by the French in 1947, became moribund. Under Diori's military successor, Seyni Kountché (1974–87), himself a Zarma prince, the ACTN was revived and the chieftaincy reimagined as an important tool for development (Abba 1990; Guillemin 1983; Robinson 1983, 1991). Under the first military regime (1966–79) in Nigeria, meanwhile, the House of Chiefs was abolished and traditional rulers' authority formally circumscribed by the 1976 Local Government and 1978 Land Reform edicts. Niger's transition to democracy via its Sovereign National Conference of 1991 sidelined the chiefs, whose inherited prerogatives now seemed incompatible with a democratizing nation. At the same time, we have seen how politically influential were Hausa chiefs in the Nigeria's Second Republic (1979–84); as formal democracy anchors itself (as evidenced by the elections of Obasanjo in 1999 and 2003, Yar'Adua in 2007, and Goodluck Jonathan in 2011), Hausa chiefs' electoral influence may be expected to expand in Nigeria.

In 1993 the (civilian) government of Niger passed new measures (République du Niger 1993) regulating the traditional chieftaincy of Niger, which had hitherto enjoyed relative autonomy. Its goal was to standardize and rationalize the institution, clearly rendering it an ancillary arm of the administration (and still subject to it; section 5 spells out disciplinary actions and sanctions that it can take against chiefs.) At the same time, the government moved to democratize the chieftaincy by changing the mode of selection: rather than appointment by the government, as had been the case since 1981, new village chiefs (eligible according to customary rules) were now to be elected by heads of family; canton chiefs (a position above) were to be elected by their constituent village chiefs. Notwithstanding the legislation's recognition of chiefs incarnating the nation's traditions and custom, for modernizing (including democratizing) elites in Niger the chieftaincy is perceived more as means to development than a cultural end to preserve for its own sake. The attitude of educated Nigérien elites, including Hausa, toward the chieftaincy may be summed up in this comment from a mayor in a newly constituted rural commune in Nigérien Hausaland: "We must make concessions—at least at the beginning" (Miles 2008).

Village chiefs—as a throwback to colonial days—were invested with the responsibility of collecting taxes (section 2, chapter 2, article 12). Their adjudicating roles were clearly limited to land disputes and customary law (but always in adherence to common law). Chiefs were now formally acknowledged as "agent, actor and partner in development" (section 2, chapter 2, article 18). But Guillemin's characterization a decade before still seem accurate, in its disconnect between "the image of a 'chieftaincy of progress,' of chiefs as 'agents of development' but also [the reality] of an institution more and more tightly controlled and directed, of chiefs [who are] 'administered' administrators" (Guillemin 1983, 124).

Among chiefs in western Niger, at least, the legislation of 1993 is associated with democratization, which is in turn linked to a breakdown in discipline and respect. "With democracy," stated a canton chief, "the people no longer consider us as respectable personalities. . . . I observe also a lack of collaboration on [their] part" (Soulas de Russel 1998).

In rural areas—and over two-thirds of Niger's population is rural—village and canton chiefs still continue to exercise considerable control, including over development projects (Olivier de Sardan 1999). They are not, however, in a position to mobilize their constituents/subjects collectively. Democratization does infiltrate the villages of Nigérien Hausaland through political parties; Nigérien parties, however, do not work the chieftaincy networks as parties do in Nigeria. Unlike their counterparts in Nigeria, Hausa chiefs in Niger are not in a position to reward politicians with titles and other honorary emoluments.

Since independence, in absolute terms the power and prerogatives of the chieftaincy, Hausa and not, may indeed have diminished in Nigeria (Davies 1990). Compared with Niger, however, Hausa chiefs in Nigeria retain considerably more prestige, security, and wealth. In borderland communities there is indeed an important common denominator: traditional chiefs and partitioned royalty possess expertise in advancing Nigérien-Nigerian transborder cooperation, peace, and security (Adnan 1993, 106; Miles 1992, xiii, 36). But colonial partition still defines geopolitically contemporary life stations and prospects, for royalty and commoners alike.

Gender

Cooper (1998) argues convincingly that women were the keepers of Islam's syncretic spirit in Hausaland. Prior to the Fulani-led jihad—and after it, in those rump states that resisted it by escape—women (including Muslims) could freely farm, practice spirit possession (*bori*), assume leadership and priestly functions, and concomitantly accrue wealth and power. Jihadist Islam, rather, entailed veiling, seclusion, and exclusion (albeit with a new opportunity to engage the Qur'an). Even where their pre-jihadic prerogatives were not entirely suppressed, women were marginalized, even prostitutionalized.

Despite a formalization of (Malikite) Islamic law under the French in ways that affected women, Hausa women in colonial and postcolonial Niger maintained an economic and social autonomy that their counterparts in Nigeria did not, at least not to the same extent. They farmed; they maintained the *bori* (spirit possession) cult; they preserved the titled position of *iya*: all practices that in Nigeria were progressively restricted as un-Islamic. Despite encroaching influence of Nigerian Islam into Niger, "the history of female participation in farming and trade makes it possible for Hausa women in Niger to be Muslim without necessarily being secluded. Hausa women in Niger, despite their relative lack of education, may be able to parlay economic power into increasing political power in ways that Hausa women in Nigeria cannot" (Cooper 1998, 35). Alidou (2005, 69) argues that with respect to formal education and Islamic teaching, French colonial policy adversely affected Nigérien women in ways that contrasted with the more benign British impact on women in northern Nigeria. Disparagement of local languages (and Arabic) in favor of French, discouragement of the Arabic script for the writing of Hausa (*ajami*), and disdain for oral culture vis-à-vis (Francophone) literacy tended to marginalize female knowledge. In these domains, women's strength had been concentrated in oral literature, Islamic-Arabic orality, and vocational (as opposed to literate elitist) education. One of her informants, Malama A'ishatu, is a Zarma-born Nigérien woman who married a Hausa man near Sokoto, where she studied Qur'an and Hausa-Islamic poetry. As she recounts, her Nigerian-learned knowledge and sources trumped a (mis)rendering of a religious poem on Niger's national radio. "Thus began Malama A'ishatu's shift from the confines of *kuble* [wife seclusion] to the public arena of national electronic media" (Alidou 2005, 35).

The significant role of Hausa women in the relatively autonomous urban spaces and palaces of the northern Nigerian emirates has been well documented.[20] The disparate function played by Hausa women in Niger's animistic subculture and "development society" has also been excellently described.[21] Between the two, in the rural borderlands dividing Hausaland, the inherited boundary again serves as stark demarcation for how colonialism and postcolonialism affect women differentially. Incidence of wife seclusion in two neighboring Hausa villages on either side of the Nigeria-Niger boundary elicited a more than threefold difference in 1986: 36 percent compared to 11 percent. Fifteen years later, purdah had advanced on both sides of the border, but the differential still held: 84 percent of married women in the Nigerian Hausa village were said to be in seclusion; 31 percent in the Nigérien one (Miles 2003d).

Within contrasting postcolonial contexts, the role and treatment of Hausa women assume different symbolic meanings (Cooper 1998). In Nigeria, Islamic "protection" of females is another way of establishing northern regional identity vis-à-vis southern and Christian social mores and political claims over the country. In Niger, women are "protected" from alien acculturation filtering in from the Western world (à la feminism) rather than from any domestic ethnoregional groups.

Alidou's research on Hausa-speaking women in postcolonial Niger leads her to identify "a new francophone Afro-Islamic modernity." She also describes the uniquely Nigérien "hybrid" outcome of French colonialism, Hausa transethnicity, and borderland biregionalism as embodied in Malama A'ishatu (2005, 42, 50). Islamic culture from Nigerian Hausaland may indeed dominate on an aggregate scale, but Nigérien identity—a contemporary byproduct of European partition and French colonialism—preserves its unique postcolonial character.

State Management of the Borderlands

Smuggling, a tendentious word in terms of its illicit connotations, has long been a respectable profession along the Niger-Nigeria boundary. Collins (1976, 1985) chronicles the continuing, undocumented transport of groundnuts from Niger into Nigeria in the decade following independence. Drought and disease devastated Nigérien groundnut growing; informal cross-border trade continued, however, with different commodities (livestock, petroleum) taking precedence. In the early twenty-first century, two other cross-border businesses came to preoccupy the Nigérien and Nigerian governments: human (especially child) trafficking and arms smuggling.

It took more than a decade after independence, but in 1971 a Nigeria-Niger Joint Commission (NNJC) was established with a rotating chairmanship and a Niamey-based secretariat. The purpose of the NNJC was to harmonize relations between the partner states. NNJC met on such subjects as road transport

(1977), industrial and agro-industrial projects (1978), culture and education (1982), and water resources, irrigation, communication, and food production (1984).

Despite sporadic periods of intensified border patrols, a civil war in one of the countries, and political instability in both of them, for nearly a quarter of a century the Niger-Nigeria boundary remained an open one. Shortly after Nigeria's New Year's Eve coup of 1984, however, the border was ordered closed for the very first time. The purpose was to thwart wanted politicians from escaping over the country's land borders. Reopened on January 23, 1984, Major-General Buhari had them shut again three months and one day later. Although ostensibly done to reduce the inflows of currency (the regime had decided to change Nigerian bill notes), the closure was maintained beyond the conversion in order to stymie the undeclared outflow of petroleum and foodstuffs. To enforce the cross-border ban, motorized border patrols were put into effect. This second border closing was to last twenty-two months.

Plans to build a network of border outposts were announced in October 1984. Eighty years after the British and French sectioned off a Nigerian colony from a Nigérien one, the successor government to the former was taking serious steps to monitor and control its northern border (see Figs. 4 and 5).

Between 700,000 and 2 million noncitizens (including 100,000 Nigériens) were ordered out of Nigeria in mid-1985. That same year, Nigeria Airways suspended its flight between the two countries' capitals. (The reasons, however, were more economic than political.)

Even with the Nigeria-Niger border still closed, the NNJC reconvened in 1985 for its sixteenth session. After March 1986, when the borders were reopened, the commission deliberated on drought and desertification (1986, 1988) and information, cultural exchange, and judicial matters (1989). One commentator claims, however, that at least until the late 1980s the NNJC was "very much underutilized" (Sanusi 1993, 31). As late as 1989

Fig. 4. New Hausaland Boundary Marker

direct telephone calls between the two countries were still being routed between Paris and London.[22]

A new institutional emphasis on the border took shape in 1989 with the inauguration (still then under military tutelage) of the National Boundary Commission of Nigeria. The commission "seeks to move away from the perception of borders as battle lines and borderlands as potential war zones. Rather, it sees international borders as bridges which can be used to achieve regional integration and co-operation" (Barkindo 1993, xvii). Among the commission's first order of activities were transborder workshops; secondly, it assembled academics, administrators, policy makers, and traditional rulers. Proceedings from that workshop resulted in the most extensive postcolonial writings on the administrative, cultural, economic, and legal realities of life in the Nigeria-Niger borderlands (Asiwaju and Barkindo 1993).

Two multilateral organizations also deal with Nigerién-Nigerian border relations: the Economic Commission of West African States (ECOWAS) and the Lake Chad Basin Commission.

Fig. 5. Nigerian Border Station

According to the first phase of the ECOWAS Protocol (1979–84), foreign citizens visiting member states for over three months were required to obtain visas. (This requirement was designed, inter alia, to control cross-border job-seeking [Labo 2000, 13]. For the tens of thousands of Nigériens working in Nigeria, such legal requirements were generally ignored. The second phase of the protocol, guaranteeing the right of ECOWAS citizens to reside and work in member countries, coincided with the closing of Nigeria's borders. Phase 3 of the ECOWAS Protocol, regulating the issuance of residence permits, also lacked implementation. Expulsion of ECOWAS aliens is supposed to respect other provisions of the protocol but to little avail. In reality, "transborder cooperation suffer[s also from] misunderstanding by border enforcement agents of the bilateral accords between Niger and Nigeria, notably . . . regarding the free circulation of people and goods [and the status of] persons in transit (Bako 1993; my translation).

The shrinking of Lake Chad has created uncertainty regarding one of the demarcation lines between Nigeria and Niger. This matter is under the jurisdiction of the Lake Chad Basin Commission. (For the same environmental reason, there is uncertainty regarding the lines of separation between Nigeria and Cameroon, Nigeria and Chad, Chad and Cameroon, and Niger and Chad.) As water evaporates or leeches away, lake turns to land and new boundary lines have to be drawn.

The National Border Commission did not replace the NNJC; in 1990, at its twentieth session, it tasked itself to implement already ratified agreements in the areas of cultural exchange, health, information, justice, and trade. Its most recurring topic for discussion, in meetings between 1991 and 2003, has been the increasing desertification of the border region. (Cross-border swarming of grasshoppers—1996 was a veritable plague year—has been another environmental concern of these bodies.)

In the 1990s security took on a greater emphasis in these binational border meetings. At the 1989 Transborder Workshop, "the greater involvement of traditional rulers in fostering border security, peace and cooperation" was recommended (Adnan 1993, 106). This policy was reiterated in 1991 during a joint border tour by the ministers of the interior of both countries. (BBC 1991). In 1994 and 1996 officials from Yobe State in Nigeria met with their counterparts in the Diffa department in Niger regarding armed banditry and criminal activities along their common border. These were believed to have been committed by Toubous.

By the mid-1990s deterioration of colonial-era boundary markers was extensive enough to warrant a new survey, redemarcation, and eventual replacement. NNJC established a Joint Standing Committee on Re-Demarcation and initially identified eight villages in Nigérien territory that actually belonged to Nigeria, and nine Nigérien ones that were erroneously in Nigeria. In addition, twenty-nine instances of individual settlements spanning the border were found. By the time the new demarcation was completed in 2006—precisely one hundred years after the original French-British surveying team finished its original act of partition—the number of villages that Nigeria realized it had to relocate from Nigérien territory had risen to thirteen. Unlike the colonial partition, however, this one recognized some material responsibility on the part of the dislocators: Nigeria was prepared to build schools, clinic, wells, and "security outposts" for villages it was relocating. One hundred new pillars were placed along the remarked boundary, at 1.2 meters depth, "to ensure that even a bulldozer would have a tough time pulling them down" (*Africa News* 2006).

Not all the ambiguity in demarcated territorial sovereignty was a matter of imprecision: in at least one case, environmental interference was at fault. In Nigeria's Borno State, farmers rechanneled the Kumadugu-Yobe River to facilitate irrigation of their croplands. Inasmuch as that waterway constituted part of the boundary, changing the course of the river amounted to the ceding of seventeen square kilometers to Niger. (In 2007 the National Boundary Commission vowed to redirect the Kumadugu-Yobe back to its original course.)

Scores of fatalities are recorded along the border every year, as Nigerian (often Hausa) farmers clash with Nigérien (usually Fulani) herdsmen. This is a persistent problem across the Sahel, however, and does little to dampen the overall amicable relations between Nigeria and Niger; the Nigerian media consistently points out that the most peaceable of the nation's borders is with Niger Republic, compared with Benin, Chad, and especially Cameroon.[23] The cross-border trafficking of children (180 were intercepted at the boundary and returned to Niger between 2003 and 2005 alone) is treated as a joint problem, not an irritant to overall relations.

Diplomacy aside, Nigeria and Niger are keenly protective of their territorial integrity. Far from negating the superimposed colonial partition, through joint surveys and redemarcation the two states are in fact reaffirming its legitimacy in the twenty-first century. Niger and Nigeria adhere faithfully to the postcolonial commandment, "I Am the State, Thy Nation": there is no question, for example, of reuniting Hausaland.

Some African elites surmise that villagers along the borderline disregard their governments' attempts to reinforce the legitimacy of the (erstwhile colonial) boundary. As one former military governor put it: "The common man whose cultural heritage as well as blood relations are solidly rooted across the borders, certainly views all international border related formalities as irrelevant and artificial" (Onoja 1993, 310). In fact, the so-called common man in the borderland is acutely aware of even the invisible boundary line as well as the sovereignty—however imperfectly exercised—on each side of it.

In July 2001 Niger's minister of foreign affairs and African integration announced, "Within the framework of cooperation on cross-border security, our two states will pursue their efforts to curb crime along the common border." The minister then broached plans for a joint anticrime border patrol and borderline tour (BBC 2001). Two months later heretofore localized interest in the Niger-Nigeria boundary took on a much broader dimension with the Islamist-inspired attacks of September 11 and the U.S. declaration of a global war on terrorism. Overnight, the "long and porous borders" of the Sahel—including those of Niger and Nigeria—came under heightened scrutiny by diplomats and security analysts from afar (ACSS 2003). Joint Nigérien-Nigerian border patrols were put into place in 2003. But the boundary as demarcator of dual paths of Islam between neighboring African states—indeed, within a single, partitioned Hausa people—had been evident long before.

Islam, Islamism, and the Border

Due to distinctive colonial policies and postcolonial continuities, Islam persevered with much greater institutional autonomy in Nigeria vis-à-vis Niger. Whereas from the outset Britain essayed to coopt Islamic leaders in Nigeria, France strove to marginalize them. There is no equivalent in colonial Nigérien history to Lord Lugard's 1903 speech in Sokoto that aimed to reassure "the natives" of the fundamental compatibility between Islam as a creed and mode of organization and British colonial rule. The secular, culturally transformative French view of religion made them view Nigérien Islam (and their marabouts) with much greater suspicion.

The relative place of sharia in the legal systems on each side of the boundary reflects this difference. For the French, keen to rationalize the judicial process, sharia in Niger was reduced to the status of customary law, with little formal recognition within the colonial court system. In Nigeria, the British took pains to preserve Islamic law while modernizing it, at least in the north where the population was overwhelmingly Muslim. By the late colonial era, and then for nearly three decades after independence, sharia in colonial Nigeria, remained an integral feature of (northern) Nigerian civil law. Although attempts to establish a Federal Court of Sharia did ultimately fail (Laitin 1982; Ibrahim 1991), the 1979 and 1989 constitutions protected the sharia system at regional levels. So does the 1999 Constitution. A Muslim Hausa who insisted on Islamic justice would have easy recourse to it if he or she lived on the Nigerian side of the border sectioning Hausaland, but much less so if in Niger.

A comparison of the constitutions reinforces this point. Article 4 of Niger's constitution (amended 1999, but on this point no different than those of 1992 and 1996) guarantees "separation of state and religion"; Article 8 assures religious equality: "The Republic of Niger respects and protects all beliefs. No religion, no belief may arrogate to itself political power or interfere in the affairs of the State." There is no mention of Islam (despite Niger being the second most homogenously Muslim nation in sub-Saharan Africa) and, most tellingly, no sharia. Indeed, there is no mention of any higher divine authority.

Nigeria's constitution takes a very different tack. The preamble situates the Nigerian nation explicitly "under God." Although Article 38 guarantees freedom of religion and Article 10 prohibits state adoption of it (Chapter 1), Chapter 7 (the Judicature) makes several provisions for sharia courts and civil law proceedings for Muslims. Part 2, Section B, Articles 275, 276, and 277, deal with state-level sharia courts of appeal; Part 1, Sections B and E, establish sharia courts of appeal at the federal level. Both parts specify appointments of kadis and grand kadis, imparting to them overall competence "in civil proceedings involving questions of Islamic personal Law."

Since transitioning to civilian rule in the 1990s, politicians in Niger Republic have pushed back somewhat (largely for electoral reasons) against the colonially inspired policy of strict separation of mosque and state. The days of corporatist subservience (religious and otherwise) to the Nigérien state that peaked under Seyni Kountché and the "Development Society" in 1980s are over. Enforcement of the ban on preaching without a license (Miles 1994b, 262–73) has also waned. Islamist associations, both highly institutional and ad hoc, have openly expressed themselves in ways previously alien to Niger (Niandou-Souley and Alzouma 1996). With regard to the former, Izala, an anti-Sufi movement of Nigerian origin (Kane 1990, 1994, 2003; Loimeier 1997, 2007), has become a prominent social and economic actor, especially in the area around Maradi (Grégoire 1992, 1993). Indeed, the spread of Izala from northern Nigeria to southern Niger may be thought of as a kind of borderland revivalism. Elsewhere in Niger, demonstrations against a proposed "family code" that would have increased legal protections for women met with unprecedented mobilization on the part of Islamic organizations (Villalon 2003). There have been Islamically inspired mass demonstrations against a government campaign to promote the use of condoms; against government ratification of the UN Convention on Ending All Forms of Discrimination Against Women; and against the hosting of International Festival of African Fashion (Charlick 2007).

Still, by and large, Islam is not the political force in Niger that it is in Nigeria. It is neither a major challenge to governance nor is it fully controlled by government. Despite the 1994 clash between Izala adepts and Nigérien soldiers, neither mass Salafist nor quasi-millenarian revolt against secular and religious authority (as witnessed in the 1980s by the 'Yan Tatsine in northern Nigeria [Christelow 1985; Hiskett 1987; Kastfelt 1989; Lubeck 1985; Pred and Watts 1992; Watts 1996]) is conceivable in Niger. Nor has Boko Haram, the Islamist terror group that began wreaking havoc in Nigeria in 2011, taken hold in Niger.

Almost as remote is the prospect of amending the Nigérien constitution to incorporate sharia. When the head of the Tijaniyya brotherhood in Niger did call for official recognition of Islamic law in 2000, he was rebuked by President Tandja, who declared, "Niger is a secular and tolerant state. We evolve as such and remain Muslims" (quoted in Charlick 2007, 31). Even if this statement glosses over the real level of collaboration between clerics and politicians, between politicized Islam and the Nigérien state, it does accurately reflect the greater pains undertaken by Muslim political leaders in Niger, in contrast with Nigeria, to outwardly respect the secular nature of the state.

In northern Nigeria, a significant shift in the colonial and postcolonial balance between civil religious and secular *criminal* law began to take shape in the late 1990s. Twelve of Nigeria's northern states (there are thirty-six in the country as a whole) elevated sharia from its circumscribed role in civil jurisprudence to codes governing criminal law. (Zamfara was the first state, in 1999, formally to legislate the transition.) World attention was galvanized by the handful of death sentences meted out (although never actually performed) to Muslim women convicted of adultery. Qur'an-proscribed amputation for repeated theft was juridically administered in some cases. Prostitution, alcohol, even live music (at least initially) were all banned. Sharia-inspired edicts against practicing traditional folkways—such as praise singing, drumming, and festive dancing—went so far that one could speak for a time of "de-Hausification" south of the border (Miles 2003b), even if strict enforcement of sharia subsequently seemed to diminish (Polgreen 2007).

Seven of the twelve "sharia-compliant" states of Nigeria bordered Niger Republic. Accordingly, some Nigérien border settlements expanded, and others arose anew, to service Nigerian clients now deprived of certain products and diversions (Onishi 2001; Kirwin 2005). "Dividends of sharia," Daniel Bach (2003) calls the political knock-off effects of Islamic law; "courtesan state" is how Matthew Kirwin characterizes Niger's role as borderline provider of sinful goods and services. A local journalist's account of the intersection of partition and sharia in the village of Doli is quite evocative. Doli is an ethnically mixed settlement (Hausa, Fulani, Zarma, and Kengawa) that sits astride the Niger-Nigeria border. Half of it lies within the Dandi local government area of Kebbi state in Nigeria; the other is subject to the département of Gaya in Niger Republic:

> [D]uring the early period of the re-introduction of the Sharia legal system . . . the administration . . . banned music and the commission of social vices. . . . Wayward youths of [Nigerian] Dole would mock the Sharia enforcement agents by simply taking a few strikes from their Dole Ingilishi[24] across the narrow drainage into Dole Faransi[25] with their instruments, and they would be in the full safety of Niger Republic to do their anti-Sharia thing however and for how long they wished. . . . The Sharia enforcement agents . . . would do nothing [because] they were politically in another country which did not practice the legal system prohibiting them from "entertaining" and "enjoying" themselves." (*Daily Trust* 2007).

Not even state adoption of sharia has satisfied the most exigent of Islamists in Nigeria. In 2004 a fanatical group of Nigerian youths, self-styled Muhajiru or Taliban, crossed the border into Niger to flee a nation that they perceived as irredeemably sinful. Occupying a borderland region between Maine-Soroa (Niger) and Yobe (Nigeria), they were eventually arrested by a joint contingent of Nigérien gendarmes and Nigerians soldiers (ARB 2004). Boko Haram has brought Islamist extremism to another level entirely.

However different the dispensing of colonial justice may have been under the French and the British, for the Muslim Hausa the Nigeria-Niger boundary now represents a firewall of sharia. Nigerian Hausa are subject to sharia far more than Nigérien Hausa. This is not to idealize the way that the actual administration of Islamic criminal law in Nigeria is perceived on either side of the border: the criticism that Murray Last (2000) relates about the politicization of sharia is shared by Hausa in both countries. Nonetheless, the juridical legacy that the British left with sharia in Nigeria, incubating for decades as constitutionally enshrined personal law, has taken on an entirely different life in comparison with its counterpart in postcolonial, neo-Napoleonic Code Niger.

West African Colonial Partition and the Contemporary African Boundary Scene

How does the experience of the partitioned Hausa, particularly in the borderlands, inform the more theoretical literature on African boundaries? The latter generally falls into two categories: descriptive and remedial.

Descriptive treatments generally acknowledge a paradox: that while the colonial boundaries bequeathed to independent Africa may have been arbitrary and illogical, maintaining them has preserved stability and furthered rationality. Jeffrey Herbst (1989) makes this argument from an elite perspective. Postcolonial African leaders have vested interests in maintaining political lines that European colonialists had useful reasons to create initially. Nevertheless, post–Cold War changes (emanating from economic and political liberalization that foster central government disintegration) have unleashed destabilizing forces that may make some boundary readjustment inevitable (Herbst 1992). Christopher Clapham (1999) acknowledges the weakness that supposed sovereigns actually display over contesting territory reaching up to their juridical boundaries. Borders, as inherited, will regain meaning and functionality when local economies recover and state power is used for equitable resource distribution. John Ravenhill (1988) focuses on (a few) instances of state territorial expansion and (fleeting) armed dissidence to highlight a growing disparity between de jure and de facto African boundaries. Nugent and Asiwaju (1996b) and Benmessaoud Tredano (1989), on the other hand, focus on the overall durability of the African frontier. Empirical analyses of the relationship between inherited boundaries and postcolonial conflict are mixed: Englebert, Tarango, and Carter (2002) find a much more direct correlation than Boyd (1979).

When one shifts to grassroots reality for Africans, scholars focus on the structural permeability at borders (Griffiths 1996) or the emergence of borderland populations (Nugent and Asiwaju 1996a). There are optimistic and pessimistic embraces of these perspectives. Achille Mbembe (2002), of the latter camp, focuses on the dark side of African border permeability: human and resource traffickers (see also Dottridge 2002), armed rebels, criminal bandits. In contrast to Mbembe's preoccupation with transborder violence, A. I. Asiwaju promotes transborder cooperation (Asiwaju and Adeniyi 1989).

Asiwaju's analyses and initiatives (1993 [with Barkindo], 1994 [with Igue], 1996, 2005) represent the remedial approach to African border studies. He wishes to do something about borderline reality, not merely study it. Remedialists can include those such as Francis Deng (1993) and Ricardo Larémont (2005), who entertain reforming or dismantling Africa's inherited boundaries. But unlike Deng and the dismantlers, Asiwaju argues for active central government, local government, and civic association involvement in recasting the African border as a bridge rather than a barrier, or as Maano Ramutsindela (1999, 195) puts it, to give "priority in the decolonisation of the map of Africa [by] changing the character of colonial boundaries rather than their physical appearance."

The partitioned West African indigenes we have examined in this chapter seem by their behavior to prefer an Asiwajian solution. They have not only adapted to being citizens of Anglophone versus Francophone polities but have evolved within their ethnicity to incorporate their nationality. The superimposed border is not an indignity to efface out of irredentist ire but rather an inherited line to traverse or exploit.

West Africa as Prototype of Partition: Implications for Overall Study

How does the overall partition of African ethnic groups (such as the Hausa) into French and British colonies fit into broader studies of postcolonial differences between Francophone and Anglophone states? Indeed, does the very distinction between former French and former British colonies still make a significant difference half a century after independence? Various scholars, studying this second question from a variety of angles, converge in responding in the affirmative.

Most of the social science literature in the first three decades following independence tended to reinforce the pan-nationalist aim of decolonization as strictly conceived: to negate the superimposed European grid in favor of overarching indigenous processes. The major paradigms advanced to understand postcolonial Africa thus glossed over Anglophone-Francophone differences in their framing of the evolution of sub-Saharan politics and society. Such phenomena as the single-party state, military rulership, ideologies of development, personalistic politics, prebendalism, civil society, patrimonialism, and neopatrimonialism have tended to elide the former French with the former British colonies (Hyden 2006; Young 2012).

Liberalization in the 1980s and 1990s—both economically *qua* structural adjustment and politically *qua* democratization—coincided with a reexamination of postcolonial legacies. The national conference phenomenon that began in 1989 in Benin, argues Pearl Robinson (1994), took its lead from an embedded Francophone familiarity with the French Revolution. By historical coincidence, the bicentennial of the Revolution coincided with the collapse of East Bloc authoritarianism: current events in Communist politics stimulated the intellectual memory of the formerly colonized. A French-language network (e.g., the magazine *Jeune Afrique*; broadcasts of Radio France Internationale) provided lubrication for resistance. By the advent of the new millennium, comparative experts could note that "In Africa, the nature of the colonial state provided a procrustean bed that determined the character of its postcolonial successor to a far greater extent than expected by the independence generation of scholarly observers of Africa" (Beissinger and Young 2002, 12).

Taking a political economy approach, Jennifer Widner (1994) focuses on the decade leading up to the regime transformation and just beyond (1982–92) and analyzes patterns in reform. Widner finds that "whether a[n African] country has an Anglophone or a Francophone heritage" shapes a variety of factors that in turn affected the likelihood of economic and political reform. The relevant factors are distribution of rents, organization of interest groups, types of electoral system, and control over media. With respect to rents, public enterprises provide opportunities for elite enrichment more in Francophone than in Anglophone countries, where tariffs and licenses provided more lucrative options. Interest groups are organized on a more corporatist basis in the former French colonies; in former British ones, unions and other extra-governmental groups prevailed. Politician-constituent linkages are stronger, say, in Ghana and Nigeria than in Guinea and Niger: the former have developed grassroots networks whereas the latter perpetrated single-party list voting, leading to greater intraparty elite politics. As for the media, central control characterizes the former French colonies in contrast to pluralism among former British colonies. Widner invokes the Ivory Coast and Kenya as exemplars to highlight these differences. The legacy of contrasts has meant that, overall, regime change in the former British colonies has been slower and more violent than in the former French ones; however, she suggests, it is probably more sustainable in the former than in the latter.

As concerns partitioned peoples throughout the developing world, perhaps we can go one step further and say along with Robert Rotberg (1997, 216), who was speaking for Africa writ large, that "In ways that are appropriate to the post–Cold War, postcolonial era, the British and French imperial legacy survives intact and is probably growing." Not only for the Hausa, but for borderlanders in Asia and Oceania, imperial legacies are part of the normal fabric of postcolonial life. For them, the colonial cuts of partition, though lands, seas, and minds, remain irrefutable. In the next chapter, we shall see how some of those "cuts"—traversing African ethnicities and Caribbean waters— remain identity-forming facts of life for the descendants of slaves in the West Indies.

3
Partition by Island
West Indies

The Negro of the Antilles will be proportionately white—that is, he will come closer to being a real human being—in direct relation to his mastery of the French language.... The colonized is elevated above his jungle status in proportion to his adoption of the mother country.
—Frantz Fanon, *Black Skin, White Masks*

When I was making my way back late that night to the hotel [in Martinique], a Negro youth shouted contemptuously: "Ey! You! You are an Englishman!" It must have been my purpleheart walking-stick—I had been limping about on one. Whatever it was, I was getting tired of the French colonial monkey-game.
—V. S. Naipaul, *The Middle Passage*

Without presuming to settle the question of basic African versus colonially superimposed identity, late nineteenth-century continent-carving was less disruptive than eighteenth- and early nineteenth-century colonialism, which resulted in the mass deportation of tens of millions of Africans to another continent. Slave-based colonialism created dozens of new polities sprinkled throughout the islands of the West Indies and on continental territories in the northeast corner of South America. Although Hispanic and Dutch-speaking descendants of African slaves are fascinating in their own right, here we are of course concerned with the differences between English- and French-speaking communities.

For reasons of geography, history, and politics, the differences in the West Indian Anglo-French diasporas are even more pronounced than on the Mother Continent itself. Prior to the "classical" colonial partition outlined in the previous chapter, Europeans had already subjected Africans to their distinct versions of imperial sovereignty. For nearly two centuries the slave trade had scattered black Africans of numerous ethnicities to dozens of West Indian islands controlled by Britain and France. For sure there were other imperial powers who did the same, notably Spain (which wound up with the macro-Caribbean territories of Cuba, Dominican Republic, and Puerto Rico) and Holland (whose Caribbean colonizing status became marginal at best). But in that cluster of islands pointing southeast from Puerto Rico toward South America—an archipelago alternately called the Lesser Antilles, the Leeward and Windward Islands, and the Southeast Caribbean—colonial history has been mostly an Anglo-French affair. A focused contrast between French Martinique and Anglophone Barbados will show just how alienating that colonial legacy is.

Geography and History

Insularity is the underlying thematic of the Caribbean, a maritime zone stretching in a gentle arc from the Florida keys and Gulf of Mexico to the northeast coast of South America. In addition to the islands, the Caribbean is commonly considered to include the three Guianas: the former Dutch (Suriname, independent since 1975), the former British (Guyana, independent since 1966), and the still French (la Guyane française). Belize (former British Honduras, independent since 1981) is also considered by most experts to belong to this region.

With the exception of Hispaniola (Haitian and Dominican) and St. Martin (French and Dutch), all the islands are uninational: a single sovereign entity oversees them. No Caribbean islands were split into Anglophone and Francophone zones. Several of them did, however, experience significant

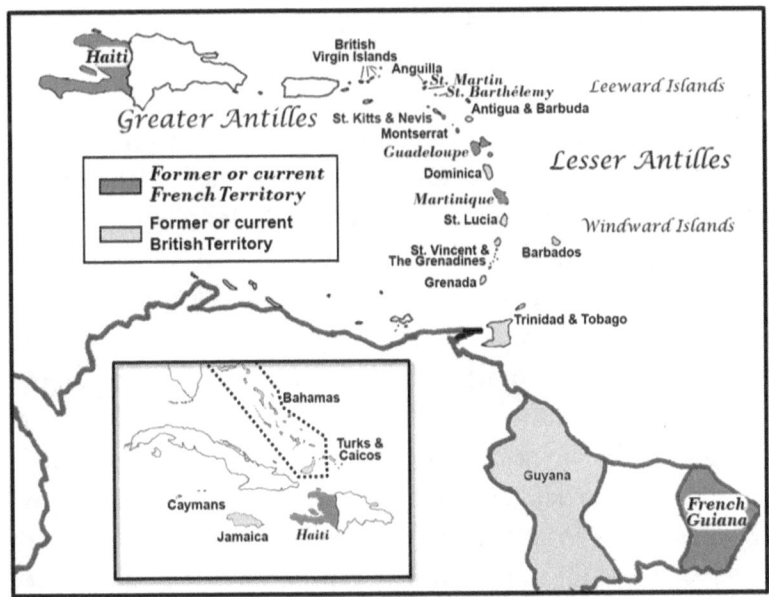

Map 8. Anglophone and Francophone West Indies

periods of French followed by British colonization. Notable among these are Dominica and St. Lucia, whose Creole language remains French-based. Such are the outcomes of competitive settlement, imperial rivalry, and naval battles between Britain and France in the seventeenth through early nineteenth centuries (see Map 8).

A dozen independent states and a half dozen dependent island clusters constitute the former British West Indies. In the former category are those inheriting a colonial "marriage" of two or more neighboring islands, usually with one dominating the other(s). These include Antigua and Barbuda; the Bahamas; St. Kitts and Nevis; St. Vincent and the Grenadines; and Trinidad and Tobago. The "standalone" island nations (even if they too have tiny offshore dependencies) are Barbados, Dominica, Grenada, and demographically the most important, Jamaica. Guyana and Belize, to repeat, are nonisland independent polities of the former British West Indies. Despite their mainland status, they share no land borders with any other Anglophone nations and thereby can claim a linguistic insularity in their respective regions.

British Overseas Territories of the Caribbean also include island clusters and single units. In the former category are the British Virgin Islands, the Cayman Islands, and Turks and Caicos; in the latter Anguilla, Bermuda, and Montserrat.

Between Jamaica, the third most populous Anglophone polity in the Americas, and Montserrat, whose volcanic explosion at one point necessitated the entire population's evacuation, the former British West Indies reflect a wide range of demographics and cultural forms. Although the majority of the inhabitants are "Afro-" by virtue of their slave antecedents, several islands (Trinidad in particular) also bear traces of important postslavery migrations from the East Indies. Trinidad (combined with Tobago) is the only former British Caribbean colony, along with Jamaica, to number over 1 million inhabitants.

The French West Indies (Antilles-Guyane) are much fewer in number than their Anglophone counterparts but only slightly less complex with respect to their geographical diversity and administrative complexity (see Map 9). The largest by far—indeed, one-fifth the size of France itself— is Guyane Française (French Guiana). It is also the least populated of the three French possessions. Located on the northeast coast of South America, French Guiana is mostly Amazonian jungle. On account of its proximity to the equator, it is also the site, in Kourou, of the European space station. Thanks to its Amerindian population, French Guiana is the only one of France's Caribbean territories to have an indigenous (albeit minority) population: the rest are populated mostly by African slave descendants and mixed Afro-Caucasian offspring.

The most heavily populated of the French islands, and the most culturally Frenchified, is Martinique. Until a form of decentralization came to the French Caribbean, Martinique's administrative center, Fort-de-France, doubled as capital of the region. Martinique is a mono-island, without dependent offshore islets.

Guadeloupe, on the other hand, is itself practically two islands

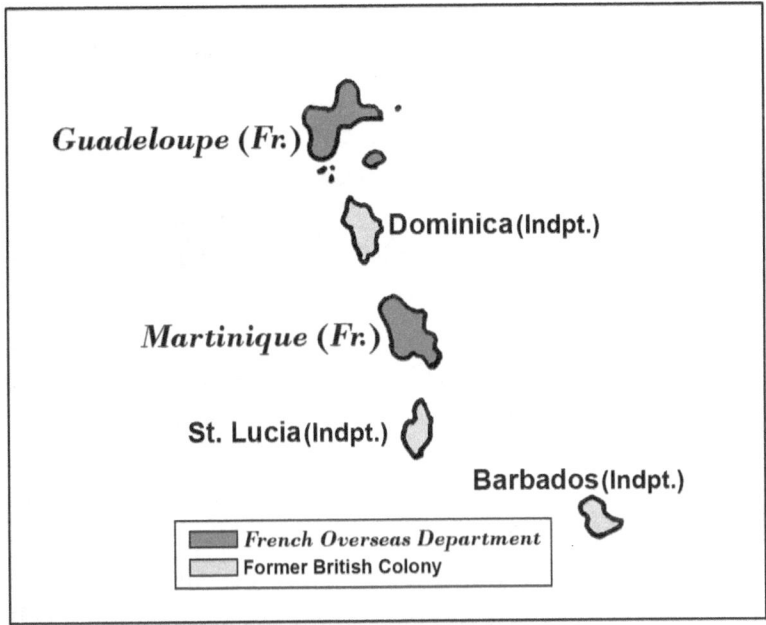

Map 9. French West Indies and Anglophone Neighbors

(Basse-Terre and Grande-Terre) joined by a narrow band of land. In addition, Guadeloupe is distinguished by having claim to several smaller island dependencies: Marie-Galante, Désirade, the Saints Islands, St. Barthélemey, and (until 2007) St. Martin. The latter island is divided into two sovereignties: French (the eastern side) and Dutch (the western).

In 1946 all three colonies, Guadeloupe, Guyane, and Martinique, were transformed into *départements d'outre-mer* (DOMs, or overseas departments) of France. This renders them the equivalents of the noncontiguous states of the United States—Hawaii and Alaska—rather than U.S. Caribbean commonwealths such as Puerto Rico or the Virgin Islands. Informally, the three are also referred to as *départements français d'Amerique*, or French States of America (FSA). On account of their insularity, each of the three is also organized administratively as a French *région d'outre-mer*, or ROM. (In metropolitan France, several departments are typically combined into a region). In 2007 the triple

"DOM-ROM" abbreviation of the French Caribbean was joined by "COM" when St. Barthélemey and St. Martin opted out of their longstanding administrative dependence on Guadeloupe to become "overseas collectivities." (The designation *collectivité d'outre-mer* already existed elsewhere among France's former colonies, such as St. Pierre and Miquelon off the coast of Newfoundland. In the French Pacific, as we shall see, there is also "POM"—overseas country of France.)

Then there is Haiti. Once regarded as the pearl in the French Caribbean crown, this Greater Antillean island took advantage of France's own revolution to shake off its colonial and slavist status at one fell swoop, becoming by 1804 the first independent black republic in the world. French remains the official language of Haiti, although relatively few Haitians master it: French-based Creole (also eventually recognized as an official language) is the lingua franca. Despite their common French Caribbean colonial origins, the DOM-ROM-COM French distance themselves (often rather vehemently so) from Haitians, given the latter's awkward juxtaposition of political independence with economic impoverishment. But not even French West Indian conservatives can deny, as Sutton puts it, that Haitians have "a distinctive national identity and a measure of cultural homogeneity greater than that prevailing elsewhere in the region" (Sutton 1986, 23).

A combination of three general features distinguish colonialism in the Caribbean from elsewhere in the world: *tabula rasa* settlement, African-based slavery, and plantation economy. Tabula rasa settlement refers to the replacement of the indigenous West Indian populations by early European settlers via expulsion, assimilation, and outright genocide. (Having exterminated the Arawaks before them, the Caribs had done something equivalent.) As a result, Dutch, English, French, and Spanish colonizers were able to recreate human society entirely in their own image, unencumbered by the cultures of previously established peoples there.

But for cheap labor the settlers had to look elsewhere: hence, African-based slavery. These slave societies were controlled, monitored, and missionized, to the extent possible, by their European owners and cultural masters. Creolized societies and peoples developed, combining mainly African, European, and after emancipation, East Indian cultural traits and genes. Ethnic differences were racialized.

Thirdly, plantations defined economic, social, and racial relations in the West Indies, both during the slave period and beyond. Hierarchical relations between (lighter-skinned) bosses and (darker-skinned) laborers carried over into broader dependencies based on clientelism and racism. Even where plantations themselves outlived their economic viability, those whose wealth was founded upon or derived from them usually managed to shift their capital into more currently profitable businesses. Thus is perpetuated the general pattern of plantation-based social and, to a large extent, political relations.

On some islands, indigenous words for places and foods survived; other islands were uninhabited at the time of the conquest and had no Carib culture to bequeath. Eradication of indigenous Amerindians was so complete, however, that there was no discernible difference in later colonial society between those islands that had had indigenous populations (e.g., Martinique) and those islands that never did (e.g., Barbados). Occupation of, and extermination in, the Lesser Antilles occurred chiefly in the first half of the seventeenth century; naval battles over these islands between the British and French continued into the nineteenth century.

African-Based Slavery

Ultimately unsuccessful early attempts at enslaving native populations encouraged Caribbean colonists to look elsewhere for labor. In the sixteenth century, Africa emerged as an economically viable choice. It took nearly a century before the African slave trade developed into the sophisticated, high-volume, immoral transnational business that it did; it took two decades after being formally abolished by the last of the major powers in the 1840s (Britain was first, in 1807) to actually cease. In the four-century interim, roughly between 1500 and 1870, over 11 million Africans, mostly from the West African coastal lands and Central Sudan, involuntarily made the Middle Passage. With the exception of the former Spanish colonies of Cuba, the Dominican Republican, and Puerto Rico, the descendants of these Africans make up the vast majority of the population of the West Indies.

The social history of the West Indies is therefore, to a great extent, the history of slave society and its aftermath. Resistance, political as well as social, also defined Caribbean slave society. Abolition, which came to the English islands in 1833 and to the French ones in 1848, was spurred both by European motives (economic and humanitarian) and periodic Caribbean slave revolts. In the meantime, new cultural styles, religions, and languages evolved on their own African-based terms.

However diverse these island cultures were to become, *all* of them are, in a fundamental sense, complete products of the colonial experience. No precolonial West Indian island cultures survive.[1] All West Indian societies, especially in the Lesser Antilles, were forged in a violent crucible of European colonialism and African slavery.

Plantation Economy

Entwined with the ethnic dimension of African slavery is the economic legacy of the plantation economy. For it was to work the plantations, especially those that would produce "King Sugar," that slaves from Africa were required in the first place. It was also the refusal of Afro-Caribbeans to work the plantations after their emancipation that occasioned—most visibly in Trinidad—the importation of indentured laborers from India.

Plantations defined the economy of the West Indies throughout the colonial period. Agriculturally based and mono-crop dependent, ordinary islanders throughout the West Indies survived when harvests were good and suffered when they—or the markets for which they were destined—were bad. Products of mixed relations ("mulattos") constituted a pivotal intermediate class between European-descendant landowners and African-descendant laborers. When the former ceded their place or actually disappeared, the "mid-colored" class stepped into the breach.

Multiple Partitions in the West Indian Context

Partition in the West Indies takes on more meanings than in West Africa, where it was usually a "simple" matter of tracing an invisible line through the sand or forest or designating a river or riverbed as a demarcation. Ethnic groups or cultural zones in Africa were accordingly split into (usually) French or British sovereignty.

In Caribbean colonialism, identity was transformed in multiple manners. The most traumatic partition emanated from slavery. Whereas partition on the African continent itself typically divided one ethnic group into two separate colonies (e.g., the Ewe into Ghana and Togo; the Hausa into Niger and Nigeria), in the West Indies a single enslaved ethnic group would find itself partitioned among a multiplicity of islands. Thus, the Yoruba, who in West Africa experienced "simple" partition between Benin and Nigeria, were partitioned in the West Indies into Martinique, Haiti, and Trinidad, among others. Slave-era records were rather inconsistent, if not lax, in recording the ethnic origins of the human "property" acquired in Africa, and we are consequently much less certain about the dispersal of African ethnicities in the New World than we are about their classic partition in Africa proper: there is still "no overall picture of the movements of ethnic groups from Africa to the Americas" (Eltis and Richardson 1997, 10). Territorial partition in Africa *transformed* ethnic identities along colonial, and eventually, national lines; colonial slave-based partition *extinguished* African ethnic identities outright.

To be sure, residues of African culture survived in the West Indies. It was the pioneering genius Melville Herskovits (1937) who began documenting them island by island. Yet however marked by African religion, language, and social patterns certain features of West Indian life may be, specific African ethnicities have long since melted into general Creole hybridity: there are no "Igbo islands," for instance, or "Ashanti-minority" societies in the Caribbean.[2] "Indigenous African cultures were all but lost in the brutal transportation process and in the slave markets and plantations that awaited the unwilling migrants" (Thorndike 1991, 111). In the Caribbean, "transformation and readjustment [of Africanisms] necessarily involved the fracturing of customs and ritual from their African institutional hierarchies of authority and governance" (Warner-Louis 1999, 21–22). No more than half the slaves brought to the British Leewards, the Guianas, and St. Domingue came from a single African region; fewer than one-third of enslaved Africans arriving in Barbados, Guadeloupe, and Martinique hailed from the same territory. "[V]arious forms of restructuring . . . have served, in large measure, to blur the ethnic distinctions brought from Africa" (Warner-Lewis 1999, 22).

Different ethnic groups predominated at different times. For example, up to the late eighteenth century, the Oyo supplied for export from the Bight of Benin Nupe, Borgu, and Ewes; in the nineteenth century, following the collapse of the Oyo Empire, the Yoruba became the ethnicity of convenience for Bight of Benin trade slavers. Enslavement and deportation of the Hausa spanned both periods, first as booty of the Oyo, then as Fulani captives of the Sokoto Caliphate[3] (Morgan 1997, 125, 129). Igbos, for their part, experienced partition from the transatlantic slave trade but not from territorial colonialism: dispersed among many islands and the American mainland as slaves, in Africa itself they escaped sectioning by coming under the single colony of Nigeria. In Barbados, on which we focus below, the earlier (seventeenth-century) partitioning enslavement brought to the island not only Igbos and Yoruba but also Adangame, Ashanti, Dahomey Edo, Ewe, Fanti, and Ga (Beckles 2006, 40).

A second level of partition in the Caribbean relates to stability of colonial overrule. In West Africa, after the early adjustment of late nineteenth-century demarcation lines, relatively few colonized peoples experienced being transferred from one colonial power over to another. The cession of German Togoland and Kamerun to France following World War I accounts for most of the exceptions. No West Africans colonized by Britain were ever "given" to the French, and vice versa. Mono-colonialism may not have been any more moral but it at least provided a certain degree of stability and predictability with respect to the national identity and overall predilections of the colonial overlord.

In the West Indies, a number of islands—and of course the African-origin slaves populating them—changed hands several times as Britain and France battled over their territories. Dominica, for example, was captured from the French by the British in 1759; nineteen years later, France recaptured it. In 1783 the island became British once again. St. Lucia experienced a similarly checkered story of colonial sovereignty. Usually, the daily life of the African slave did not substantially change when the Union Jack flew over them rather than the fleur-de-lis or the Tricolor. But the contrasting fates of Martinicans and Guadeloupeans during the French Revolution does illustrate how traumatizing unstable colonial overrule could be. Martinique (which had once before been captured by the British, in 1762) was "immunized" from *la Revolution* and its emancipatory declarations by a British occupation (negotiated by the island's slaveowners). Guadeloupe, on the other hand, did experience abolition—that is, until Napoleon restored slavery in 1802 after taking power. In the meantime, Guadeloupean slaves tasted freedom (and slaveowners literally lost their heads, casualties of Victor Hughes's version of overseas Jacobinism). Whether a few years of freedom followed by two generations of re-enslavement was more or less cruel than uninterrupted slavery is a matter of philosophical debate. With respect to partition, enslaved Africans who had already lost their ethnic identity through deportation to and dispersal throughout the West Indies not uncommonly also experienced uncertainty over the identity of their ultimate overrulers.

Beyond effacement of ethnic identity and uncertainty of colonial overrule, one may speak of a West Indian "triple partition": vagaries of colonial history that have divided West Indians between those who belong and those who do not belong to independent states. There is a trade-off between material benefits and economic security on the one hand, as enjoyed by French Guianese, Guadeloupeans, and Martinicans, and the psychic satisfaction of political independence, as experienced, for instance, by Bahamians, Barbadians, and Barbudans. This is a divide that is rarely discussed between "independent" and "nonindependent" West Indians but nevertheless underlies interactions between them.

There is a fourth degree of West Indian separation—linguistic partition. In many West African nations the official language is spoken fluently by relatively few citizens but indigenous linguae francae (such as Hausa) and pidgins (usually English-based) span borders as well as ethnicities. In the West Indies, there is no lingua franca. Although St. Lucians and Dominicans share a variant of French Creole similar to that of Martinicans and Guadeloupeans, most French West Indians cannot communicate with, say, Barbadians or Trinidadians. Not even Creole-speaking Haitians (relatively few master French) are easily understood by Creole speakers of Martinique.

If political unity within the Anglophone Caribbean has proven well nigh elusive, unification between English- and French-speaking West Indians—descendants of Africans in their great majority—belongs to political fantasy.

From Emancipation to the Global War for Freedom

The fifteen years separating the definitive abolition of slavery in the British and French islands (1833 and 1848, respectively) were but one indication of how differently former slaves and their descendants would experience "freedom." Abolition for the British empire emerged out of a persistent but gradualist campaign led by William Wilberforce (1759–1833). France, too, had its humanitarian abolitionist in the person of Victor Schoelcher (1804–1893). But whereas emancipation by the British was an outcome of prolonged moral suasion and painstaking parliamentary process, *l'abolition* for the French was a tempestuous byproduct of the wider democratic revolution of 1848. Periodic slave rebellions in both the British and French West Indies added to domestic pressures to ratify an end to the "peculiar institution."

The French and British, abolitionists included, had quite different understandings of what emancipation from slavery would entail for the newly freed islanders. Former British slaves were regarded as second-class subjects, eventually eligible for equality with all the King's subjects but only after a practical (and prolonged) period of tutelage and education. As an expression of the radical idealism prevailing in Paris, freed slaves were immediately made citizens, with all the rights and prerogatives thereof—including universal (male) suffrage.

As with the initial abolition of slavery by France in 1794, voting rights for the freed French slaves were to be rescinded: the Second Empire, which in 1851 superseded the Second Republic, made short shrift in doing so. Still, the "radical" notion that former slaves should be full citizens profoundly distinguished French emancipation from British.

In 1870 former slaves and their descendants regained the right to vote in the French West Indies; the right to elect representatives to the legislature in Paris was restored in 1875. In the British West Indies, an equivalent right of suffrage would not be fully extended for another three quarters of a century. But even more important than the disparity in voting rights was the difference in forum of representation. When they *could* vote, black British West Indians did so to send representatives to their island assemblies; French West Indians sent parliamentarians to the National Assembly in Paris in addition to councilors for their local municipalities.

Under the Third Republic of France (1870–1914), universal education was extended to the French West Indies in all its assimilating grandeur. This was the period, as we have seen in chapter 2, that corresponded with the colonial partition of West Africa and the extension of the *mission assimilationniste* there. By the time of the Berlin West African Conference in 1884–85, Guadeloupe and Martinique had been part of France for 250 years already. Not only had slavery (of Africans and their descendants) been abolished two generations before, but French West Indians by then had a decade's worth of full citizenship, as testified to by their exercise of voting rights. The education that French West Indians were being exposed to, then, was an integrationist one: as in the metropole, it was free, secular, obligatory—and French. As one metropolitan contemporary expressed it:

> Are not the colonies French? Are they not part of the great family? They were founded by the French, and have been inhabited by the French . . .
> The Colonies *are* France. (Gaffarel 1880:18)

It is no wonder that soldiers and administrators from these older French colonies would go on to assist in the colonization of the newer ones in West Africa.

Although there were wide disparities in cultural assimilation among the British islands (Jamaica and Barbados being on the Anglophile side of the continuum, Dominica and Tobago more on the Creole side), there was no parallel policy emanating from London either for equal rights locally or full integration within Britain as a whole. To the contrary: freedom to African slave descendants would have to be extended gradually through a process of tutored self-governance. White elites of the plantocracy managed to forestall this, at least for a while: during the quarter century that French West Indians actually starting to exercise their franchise (1875–1900), most of the British West

Indies reverted to rule from the Colonial Office. Education in the Anglophone Caribbean—a precondition for voting—was far from a priority. Originally it was a privately funded luxury for the elite, not a right for the masses. "The prospect that men of African descent might dominate [British] Caribbean lands was as repugnant to many in the Imperial Government as it was to West Indian whites" (Lowenthal 1972, 65). Even when the principle of free public primary education was accepted in the 1870s, religious denominations rather than government departments shouldered the greater responsibility. This situation prevailed until the 1950s. In contrast to a French Caribbean educational system perpetuating an implausible myth in Gallic ancestors and creating "Black Frenchmen" (Murch 1971), that of the British West Indies "created a cadre of leaders throughout the region [with a] strong sense of local identity and acute knowledge of British political institutions."

The differences between the *plural society*, as M. G. Smith (1965) describes the British West Indies, and the *assimilationist* policy of the French ones, are illustrated by the respective fates of East Indians. In Trinidad and British Guiana (now Guyana), descendants of East Indian wage laborers have come to constitute a well-defined, endogenous social group. Domestic politics reflect their continuing electoral clout. In Guadeloupe and Martinique, the situation is quite different. While one can still find traces of East Indian cultural identity and Hindu religious rites, French West Indians of East Indian descent play absolutely no political role as such. To an extent far greater than their Anglophone counterparts, they have blended—one is tempted to say assimilated—into the overall social and, especially, political scene.

Pluralism in the British West Indies can also be discerned in the colonial structures of government. Three patterns emerged (Knight and Palmer 1989). Crown Colony government, which entailed rule by officials directly appointed from London and virtually no local democracy, was originally instituted in the islands that had been most recently under French and Spanish sovereignty (i.e., St. Lucia and Trinidad, respectively). Minimal local governance was institutionalized, through island-wide assemblies, in those islands that France ceded in the 1764 Treaty of Paris (e.g., Dominica, St. Vincent). Those islands experiencing the longest (and uninterrupted) periods of British rule (Barbados, for instance, and Jamaica) enjoyed the most robust institutions of local government. In contrast, French centralism (in Cartesian terms, a synonym for rationalism) meant that the structures and mechanisms of governance were virtually identical from Guadeloupe to Guyane to Martinique. Note that Martinique's geographically closest Anglophone island neighbors—Dominica to the north, St. Lucia and St. Vincent to the south, and Barbados to the southeast—all experienced, before independence, rather different systems of government, even under the same British crown.

Until World War I, British policy toward its West Indian islands remained more a matter of perpetuation than transformation. Within a framework of property and income qualifications, middle-class islanders were content to achieve representation to local councils and colonial legislatures. Change remained a matter of individual promotion, reinforcing social conservatism and militating against structural transformation.

The British West Indian status quo continued up until the 1930s, overlapping with Fourth Republic socialist and communist agitation in the French islands. Economic shocks associated with the worldwide depression fanned political grievances in the Anglophone islands, leading to demonstrations and riots, some resulting in fatalities. Labor unrest was best understood and politically channeled by those few Fabian intellectuals and activists who had managed, against odds, to receive instruction in Britain. Not even World War II could delay the release of the Moyne report, commissioned by the Colonial Office in response to the unrest. While eschewing the term "independence," its recommendations led to modest institutional changes that presaged the beginning of British disengagement from the region.

The Second World War had a much more catalyzing effect in the French Antilles, though not toward independence. Subject to Vichy from 1940 to 1943, French West Indians suffered racist rule under the guise of "National Revolution" (Jalabert 2004; Jennings 2001b, 2001c; Miles 2005a), and on account of American naval blockade, severe material deprivation. France's liberation (which owed partially to French West Indians who had rallied to Charles de Gaulle) reinforced affective ties with, and appreciation of their economic dependence on, the metropole. The war's aftermath was to crystallize the different mindsets and frameworks fashioned by over three hundred years of British vis-à-vis French colonialism. Whereas for British West Indians the lesson of anti-Nazism was freedom and racial equality through national independence, for French West Indians Nazi occupation reinforced patriotism for a violated France, republicanism as an ideal worthy of sacrifice, and racial equality through political assimilation.

West Indian Decolonization: Anglophone Independences and French Departmentalization

At the request of the elected French West Indian representatives in Paris, on March 19, 1946, the National Assembly passed the "law of assimilation." In one fell swoop, the three French Caribbean territories of Guiana, Guyane, and Martinique (along with the Indian Ocean island of Réunion) were transformed from old colonies into overseas departments. This was the ideal of French decolonization: not independence (which, according to French logic, would be a form of ungrateful rejection) but rather full juridical integration into the Republic, as voluntarily requested by the formerly colonized. As expressed by one of those French West Indian parliamentarians: "[T]his demand for integration constitutes an homage rendered to France and her genius (especially at this time of doubt) about the solidarity of the Empire." These words were uttered not by any petty politician oblivious to the injustices of colonialism or the legacies of slavery, but by Aimé Césaire, founding partner with Leopold Senghor of the prewar négritude movement. When he proposed the law of assimilation, Césaire was still a member of the French Communist Party. His desire to see his French West Indian brethren achieve full freedom and development reflected a profoundly French approach to leftist politics: that interracial equality and human dignity is a universalist aspiration best achieved, not via separation from like-minded idealists, but by full incorporation within a great and liberal civilization. For the small, impoverished, and long-despised peoples of the French West Indies, that civilization could only mean France. Such a model of decolonization was classical from a French perspective, if retrograde from an Anglo-Saxon one.

Aimé Césaire was no color-blind assimilationist. More than any other French West Indian, through his prose and poems (especially his 1939 classic *Return to My Native Land*) he strove to elevate the dignity of the black, a person whose roots in Africa Césaire broke local taboos by glorifying. Despite subsequent chinks in his faith in France, and his (unfulfilled) aim to achieve a status of institutional autonomy, Césaire never renounced French ties or embraced independence. While the structure of local governance has greatly expanded since 1946, the DOM remains firmly ensconced within the French Republic. There is no such thing as Guadeloupean citizenship or Martinican nationality: the islanders are citizens of France.

In the Anglophone islands, decolonization has proceeded along a much-expanded time frame and with a completely different approach. There was little question, either from the British or the islander side, that decolonization entailed self-government that was a way station toward independence. Postwar Britain, as pragmatic as ever—particularly in matters colonial—realized no economic benefit from continuing its tutelage role. For decades, local leaders and emerging classes had been jockeying for greater and greater power—not within Britain but in their respective islands.

To facilitate its progressive renunciation of colonial responsibility, Britain midwifed its "maturing" colonies into a confederation. The West Indies Federation (1958–1962) did not survive, however, on account of economic imbalances among its ten constituent members and inter-island rivalries among its leaders. Breakup of the federation heralded a string of typically drawn-out transitions to independence (gradualism had always marked change in the British West Indies).

Sixteen years after the French West Indies became, at one fell swoop, overseas states of France, Jamaica and Trinidad (and Tobago) in 1962 became the first independent Anglophone Caribbean countries. Barbados followed suit four years later. In the 1970s five more left the British colonial fold: the Bahamas, Grenada, Dominica, St. Lucia, and St. Vincent and the Grenadine Islands. The 1980s saw another two pronouncements of independence, albeit in problematic pairings: Antigua and Barbuda, and St. Kitts and Nevis.

Five remaining Anglophone groupings (Anguilla, the Caymans, Montserrat, the British Virgin Islands, Turks and Caicos) remain British Overseas Territories, a designation that took effect in 2002. Their future status is uncertain. But "the appeal of independence seemed . . . to have been widely replaced by a determination, substantially less heroic, to hang onto the tangible benefits of imperial protection" (Payne and Sutton 1993, 20). In the meantime, during the nearly half-century process of Anglophone islands achieving independence, Martinique, Guadeloupe, and French Guiana have become increasingly absorbed within French, and ipso facto European, political procedures and economic institutions. Whether the culture and psychology of these French States of America are more akin to France or the Caribbean remains a more complicated question; that it *is* a question at all speaks to a fundamental difference between French and Anglophone West Indians. For its part, the Commonwealth Caribbean, comprising all the Anglophone islands (independent or not), continues to reflect considerable internal diversity, with this caveat: independence has been uniformly accompanied by gradual Americanization, replacing, particularly in the realms of culture and economy, colonial British influence. Departmentalization in the FSA, in contrast, has precluded any other power from substituting for France.

Emigration patterns both reflect and reinforce this postwar contrast in metropolitan influence. After the 1950s wave of Caribbean relocation in the United Kingdom, British restrictions on immigration in the 1960s induced would-be Anglophone migrants to seek opportunity elsewhere. This accelerated movement to elsewhere in the West Indies, Canada, and especially the United States. One year after Parliament passed the restrictive Commonwealth Immigrants Act (1962), France established an agency (BUMIDOM—Office of Overseas Departments Migration, existent until 1981) to *encourage* "her" West Indians to resettle and work in the metropole. There are no visa requirements for French citizens traveling between the FSA and metropolitan France: proof of French citizenship is sufficient for entry, residency, and employment. For sure, racial discrimination exists in France as well as Britain. "Yet despite the general similarities in the abusive treatment experienced in both England and France by West Indian immigrants going 'home,' West Indians in the latter country probably have fared better" (Richardson 1989, 218). This, Richardson attributes to the greater number of minorities of North African descent, but a greater legacy of French assimilationism, based more on language than color, also plays a part.

In short, the upshot of such divergence in Caribbean decolonization was "a political landscape still deeply marked by fragmentation. Each imperial power can be said to have done it its way" (Payne and Sutton 1993, 8). Gordon Lewis (1985, 225) vividly describes the outcome as a "crazy patchwork quilt." Decolonization along strictly nationalist (and subnationalist) lines not only maintained distinctive, colonially inherited traditions but actually strengthened them. The West Indies Federation of ten territories, which subsisted from 1957 until 1962, was "doomed from the start by lukewarm popular support . . . foundering on uncompromising insular interests" (Knight and Palmer 1989, 15). Erection of a "common political culture across the region" (Payne and Sutton 1993, 8) has remained a pipe dream.

In the smaller Commonwealth Caribbean islands in the vicinity of Martinique and Guadeloupe, Britain had envisioned an internal self-government solution: associated statehood. Anglophone islands would be in full control of their internal affairs, but foreign relations and military defense would remain the purview of the Crown. Ironically, this is akin to what, under decentralization, the DOMs have undergone. Britain, however, saw its islands achieve complete independence—absent which they would have continued to suffer "inadequacy," psychological and well as economic (Sutton 1986, 12). Writing in 1986, Sutton described the framework for governance within the Eastern Anglophone Caribbean as one of "pragmatic conservatism" and went on to observe: "A more British approach, stereotypically, could scarcely be imagined" (13).

Postwar Democracy, Sovereign and Not

An enduring hallmark of politics in both Anglophone and Francophone Caribbeans—one that distinguishes them from elsewhere in the Third World—is democracy. Scholarship on democracy in the developing world points to commonalities within the Commonwealth Caribbean—small size and British colonial heritage—as factors favorable to the consolidation of democracy. Britain's legacy of Westminster-style parliamentary politics has persevered in the West Indies as it has not in West Africa. Indeed, the strength of West Indian adherence to Westminster-style politics and practices has given rise to the sobriquet "Afro-Saxon" (Ryan 1994, quoting Lloyd Best). This is especially the case in the Lesser Antilles, where with few notable exceptions, the tensions of class and race have been subsumed within a generally two-party, nonviolent competitive alternation of power. The two major exceptions are Grenada in the early 1980s and Trinidad in 1990. In the former instance, the Marxist-inspired New Jewel Movement, having taken power in a 1979, degenerated into violent factionalization and the 1983 assassination of Prime Minister Maurice Bishop and six of his cohorts (precipitating U.S. invasion of the island). In the latter, a group of Afro-Muslim radicals attempted in 1990 a coup d'état, in the process seizing parliament and taking hostage the prime minister and other lawmakers.

However heralded by most outsiders, Westminster-style democracy in the Commonwealth Caribbean by the 1980s was "far from unblemished." Domestic political corruption, outside electoral cash, internal racial divisions, and an "old colonial taste for messianic leadership" vitiated the model (Payne and Sutton 1993). In the 1990s, the collapse of the Soviet Union further extinguished the hope, harbored by certain Anglophone politicians, that radical egalitarian ideologies could take hold even in small states (Meeks 2001). Elections in Jamaica can still be a nasty and violent affair. Still, Westminster-like democracy continues to prevail throughout the Anglophone Caribbean.

In the two decades between French West Indian departmentalization (1946) and the onset of Anglophone West Indian independence (1966), a curious combination of communism and Gaullism held sway in Guadeloupe, Guyane, and Martinique. Leftist politicians, having successfully spearheaded the move toward departmentalization, continued to win FSA support for the (French) Socialist and (French) Communist parties in legislative elections. Charles de Gaulle, for his part, represented liberation from (racist) Nazi occupation and collaborationist Vichy rule. De Gaulle acknowledged, in Gallic grandeur, the Frenchness of the overseas French: "My God, my God, how French you are!" he famously exclaimed in a 1964 public rally.

In 1965, the first presidential election of the Fifth Republic conducted by direct vote, de Gaulle swept the FSA in a landslide. In the next three presidential elections, which overlapped with the slow wave of successive Anglophone island independences up to the last one (1983), the FSA continued to back de Gaulle's political heirs: Pompidou in 1969 and Giscard d'Estaing in 1974 and 1981. Aimé Césaire understood why, despite his strong support for the Socialist Mitterrand, Martinicans backed Giscard: fear of imposed independence and ensuing material deprivation. "Metaphysical considerations can come later, but the people have children to feed"(Miles 2009).

Five major differences in democratic structures and stakes between the Commonwealth Caribbean and French States of America should be noted. First, whereas citizens on independent Anglophone islands have from the outset (1966) always voted for their chief executive *indirectly* via parliamentary majority, over the same time span French West Indians have experienced *direct* election of their president. Second, whereas Anglophone West Indians (excepting Guianese and Trinidadians) vote according to first-past-the-post electoral rules that reinforce a two-party competitive system, French West Indians participate in a multiparty system of comparatively breathtaking variety: six presidential candidates in 1965, seven in 1969, nine in 1988, ten in 1981 and 2012, twelve in 1974 and 2007, and sixteen in 2002. A third difference relates to the scope of the parties: in the Commonwealth Caribbean, the parties are unique to each country (e.g., Barbados Labour Party, Jamaica Labour Party); in the FSA, most political associations are local branches of French national parties and are thus transatlantic as well as trans-FSA. Fourth, unlike the independent Anglophone Caribbean nation, in a French State of America there is no single governing elected official (i.e., prime minister): there is both a president of a regional council and president of a general council, neither of whom is directly elected. (There is also a prefect in each FSA, appointed by Paris, but under post-1981 decentralization reforms he has come to play more of a coordinating than executing role.)

The fifth and most important distinction, of course, is that the ultimate winner of a national election in a Commonwealth

Caribbean contest governs that country and that country alone. When citizens of an FSA vote in a presidential election, the overall winner (whether or not he was favored in that particular FSA) becomes president over not only that FSA, but over the other two, and not only president of the three FSAs, but president of the entire French Republic (Miles 2003c).

For reasons of scale and access, national political campaigns in the former British West Indies have a different feeling from that in the French West Indies. In the former, campaigns have a revivalist feel to them, sometimes blending into carnival fever. Direct access to political leaders, who are just as likely to be national as local, is the norm. Contrast that with French West Indian election to the national assembly in Paris, for instance: local politicians campaign vigorously, for sure, but then need to cross the Atlantic to perform their more critical public duties.

Since 1983, year of the last Anglophone island independence, French West Indians have participated to date in five more presidential contests: 1988, 1995, 2002, 2007, and 2012. Even as the FSA have turned more to the left, the additional quarter century of participation in French democracy as full-fledged *départements* has reinforced the general sentiment that departmentalization remains the only option for the foreseeable future. This is a sentiment shared even by the minority of French West Indian independentists who now freely (unlike in the 1960s) demand sovereignty from France.[4]

For sure, the cultural nub of French West Indian identity has evolved. From being fundamentally French with an overlay of Caribbean ethnicity, the trend is toward seeing themselves primarily as West Indians who happen to have French citizenship.[5] Still, the institutional question of belonging to a French republican democracy seems squarely resolved. Although the majority of French West Indians favored Ségolène Royal for the presidency in 2007, for example, none in the FSA espoused secession from France on the grounds that Nicolas Sarkozy was the eventual victor and therefore not the chosen leader of the Martinican majority; Socialist candidate François Hollande's 2012 victory over the conservative Sarkozy would have in any case nullified such logic. Independentists, for their part, will boycott presidential elections but are selective about the particular French national elections in which they will indeed participate.

With respect to colonial continuity of maritime partitions, more important than the outcome of individual elections is the parallel perpetuation of European political systems and the cocoons of connectedness. "The Westminster tradition of parliamentary government, inherited and substantially absorbed by most Commonwealth Caribbean countries," combined with the "insertion into the French Caribbean of the major political parties and debates of metropolitan France," resulted in the cutting off of neighboring territories from each other (Payne and Sutton 1993, 8–9). Outside the French Antilles, an intellectual giant such as Aimé Césaire—also a prominent political and literary personage in France itself—becomes a virtual nonentity in nearby Anglophone islands. The same is true of Christiane Taubira, French Guianese female parliamentarian who was a presidential candidate in 2002. Conversely, otherwise notable Anglophone Caribbean politicians past and present, like Marcus Garvey, Michael Manley, and Edward Seaga in Jamaica, or Grantley and Tom Adams in Barbados, or Eugenia Charles in Dominica, are unfamiliar names in Guadeloupean, Guianese, and Martinican popular consciousness.

Caribbean Culture: Assimilationists to Creolists to Cricketers

Literature suffers from a similar geocultural partition as politics: rare is the French West Indian bookworm who has read C. L. R. James (Trinidad), Jamaica Kincaid (Antigua), George Lamming (Barbados), V. S. Naipaul (Trinidad), Walter Rodney (Guyana), or Derek Walcott (St. Lucia). Even translated into English, Guadeloupean authors Maryse Condé, Simone Schwarz-Bart, and Edouard Glissant of Guadeloupe go unread in Antigua and Jamaica; Martinican novelists Jean Bernabé, Raphaël Confiant, and Patrick Chamoiseau are similarly unknown quantities in Trinidad and Barbados. Yet all suffuse their writing with a common West Indian historical fount and emotive sensibility that otherwise ought to transcend sea channels and colonial language patterns.

The authenticity and identity of Anglophone Caribbean culture is incontestable: who will claim that Bob Marley or the Mighty Sparrow were British musicians, or that George Lamming and C. L. R. James write as Englishmen? In the case of French West Indian cultural artists and intellectuals, the issue is more complicated (Burton 1992, 1993a, 1993b). Even as Jean Bernabé, Patrick Chomoiseau, and Raphaël Confiant claim in their essay (1990) and novels that Martinique is fundamentally a Creole society, they do so ensconced in a French linguistic, literary, intellectual, and academic culture and context that belie their pretensions to trans-Caribbeanness, let alone universality. The same can be said for Guadeloupean writers Edouard Glissant (1981) and Maryse Condé, despite their recognition within rarefied North American circles of literati. Even the more accessible music of *zouk* (through bands such as Kassav' and Taxikréol) as well as Malavoi and Kali is better viewed as commodification of a French subculture rather than the emergence of an autonomous Caribbean cultural movement.[6] In short, in ways alien to an easily recognizable Anglophone Caribbean culture, ambiguity permeates the *antillais* cultural movement supposedly counterhegemonic to French cultural domination. To take another example of Anglo-French West Indian differentiation, there is no unifying Rastafarian language. More likely than not, a Rasta from Jamaica would have a difficult time communicating with *un rasta de la Guadeloupe*.

John La Guerre (1986) personalizes the dual legacy comparison by contrasting two representative political-literary figures: the French West Indian poet-politician Aimé Césaire and the Anglophone West Indian writer C. L. R. James. Both towering figures are situated within their respective colonial contexts, which La Guerre breezily captures thus: France—a civilizing mission; a singular and indivisible empire; colonies as overseas France; cultural standards identical with the metropole. On the other hand, the British, "beyond occasional dicta and 'Lugardisme[,]' were never able to work out a coherent theory of colonial rule along the lines of the French."

However unarticulated, the British still had, according to James, some overarching colonial principles: belief that representative government is a good, but it needs to be achieved by the colonized, not imposed by the colonizers. Constitutional evolution (in contrast with French revolutionary struggle) therefore has to be gradual. Good government requires certain values, standards, and even prejudices (those that the ruling class back home embody). In short, Britain is bound to lead her colonies to self-government, the precursor to independence.

Both Césaire and James wrote ripping critiques of colonialism, the former in French, the latter in English. La Guerre contrasts their views on race and liberation. Regarding the racial question, he finds that James, an unambiguous Marxist, subsumes race to class ("The race question is subsidiary to the class question in politics, and to think of imperialism in terms of race is disastrous"). Césaire, also deeply steeped in Marxism, nevertheless breaks with the Communist Party on account of "its inveterate assimilation; its unconscious chauvinism; their current, though understandable conviction—which they share with bourgeois Europeans—of the omnilateral superiority of the West."

With respect to decolonization, James believed in the integrality of colonial revolution and world revolution. Following Trotsky, no single country could be truly freed until all other oppressed nations were liberated. Césaire, rather, believed that each revolution was *sui generis*; even within the colonies, each revolution followed its own logic, its own trajectory, its own "different impulses and objectives" (La Guerre's characterization).

How these contrasting visions of race and colonial liberation are linked to, or derive from, the colonial traditions out of which James and Césaire emerged is not made explicit in La Guerre's otherwise insightful chapter.

Perhaps the easiest contrast in Anglophone and French Caribbean culture is in the realm of sport. Cricket and soccer represent completely different modalities of participation, from the pitch to the field to the global athletic community. For C. L. R. James, cricket provided a mental grid that extended far beyond the centuries of the game: "I knew best the British way of life," he writes in *Beyond a Boundary*, "not merely in historical facts but in instinctive responses. I have acquired them in childhood and, without these, facts are merely figures." Fair play, patience, gentility: these are traits associated not with the fast moving contact sport of international soccer but of Commonwealth cricket. For French West Indians, *le football* provides an outlet for celebrity and international recognition; hence the political ramifications of the soccer World Cup in 1998, won by a French team made up of French West Indians and other players hailing from the former colonial empire (Miles 1999a).

Cricket and soccer alone stand as a powerful rebuff to those who would argue that there exists a Caribbean political culture transcending national differences. Is there a fantasy more ludicrous than that of a Guadeloupean cricket team?

Economy and Development

In contrast with the "important and enduring contradiction between a legacy of political fragmentation," experts of the Caribbean also accentuate the "economic uniformity" that defines the region (Payne and Sutton 1993, 4). Tropical primary agriculture (principally sugar) grown by slave labor gave way to tropical primary agriculture (sugar, bananas, cocoa) grown by a peasant class. Exploitation of peasants and factory workers was chronic, and sporadically precipitated strikes, riots, and other labor disturbances; those in the British Caribbean between 1935 and 1939 resulted in the palliative Moyne Com-

Table 3. Material Outcomes—West Indies

	GDP per capita (dollars, 2008)	Life expectancy (years, 2005–10)	Adult literacy (%)
Former British colonies			
Antigua and Barbuda (87)	14,048	75.3	99.0
Bahamas (338)	22,102	73.4	—
Barbados (255)	14,422	77.0	—
Belize (10)	4,569	76.3	75.1
Caymans (56)	50,716	80.6	98.0
Dominica (67)	5,447	75.8	88.0
Grenada (104)	6,221	75.3	96.0
Guyana (763)	1,543	67.0	—
Jamaica (2,708)	5,571	71.9	86.0
St. Kitts and Nevis[a] (51)	10,874	74.4	97.8
St. Lucia (170)	6,017	73.8	94.8
St. Vincent and Grenadines (106)	5,515	71.7	88.1
Trinidad and Tobago (1,333)	18,153	69.4	98.7
Turks and Caicos[a] (36)	23,768	75.6	98.0
Former French colonies			
French Guiana[a] (220)	15,955[b]	76.3	—
Guadeloupe[a] (464)	21,704[b]	79.1	—
Haiti (9,876)	717	61.3	62.1
Martinique[a] (403)	24,028[b]	79.4	—

Note: Number in parentheses next to country refers to population, in thousands.

[a]Nonindependent

[b]In 2006

Sources: UN Data, Country Profiles (http://data.un.org); UNDP Human Development Index 2009 (http://hdrstats.undp.org/en/indicators/89.html); CIA *World Factbook* (http://www.cia.gov); Institut National des Statistiques Economiques (http://www.insee.fr/fr/insee_regions); IRS Euro to Dollar (http://www.irs.gov); Turk and Caicos Island Department of Economic Planning and Statistics (http://www.depstc.org).

mission. More recently, diversification in the services sector has provided offshore banking opportunities to some islands, and to virtually all of them, a tourism industry. Although the structures of economies may look similar, the outcomes have been extremely varied (see Table 3).

While Britain made some sporadic attempts to unite her British possessions into some kind of economic union, her impetus was far from consistent. Colonial allergy against creating trading blocs that would crosscut imperial divisions persists in postcolonial economies. Notwithstanding their geographic proximity, commerce between the Commonwealth Caribbean and the French States of America is meager. "History and culture coincided to create insular divisions, even as they were producing the broad context against which the particular evolution of each society would take place," write Franklin Knight and Colin Palmer (1989, 4). For Thorndike, the "whole fabric of the colonial system not only tolerated insularism but actively promoted it" (1991, 125). Caribbean insularism is material as well as mental.

Such insularism is remarkable in light of the common dangers facing the Caribbean economy: globalization, dematerialization of industry, NAFTA, the EU, the Pacific Rim growth pole, and Third World debt. The "prospect of the Caribbean being left to fester on the edge of the world system" persists (Payne and Sutton 1993, 25, 26).

Both French and former West Indian economies are dependent. But whereas the former are dependent on a France that can be relied upon to buttress them, the latter have no metropolitan crutch on which they can rely. Guaranteed welfare support, on the individual as well as departmental level, imparts to the French West Indian an economic security that her Anglophone counterpart does not enjoy. Whereas both suffer dependency, the latter's is more cultural and psychological; the former's, more material and economic. National governments in the former British West Indies struggle with trade deficits and import bills; the general and regional councils of the FSA are indifferent, if not oblivious, to them. Such economic dependency has split the Anglophone islands. "Whereas Barbados opted for sovereignty as an expression of nationhood, after it was clear that a planned federation of the south-eastern Caribbean islands would never materialize, the others agreed with Britain that they were too small to support independence" (Thorndike 1991, 122–23). Since 1958, the French States of America have experienced progressive economic integration into the metropole, evoking major distortions of local economy—and culture.

Political Culture in the Anglophone Caribbean

Tony Thorndike sums up the political culture of the Anglophone islands of the southeast Caribbean in one cruel word: mimicry (Thorndike 1991, 128). Political institutions still bear the stamp of Westminster—inappropriately so, according to Maingot (1989). Indeed, the peculiarly British form of democracy "was eventually regarded as an autochthonous form of government, its origins across the ocean being virtually forgotten" (Thorndike 1991, 117). Even though the cultural model of the metropole has shifted from United Kingdom to United States, politics and procedures remain basically British. No nation within the former British West Indies has come close to Nigeria in moving away from its independence-era parliamentary system of government toward an American-style presidential one. Not that the latter is intrinsically superior, or even better adapted to either context: it is institutional conservatism that distinguishes the West Indies from West Africa. (Bureaucracies and armed forces that are "nonpartisan and corruption-free" provide a different kind of contrast with Nigeria and West Africa writ large.) Whether parliamentary or presidential, first-past-the-post electoral systems in small island constituencies have often distorted the popular will; there is no question of changing them, however (Thorndike 1991, 116, 118).

Thorndike, following Beckford (1972), attributes such conservatism (and psychological dependency) to slavery. Plantation systems, through authoritarianism and hierarchy, engendered a complex of inferiority. Radical Anglophone revolutionaries such as Maurice Bishop of Grenada and Patrick John of Dominica have been atypical of former British West Indies politics.

According to Thorndike, with deference to authority has come cynicism toward government, but distrust of politics and politicians is hardly unique to democracies in the Caribbean. More useful is the acknowledgment of relatively high electoral turnout and a tendency to "throw out the rascals" via the ballot box: "at least at the working-class level . . . is a genuine belief that politics *matter*" (Thorndike 1991, 114, emphasis in original).

Theirs is "a political culture that is essentially inward-looking and insular, where the surrounding sea is a barrier rather than a highway" (Thorndike 1991, 110). Anglophone West Indians are acutely conscious that they are pawns in international politics. They must support the West, and especially the United States, believing that development will occur only by renouncing independence in foreign policy. French West Indians, in contrast, by virtue of being part of France, are also free to rail against metropolitan politics. They delight in criticizing American foreign policy, whether or not the French government supports the regime in Washington.

"These islands have an enviable record since the 1940s in human and political rights, particularly when set against those of other parts of the Third World" (Thorndike 1991, 128). The British tradition of local adaptation and devolution in governance is in great contrast to the French. "Arguably, and unanswerably if judged by results, the British model has permitted a more workable decolonization in the [Caribbean] than the French, even if Britain remains perplexed as to what to do about its very smallest colonies" (Sutton 1986, 17). Still, according to Sutton, both systems bequeathed essentially conservative, if not reactionary, legacies.

The unique "population mélange" (Knight and Palmer 1989, 1) of the Caribbean ethnically has given way to political fragmentation: independent states, associates states, and colonial dependencies. Ninety percent of the region's overall population reside in independent states—though this is a formal independence belied by economic dependency. But independence-dependence is not a clear-cut dichotomy with respect to popular will. Take the case of independence embarrassment for Anguilla, from which "rebels" (ostensibly with Mafia money) declared secession from St. Kitts and Nevis, with which Anguilla was linked. No evidence of outside interference was indeed found after the British military occupied the island. They did find, however, popular sentiment that Great Britain should recolonize Anguilla.

The Comparison: Martinique and Barbados

For reasons of geographical proximity and certain structural and historical similarities, the islands of Martinique and Barbados are quite suitable for purposes of comparison. Unlike some of the more strongly contested islands of the Lesser Antilles (e.g., St. Lucia and Dominica, control of which changed hands dozens of times in the eighteenth and nineteenth centuries alone), both Martinique and Barbados have been occupied without significant change for over three hundred years by their original settlers. (D'Esnambuc took possession of Martinique for the French in 1635; Captain John Powell took possession of Barbados for the British in 1625.) Both colonies were constituted juridically as the properties of charter companies but were to be ceded to their respective royal crowns. Neither suffered from "absenteeism": that is, large landowners, exploitative as they may have been, did live on the island and socially creolized to an extent that corporate representatives did not. Both were to experience rapid population increases in the seventeenth and eighteenth centuries from the slave trade, establish plantation economies based on a sugar monoculture ("King Sugar," as it was called in Barbados), prosper as the principal suppliers for their respective metropoles, and decline as economies of scale, technical advancements, and competition from sugar growers in Europe, America, and other Caribbean islands relegated them to marginal economic significance. Both regained a modest prosperity in the wake of postwar development schemes. Both remain home to the most powerful of historic white minorities in the Caribbean.

Today, Martinique and Barbados rival each other in their accession to the perquisites of a modern-day society and in their exposure to the outside world. Thanks in part to relatively early mass schooling,[7] both boast a 98 percent literacy rate, an educational infrastructure up to the university level, the highest per capita radio, television, and cinema rates in the Caribbean, developed road, transportation, and telephone networks, and free access to foreign and domestic newspapers, journals, films, and books. Certainly the average Barbadian, with a GDP per capita income of nearly $17,300, is not as financially prosperous as her Martinican counterpart with 16,370 euros (and who benefits from a social and wage structure linked to that of the French metropole), but a lower cost of living makes any strictly statistical comparison problematic. According to the United Nations human development index (which does not include France's nonindependent territories), Barbados ranks higher than any other Caribbean country and is well within the top half of "high human development" nations. (Bahamas has a higher GDP per capita income but ranks lower on life expectancy and education.)

Even the most casual visitor to the two islands, separated by a mere 125 kilometers, will acknowledge that Barbados is far from being an "English Martinique" (or Martinique a "French Barbados"), and that there is a substantially different feeling to the two islands. A more critical observer will note that as far as political culture and national consciousness are concerned, the concerns, attitudes, and behavior of the respective populations are quite dissimilar. The more we examine the origins and expression of these differences in their political cultures, the less we can be satisfied to reduce the differences to the fact that Martinique has been a French department since 1946 and Barbados an independent state since 1966.

Geography and Topography

Barbados, while part of the Windward Islands chain (as is Martinique), is the sole island that lies outside the fine curve of the archipelago. In an era when transportation was undertaken entirely by sailing ships, and inasmuch as the trade winds blow from arid easterly to westerly direction (limiting movement from the other islands toward Barbados), Barbados enjoyed a geographic immunity from the otherwise stormy battles for sovereignty over the West Indies. Geography is the first of Blackman's (1998) "several 'fortunate' accidents produc[ing] for the island a leading place in the Caribbean."[8]

Barbados is also the most easterly island in the entire Caribbean, and thus benefited as the first port of call for British trading ships, at least in the Windward Islands zone. Geographically isolated from the other islands, and buttressed by its prominence in the British trading circuit, Barbados developed relatively early a sense of separateness, of difference. From early literature in the British empire, it was cast as the "first" and "ideal" plantation society: "The model of sugar and slavery was perfected here, and exported to other parts of the West Indian complex" (Beckles 2004, 155). Over the years, such feelings developed into a feeling of splendid isolation, bordering on pride.[9] "Individual pride is clearly associated with economic status and has been cited as a reason for Barbados' early economic success, which surpassed that of the Windward Islands." With that work ethos has come, with the British model, a stratified and class-conscious society (Meyerson, Hornbeck, and Haggerty 1989, 393). Reinforced by economic and cultural achievements, pride has become an integral feature of "Bajan" (informal nickname for Barbadian) national character.

Martinique, too, claims its own measure of cultural and historical specificity (although distinction as the earliest and most heavily colonized of the Vieilles Colonies is perhaps a dubious honor). But by virtue of its geographic integration with the Lesser Antilles, Martinique was more subject to the never-ending contention of British and French imperialism in the region, and could less divorce its consciousness from both the local warfare in the Caribbean and the interplay of politics in distant Europe. Martinique also shares a linguistic and cultural similarity (through Creole) with her northern and southern neighbors (St. Lucia and Dominica), as well as with her sister overseas department, Guadeloupe. The geographic isolation of Barbados has deprived it of any comparative cultural integration with nearby peoples and heightened its sense of distinction. (The particularity of the Barbadian accent is cited locally as a mark of distinction, and indirectly, a matter of linguistic superiority.)

Martinique, an island of volcanic origin, possesses a mountainous landscape offering seclusion and retreat for those so desirous. Her landscape was so exploited, first by the *marrons* who, escaping from their slave habitations, sought the refuge offered by such mountain retreats, and afterward by freed slaves who, still wishing to flee the reminders of their earlier condition, left the plantations to settle their own homesteads in more marginal and theretofore unexploited land.

The Barbadian landscape, however, disallowed the topographic exploitation of land for migratory purposes; indeed, "of all [the British West Indian] colonies, Barbados was topographically the most unsuitable for rebellion" (Buddan 2001, 37, quoting Hart 1998, 36). Of coral formation, and at 166 square miles less than half the size of Martinique (421 square kilometers), Barbados is generally flat, precipitating the early and exclusive development of plantation settlements throughout the island. Escape is only feasible where there is a place one can escape to, and without any natural shelters, the Barbadian slave was barred the option of physical flight. Since virtually all the land was already divided into plantations by the time emancipation came in 1838, the freed Barbadian slave was constrained to stay and work on the same plantation where he had labored under his former status. A paradoxical benefit derived: "Barbadians have a cultural propensity to access knowledge because they received the rawest deal at emancipation, a landless freedom that drove them to rely upon education to escape the entrapment of the estates" (Beckles 2004, 175).

In short, the argument goes, the Barbadian, if for topographic reasons alone, developed a sense of compromise and acceptance in terms of physical environment. Unlike his or her Martinican counterpart, for whom the possibility of escape from an oppressive reality was (and is, according to the psychological analyses we shall examine) a matter of individualistic revolt and rejection of the other, the Barbadian was more inclined to adapt to the given situation and make the most of it.

Today, with 280,000 inhabitants, Barbados is also not only the most densely populated island in the West Indies but also one of the most densely populated communities in the world. Unlike Martinique, whose population (approximately 400,000) is clustered within definable spatial limits, separated by kilometers of tropical forest or flatter land expanses, the swollen population of Barbados is more uniformly spread throughout the island (giving rise to the adage "Barbados is a city where sugar grows in the suburbs"). Emigration is a necessity almost as much for reasons of demography as for unemployment. But unlike in Martinique, where emigration used to be cast as part of a policy of "genocide by substitution," the considerable Barbadian presence abroad[10] is seen rather characteristically as a matter of welcome expedience, if not a diffusion of Barbadian generosity. (The long-time existence of Barbadian lineage in the southern United States, as well as the existence of important Barbadian communities in New York and Canada, are often mentioned in this connection.)

In the long run, Barbadian topography (and resulting demography) have contributed to a temperament that rejects radical solutions (the resistance of *marronage*, for example) in favor of practical solutions and compromise. In the words of *Daily Sun* columnist John Wickham in Bridgetown, the result is an "island mentality" and the recognition of the "need to share a common landscape." The recognition of the need for solidarity in an otherwise limited environment also helps explain, according to the same observer, the erosion of the black-white dichotomy: the "we're all in the same boat" attitude.

However intriguing, arguments based on comparative geographic and topographic constraints at best reinforce those driven by colonial policy and postcolonial politics. For it is in the history, psychology, and economy of both colonizer and colonized that the fundamental differences between Martiniquais and Bajan emerge.

Psychological Aspects: Consequences of Slave Society and Postmodernity

[The Barbadian] possesses flexibility of mind, an almost instinctive capacity for creative response to fresh situations and challenges. (Will 1972)

[S]omeone from Martinique . . . told me with considerable resentment that some Guadeloupe Negroes were trying to "pass" as Martinicans. But, he added, the lie was rapidly discovered, because they are more savage than we are; which, again, means they are farther away from the white man. (Fanon 1967, 26)

Much has been written about the French West Indian mentality, the most famous being that of the Martinican doctor Frantz Fanon. In *Black Skin, White Masks*, written from the perspective of engaged psychiatry, Fanon strips away the inauthenticity of the Martinican who denies the reality of his race, history, and geography in a futile struggle to be French like those of the metropole. André Lucrèce (2000) chronicles the psychological effects of three post-Fanon decades of Western-style "development" and "modernity" upon French West Indian society. Salient symptoms are nervousness, excitability, impulsiveness, feverishness, instability, and compulsiveness.

Bertrand Edouard (1972) stresses the transgenerational influences of slave-plantation history. He attributes to the Martinican the following traits that come directly from the slave-era past: antiwork ("The Martinican reactivates the same behavior towards work as his ancestors, for whom passivity was a means of opposition"); individualism ("When it comes to action, the Martinican retreats into an individualism. . . . Only fear of authority allows the maintenance of collective harmony"); ostentatious consumerism ("For want of true, lasting power, the Martinican seeks self-esteem in external signs of wealth: large parties, luxurious automobiles, jewelry, presents"); racial tension ("The colonial past touches off a superiority complex in the Metropolitan, and an intolerable trauma of slavery in the Martinican"); even sexism ("In those rare moments when the man is at home, he erects an obvious master-slave relationship between himself and his woman, conducting himself as a domestic tyrant"). It is self-evident for Edouard that the most outstanding features of the Martinican personality (antiwork, individualism, ostentatious consumerism, racial tension, sexism) can be reduced to the residues of a slave mentality (reincarnation of "his ancestors," "fear of authority," "the search for true power," "the colonial past," the reestablishment of an "apparent master-slave relationship"). Does the Barbadian, also with a slave past, manifest the same personality traits?

There is no contesting that early Barbadian history was at least as harsh as Martinique's: "[Barbados] was a greedy, cruel place, like any other West Indian sugar island" (Will 1972). Unlike Martinique, whose earliest plantation owners at least included dukes and nobles (and were therefore "civilized," by European standards), Barbados from the beginning was considered "the dunghill whereon England cast forth its rubbish, its rogues and prostitutes" (quoted in Simmons 1976, 10). Even today, the respective indigenous white populations demonstrate the difference in colonial personality and origins: whereas Martinique's *békés* are a quasi-aristocratic caste of prosperous landowners and traders, those in Barbados also include "Red Legs," a poor, disparaged lot of outcastes, working small plots of land in a kind of rural ghetto on the northwestern part of the island.[11] If slavery as an institution was no less pronounced in Barbados than in Martinique, racism as a sociological fact was no less real, either: Barbados was "the most racially and class-divided territory in the Commonwealth Caribbean" (Will 1972, 85).

So why have the legacies of slavery and racism been of one sort on one island, and of another sort on the other? Was English slavery in Barbados different from French slavery in Martinique?

It would be fatuous to propose that one kind of slavery was, or could be, "better" than another, and no portraits of Caribbean slave society purport to do so.[12] Nevertheless, Marvin Will suggests that an alternative model to the otherwise miserable slave masses was portrayed by that section of Barbadian society (other than the Red Legs) that pretended to a certain culture or class. Will speaks of "certain proprieties, a certain sense of style" in matters of home life, and a "gentility" in domestic and public "manners" which were observed by a large proportion of Barbadian society. John Hearne (1967, 7) in his essay on Bajan national identity claims that "any slave society takes its tone and customary behaviour from the masters."[13] These cultural modes presumably would have been internalized and passed down in postslavery generations. It is in this context that the most visible difference in English and French "styles" of slavery merits mention: tendencies toward miscegenation.

The CIA *World Factbook* provides the following breakdown of the Barbadian population reveals the following statistics: African ancestry, 93 percent; European ancestry, 3.2 percent; mixed, 2.6 percent.[14] A similar breakdown for Martinique—where rare is the family entirely bereft of a chromosomal French heritage—would be a hazardous task indeed. Neither would we venture a hypothesis into the respective sexual mores of the French and English in their colonial possessions. But if the prerogatives of slaveownership took on a markedly less intimate tone in Barbados[15] than in Martinique, we would do well to repose our earlier suggestion. Is not the style of a slave institution, rather than its existence per se, the key to an understanding of its present-day residues?

Much more than in Barbados, slavery is memorialized in Martinique. Museums, sculptures, murals, and slave-era architectural restorations all bear witness to the concerted effort by Martinican individuals and local government to reclaim the memory that official French historiography had eclipsed (Reinhardt 2006). The 150th anniversary of the French abolition of slavery (1998) galvanized this movement (Miles 1999a). Efforts in Barbados to restore recognition of African and slave-era identity are commensurate in intention but lag way behind Martinique in terms of collective consciousness and governmental support.

Cultural Aspects: "Assimilationism" and Afro-Saxonism

Particularly in the West Indies, it is tempting to reduce the differences between British and French colonialism and decolonization to its most stripped down form: "When the French colonize, they try to turn their subjects into Frenchmen themselves. When the British colonize, they take what they want, take off when they've finished, and let their former colonies fend for themselves." The psychological result of these colonial philosophies, presumably, is that the French West Indies, being more thoroughly assimilated to French culture, lifestyle, and politics than their English-speaking counterparts are to British culture, lifestyle, and politics, are more reluctant to leave the *mère-patrie* than *les Anglais* are to be independent of their "mother country."

It is not merely by poetic or touristic hyperbole that Barbados is dubbed "Little England." Unlike Martinique, whose settlements of Carib Indians at the time of white colonization and discovery attest to a pre-European and pre-African culture, Barbados, lacking such an indigenous population, is solely the product of British settlement and slave society. Whereas the origins of French colonization over Martinique lay in conquest, Barbados was founded less violently, as a settler colony (Buddan 2001, 36). And just as Martinique is often said to incarnate the mores and customs of *la Vieille France* (Old France), Barbados is said to be "more traditionally British" than Britain itself. Barbados "borrowed more of her political culture and structures from her colonizer than any Caribbean territory" (Will 1972,

12). Bimshire is the sobriquet for the island that, before independence, the local elite popularized among slave descendants to reify an old English model for a West Indian island.

In French colonial history, the term is *assimilationisme*; for the British, especially in Barbados, we could as easily talk about saxonization. ("Barbadian blacks have been 'saxonized' by nearly three and one-half centuries of British colonialism" [Will 1972, 12].) An "affinity to things British," "stability," "resistance to rapid change," a reliance on "tradition," and "orderly change"—express characteristics of Barbadian culture—more strongly evoke the image one has of English values and temperament, and less the stereotyped image of steel-band music, jump-up carnival, and Rastaman that many have of the Anglophone Caribbean islands. Indeed, disdain for counterculturalism, as embodied in Rastafarianism (and "rebel music"), runs deep. While Barbados holds an annual African Liberation Week, its resonance should not be exaggerated: the *Barbados Advocate* criticized the local "Africanist lobby [as] usurpers who had declared the need for social revolution and who are conditioning the people's minds to believe that somehow they are victims of injustice" (quoted in Buddan 2001, 43). Even in its most conservative days, it is hard to imagine *France-Antilles* taking such an overtly conservative position.

A psychological identification with the colonial personality is not relegated, moreover, only to the French West Indian "black skin, white masks" phenomenon described by Frantz Fanon. *English Rustics in Black Skins* (Greenfield 1966) is not only the title of a study of West Indian elites but a description of a process of cultural identification that is more popularly referred to in its modern-day Barbadian manifestation as "Afro-Saxon culture."[16]

But there is a difference, and even a paradox, to the respective assimilations as experienced in Martinique and Barbados. For whereas both *assimilé* and "black Englishman" were supposed to represent the apogees of cultural evolution in the French and British West Indies, the former term has a negative, sometimes scornful connotation that the latter does not. This holds true not only for a minority of radically assimilated individuals but also for the society as a whole. "Barbadian . . . Englishness . . . is a source of real psychic strength. It is one of the inheritances that give [Barbadians] their extraordinary self-confidence and self-discipline. . . . There is a "wholeness" to the Barbadian . . . not found in any other British Caribbean territory, an awareness of himself as a person that is remarkable, enviable and, in every sense of the word, good" (Hearne 1967, 8).

Strength of identification with home island may have to with the earlier creolization of Bajans vis-à-vis other British islands. "By 1817 only 7 percent of Barbadian slaves had been born in Africa; the comparable proportion was 36 percent in Jamaica and 44 percent in Trinidad" (Gmelch and Gmelch 1997, 38).

Herein lies the paradox of the respective policies of cultural assimilation pursued in the British and French West Indies: whereas the intention of the French, more than the British, was to create subjects (or citizens) who are culturally if not politically similar to themselves, the result has been a much greater ambivalence between those who spouted perfect equality, despite racial difference, as an ideal and policy (colonial assimilationists), and those who have resisted the withering away of Creole identity and culture (the proponents of West Indian négritude). The problem of French departmentalization in a Caribbean society is "the unfinished project of political creolization" (Périna 2003).

We cannot limit our comparison to the intentions and results of European policies of cultural identity. Beyond a historical (and Eurocentric) explanation of present-day tendencies, political culture must take account of a people's own conception of identity. A further question, therefore, calls for a response: how do Martinicans and Barbadians see themselves?

Sociological Characteristics: National Character and Perceptions of Self

The tragedy of the Martinican condition, as described by many of her writers, is that the basic solution to the deformed and exaggerated individualism—acquisition of a national identity—is lacking but in its most nascent form. La Martinique may exist as an island, a department, even a region (according to the prevailing administrative vogue), but the appellation "nation" comes naturally to few when referring to Martinique (Miles 2006). The development of a political culture entails, more than anything else, the recognition of a personal identity with a larger (nonfamilial) group, which serves as a source of solidarity, strength, and meaning. "Patriotism and a sense of culture . . . are only smaller partners with one's personality " (Allsopp 1972, 6). Lacking this national identity as a fundamental basis, a formalistic designation of "nationhood" or "independence" is devoid of content. While this sense of national identity may be linked with a formal status of independence, it does not automatically follow it.

Barbados, on the other hand, thinks of itself as "a new state but an old nation." From the outset, a respect for protocol, traditional procedures, and a historical awareness have created a strong sense of community and a specific sense of Barbadian pride. Far from emanating from the accession to independence on November 30, 1966, this strength of political culture is the result of a centuries-old evolution. "Political independence hasn't made a hell of a lot of difference in identity. Independence (as an event in and of itself) wasn't a big thing"—there was rather a "lukewarm" response to it (Wickham 1981).

According to Richard Allsopp, the uniqueness of Barbados resides in its fidelity "to those very political and religious principles (democracy and Christianity) that had been so gruesomely negated by the teachers themselves." Barbadian prudence and realism is a matter of historical record as well: "Where our forefathers could rebel they did so, and where they couldn't they compromised to survive." But Barbadian patriotism does not preclude identification with a broader Caribbean history and culture: "My joy is in the totality of our Caribbean culture of which Barbados is inescapably a part" (Allsopp 1972, 7).

The traits of a "distinct Barbadian culture [are] easy to trace. . . . Barbadian customs are notably landbased and little affected by the surrounding sea. . . . The Barbadian character has a customary absence of intransigence, a notable ability for compromise, and even tiresome proneness to see two sides when the more popular and 'progressive' tendency is to see only one" (Allsopp 1972, 8).

A leading columnist of Barbados's *Daily Sun* characterizes the Barbadian personality thus: "Barbadians are attentive to the *organization* of things. They incarnate a respect for property. . . . Roads [for example] are tidy." Even in terms of household budgets, the Barbadian propensity toward frugality contrasts with the ever-increasing consumerism of Martinican society where, thanks to the incentives of credit or loan institutions, all goods are more readily seen as obtainable to the interested consumer. Although a certain change in attitude is slowly surfacing, the Barbadian, in contrast, still possesses a "peasant kind of thrift. He does what he can afford." Such cultural conservatism (linked to class rigidity) has been a source of criticism for some Anglophone Caribbeans (Buddan 2001, 42). "Barbadians pride themselves on being a model of stability and prudent management, perhaps even to the point of arrogance" (Lewis 2001, 145).

Barbados has adopted a consistently conservative political stance. The difference between the two political parties, the Democratic Labour Party and the Barbados Labour Party, which have democratically vied for power since independence, is more one of style than ideology.[17] Radical political parties are negligible; little remains of the People's Progressive Movement and allied Marxist black nationalist organizations of the 1960s (Lewis 2001, 156–57). This is in direct contrast with the Martinican political scene, which is dotted with sundry leftist groups of various radical tones. If in Barbados there is "a preoccupation . . . with stability above acts of contestation" (Lewis 2001, 158), contestation is said to be a veritable hallmark of the Martinican national character: "The first trait characteristic of Martinican identity," replied the mayor of Fort-de-France, soon to be elected to the French National Assembly as one of four Martinican parliamentarians, "is resistance" (Sabra 2007).

There is a general consensus that, apart from a "residual hang-up in color" (such as a disappearing preference for lighter skin pigmentation in hiring practices), there is "no underlying racial tension."[18] Whereas historically segregation was very pronounced on the island, it is believed that modern-day Barbadian society has "purified" itself of racism. "Barbadian feeling of national pride" is seen as contributing to this lack of racial tension. It does not, however, replace a supposed "crisis in political authority":

> Political leaders are depreciated, especially if they inherit their top leadership position . . . from the colonial era. The courts have been put under pressure from the economically powerful, drug barons, and politicians themselves. Religion, especially the established denominations, has begun to lose its controlling sway. . . . The social fabric appears to be disintegrating into an alarming and persistent . . . outbreak of crime, child abuse, spouse beatings, suicides, increase in pathogenic disorders . . . drug abuse [both legal and illegal], poor service and interpersonal relations, absence of retraining standards, and rampant consumerism. (Duncan 1994, 86)

Economic dependency defines both islands but in different ways and with varying consequences. Barbadian welfare depends on the vagaries of a diffuse external economy (North American and western European), particularly as it affects tourism. Martinique's depends on France. The former leads to adaptation, both on the macro and individual level: Gmelch and Gmelch (1997) stress the multiplicity of sources of income that rural Barbadians use to make ends meet. Dependence on a single country personalizes the dependency complex; Martinicans can hail or rail against France, but they cannot deny her role in their material survival. Barbadians may suffer from periodic international economic recession but are less inclined to channel their frustrations toward any specific nationality.

Unemployment, particularly among young males, is high on both islands. In Barbados, a variety of family and social mechanisms enable young male islanders to "lime" (hang out) indefinitely. In Martinique, what enables the unemployed to survive is *l'Etat*—the (French) state. The social and psychological consequences are less benign: "'Why should I work,'" paraphrases a Martinican deputy to the French National Assembly, "'when I am paid every week not to?'" (Miles 2007).

Religious Differences

Nearly four centuries of colonialism have bequeathed contrasting religious heritages to Barbados and Martinique. But this not a mere question of denominational difference: it is the general importance of religion in the overall society that gives rises to further distinguishing traits. In Martinique, against the long tradition of Roman Catholicism—nevertheless mitigated by deep-rooted Africanist folk practices (*quimboiserie* [Affergan 1989; Alexis 1976; Bougerol 1991; Degoul 2000a, 2000b; Delawarde 1983; Henry-Valmore 1983, 1989; Jardel 2000; Leti 2000])—there is a French cultural overlay of *laïcité*, or secularism. Barbados's colonially superimposed variety of Christianity—Anglican Protestantism—has been challenged in recent years by more evangelical expressions of the faith (African religious survivalisms taking the forms of duppies [spirits] and *obeah* [witchcraft]). But despite a democratically generic separation of church and state, Barbados has no competing national or historical ethos, as do the French Antilles, of anticlericalism, hardcore secularism, or outright atheism.[19]

Anglicans in Barbados constitute a plurality (28 percent) of practitioners. Major growth has been occurring in the Pentecostal churches, which are now the second-largest drawer of worshippers (19 percent). The expressive, populist brand of Pentecostal worship, successfully competing with the more staid "High Church" of Anglicism, has its parallel in Martinique; there, the Seventh-day Adventists and Jehovah's Witnesses, with an even more millenarian appeal than Barbadian Pentecostalism, have been to encroach on the Roman Catholic parishes (De Vassoigne 1994; Hurbon 1989; Massé 1978a, 1978b; Massé and Poulin 2000). Upwards of 85 percent of Martinicans are nevertheless still identified as Catholics, compared with only 4 percent of Barbadians.

Compared to, say, Jamaica, Rastafarianism is a marginal phenomenon in both Martinique (Yerro 2000) and Barbados; at least in numbers. Rastas nevertheless represent a present psychological threat to middle-class Caribbean society—be it a conservative indigenous social society of Barbados or a European-emulating one in the French Antilles. On both islands, Rastafarianism is seen not only as a drain of young adherents from "good" religion but also as an enclave of drug culture and criminality. Gmelch and Gmelch (1997) observe that some islanders manage to distinguish "true Rastafarians," whom they respect for their idealism, Africanism, and nativism, from the merely dreadlocks-and-tam-wearing hooligans who "dress dread" to cloak their criminality in a patina of coolness.

Despite parallel challenges to the predominant religious orders, overall the Catholic stamp of Martinique still sharply differentiates it from the Protestant culture of Barbados. From the earliest colonial times until today, Roman Catholicism has constituted in Martinique an institutional and ideational monolith without denominational equivalent in Barbados (ADM 2001). Protestantism in Barbados, even with its Anglican ascendance, has been more variegated and institutionally disparate than Catholicism in Martinique. A hierarchical religious structure—one tied so strongly to France's ecclesiastical structure, no less—has been quite compatible with an overarching colonial philosophy preaching centralism and direct rule. Max Weber's otherwise contested theory of an otherworldly Catholic worldview that fosters fatalism above resistance may very well apply here: unlike elsewhere in Latin America, liberation theology did not take hold among French Catholic West Indians.

On account of France's (over)generous welfare system (a byproduct of Martinique's overall institutional integration within France), Martinican critics of various ideological stripes bemoan the culture of dependency that presumably afflicts the work ethic of the Martinican people. A religiously based comparison with Barbados raises the additional question whether lack of a Protestant work ethic in Martinique might also explain part of the industriousness differential between these two Windward Island peoples.

The significance of Christian legacies of colonialism will resurface in the next chapter. There we shall find that the Catholic-Protestant partition prevailing between neighboring Martinique and Barbados in the Caribbean being replicated *within* the same island nation in the South Pacific (Vanuatu). Although denominational outcomes are somewhat different in that religious borderland, French Catholic allergy to political independence, at least initially, distinguishes itself yet again from Anglophone Protestantism.

Political Aspects: Evolutions of Government

Both the philosophy and implementation of government in Barbados and Martinique have followed distinctively separate paths, yielding distinctively separate results. A thorough comparative history of Barbadian and Martinican governance is of course not possible here, but inasmuch as an understanding of the present-day political cultures of the two islands must take into account their political histories, we will limit ourselves to highlighting the pertinent differences.

From the beginning, the juridical status of Martinique (and its inhabitants) has swung between two poles of metropolitan ambivalence. Even if the cultural tenets of *assimilation* as a colonial philosophy were rarely questioned, their implications as an administrative policy were less clear.

It is true that from the Third Republic on, the tendency was to apply French civil, penal, and military codes to the judicial apparatus in the colonies. Yet formal acceptance of Martinique (and the other "Old Colonies") as full departments, on the same level as the metropolitan territories, took fifty years between the proposal of departmentalization by Senators Isaac and Allègre in 1890, and its ratification by the National Assembly in 1946. In the meantime, and even since decentralization of the 1980s, governance in Martinique remains essentially a matter of the proclamation or passage of laws by metropolitan executives or legislature (as kings, emperors, or assemblies), their application, enforcement, and supervision by the government's chosen representatives (be they governors or prefects), and adjudication by metropolitan-chosen judges (themselves mostly metropolitan), interpreting according to the Napoleonic Code. Only in budgetary allocation have the local regional and general councils assumed a substantially increased measure of local initiative. Tellingly, referenda in 2003 and 2010 that would have modified and liberalized Martinique's administrative status within the French Republic—a far cry from separatism—were decisively rejected by the local electorate.[20]

Barbadian administrative history differs both from Martinique's history and from that of most of the other former British colonies. For while most of the British West Indies were ruled by Crown Colony governments, Barbadian political history is unique by virtue of its independence from metropolitan interference and control and its development of an indigenous structure of government with particularistic nationalist sentiments.

For most of the British West Indies, Crown Colony government entailed the establishment of a local legislature, whose members were either exclusively nominated by the government in England—a pure Crown Colony—or a semirepresentative system, by which the legislature was partly chosen by the electorate and partly nominated by the government. In either case, the legislators were but straw men, in that they were committed to support the government's policy and obliged to vote according to orders given by the executive. True power lay with the governor who, limited only in theory by the Colonial Office, ruled as a virtual autocrat, siding with the upper against the lower classes, and considering the maintenance of law and order as his primary duty. Inasmuch as the government was seen as the institutionalization and consolidation of the already established interests (and not as the representatives of the people), the result was an underlying political tension between the government and the people on the one hand, and "moral havoc" on the part of the impotent legislators on the other. Political life was seen in a jaded light by participants and "represented" alike, since the legislatures gave the illusion of power without any real responsibility. "Colonial government was negative government. Its institutional arrogance bred popular irresponsibility" (Lewis 1967, 8).

In Barbados, however, Crown Colony government never took hold, and the Old Representative System prevailed. The Barbadian House of Assembly, which is still today the political institution of Barbados, was established in 1639, making it the oldest elected legislative chamber in the Western Hemisphere, and the oldest continuously elected parliament in the Commonwealth. The Barbadian House of Assembly has from its inception been a fully elected legislature: its independence from both London and London's representative was challenged only once, and unsuccessfully at that, when Barbados rebelled against the imposition of Cromwellian rule during England's Civil War. Otherwise, the House of Assembly was more powerful than the governor, limiting both the governor's militia and his summoning powers. In fact, the parliament in Barbados had more power, and greater independence, vis-à-vis the executive than its counterpart, the House of Commons, had in England itself. Politically, Barbados was characterized by "the complete Rule of Law, and Barbadian law at that."

The political independence of Barbados also benefited from another fact: Britain's own lack of interest in Barbadian affairs. British policy toward Barbados in the seventeenth and eighteenth centuries was perhaps best characterized by Edmund Burke, who termed it "salutary neglect." Control of internal political affairs in this early English settlement was generally left to the Barbadians themselves, leading to a kind of "New World incubation, and eventual creolization of both attitudes and structures" (Will 1972). It is no wonder, then, that the advent of independence made little difference in the form of the Barbadian political structure, which retains the common law courts, executive department, parliament secretariat, and House of Assembly which tradition itself bequeathed. Postindependence Barbados has experienced the rivalry of the Barbados Labour Party and the Democratic Labour Party, which have been vying for legislative supremacy for four decades in nonviolent, free and fair democratic alternations rarely seen elsewhere in the independent islands of the Caribbean.

The most comprehensive comparison of Martinique and Barbados from an administrative and institutional point of view has been conducted by Fred Reno (1989). Reno asks why the antiestablishment political elites of Martinique and Barbados would have come to such different demands with respect to decolonization: statehood with the former colonizer for Martinique, independence from the former colonizer for Barbados. For Reno, different colonial policies emanating from France and Britain created different kinds of local struggles. In Barbados, British reluctance to interfere in colonial rivalries channeled nationalist frustrations against the local "agro-bourgeoisie": the few whites families who maintained post-emancipation hegemony. Sleeman's (1986) sugar-based comparison parallels Reno's analysis here: an agribusiness bourgeoisie in Martinique, without formal power in the political system, successfully and strategically replaced sugar with commercial industry. In Barbados, diversification by this class has been "uneven and incomplete."

Barbadian decolonization hence entailed wresting political control, via independence, on behalf of the black masses (albeit by a predominantly brown middle class) in order to raise living standards for both groups and social standing for the latter. In Martinique, the greater struggle was with an ever-centralizing and culturally moralizing France who still preached liberty, equality, and fraternity. Martinican activists (unlike in Barbados, composed mostly of civil servants) demanded that France materially realize her promises by granting full parity—politically through departmentalization, economically through subsidies and other welfare transfers. Even when the benefits of departmentalization proved disappointing—income and social gaps between Martinique and the metropole proved stubbornly ineradicable—nationalist politicians (still French-employed *fonctionnaires*, for the most part) demanded different kinds of administrative reforms (regionalism, autonomy, decentralization, confederation) to fix the Martinique-metropole misfit. Reno fully recognizes the ambiguous and paradoxical nature of such nationalist demands: "acceptance of the French presence and criticism of politics directed from the [French] center" (Reno 1989, 26); "affirming the existence of the [Martinican] nation, while refusing for it an independent political expression" (30). Politically, says Reno, Martinican nationalism suffers from being a "prisoner of [French] state universalism" (29) and economically from being "prisoner of State resources" (31). Reno attributes the persistence of three seemingly contradictory goals for Martinique to the dialectical brilliance of Aimé Césaire. Thanks to "Césairien thought," Martinicans can simultaneously demand recognition for Martinican cultural and national specificity, criticism of statehood *qua* departmentalization, and continued belonging to greater France (30). In the meantime, Barbadian postcolonial political struggles take the form of partisan rivalry between two moderate, ideologically similar parties, each preferring to command the polity and economy by (and, some argue, for) itself.

Reno omits from his otherwise perspicacious comparison three other noteworthy political currents. Although they have gradually lost overall electoral dominance since the 1980s, Martinican departmentalists—staunch opponents to change in Martinique's administrative/juridical status with France—remain a local force with a significant following. Although even departmentalists have accepted the reality (if not the discourse) of a cultural Martinican reality distinct from that of metropolitan France (unlike, say, the classic assimilationists like Victor Sablé [1955, 1972]), they continue to articulate neo-assimilationist views.[21] Neo-assimilationists more straightforwardly argue that Martinique's welfare lies with France rather than without it, and they more comfortably envision incorporation within the EU (European Union) rather than, say, CARIFTA (Caribbean Free Trade Association).

Reno also pays little attention to the small but vocal independentist movements in Martinique. By far and away the most prominent is the Mouvement Indépendentiste Martiniquais (MIM). So associated is the MIM with its charismatic leader that the one book dedicated to analyzing the MIM is subtitled "presentation on Marie-Jeannism." Despite its electoral breakthrough since 1997 (Miles 1999a, 2003a, 2003b, 2006, 2007), MIM's success should be seen more as the result of protest votes than as authentic expression of populist desire for independence. It is hard to find a Barbadian equivalent to this brand of radicalism—except, perhaps, that wing of Bajan nationalism that calls for an out-and-out republic to replace the continuing colonial symbolism of fealty to the Queen of England.

Third, there are also Barbadian activists (more academic intellectuals than party politicians) who wish to redirect Bajan nationalism back to its original independence aims: sovereignty for the sake of a more equitable redistribution of local resources. These writers and activists,[22] led by the "new breed of historians" at the Cave Hill campus of the University of the West Indies (Welch 2003, 39), again put the problem of race front and center for a Barbados still economically dominated by a few white families who since independence have been protected by a collaborationist black middle and governing *comprador* class "deluded by distorted notions of their own relative autonomy" (Lewis 2001, 150). Bajan black nationalists and "counterhegemonic" intellectuals advocate a radical intervention by the state for the sake of more equal distribution of Barbadian wealth—a goal that, presumably, decolonization was supposed to achieve anyway.

Decolonization, we have observed earlier, is a process, not an event. In Barbados, the unfinished business associated with decolonization revolves around race; in Martinique, while race is also a social feature, the larger question is sovereignty.

Back to Haiti

Lurking in the psyche of the French West Indies is the experience of Haiti, the first Caribbean island to achieve independence (by revolting against France) and for long the poorest polity in the Western Hemisphere. Why an independent political future would resemble the experience of Haiti rather than, say, Barbados is rarely mooted. Perhaps it is because British West Indian history is given short shrift in school compared with that of the French Antilles; or perhaps because of the linguistic proximity afforded by Creole. That a virulent anti-Haitian immigrant movement headed by a disc jockey-turned-politician Ibo Simon took hold in Guadeloupe (to the point of being a factor in post-millennial elections there) is a reflection of continuing phobia over Haiti. In any event, Haiti remains a tacit reason for Martinique's continuing attachment to France.

Lawrence Harrison (1985) also invokes Haiti in his cultural explanation for Latin American underdevelopment. As in most comparative analyses of Haiti, Harrison calls up the Dominican Republic, with which Haiti shares Hispaniola, to emphasize the contrasting legacies of slavery, race, and religion (Vodun). But Harrison uses a chapter to contrast Haiti with Barbados, pointing to the post-emancipation tutelary attitude adopted by free coloreds toward blacks (as opposed to continuing denigration in Haiti), the expansion of education[23] and health services, the foundations of a robust economy, and a democratic process responsive to the aspirations of an economically modest black majority. For Harrison, the overarching reason for Barbados's success lies in its absorption of British cultural values. The "absorption by the colonized people of the colonial power's values and attitudes *over an extended period*... gives vitality and durability to the imported institutions" (Harrison 1985, 98, emphasis in original). Haiti has been survivalist; Barbados, progressive. External pressures forced the former into isolationism; the latter has been internationally open. Work is a positive ethic in Barbados; Haitians view it ambivalently, if not negatively. Outside the family, people are mistrusted in Haiti. But in Barbados, a civic culture has taken root.

Harrison takes the controversial position that descendants of slaves in the British Caribbean have fared better than their cousins who remained in West Africa (101). By the same token, and using the same statistical indices, one could argue that the best off of all are the descendants of West Indian slaves to whom France extended full citizenship and economic integration. How does one weigh the psychic benefits of sovereignty vis-à-vis more tangible gains of income or health services? Who decides if possessing a singular nationality (albeit of a small island) is superior to membership in the European Union—at the cost of homeland independence? In the square-off between Martinique and Barbados, between the benefits of French versus British (de)colonization in the Caribbean, Haiti represents the uncomfortable but undeniable variable: a people deprived but proud, a historical paragon of liberty in an age that professes racial equality but remains leery of recognizing the material trade-offs that black freedom entailed.

Differential Insularity: Implications for Postcolonial Legacies

Whereas Barbadian political history has been characterized by continuity, isolation, and particularity, that of Martinique has been more closely tied to the institutions, philosophies, and politics of the metropole. The governmental structure in Martinique has evolved according to the changes in France's own political history; the Barbadian political structure has remained virtually unchanged for close to four centuries. Martinican events have been observed and molded by a keenly interested metropolitan government; the evolution of Barbados has largely developed independently of metropolitan events and interference. Martinican political institutions are the transplants or replicas of French formulae; Barbadian political institutions are the result of the "creolization" of European institutions.

It would not be surprising if the political culture of Barbados were characterized by a greater interest in, and identification with, the formal institutions of government than in Martinique, where national elections are often seen as alien or externally generated occurrences. If this contrast does hold true (as electoral statistics tend to show), we are only partially justified in attributing it to the hypothesis that Barbadians are more interested in Barbadian elections than Martinicans are in French elections. Independence alone cannot explain a people's participation in or attitude toward the political process. The origins, evolution, and symbolism of the institutions of government are at least equally important in evaluating a society's attitude to the political act and its participation in the electoral process. The West Indies serve as a quintessential model for comparing different colonial models.

No matter how divisive the partition of the African continent in its creation of separate colonial and national identities, at least the colonized there remained African. Long after Kwame Nkrumah's utopian vision of unifying the continent faded, pan-Africanists still maintain that Africanity trumps colonial legacy. Superimposed national identities, they aver, do not supersede the basic essence of an African soul or cultural fount. However problematic that argument may be from a continental African point of view, it is all the more difficult when transplanted to the New World.

Slave descendants in the French Antilles today experience a very different reality than do their counterparts in nearby Anglophone islands. In the Caribbean, France still practices decolonization without independence. Slave-based colonialism bequeathed fewer options for postcolonial transformation than in colonial lands of ethnically indigenous populations: the West Indies do not display the diversity of political pathways that West Africa does. Whether independent or not, Anglophone and Francophone Caribbean societies reflect the image of their colonial pasts more than we have seen in West Africa, and more so than we shall find in Asia and Oceania. Our focused comparison of Martinique and Barbados, following general discussion of the (former) British West Indies vis-à-vis the (still) French ones, bears this out. "Assimilation" and "Saxonization" may be unfashionable terms today, but they still evoke, respectively, generally efficacious French and English modes of psychological transformation.

The Caribbean scenario of French and British postcolonial legacies raises poignant questions about the value of independence in an era of globalization. Globalization provides tremendous opportunities to individuals who manage to navigate new international pathways for insight and profit. Yet for poor and small nations, globalization also lessens choices and aggrandizes shocks: the international economic system displays little mercy for higher-priced diversity. Material prospects for tens of millions of workers worldwide can be instantly jeopardized by the shift in a few percentage points in economic indicators, exchange rates, or commodity prices.

What, today, are the relative trade-offs between sovereignty and security? What is the modern relationship between freedom and decolonization? And what are we to make of island polities where French democracy thrives but national independence is eschewed or denied?[24]

Are islanders in the West Indies conceivably better off, overall, when cushioned from international economic tsunamis by virtue of their status as overseas states? What about real environmental catastrophes in maritime polities projected by global warming and rising sea levels—who will assume responsibility for the spillovers?[25] Does citizenship in a sovereign homeland provide the same moral and psychological benefits in the twenty-first century that it did in the middle of the twentieth?

Contrasting postcolonial legacies of Britain and France in the Caribbean borderlands is not merely a matter of differentiating, for example, Bajans from Martinicans today. It is about anticipating how the respective inhabitants of neighboring islands will weather future shocks as they are bound to hit, either from economy or ecology. The unfortunate reality is that that they will do so in mutual ignorance of each other's deep culture, politics, and mentality. It is in this sense that, beyond the dissolution of specific African, Indian, and other ethnicities, West Indian scars of partition run the deepest.

For the bandages that cover those scars, France spares no expense.

4

Political Arbitrariness of Archipelagoes
The South Pacific

> Between peoples with temperaments as dissimilar as the French and the English, [joint colonial rule in the New Hebrides] was doomed to disaster from the beginning. There is a complete lack of that sympathetic cooperation so essential in such an obviously exacting enterprise; neither trusts the other for a minute.
> —A. J. Marshall, *The Black Musketeers*

As in the West Indies, the islands of the South Pacific were also arbitrarily parceled largely into French and British colonial zones. However, three major features distinguished the Anglo-French partition of Oceania from the Caribbean. For one, whereas colonialism in the Caribbean gave way (mostly) to separate postcolonial independences for discrete islands, the South Pacific has remained clustered into groups of islands according to prior colonial partition. Compare, for instance, the Lesser Antilles in the West Indies to the New Hebrides in the South Pacific (Map 10). Both measure roughly four hundred miles from north to south. The former archipelago is today the home to eight independent island nations, four French jurisdictions, three Dutch dependencies, and two British colonies. The latter, with a greater number of islands, is a single country.

Second, inasmuch as the West Indies were repopulated by African slaves (who involuntarily occupied the space of indigenous Caribbean peoples) colonialism there entailed the cre-

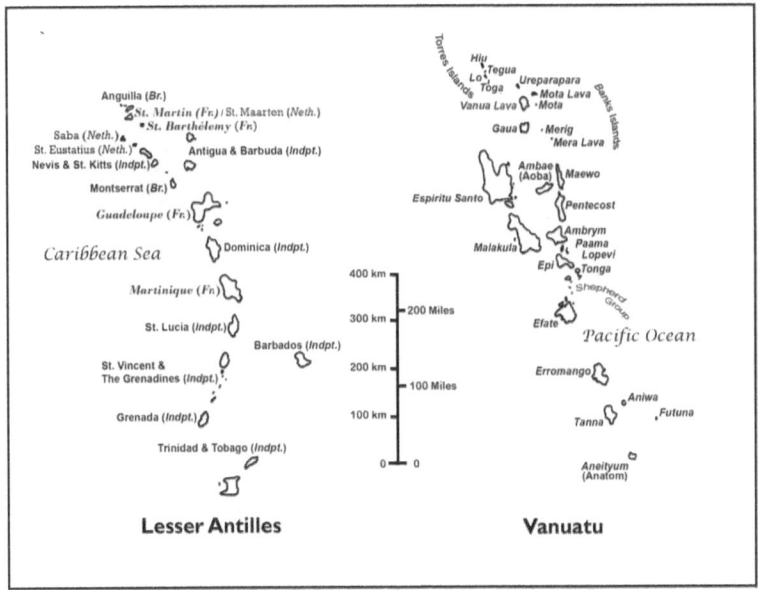

Map 10. Vanuatu and Lesser Antilles

ation of entirely new Creole cultures. Not so the South Pacific, which highlights the third main difference: partition in the South Pacific has entailed the political separation of otherwise ethnically related indigenous islanders whose cultures (hundreds of languages' worth) have nevertheless survived. In West Indian colonialism, as we have seen, partition was diasporic, separating African slaves not only from their own people but from their very own culture.

With respect to sovereignty, however, as in the West Indies, so goes the South Pacific: oceanic independence is mainly a condition of former British islands; French-speaking South Pacific islanders—with one significant exception—are still citizens of France.

Geography and Colonial History

The South Pacific is a vast expanse that is conventionally divided into two zones: Polynesia ("many islands") and Melanesia ("black islands").[1] How within the overall framework of the South Pacific

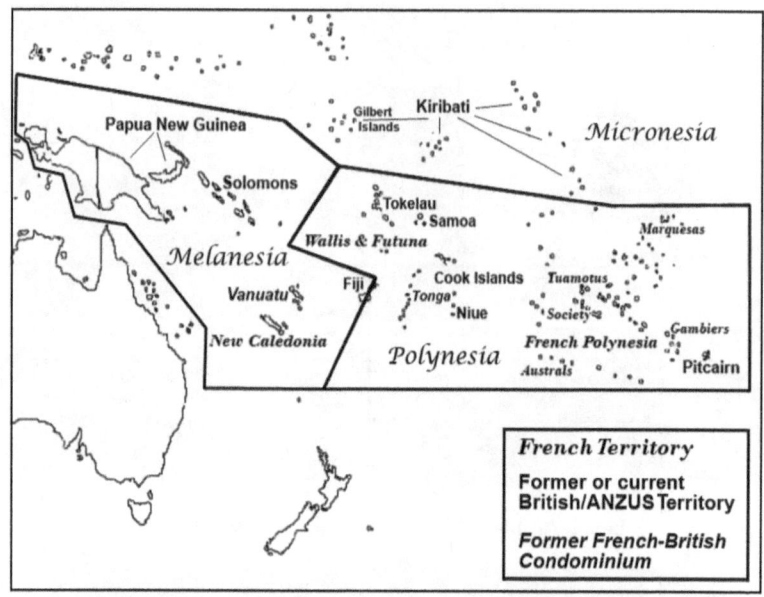

Map 11. Anglophone and Francophone South Pacific

to classify Australia, which Great Britain declared a colony in 1788, is a matter of geo-semantic debate. As a continental settler colony, Australia is unique in many ways. A member of the Commonwealth, it was "outsourced" long ago to take on colonial responsibilities over smaller islands that Britain did not or no longer wished to administer. (To a lesser extent, the same is true of New Zealand.) Some of those responsibilities continue to this day. (See Map 11.)

Polynesia

As with West Africa, colonial conquest of the South Pacific was largely a mid- to late nineteenth-century affair. Not wishing to cede the entire region to Great Britain, France initiated an annexation policy to counterbalance the massive British fait accompli over Australia. Beginning with the "protectorate" of Tahiti in 1842, French Polynesia grew into an agglomeration of 130 islands in five clusters: the Society Islands (including Tahiti, and comprising 85 percent of the overall population), the Gambier

Islands (east of which lie the Pitcairn Islands, a rare example of a British settler colony for the southeast Pacific); the Tuamotus, the Marquesas, and the Austral Islands. Different islands at different times have come under juridical statuses: colonies, naval governments, overseas territories, territorial collectivities. As of 2004, French Polynesia has been designated an overseas collectivity. Although their islands do not have the same administrative status as those of the French West Indies (that is to say, "departmental" status on a par with metropolitan France), French Polynesians are full French citizens. They vote in French elections and receive French social welfare benefits. French, of course, is the official language of government; culturally, they share an eastern variety of the Polynesian language.

A smaller cluster of French islands in Polynesia (although not administratively part of French Polynesia proper), is Wallis (also known as Uvea) and Futuna. Whereas official colonization of four of the five clusters of French Polynesia was a matter of the 1840s, that of Wallis and Futuna was that of the late 1880s. The long administrative yoking of Wallis/Uvea to Futuna demonstrates the negative converse of partition: colonial consolidation of dissimilar cultures. Linguistically, culturally, and historically, Uvea is linked more closely to Tonga (a rare Polynesian kingdom never to be colonized). Futuna, on the other hand, has more supracolonial affinity with Samoa.

Samoa, for its part, considers itself the "cradle of Polynesia." Its four inhabited (out of nine) islands are populated by people of yet another distinctive ethnicity. Colonized on the eve of the nineteenth century by Germany, Samoa was taken over by New Zealand at the beginning of the First World War. In the 1920s and 1930s the Mau ("strongly held view") rebellion reflected Samoan dissatisfaction with foreign overrule. In 1962 Samoa became the first Pacific nation to regain independence.[2]

The fifteen Cook Islands are home to two indigenous Polynesian languages, Samoan and Maori. In 1888, ostensibly for fear of French colonial intentions, some island chiefs (prompted by Anglophile incentives) requested protection. Great Britain was too happy to oblige: thus began a British protectorate that grouped northern islands that are culturally closer to Samoa than they are to the southern Cooks. In 1901 the Cook Islands underwent transfer to or annexation by New Zealand, a status that was upgraded in 1965 to that of associated state. (A similar situation obtained in 1974 for the nearby mono-island entity of Niue.) These Polynesian islands accordingly are regarded as "sovereign," but New Zealand is still responsible for their defense, and extends automatic citizenship. Indeed, there are more Cook Islanders in New Zealand than in the Cook Islands themselves.

The geographical relationship between the Cook Islands and New Zealand invites a commentary on partition in Polynesia. Only 750 miles west of the Society Islands of French Polynesia, the Cooks are a considerable two thousand miles to the northeast of the New Zealand with which they are politically associated and to which they are economically tied. Culturally, of course, they are more Polynesian than New Zealander. Tokelau is even more closely tied to New Zealand than are the Cook Islands (New Zealand enjoys full sovereignty and extends citizenship to the islanders) but are even farther away—four times as distant than they are to the French islands of Wallis and Futuna.

Tuvalu, an archipelago of ten islands and atolls, is just as close to Wallis and Futuna as it is to the (Micronesian) Gilbert Islands, of which it was a part, as a British colony, until the mid-1970s. Polynesians speaking a language close to Samoan, these islanders of the erstwhile Ellice Islands became independent, as a constitutional monarchy, in 1978.

Melanesia

In terms of population, the South Pacific is mostly Melanesian: three-quarters of all Pacific Islanders hail from this more westerly region of Oceania. Ethnolinguistically, Melanesia is much more heterogeneous than Polynesia: it is here that one finds the

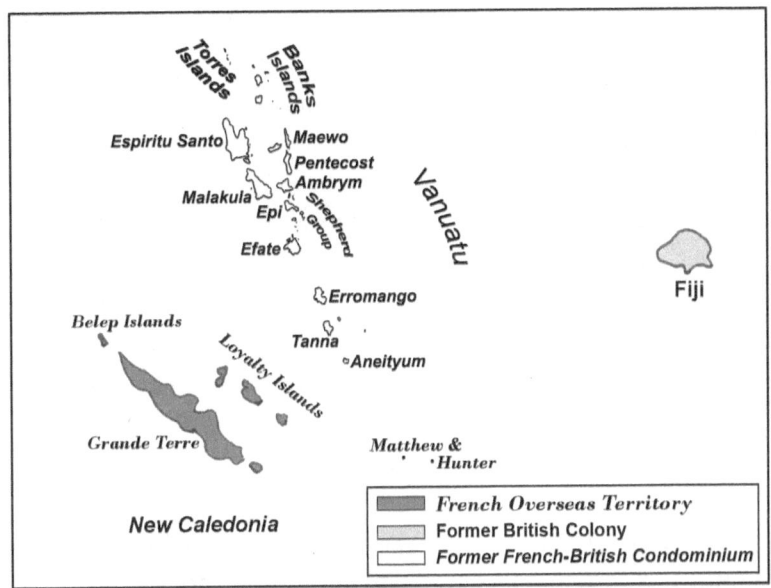

Map 12. Southern Melanesia

greatest number of indigenous languages per polity. (While it is relatively easy to draw geographic markers between Melanesia and Polynesia, culturally and ethnically there is overlap: Fiji and the Solomon Islands exhibit traits of both Pacific regions.)

From a colonial vantage, the history of Melanesia is akin to that of Polynesia: mid-nineteenth century forays by France to establish an early beachhead, with intensified French and British colonization toward the end of the same century.

New Caledonia is both a forerunner and outlier in Melanesian colonialism (see Map 12). France declared sovereignty over Grande Terre ("Big Island") in 1853. In the two succeeding decades, France extended its self-proclaimed New Caledonian writ (challenged by indigenous uprisings until 1917) over smaller islands in the vicinity of Grande Terre: the Loyalty Islands, Belep Islands, and the Isle of Pines. Paris eyed New Caledonia as the French answer to Australia—a settler colony encouraged by involuntary European servitude. During the last four decades of the nineteenth century, New Caledonia accordingly served as a penal colony. Although indigenous Melanesians (called Kanaks in New Caledonia) constitute a plurality of the population (over 40 percent), French settlers (Caldoches—many of them descendants of *deportés*) retain a significant demographic (34–37 percent) and political presence. Violent clashes in the 1980s (both Kanak-Caldoche and intra-Kanak) forced France to renegotiate New Caledonia's status (as an overseas territory) within the French Republic. That process, encapsulated within the 1998 Noumea Accords, has not ended, and New Caledonia remains under French sovereignty as an "overseas country" of France (*Pays d'outre-mer de la Polynésie Française*). Three referenda are scheduled between 2013 and 2018 to determine popular desire for full independence.

Fiji is also a (mainly) Melanesian nation that has experienced significant nonindigenous settlement. Here, though, the "settlers" (roughly the same proportion as Caldoches in New Caledonia) are not of European origin, but rather Indian. Descendants of British-encouraged immigration from the 1880s to 1920s, Indo-Fijians have advanced economically and politically from their former status as indentured plantation sugarcane cutters. Although in the late 1980s they lost their half-century-long demographic superiority over indigenous Fijians, they remain the object of political resentment and suspicion by certain Indo-Fijian elites. Those in the military have mounted at least three coups in the last three decades to ensure indigenous Fijian hegemony, even at the cost of constitutional democracy.

Such is one outcome of British colonialism in the South Pacific, a process that began over the roughly three hundred Fijian islands with the cession of power of the chief of Viti Island in 1874. Fiji achieved independence in 1970.

Nearly one thousand islands make up the Solomon Islands, declared a British protectorate in 1893 to forestall anticipated French annexation. The most violent invasions of the Solomons occurred during World War II, when they were occupied by the Japanese and then retaken by Allied forces beginning with the 1942 Battle of Guadalcanal. A nationalist movement hastening independence held sway from 1944 until 1952. Independent from Great Britain since 1978, Solomon Islanders use an English-based creole that facilitates communication within an archipelago that is home to seventy indigenous languages. Despite a British colonial legacy that is often thought to buttress democracy, late 1990s military coups in the Solomons and Fiji led at least one commentator to invoke the specter of "Africanisation of the South Pacific" (Reilly 2000).

If Melanesian colonization by the British in Fiji and the Solomons had a relatively light touch, in what became Papua New Guinea it was hands-off from an early stage. Australia was handed colonial responsibility of the eastern half of the island in 1906, an administrative task it bore fitfully until acceding to Papua New Guinea's independence in 1975. The island of New Guinea remains partitioned, its western half under Indonesian sovereignty (a legacy of the original tripartite British-German-Dutch partition).

As in Polynesia, colonial partition in Melanesia was mainly a matter of colonial powers appropriating entire archipelagoes to themselves. Where one archipelago ended and another began was not merely a geographical question, however. Islands were grouped together according to colonial convenience, not on the basis of cultural affinity. In terms of Anglo-French Pacific colonization, one Melanesian archipelago stands out. The New Hebrides is the one cluster of islands that for almost a century was jointly administered by France and Britain as a condominium. Due to its specific character as the embodiment of both French and British colonialism in the South Pacific, I shall focus on Vanuatu, as it came to be known after its independence in 1980, separately below.

Prior to political colonization, the Pacific islands had been fertile grounds for a half century of Christian proselytizing. Catholic missions (especially the Marist Order) and a multitude of Protestant churches (spearheaded by the London Missionary

Society) had already put their stamp on islands large and small; so had commercial agents, whalers, and labor recruiters. Culture contact between Pacific islanders and European adventurers did not begin with declarations of sovereignty. By the time Britain and France dubbed these islands "protectorates" and "colonies," their expatriates, religious and entrepreneurial, had already shown the stripes of their respective homelands.

Colonial Policies, Indigenous Responses

Sir Arthur Gordon was to the Pacific what Sir Lugard was to West Africa: the British colonial governor who put his administrative stamp on the region. Mindful of the expropriation of the Maoris by European settlers in New Zealand, he saw his task in Fiji (to which he was appointed in 1875) as creating a protected and enabling environment for the islanders, even as whites developed plantations. Foreshadowing Lugard's use of traditional authorities in West Africa, Gordon appointed indigenous Fijian chiefs as village, district, and regional officers. The method of taxation that he introduced was collective, creating incentives for villagers to pool their produce in a way that benefited their village and spared them from plantation wage labor. (Hence the resort to imported Indian sugarcane cutters.) Gordon's land system protected (and in some instances repossessed) vast tracts in the name of native inalienability. This "humanitarian tradition of colonial government"—replicated in New Guinea (even after formal transfer to Australia)—antagonized settlers who viewed it as inimical to prosperity and "completely wrongheaded about what was best for 'primitive' peoples" (Campbell 1989, 162). Less populated archipelago colonies under the British enjoyed less oversight and solicitousness. In the Solomon Islands, for example, social services were left to missionaries and economic policy to Lever Brothers.

Resistance to French colonialism in the Pacific was more violent both at the outset and in the long run: until 1847 Tahitians forcibly resisted occupation, and as late as 1988 Kanak nationalists in New Caledonia expressed their antagonism by taking hostages (resulting in the hostage takers' death by French government forces). In the interim, two distinctly different governance patterns emerged between Polynesian and Melanesian France. Whereas the latter became the locale of significant settlement and economic exploitation, the former was consigned to relative neglect: early "French administration was a ramshackle business of local feuds between resident tradesmen and of Paris' ineffectual foreign policy which lacked vision and guidance" (Fischer 2002, 135). Missionaries provided the will and commitment that the French government could not. Between 1882 and 1914, Paris had to dispatch no fewer than twenty-four governors to ensure the tricolor was saluted at the highest level. Having overthrown the Tahitian-based Pomare monarchy in 1843, France had assumed the burdens of micro-governance at macro-distance. Until the first half of the twentieth century, her Polynesian policy was a matter of "benign neglect" (Fischer 2002, 188).

New Caledonia, in contrast, loomed as land for settlement and ranching and mineral exploitation: copper, cobalt, and especially nickel. After an 1878 revolt led by Chief Atai of La Foa, Kanaks were dispatched to and divided among 150 reservations. The status of landownership had been an issue before, and has been ever since.

So has the question of Kanak identity vis-à-vis France. Conscription into the French army led to a revolt in 1917, crushed at the cost of a thousand Kanak lives. Within a decade, as a result of land alienation, physical disease, and cultural malaise, fewer than thirty thousand indigenous New Caledonians were still alive.

By the end of the First World War and the attendant uprooting of German colonial aspirations, colonization in the South Pacific was mainly an Anglophone-Francophone matter, the term "Anglophone" in this context also encompassing Australian and New Zealander accents and nuances. British interest in colonizing the Pacific was hardly as keen as it was in Africa and the Caribbean before that. "[S]eemingly forever dedicated to the principle of insular indifference," Britain reluctantly found itself with the "largest colonial encumbrance" in the region (Fischer 2002, 167). France, though initially more motivated, progressively "wilted into administrative ennui" in Melanesia as well as Polynesia. Schooling was relegated to voluntary Christian efforts, the notion of self-governance an inchoate British ideal. The Second World War was a rude wakeup call regarding the burdens that distant, colonial archipelagoes entailed. For Pacific islanders, it crystallized notions of political identity that were framed in colonial terms before taking on nationalistic ones.

World War II: National Consciousness and Cargo Cults

Early Japanese advances in the northern Pacific (Philippines, New Guinea, and Guam) turned the South Pacific into a major arena of World War II conflict. Unlike French West Africa and the French West Indies, whose initial war years were spent as Vichy outposts, French Polynesia and New Caledonia rallied to de Gaulle as early as September 1940 (forcing the governor of the latter into exile in Indochina). Both became important Allied staging grounds, Bora Bora and Noumea constituting half the United States' major supply bases in the Pacific. (The French colony of Wallis and Futuna joined Free France after Pearl Harbor, Wallis alone housing thousands of American troops between 1942 and 1944). In islands both French and Anglophone, World War II Americanized Pacific perceptions of the "white world" in revolutionary ways.

Anglophone islands in the South Pacific (not to mention Micronesia) experienced the most savage fighting: Guadalcanal in the Solomons, Buna and Gona in New Guinea. Compared with Melanesia, Polynesia escaped World War II relatively unscathed. But Polynesians as well as Melanesians, Francophone islanders as well as Anglophones, all took from the war the consciousness of a global struggle in which their region played a major part.

That struggle included notions of political freedom and self-determination. Allied bases brought more than hardware and cargo to such remote Polynesian archipelagoes as Tuvalu and the Cook Islands: they planted seeds of sovereignty and aspirations for development. Indigenous veterans returned to their islands with even more gusto for change.

The colossal scale of Allied, and particularly American, implantation throughout the Pacific touched even the most far-flung islanders, reviving and stoking cargo cults. Indigenous prophets or gods would arrive, went these neoreligious beliefs, bearing goods and heralding an era of unprecedented prosperity. So ecstatic, and also revolutionary, were these cargo cults that colonial administrators periodically strove to suppress the organized groups and leaders that sprung forth from them. But massive American airlifts of supplies for the war effort *were* fantastic spectacles to communities hitherto in thrall to subsistence life, and who was to say that Melanesian prophets had not magically taken the form of white soldiers?

New and reinvigorated cargo cults represented but one side of the indigenous reaction to the political seisms introduced by the Second World War. Cargo cultists themselves would not lead struggles for sovereignty. They did, however, reflect the depth of change that the war brought to the islands, archipelagoes, and future island nations.

Postwar Paths toward Decolonization

Under New Zealander tutelage, in 1962 Western Samoa became the first Pacific nation to achieve postcolonial independence. Not all wards of Auckland desired outright sovereignty. Inhabitants of the Cook Islands and Tokelau have preferred remaining citizens of New Zealand. But these are Anglophone anomalies. Britain and Australia have successfully pursued postwar paths of decolonization through independence, both for high-minded reasons of international justice and as pragmatic concessions to downsized national budgets. In the light of a world war whose Pacific theater experienced the costs of occupation, empire and colonization appeared anachronistic and expensive—at least to Anglo-Saxons from Europe and Down Under. Solicitous of the delicate balance between indigenous islanders and East Indian immigrants, Britain shepherded Fiji toward independence through painstaking constitutional arrangements; Australia amalgamated Papua and New Guinea with an aim toward better administration, economic commercialization, and eventual self-government. Here, the tensions were not based on ethnicity (as in Fiji) but education and acculturation: westernized Melanesians demanded development and independence right away; nonwesternized Melanesians reacted by forming new cargo cults. A 1987 military coup in Fiji and secessionist violence a few years later in Bougainville, Papua New Guinea, exposed lingering postcolonial grievances in these two most influential Anglophone indigenous ex-colonies of the Pacific. Despite British and Australian intercession and intervention, however, recolonization was never contemplated. Independence was forever, for English-speaking islands large and small. That was the ineluctable postwar path. But not for France.

Initially, with the establishment of the French Union in 1946 it did seem that France's major territories were similarly heading toward sovereignty. Both in New Caledonia and French Polynesia, citizenship was universally extended and representation to the French parliament was granted. Both were elevated from colony to "overseas territory," a mark of autonomy. Pushback soon came, however, both from discontented locals (Caldoches in New Caledonia) and from anti-independentist Gaullists (French administrators in Polynesia and Paris). With the advent of the Fifth Republic in 1958, local powers were scaled back and a reassertive France put a national stamp on her Pacific islands. Foremost was the development of Polynesia as a French nuclear testing basin. Second in importance was retention of the nickel mines of New Caledonia. Undergirding both objectives was prestige: France's postwar (and Cold War) image as a world player was bolstered by maintaining sovereignty over large swaths of the Pacific. Caledonian mineral wealth and nuclear power status were key elements to that greater aspiration.

International pressure (including the Rainbow Warrior scandal) has mothballed France's nuclear testing in Polynesia, and unrest in "Kanaky" (independentists' preferred name for New Caledonia) has yielded concessions on the principle of sovereignty. However, three generations after the end of World War II, and more than a century since colonization there began, most Pacific Islanders still fall into one of two jurisdictional camps: citizens of independent island nations formerly administered by Anglo-Saxons, and citizens of France. The major exception—where the quintessence of French vs. British colonialism converged—crystallizes the differences between the two colonial mindsets and their postcolonial legacies.

Colonial Convergence Point: Condocolonialism in the New Hebrides

In one sense, administration over the New Hebrides was an anomaly. It was the only instance in Anglo-French colonial history in which Britain and France jointly administered the same territory for a significant length of time (three-quarters of a century) as equal tutelary powers over an indigenous, stateless people. This unusual arrangement of joint rule was known as *condominium*; accordingly, I refer to the unique process of combined Anglo-French governance there as *condocolonialism*.

In another sense, however, the New Hebrides (or Vanuatu, as the Melanesian archipelago has been known since independence) was a microcosm (Miles 1998): a close-up, miniature imperial model highlighting the differences between French and British colonial rule in a protracted state of reluctant jurisprudential coexistence. In their respective dealings with the same "natives" and with each other, the agents of condocolonialism glaringly reflected the quintessence of their own as opposed to their partners' styles, methods, and mentalities.

Condocolonialism did not the illuminate the overall contrast between French and British imperialism only for the South Pacific. By the time of the critical and final phase of the condominium—the two decades before independence (1980) bequeathing the most potent of postcolonial legacies—many of the administering "residents" and district agents of the condominium had seen service in Africa (Bresnihan and Woodward 2002). Their perspectives, as well as those of the New Hebrideans themselves, reinforce the microcosmic nature of the condominium, not only with respect to French and British policy in the Pacific but also for the colonial, and postcolonial, world writ large.

Condocolonialism refers not only to the policies and (in)actions of the condominium and its two partnering national governments.[3] As throughout the South Pacific, religious missions had enormous influence, and for roughly the first half of the condocolonial period (at least up to the Second World War) provided most de facto government and services outside of the capital of Port Vila.[4] Although missionary installations and religious denominations were numerous (Anglicans, Church of Christ, Presbyterians, Marists, Seventh-day Adventists, etc.), in effect they mirrored, and reinforced, the dual nature of the condominium. Roman Catholic missions from France, spearheaded by missionaries of the Marist order, imparted French language and, indirectly, formed Francophiles. Protestant churches, founded by preachers from Australia, England, Ireland, and Scotland, evangelized in local languages, fostering local attachments, a vague appreciation for "English ways," and anti-Papist (i.e., anti-French and anti-Catholic) beliefs. Religious missions were not attached to or controlled by either of the governments constituting the condominium. In effect, however, they created two linguistically defined camps of New Hebrideans, whether or not they could actually speak English or French: so-called Anglophones (i.e., Protestants) and Francophones (i.e., Catholics).[5] By the eve of independence—a movement led, not coincidentally, by Protestant pastors—"Francophone" Catholics constituted about 15 percent of the population (as did "Anglophone" Anglicans). Over one-third of the population identified with "Anglophone" Presbyterianism. Condocolonialism therefore refers not only, or principally, to the competitive partnership of Great Britain and France in administering the New Hebrides/Vanuatu, but to the entire process by which the indigenous population of the roughly dozen inhabited islands were divided by intra-European jockeying, linguistic affiliation, and theological competition. The "boundaries" that divided New Hebrideans up to independence were not so much territorial as they were ideational.[6]

Greater partition superimposed by colonizing Anglophones and Francophones was thus not spatial but mental. In Vanuatu, postcolonial politics is about constructing a national identity where no single previous (condo)colonial one existed. Although the European division of the New Hebrides began at the same time as in West Africa and Southeast Asia, and for similar reasons, postcolonial legacies have this essential distinction from Hausaland and the Golden Triangle: here, although the colonized were divided into separate camps, they did not inherit separate countries.

Condocolonial Origins

As we have seen earlier, France viewed the New Hebrides as additional Pacific territory from which she could balance perceived late nineteenth-century Anglo-Saxon hegemony spreading from Australia. Britain was not keen to dissipate imperial responsibilities by extending her sovereignty to other far-flung small islands. But Australia, uncomfortable with the growing French presence in relatively nearby New Caledonia, pressured her reluctant mother country to act. Activist Protestant missionaries, from Oceanic and British Isles alike, also forced the hand of a hesitant colonial bureaucracy. The "martyrdom" of the early ones (beginning with the probable 1839 cannibalizing on Erromango of the Reverend John Williams of the London Missionary Society) provided moral capital, eventually strengthening the evangelical lobby.[7] Two other precondocolonial activities creating an Anglo-Hebridean relationship were commerce (notably the extraction of sandalwood) and blackbirding, the recruitment (sometimes forced) of islanders as laborers for Australian plantations. With respect to actual settlement, however, more European planters hailed from France than Britain or Australia. Land acquisition for the French was aggressively pursued in the 1880s by an Irishman-turned-Frenchman, John Higginson, under the auspices of the Compagnie (later, Société) Calédonienne des Nouvelles Hébrides. At around the same time, (French) Catholic missionaries succeeded in creating a local alternative to (Anglo) Protestant versions of Christianity. Anglo-French competition in the New Hebrides was thus over souls as well as land, labor, and power. With neither side willing to cede to the other, a stalemate over sovereignty arose. Yet neither government was prepared to challenge the other by force, even as both recognized the necessity to impose a system of law and order. Compromise took the form of condominium.

The Condominium

Precursor to the Protocol of 1914 setting up the condominium were the 1906 Convention and the 1887 Anglo-French Joint Naval Commission. All three agreements precluded territorial partition: jurisdiction was shared; no islands were officially ceded to either party. Informally, however, individual communities, and sometimes entire islands, were understood to be Anglophone or Francophone by dint of missionary and educational activity. (During most of the condominium, the two were inseparable: schooling was consigned almost entirely to the missions, at least until the 1960s.) Thus, for example, the largest island—Santo—was thought of as Francophone whereas Efaté (seat of the capital)—was considered Anglophone.

British subjects were subject to common law, French citizens to the Napoleonic Code. The New Hebrideans themselves were stateless, subject to a combination of customary law, joint Anglo-French adjudication, and as often as not, improvised happenstance. Since British and French district agents (each of the four island districts had its own pair) rarely toured together, islanders with complaints (land being a common cause of dispute) could "shop" for favorable judgment. If an islander did not like decision of the British district agent, he might go to the French district agent for a better outcome (and vice versa).

Residents and visitors from third countries had to opt for one of the national systems of justice. Inasmuch as French justice was perceived as more lenient toward westerners than British law, an Australian planter might declare himself an *optant* under the French. A joint court, whose president was supposed to be appointed by the king of Spain, was set up to adjudicate land and other disputes between westerners and Melanesians. For the four decades leading up to independence the post remained vacant, the Spanish judge deemed to be on "temporary leave." It is no wonder that the more popular descriptor of condominium became "pandemonium."

Land alienation in the New Hebrides before and especially during the condominium created conditions of quasi- and micropartition that would ignite politics in the two decades leading up to independence and beyond. Reclamation by traditional custom owners of land supposedly purchased by companies and settlers would come to split islanders into competing camps of claimants. Undoing the partition of plantation and grazing land from "dark bush" would become one of the thorniest legacies of condocolonialism. Rodman (1998) perceptively considers the complexities of "colonial space" within the New Hebrides/Vanuatu memory.

The 1920s were marked by import of laborers from Vietnam[8] and the expansion of French plantations, whose main export product was copra, dried coconut flesh. The decade also saw the first expression of organized antisettler sentiment when the would-be king, Ronovuro, tried to expel whites from his native island of Santo. In the 1930s a similar movement was led by Chief Samuel Kora on Tongoa. In the main, however, the condominium remained an insouciant backwater for Britain and France alike. Beyond official shows of formal authority (mostly through tours of the outer islands by British or French district agents), both powers were content to leave day-to-day service provision, such as it was, to the missionary establishments. Christianization (as well as high condocolonial mortality rates) led to the erosion of traditional Melanesian culture throughout much of the New Hebrides. Loose affinities developed, not surprisingly, between British officialdom and Protestant missions on the one hand, and French officialdom and Catholic missions on the other. With respect to governance, the two powers operated more parallel to, rather than in tandem with, each other. Each national administration was headed by resident commissioners, the personal chemistry between whom largely determined the success of the condominium at any particular time. In the 1940s, however, a new Western power appeared that upset the overall condocolonial inertia and stasis: America.

World War II

Although not a battleground itself, the future Vanuatu was a staging site for major campaigns on the Pacific Front. Virtually overnight, the island of Santo was transformed by GIs from a lonely outpost to a major U.S. military installation. Not only the tonnage, diversity, and ingenuity of hardware mesmerized islanders but also the easy bonhomie that Americans exhibited toward New Hebrideans; it was in startling and liberating contrast to the condocolonial coolness that emanated from colonial officials and missionaries alike. Affinity for Americans and thrall for their matériel combined to revivify cargo cults such as Ragrag Charley on Malekula and Bule John on Pentecost. The most politically significant, though, was John Frum of Tanna. Frum ("from America?") was a Melanesian messianic myth who emerged shortly before the war itself. Alternately described as an incarnation of a Tanna mountain god and a dusky American, he reputedly inveighed against missionary Christianity (although not against belief in Jesus) and condocolonial capitalism (as evidenced by his adepts' frenetic disposal of cash). The massive influx of real Americans and their prodigious prosperity could only confirm the Frumites' beliefs. Frum fervor, in turn, greatly alarmed condominium officials. John Frum leaders were imprisoned and exiled. Although their movement was repressed, it was never eliminated: more than a decade after independence, followers of John Frum still pined for a Frumerican liberation, rejecting that of independence.

World War II turned into a wake-up call, and not only for cargo cultists. By the 1950s Great Britain had accepted the ineluctability, if not the desirability, of decolonization in the South Pacific as elsewhere in the empire. This might have to be a gradual process, but the end result of self-governance was clear. It would first require economic and infrastructural development as well as tutorship for self-government. An advisory council for the condominium, and local councils in the islands, were set up and began initiating Melanesians into modern modes of government and administration. Both sides could agree to that. But Great Britain was married in the New Hebrides to a French wife who did not share the same vision of postwar life and was not prepared to give up the estate. Nor were their wards of one mind, either. Whereas Anglophones would easily embrace nationalism as an ideology and sovereignty as a goal (was freedom not a value that New Hebrideans helped the Allies preserve?), Francophone islanders feared what an Anglophone (and Protestant) independence might mean for them.

Rivalry, Resistance, and Independence

Three major trends arose in the 1960s. One was the coming of age of Anglophone intellectuals, schooled principally by missionaries elsewhere in Oceania. These were sensitized to the winds of political change throughout the Pacific, as well as somewhat more progressive theological ways of viewing their cultural antecedents and traditions.

A second trend was a resurgence of land clearing by settlers (essentially for cattle grazing) and the emergence of an organized opposition to it. This movement, Nagriamel, rapidly evolved from a land protection movement to a virtual counterculture espousing a return to *kastom* (traditional Melanesian ways of life). Under the leadership of Jimmy Stephens, of mixed European-Polynesia heritage, Nagriamel represented a much more serious challenge than John Frum to the powers of the condominium, missionaries, settlers, and Westernized local elites.

A third major trend of the 1960s was a major French push to establish schools throughout the islands. Education—that is, modern, free, and *French* education—was deemed a major bulwark against remedial, parochial, and independentist Anglophone schooling. In contrast to the mission and British-subsidized (but still fee-assessing) schools made of local materials and employing local teachers, France expended considerable sums to ship impressive prefab structures in which young Frenchmen (as an alternative to military service) taught young New Hebrideans as if they were French kids.

All three trends converged in the 1970s to create a dynamic, if not combustible, atmosphere. Anglophone-trained elites returned home and founded a cultural association that soon morphed into a political party (New Hebrides National Party, precursor to the Vanua'aku Pati). With tacit (and not so tacit) British encouragement, these Anglophone nationalists pushed for free elections as a run-up to out-and-out independence. As counterweight, France actively supported an amalgamation of Francophone parties, known as "les Modérés" (for they were more "moderate" in their demands for political change.) New Hebridean graduates of Francophone schools, as well as French citizen settlers, constituted the core of this camp. Nagriamel, for its part, came to view Anglophone independentists as a greater threat to their way of life (which by now came to include business deals with American entrepreneurs and speculators) than it did the French government or French settlers. French support for anti-independence elements increasingly rankled their less well endowed pro-independence British counterparts and, especially, Anglophone islanders. Inasmuch as loyalty poaching took the form of school sitings, rivalry and jealousy between local school administrators and teachers were particularly keen. But even such an ostensibly nonpartisan institution such as chieftaincy became politicized along Anglophone versus Francophone lines (Bolton 1998).

In addition to pleasing her local planters and keeping her Pacific presence intact, France had an additional reason for resisting independence: New Caledonia. More than losing a half share of a condominium, France feared losing an entire territory—one whose mining, cattle, and settler interests were much greater than in the cumbersome condominium. Subscribing to her own Pacific version of the domino theory, France imagined the "loss" of les Nouvelles Hébrides as precursor to that of New Caledonia. With French Melanesia gone, French Polynesia—including strategic nuclear testing sites—would similarly be in jeopardy.

In the end, these calculations could not indefinitely fend off local Anglophone agitation for independence, British reluctance to preserve the condominium, and backlash against heavy-handed French tactics (governmental and private citizens') to "moderate" demands for full sovereignty on the basis of universal suffrage. The latter included initial support for Nagriamel secessionism.[9] In the run-up to Vanuatu's independence in 1980 (under Father Walter Lini and the Vanua'aku Pati), French paratroopers joined British Royal Marines in putting down Nagriamel's takeover of Luganville, the nascent nation's second-largest town. France came to terms with Vanuatu independence—more easily than did ni-Vanuatu Francophones (Miles 1994a, 1994c).

Voices of the Partitioned

Given that the partition between Anglophones and Francophones in the New Hebrides was not a matter of geography but rather affinity (religious, political), *everyone* was a borderliner of sorts. Island origin did not necessarily define condocolonial identity. Members of the same family experienced this bifurcation. Some families actually opted for it, in the interest of hedging one's condocolonial bets.

The relative recency of Vanuatu independence allows for a higher quality of contemporary oral history in comparison with our other instances of Anglo-French colonialism and decolonization.[10] Two full decades separate the independence of Vanuatu from those of Nigeria and Niger. The other great decolonizing shift of that era (and same year)—the transformation of Rhodesia into Zimbabwe—did not have a French connection: neither have any of the subsequent independences.

Indigenous Views of the Condominium

Chief Keil Johnson of Lawliyuliyu, Tanna, reflects the indigenous Anglophone view of Vanuatu history.[11] Born in 1905, he recounts that his own grandfather was a warrior, fighting with arrows made out of bone, the *kasowaso* (a deadly hurling stone), and the *nal-nal* (bludgeon). "In those days, people killed their own children." (Twins, for example, were believed in some indigenous communities to be a spiritually malignant manifestation.)

"Then the Europeans came, some buying land in exchange for stick tobacco and muskets. Others brought the 'good news' of the missionaries, saying that eating people was no good. . . . The Presbyterian Church came and built a hospital and church. Then came a school—in English. Only Bible study was taught there. . . . Then Dr. Nickerson came to announce the 'Two Fellow Government' [*tufala gavman*, i.e., the condominium]. Mr. Wilkes was posted to White Sands. After him, Mr. Nichol—he made a road so he could travel in his horse and buggy."

In 1935 Johnson entered the British-run police force, in which he served until 1937. Soon the French came, too, to catch up with the British by building their own hospital and setting up their own police force. In 1938 Johnson joined the French police, providing a rare, insider's insight into both sides of the condominium.

According to the future chief, the French were more devious in their methods: "They would 'sweeten' [i.e., bribe] people, in an attempt to take over, to control, the land." Yet the French were also somewhat more severe than the British. "They had the guillotine," after all, whereas the British punished only with prisons. Perhaps more important, the British didn't work their employees as hard: Mondays through Saturdays, with half-days (after 11:00 AM) on Saturdays. But the French? Full work-weeks, including Saturdays, and only Sunday afternoons off. Johnson preferred working for the British police on account of the greater time off. Moreover, "British officers used Bislama. French ones didn't understand" it.

"With 'Two Fellow Government,'" Chief Johnson reflected, "one would say 'no,' the other would say 'yes.' Independence was necessary to clarify matters. Without it, education would remain of low quality. Now, the doors are open for other countries to provide us with assistance."

On the island of Malekula, David William (aka Apia) recollected how unceasingly competitive the two governments—supposedly "working together to solve a problem"—actually were: "The British government would agree and then the French would stand behind the back [of the British] and disagree, and start gossiping. . . . We once had a French government district officer named Q. who told me, 'If I got hold of Wilkens—the British district agent—I'd tear him [up].' So I told Mr. Wilkens what Q. had said, and he answered me, 'That's all right. Don't worry, just keep quiet. The only thing I want is for you all to be well educated so that you take over my position. Your country must become independent.'"

Apia sums up the condocolonial dichotomy: "The French thought they would rule [indefinitely] while British worked quietly with the people and taught them how they could become independent. . . . During the Condominium, their minds and work didn't go together. Independence is really a good thing." Still, he looks back with nostalgia to a time of limited patronage. For after independence, "government workers chose their own relatives to work in government. Not other well educated people."

An Anglophone[12] (i.e., Protestant) on Santo provided a chilling narrative of the early days of the colonial land grab: "Europeans beat the natives using hammers and bull testes. They shot them with muskets. They also tricked them into buying, on Saturdays, bottles of wine mixed with poison. Most of the natives, after getting drunk, slept forever. At Aore, the French poisoned all of the people until there were none left. They treated the people of Malo the same way." The goal of the French, this informant went on, was "to gain the whole of the New Hebrides." In contrast—and citing South Santo as a local example—"the British only had limited land area." Eventually, they ended up disputing between themselves.

"In the process, the French decided that they would build permanent classrooms, using bricks." (Anglophone schools were made out of less durable, local materials.) "This was also to gain land. The British government had no choice but to educate the natives. With a determined mind, the French government continued with development projects, like coconut plantations and more permanent buildings."

Chief Tuk, a prominent leader from Yakukak, Tanna (neither a French nor English speaker himself), had a diametrically opposite position: The Brit was a "rubbish" man. When he arrived, he didn't want to have anything to do with blacks. He kept them at a distance, even throwing away their utensils, their drinking cups. Tuk had a personal reminiscence regarding a certain Craig: "When I was a small boy, I once leaned on his patio. When Craig saw, he chased me away, cursing. He had his housegirl get a bucket of water and wash the spot against which I had leaned. . . . But the Frenchman—he came after the

Brits, but when he did, he ate, drank kava, and slept with the black man. He was his brother."

Ignace Liatlatmal[13] said: "Believe me, France and Great Britain crammed our heads with ideas. Myself, I speak French. Because I'm a Francophone, automatically, I wouldn't want to even see an Anglophone. There was this hate, this atmosphere. Sometimes, if we'd wind up at the same bar, we'd exchange blows [if I'd say] I am proud of Francophonie!"

Liatlatmal well distinguishes the two camps in terms of mentality and thought process, perhaps the most significant of post-condocolonial legacies. Unlike the Anglophones, "I embrace questions, I can tackle them. . . . These people, quite often, are like robots. They're just *'Yes, sir.'* No capacity for critical thinking."

Leader, Elite, and Expat Recollections of the Condominium

After losing his position as prime minister, Walter Lini could take the time to reflect on the condominium and its legacies.[14]

> Condominium to me was a system which the British and French established just to take Vanuatu and protect the nationals of the[ir] two countries. There was no plan for indigenous ni-Vanuatu, no conception of trying to do anything fruitful for the future of the New Hebrideans. . . . It left the ni-Vanuatu in the middle to make their own choices. In a way, I think that continues today. You can find that some people want to make French choices, other people, British choices. Some people like me want to make a ni-Vanuatu choice. . . . So the Condominium, even though bad, was good in that a ni-Vanuatu person, man and woman, was able to make their own free choice.

Jimmy Stephens, head of the Nagriamel movement and rebel leader, went to prison for over a decade for opposing the Lini-led independence of Vanuatu. (Stephens advocated a confederation rather than a "general government," fearing it would take land from the people.) Yet Stephens's views on the condominium, if more evocative, are not all that different from Lini's:[15] "Britain and France were like two wild dogs, with a bone in between—and we were the bone. They didn't work together but rather pulled each other in different directions." Alienation resulted, as the islander subjects were similarly pulled apart: "You have a black Frenchman, you have a black Englishman, but you don't have a black *kastom* man."

Frank King, an Australian-born travel agent who has taken Vanuatu citizenship, claims that not all the violent Anglo-French confrontations in the lead-up to independence were even reported.[16] One of them started out as a minor traffic accident between an old-time French resident of Port Vila and a local taxi driver. The taxi driver chased the Frenchman all around the capital but the French driver wouldn't give up, even after getting to his home. Along the way, a whole lot of other taxi drivers joined in the chase, out of solidarity with their fellow taxi man. In the end—and for no discernible reason—the Frenchman took refuge in the British police station. But since he was a French national, the police there claimed they had no power to protect him or restrain his pursuer. Although he protested he would be beaten to a pulp if he left the station, that's precisely what he was forced to do. He reported his ensuing beating to the police under French employ, who responded by stoning the windows of the British police station.

King also relates the meticulous practicing of the flag ceremony prior to the July 1980 independence ceremony, lest even a few seconds gap between the lowering and folding of the Union Jack and Tricolor be given a political misinterpretation. The ceremony went off without a hitch, the British and French flags being struck simultaneously. Then, according to condominium protocol, the national anthems were also played—simultaneously. The condominium went out as discordantly as it had been administered all along. Nevertheless, the British tried to take one last dig at the French by having their warship in Vila Bay take off at full speed leaving the French ship to take the awful wake that the

British captain knew would result. Waves hit the boardwalks and caused damage; King claims that the captain, despite his nationalistic intent, was reprimanded for his rashness.

Former president Ati Sokomanu bemoans the British tendency to "get rid of their colonies quickly." He accepts the view of the advisability of first being economically viable, of having adequate social services prior to independence. "Most people thought that as soon as the British and the French leave us, they will give us so much [aid] that we would be able to live without thinking what would happen in the next ten years. Well, it didn't happen. Because from 1980 [to] 1985, they started cutting, chopping down the aid to the country. It's too late."

Walter Lini distinguishes between the benefits of the condominium upon individuals as opposed to the collectivity: "In terms of nation, it is a good thing to have [both] the French and British influence." For individuals, however, "the rivalries are still there." During his eleven years as prime minister "we tried to unify the country. We would have been able to do it by Bislama. But in terms of mentality, of considering whether you are French- or English-educated in Vanuatu, it is still very strong. . . . We are [now] led by a Francophone party. We have a coalition government but deep down, spiritually and within my soul, I am not totally in unity with the Francophones. It is still deep, very deep."

Within a year of Lini's exit, Maxime Carlot became Vanuatu's first Francophone prime minister. Although admitting the Anglophone-Francophone cleavage still existed, he attributed it principally to the influence of foreigners. But within the country itself, he claimed to be "in the process of creating an atmosphere so that there is no difference between the Anglophone and the Francophone. Today, an Anglophone and a Francophone are equal citizens."

Still, Carlot admitted that "there is distrust among those who took a political position in favor of Anglophonie. They say, 'Careful, they [Francophones] have come for revenge!'" For Carlot, it is not a question of revenge but of balance: "Francophonie was lost for eleven years at the level of those who ran the government. There was reason to think that the proportion of Francophones was falling and that, little by little, the French language was disappearing. It's true."

It is a constitutional question for the Francophone prime minister to ensure "a fair share" for those who wish to study and work in French. "This government is there to give a chance for every family to choose, in complete freedom, one's language."

Like Lini, Carlot acknowledges the importance of Bislama as a lingua franca between colonial language communities and among islands. But as a Francophone, he is sensitive to the English vocabulary base of the language, and accordingly "should be careful that the Bislama that we develop is the real Bislama of the islands, and that we not introduce English words at every new occasion. On the radio, they just throw in an English word into a Bislama phrase and all Vanuatu talks that way. Real Bislama is not the Bislama that is currently spoken, this 'broken English.'"[17]

Carlot was not so far from Lini in acknowledging the dual legacy of the condominium: "It is necessary to continue this advantage that we have, of two languages, that after independence become the property of Vanuatu. . . . I am not here to defend Francophonie alone."

Outer Island Legacies

The view from the outer island Maewo is different from the capital Vila. For sheer practical reasons, there is no need for French. "There's no use for it here," stated Chief Mark Meliu.[18] "There's no Catholic mission," he declared, invoking the long-standing link between language and religion. "What can you do with French on Maewo? You can't even continue schooling in it—you've got to switch to an English [medium] school."

Far to the north, at the Anglophone Arep school on Vanua Lava (Banks Islands), French teacher Norbert Napong notes a similar parental disaffection from Francophonie. After independence fees were introduced in all schools (previously free at French ones), Francophones couldn't find work; promotion was more likely for English speakers. Internally, administrative protocol also favored Anglophones. The principal of the Anglophone secondary school had his own budget, ordering supplies directly, whereas the Francophone primary section had to apply to the (Anglophone) regional education officer, who may or may not honor the request.

Yet Norman Wilson, a nearby educator in the Banks, has no truck with retaining French. The language ought to be dropped for two reasons: (1) "the French were against the country's independence" while "the English" promoted it, and (2) since one party, the Union of Moderate Parties (UMP), wants to maintain it, the language is a source of political division.

Wilson's responses reflect common residual resentments of condocolonialism. From the Anglophone perspective, the French government spoiled Francophone New Hebrideans to the point of compromising their souls. Free tuition, free room and board, pocket money, even professional disciplinarians (*surveillants*) came at the cost of dignity, self-respect, and national pride. French-schooled islanders had it easy, too easy, and independence is an opportunity to bring them down several notches.

Francophones naturally view the situation differently: while accepting the reality of independence, they can't help viewing their education, past and present, as superior. ("The reason they've hurt the Francophones?" rhetorically rasps the headmaster of the Orap (Protestant) Francophone school. "Because they're jealous. Jealous of our superior education.")

Unifying the separate government services from the three that existed previously (British, French, condominial) has been a major administrative challenge. Merging Anglophone and Francophone schools has been most sensitive, particularly given the role of schools as agents of condocolonial socialization.

Pastor Nawayang of Lowniel recalls the peculiar punishment meted out at the French school: rice bags were filled with sand, which truant pupils were compelled to carry. But attendance at the French schools was free, compared to the Anglophone mission ones that required fees. Still, Pastor Nawayang eventually renounced the (mostly Anglophone) Vanua'aku Pati (VP) after it refused to make reparations to the family of Alexis, a UMP militant whom VP enemies killed. "UMP didn't shoot anyone, so I joined them."

Up until the 1960s and 1970s, education for Anglophones invariably ended with primary certificates from their home district schools. Those being groomed for preaching careers might go off to mission schools in Australia. Gifted Francophones, on the other hand, could continue their secular studies at the secondary level by being sent to New Caledonia—if family permitted it. (After independence, the separate English and French school systems were unified under a single national education ministry, which maintains parallel streams for total curricular instruction in either English or French).

"After my elementary school certificate," recounts Ignace Liatlatmal, "I was to go to Noumea. My father was very angry and came see Father Soucy," young Ignace's Catholic priest mentor. "'Father,' he said, 'You want to send my kid over there? Make one yourself, and send him instead!'" So Liatlatmal did not leave Vanuatu. Instead, he completed six years of correspondence courses with the Academy of Nantes. "After that, my father pushed me to get married." Which he did. Teacher training courses in Port Vila followed, and then a career in teaching itself. In 1968–69, at age twenty-three, he became the first ni-Vanuatu to teach the intermediate levels of elementary school. "I'm waiting for my father's death so that I can finally go to Noumea," he laughs.

Liatlatmal continued: "As head of the education department I would visit both Anglophone and Francophone schools. What weakness in the Anglophone ones! These people are not educated, they aren't motivated, they aren't sufficiently prepared really to teach a foreign language. They just wait for the end of the month [to be paid]. . . . If we had waited another ten years for independence, the English schools would not exist anymore because the teachers were all speaking Bislama. 'A blind man cannot lead another blind man.' We know that education is the development of physical, intellectual, and moral faculties. But Anglophones don't know how to go about it. I tell you frankly, Anglophone education is in the process of falling apart."

Chief John Peter, president of a local government council and who "schooled English," takes a contrary position: "I like the English system of education more than the French system. That was the main reason why I had to divorce my first wife, Vitaroki, who I bought. My second wife was born as a [Seventh-day Adventist] member. . . . From my point of view, the French education system is too weak. Those who were educated in it had a weak level of planning ahead. The French did not educate its students in reality. It deceived people by giving them money, but in the long run, it was not worth it. Education is better than money."

Liatlatmal has a different take entirely on the mental faculties cultivated by graduates of French schools in Vanuatu. They embody a critical (Cartesian?) spirit that the Bible-schooled Anglophones do not.[19] "If I want to swear, I will." In Liatlatmal's case, that mentality included taking a critical stance toward the French themselves, when appropriate.

Francophone Liatlatmal recalls a demonstration that he organized in 1974—when "politics began to appear"[20]—with the aim of forcing the condominial government to build an airstrip on his part of Malekula Island. "I went to see Monsieur Lecuillet, the French delegate, and told him, 'Listen, if really you are incapable of administering the district, then take your pen and resign, go away.' Oh, did he turn red! [Laughter.] They almost arrested me there and then. We went a little beyond our education, it would appear."

"I am proud of Francophonie. If I inquire deeply into questions, I can answer them, whereas I don't see this among the Anglophones. I don't want to underestimate them, but these people, sometimes, you can say they are robots. They are all 'Yes, Sir.'"

After independence, Anglophones ill accepted being supervised by Francophones. Liatlatmal recalls what it was like being a Francophone in charge of Anglophone civil servants: "They couldn't swallow it, that a Francophone be head of department. They did everything to take my place but their level of education was so low. Really, just to write an administrative letter, they would take two, three hours!"

Liatlatmal sees a microcosm between the two neighboring communities constituting the district of Walarano. "On the island of Rano, they are 'progressive'—making a lot of noise to say nothing. They talk about women but, with respect to work—zero. The people of Walla don't talk, but they work."

Titus Path, influential pastor at Hog Harbour, notes that on Santo, the previous split between Anglophones and Francophones remains "quite marked." Serge Vohor, UMP activist and future prime minister, observed that more than a decade since Walter Lini and the Vanua'aku Pati came to power, "the government had such an influence from the Anglophone side that it leads a policy towards the destruction of Francophonie." Vohor creates an interesting parallel between language group and race. "Personally, I am not a racist, but the fact is that certain universities in the Pacific, and educational institutions here in Vanuatu, have propagandized against the richness of the French language, the richness of Francophonie. There has been practically a system of brainwashing to say that Francophonie in Vanuatu has no future. Since independence, Francophonie has become a matter of private property. . . . We represent all ethnic groups and religions. With UMP, tomorrow there will be no more discrimination." Discrimination against Francophones is a common theme, as reported by Watt (1995) and Virelala (1995).

More than a decade after independence, at the Naboutariki school on West Ambae, the continuing tension between Anglophones and Francophones was palpable. Naboutariki is a typical outer island public school, where English and French medium students and faculty were merged. The French language teacher testified:

> The Anglophone principal would not introduce me to his number two, the head of the Francophone primary school. The [latter] told me in no uncertain terms that they were not on speaking terms—never had been.
>
> From the outset, the principal wouldn't look at me, wouldn't talk to me. When he wants to communicate to me, he does it by letter. . . .
>
> I received a memo from the ministry [of education] instructing me to remove my students from one of the classrooms. They wanted it for the Anglophone secondary school. That was too much.
>
> So I [informed] the inspector for education and told him to come and see the situation for himself. He really didn't want to get involved, but I insisted. . . . In the end, another memo was sent out retracting the first. But it was not an easy time.[21]

The teacher's concluding remarks reflect the heavy dilemma inherited by postcolonial professionals: "I didn't come here to get involved in such entanglements. I'm a [French] teacher. My job is to teach French. I'm not here to battle for the survival of Francophonie, but look at the position I'm put in."

Younger teachers who did not come of age under the condominium are somewhat befuddled by the superimposed language-based hostilities. Mistrust and mutual ignorance between Anglophone and Francophone educators is gradually eroding; the rivalry is residual, not primordial. It is now rare to hear Francophones refer to Anglophones with the epithet *poken* or *boken* (derived from "spoken"). But even younger Francophone schoolteachers feel that they are on the defensive as an embattled minority. For many, that serves as a prompt to approach their job with greater drive and a sense of mission.

A posted note by the principal at the Francophone school in Nasawa, on the island of Maewo, reflects the continuing demanding nature of instruction in French, a pedagogic policy without parallel in English medium schools: "Teachers will be strict. Students must speak *French* in class or during the diverse activities at school. Students who do not respect this obligation or rule will be punished." The (expatriate) headmaster at Rensare Junior Secondary School on Malekula expressed a Francophobic pedagogical view: "French 'education' is merely a protracted language drill. Real education is only second in importance [to them]."

Norbert Napong notes the advantages and disadvantages of unification of the Francophone and Anglophone systems of education. On the one hand, parents became less worried about choosing the wrong track for their children. With qualifying examinations demonstrating a higher success rate for Francophone-stream students, parents feel freer to choose the "minority" option. (They also note that Francophone schoolchildren study English with much more gusto than the converse.) On the other hand, Anglophone methods of pedagogy viewed as inferior, such as memorization and the "hole method" of evaluation (i.e., multiple choice), are perceived to dilute the rigor of Francophone approaches, such as calculation.

Linguistic "unification" is a noble principle, but one whose difficulty in practice the headmaster of the school on Epi embodies. A Francophone, he is responsible for Anglophone- as well as Francophone-stream students. But he cannot communicate with his own Anglophone students—not according to regulations, at any rate, for the students are officially forbidden from speaking "pidgin" on school grounds. Such is an unacknowledged (and ironic) consequent of school unification: rather than strengthening the two languages of instruction, it unwittingly promotes Bislama.

A Case of "Mixed" Marriage

Not all relationships between Anglophones and Francophones are so fraught with tension. Take the case of the Arutungais. At Saratamata, on the island of Ambae, Jeanne is married to Selwyn, a teacher and Anglophone. She, however, is from Mélé, a famous Francophone redoubt on Efaté Island. After finishing primary school, she pursued a vocational training track (studying cooking and sewing) at the Ecole Colardeau in Vila. Jeanne and Selwyn have one child, a daughter named Lavigna. Although haltingly (probably from lack of practice), Jeanne speaks very good French—much better than an Anglophone counterpart with a similar level of education.

Jeanne might have wanted to send Lavigna to a Francophone school, but Selwyn is against the idea: he wouldn't be able to tutor her. Jeanne herself does not teach Lavigna French, and does not really care that her children will be Anglophones.

It is impossible to know how many other "mixed" marriages like this dot the Vanuatu landscape. Familial linguistic détente nonetheless provides a hopeful basis for political reconciliation.

A Francophone's Progress—and Dilemma

As a child, Anatole Hymak was schooled at the Protestant mission on the island of Malekula.[22] Kanak missionaries asked his parents permission to take Anatole back with them to New Caledonia to continue his education. Permission granted, he remained in the French territory until the age of eighteen, returning in 1979, a year before independence. Uncertain of the future within an independent Vanuatu, he took his chances with a competitive examination to study in France. He succeeded, and spent seven years in study (Bayonne, Orléans, Bordeaux), earning a degree in tax law. He might have remained in France but preferred to return to his homeland, in order to "make things move," to offer "fresh thinking," to provide "new ideas." His country needed him, he thought, for whatever contributions he could make.

But Anatole was "welcomed" with suspicion, particularly by the Anglophone establishment. His young age, his overseas experience, his education—all this was held against him, and he could not land a position in the private sector. Eventually he secured the position of first deputy clerk of the Parliament. As a civil servant, he knows he is not supposed to actively engage in politics. Still, he believes the distinction between that prohibition and the constitutional clause protecting freedom of expression is loose enough to allow him to carry his attempts to "change things."

Francophonie in Vanuatu, according to Hymak, is "in agony, undergoing a slow death." Residual tension between Anglophones and Francophones makes life difficult.

> When I walk into a room of Anglophones, I feel a certain tension, a sense of skepticism. Not outright suspicion or hostility, but something [negative] nonetheless. . . . The fault lies with the older generation, which imbibed the divisions created by the French and British. It is disappearing slowly, but the holders of power still have it. . . . You must understand the terms "Anglophone" and "Francophone" in the largest sense. An "Anglophone" can mean no more than someone who had a grandparent who once spoke English. Or someone who was raised as a Presbyterian.

Custom

The relationship with *kastom* (custom)—that is, indigenous folkways and religion—is a major distinguishing factor between the (Protestant) Anglophones and (Catholic) Francophones. Vanuatu's experience was the converse of what we have found elsewhere, where British Indirect Rule entailed a persistence (if not a flourishing) of local customs in contrast to the more assimilationist French style. Here, however, colonialism was much more a matter of denominational theology than colonial policy. Longstanding attempts by Protestant denominations to expunge the devil were much more radical than Catholic missions' attempts to win souls.

The island of Tanna is reputed to be the fiercest protector of indigenous culture. There, Chief Samuel of Lawnapunga described the Presbyterians as "half-half" with respect to *kastom*, whereas Catholics were "full up" with it.[23] There were various customs including dancing, drumming, and singing that the Presbyterians and other transformational Protestant denominations attempted to eradicate.[24] One of the social activities most specific to Melanesia was the ritualistic drinking of kava, a seminarcotic derived from the root of a tuber. In a *nakamal* (men's club house), the traditional link between death, God, and kava—a linkage Anglophone Protestant missionaries attempted to tried to eliminate—was explained to me thus:

"When someone dies we are supposed to bury the body inside the nakamal. Later, when the body is all worn out, our elders would take the bones and place them on a long post inside the nakamal. Then they would take a flat stone and place the head against it. So if one of us stopped drinking kava inside the nakamal as it should be, the dead man's bones would be angry. According to our *kastom*, we had made those bones our god. And he would be angry because he too was thirsty when we stopped drinking kava. He too wanted to drink. But because we stopped, he would kill one of our children, a man or a woman."

Even more problematic, from the missionary perspective, was the practice of headhunting and cannibalism. Pastor John Peter recounts: "The Seventh-day Adventist Church was brought to our island in 1913 by a Pastor Parker. He originally asked if he could build a church in Vila. But Mr. King [the British district agent] answered that the Presbyterians and the Catholics had already established themselves there." King recommended that Parker try the island of Malekula, where the practice of headhunting was strong. "So at first he established an Adventist station at Tanmaru, on Atchin Island off the coast of Malekula."

Pastor Parker wished to see the chiefs of the inland areas. But arriving to see one of them, "his hands and legs were tied and they were ready to put him on the earthen oven as soon as they cut his neck and his head off.

"As he started to bake, Pastor Parker noticed that one of the bush natives had an ulcer on his knee cap. He requested that they let him treat the ulcer before killing him. At the sound of his words they stopped their activities to see the steps he would take to heal the ulcer. A man then asked the chief if the pastor's life could be spared." Parker was released, and returned to successfully missionize his would-be diners.

There are not many prime ministers in the world who take a position on cannibalism. Walter Lini, a staunch proponent of custom, however, did so: "Cannibalism was done not just for killing and eating, but religiously. People killed and ate the enemy not just for the meat, but to show that they have completely overpowered him."

One feature of Melanesian culture that receives insufficient attention is the tendency for corrosive jealousy to separate neighboring communities. The basis of jealousy can be material or intangible. The headmaster of a Catholic mission school on Ambae, for instance, declares that Anglophone teachers are jealous of Francophone ones for two reasons: (1) the education of Francophones is superior and (2) prior to independence, Francophones didn't have to pay school fees.[25]

Anglophone nationalists, particularly politically progressive pastors such as Walter Lini, reconciled custom with Christianity. For them, modern Protestantism not only joined the yearning for spiritual freedom with national liberation, but it also blessed *kastom* as a divine expression of cultural diversity. Some older customs—head hunting, cannibalism, infanticide—remain anathema, but not those cultural activities (e.g., traditional song and dress, kava drinking) that Protestant missionaries had misguidedly suppressed.

Shortly after his release from prison, Jimmy Stephens, custom leader, was already expressing his concern for the future that modernization would bring: "Something from the outside world will come in and spoil not only Vanuatu but the whole Pacific." The white man, he conceded, was clever: "He can go around the world in five minutes, to the moon in two or three hours." But the Western world's effects on culture and tradition are deleterious. "School spoiled custom" (i.e., Western education has damaged the traditional ways). Even if the modern educated have political strength, "custom man is strong with spirit."

Stephens may have underestimated the possibility of syncretizing politics, custom, and education. A front-page photograph from Vanuatu's newspaper shows the French-educated Maxime Carlot on an official visit to some outer islands.[26] Bare-chested, with a loincloth over his dark slacks, the picture captures the prime minister plunging an axe into the skull of a roped up pig. (In symbolic terms, this is the equivalent of an American politician kissing a baby while on the stump.)

Bislama and Other Linguistic Hangovers

Reinventing *kastom*, however useful from a political point of view, is problematic from a cultural one: in an archipelago that encompassed a multitude of pre-Western religious traditions—many of which had been extinguished by aggressive Christian missionizing—which varieties of *kastom* would be revitalized and which ones would be consigned to oblivion?[27] What about kava, still reviled by some indigenous churches yet used in official government ceremonies as a hallmark of *kastom* and reconciliation?

In terms of bridging the Francophone-Anglophone divide, it would seem that more straightforward would be the adoption of Bislama as Vanuatu's national language. But not even its designation (along with English and French) of this lingua franca as an official language is innocent of condocolonial legacies.

The term Bislama is thought to derive from the French term for the sea delicacy *bêche-la-mer* whose English translation is distinctly nondelicious: sea slug. An early commodity in the Melanesian maritime trade incentive of the nineteenth century, it stimulated rudimentary commercial communication between European seafarers and native islanders. Bislama is actually a pidgin variety of English whose variant in Papua New Guinea is called Tok Pisin (literally, "talk pidgin").

In a country with more indigenous languages per capita than any other in the world, upon which standard English and French were imposed upon the small condocolonized elite, Bislama has been an indispensable unifier. Should circumstances ever bring together islanders from the Banks and Torres to the far north with those from Aneityum, the most southern, they could communicate in Bislama. String bands, a popular form of music, also perform in Bislama, sometimes to reinforce in their lyrics message of national unity and harmony. But not even Bislama is completely without its own condocolonial baggage.

As a "mere" pidgin—and one derived from English no less—Bislama has not been accorded the same social status by Francophone elites that Anglophones have. During the condominium, British district agents commonly learned Bislama whereas French ones did not. This is not entirely due to the greater familiarity of Bislama for a native English speaker. In Africa, British administrators were encouraged to learn local languages in contrast to their strictly French-speaking counterparts. French-speaking New Hebrideans learned to speak Bislama as well as Anglophone ones, but many of them did inherit the prejudice held by the French against the "broken" language. Educated ni-Vanuatu Francophones decry the slippage between English and Bislama that they detect among their Anglophone counterparts and especially their students. Francophones recognize Bislama as indispensable; they do not, however, easily accept its gradual predominance as a language of prestige over "correct" European ones. It is, according to some, no better than *un charabia anglais* ("an English gobbledygook") or *l'anglais batârd* ("bastard English").

The triangular relationship among English, French, and Bislama is not the same for Francophones as it is for Anglophones. All speak Bislama; that is a given. European-language bilingualism, however, is much more the preserve of Francophones than Anglophones. Ni-Vanuatu schooled in the French track are often obliged, out of professional necessity, to speak English. It is rare, however, for islanders originally schooled in English to also learn French.

Despite the presumed constitutional mandate for doing so, maintaining equality between French and English is begrudged by influential Anglophones—not only by ni-Vanuatu Anglophones but by expatriate advisors and scholars (Early 1999). It is true that translating all laws and parliamentary deliberations (most of which occur in Bislama) into both English *and* French for publication does constitute a significant financial obligation upon the resource-strapped state. Condocolonial legacies of partition are budgetary as well as political.

Given its ratio between population and vernaculars (approximately 130), Vanuatu has the greatest number of languages per capita of any country in the world. Few ni-Vanuatu are literate in any of these indigenous languages, many of which face extinction. Bislama is the major culprit: urban drift results in the loss of island languages in Vila and Luganville, and governmental services (except education) are delivered almost exclusively in Bislama. Had condocolonialism not bequeathed forces vying for the maintenance of French vis-à-vis English, greater political and economic capital might be expended on behalf of the vernacular tongues. Vanuatu's cultural treasure of indigenous languages is an indirect casualty of the legacies of British-French partition in the New Hebrides.

Assimilation or Sophistication? Mental Boundaries

More than a decade after independence, Ignace Liatlatmal reflects on the postcolonial meaning, for a ni-Vanuatu, of having been exposed to French education: "Thanks to Francophonie I know my way around somewhat. For example, at a restaurant, I know I must first order an *hors d'oeuvre*. Then the *plat de résistance* [main course] and then the dessert. After that will come the *café*. That's what I learned at school; it is this mentality that is bound up with the French language. . . . A Frenchwoman is seated at the table and drinks wine. Anglophones don't drink wine, you see? Tea perhaps, I don't know."[28]

Yet for all his Francophone *savoir faire*, Liatlatmal is no *assimilé*. He is emphatic that he is "Melanesian first and Francophone afterwards." His differences with Anglophones come out in town. But in the village, he is as Melanesian as any other. Just as important, he opposed the French as much as he did the British government dominating Vanuatu.

His party, the Tan Union, was created for the purpose of "preparing" independence but to "not go precipitously into independence." Similarly, the other Francophone party, UMP, also asked for "five years of internal autonomy" to prepare independence" (Vohor). To this (Francophone) notion that independence must be prepared, one Anglophone pastor-politician rhetorically asked: "When you get married, do you know you are ready?" In other words, when the time is right, one (individual or country) plunges into the next phase of life. For the Anglophone, independence is like marriage: an unfolding process to which one accommodates, adequate preparation for which is impossible.

Serge Vohor, longtime militant for the Francophone party, notes: "What we need in Vanuatu is to accept what we are—a Melanesian people pure and simple." Vohor reverses the usual identification between Francophonie and assimilation: "The Anglophone Melanesian in power represents solely the image of the Australian." According to Vohor, since independence Vanuatu has experienced the same Anglophone neocolonialism (through cash and advisors) as the Solomons: "Australians are pursuing a policy of occupation in Melanesian territories. Here in Vanuatu, the policy of Australia is to expel the French and to replace them with Australians. This is not an independence. And it's exactly what will happen to the Caledonians, if they aren't careful. . . . Nowadays, despite all the good that France has done, she gets spit upon."

Unlike in New Caledonia, no faction in the New Hebrides advocated indefinite juridical belonging to France. Even for Francophones, independence was inevitable. While politics pit

Anglophones against Francophones, member of both camps recognized that they were Melanesians. Assimilation in Vanuatu was never tantamount, as it was in Martinique, to rejection of sense of place in favor of (condo)colonial identity. Educated Francophones in Vanuatu nevertheless demand recognition for the difference, for the specificity, that their distinct brand of Westernization has entailed.

Religion

At the eleventh anniversary of independence, on the island of Malakula, a number of local dignities delivered speeches. Warm-up talks were given before the (juice) cocktail honor. After the address by the representative of the chiefs, one from the local government began, welcoming the assembled (including the secretary and vice president of the council, the heads of department, pastors and police chiefs) "in the name of God in heaven, the Son, and the Holy Ghost."

The overt invocation of religion in Vanuatu politics at the grassroots is not surprising, given the conviction expressed at even the highest levels for adjoining the two. Here is how the first prime minister and founding father of Vanuatu, Walter Lini, put it: "I for one do not believe that it is right to separate politics and religion. . . . A person is a religious being and also a political being. Because of the background we come from, we cannot separate the two. In our [traditional] society any leader is both a religious and political leader."

Lini applies these theo-politics to himself: "I believe firmly that as a priest and also as a political leader in Vanuatu, I have a duty to continue to be a religious leader and do my duties as [one]. As a politician, a political leader, I also have a duty to make sure that I represent what I believe to be Christian, and to be justified politically for the people of Vanuatu, even if they are of a different religion. As long as human rights are respected."

On the island of Santo, the Second National Arts Festival—a platform to highlight the traditional customs of the different islands—took pains to legitimize custom in Christian terms.[29] Opening remarks (in Bislama) were akin to a prayer service: a sermon with a reading from Genesis, the thrust of which linked *kastom* to creation: "God, in creating the world, gave it many different kinds of animal, flora, fauna, colors. Identity for each distinct people, too, comes from God. God allowed for a multiplicity of human customs and traditions. They are part of life itself. Art is God-given."

In addition to the Old Testament reading from Genesis, there was a New Testament lesson from Corinthians. Here, the message was a warning. Some things are for God alone to judge; individuals should not condemn the practices of other groups.

> Who is to judge which is a Christian life, compared with a traditional one? Tradition and customs are ways of praising God, by practicing people's God-given talents:
>
> Glory, Glory, Glory to God ... Art, culture, custom, tradition all go together, all glorify the Lord!

Head of the National Chief of Councils, Chief Willy Bongmatur, reinforced this message, from a traditionalist perspective. "God has made all peoples, all beliefs. It is not true, as some have been claiming, that some customs are satanic. . . . Long Live Custom of Vanuatu. Long Live God's Blessing."

President Fred Timakata opined in Bislama that "culture is the root of values. It gives us respect, it gives us honor. Different kinds of dances, of cooking, of songs, of drum-beating give us the opportunity to respect them all. But one custom is all-unifying. It is a *secret message* [spoken in English]. This is pig-killing. By this, we leave all divisions behind."

The minister of education, after comparing Vanuatu to a banyan tree (its roots are in custom; young people need to rejuvenate the old roots and plant new ones), injected an international dimension to the festivities: "Neocolonialism is a process that harms culture. It prevents the old roots from giving strength to the tree. We need to fight against this neocolonialism, by which large countries, big societies, replace or deaden our own customs. . . . Vanuatu is a country combining *kastom* and Christianity. We have rights. We have power."

At the closing ceremony, Prime Minister Lini reinforced these themes by giving more concrete examples: "Culture and custom is God-given. It is the path to unity and peace. . . . People mustn't think that the culture of Vanuatu is the culture of the Chinaman, of the Indian, of the Frenchman, of the Englishman, of the African, . . . In school, children need to learn not only English, French, math, etcetera, but *kastom* as well. *Kastom* is the root of life," concluded the pastor–prime minister.

According to Titus Path of Hog Harbour, "the older generation of pastors are in government now—prime minister, minister of home affairs, minister of finance, minister of agriculture. We still have to liberate the economic side." After political independence comes economic independence. "The standard of living of Vanuatu is very low. People are struggling."

Protestant denominations, having succeeded in helping achieve independence, did not then withdraw from the political sphere. Few countries operating by democratic procedure experience as much direct comment in the day-to-day partisans operations of their government. Take, for example, this statement from the executive assembly of the Presbyterian Church of Vanuatu, addressed to the Prime Minister Lini in May of 1981, observing "with deepest regret and concern the mass dismissal of government ministers, political secretaries and public servants and the absence of ombudsman." The theological justification was that "We as the Church are concerned about life and good of the people you dismissed without warning. . . . The increase in nepotism in your government is alarming and the Church considers this undemocratic and unchristian. . . . The Church is concerned that you have not made the post of ombudsman attractive enough to interest capable ni-Vanuatu to apply for the position."[30]

For sure, liberation theology throughout much of Asia (including the South Pacific) and Latin America has galvanized churches, including Roman Catholic ones, to enter the political fray when governmental injustice crosses theo-political lines. A change in regime (colonial, as in the case of South Africa, or indigenous, as in the Philippines) usually is a signal to churches to "privatize" their activities (i.e., to return to pastoral priorities rather than public ones [Haynes 1994]). The strong role played by the Protestant (and Anglophone) Church in pre-independence Vanuatu, in contrast, has bequeathed a continuing involvement in the micropolitics of that nation.[31]

New Caledonia and Ni-Vanuatu Francophonie

Administratively, New Caledonia and the New Hebrides were never linked. Culturally and psychologically, however, the presence of other French-speaking Melanesians was mutually reinforcing in condocolonial times. After Vanuatu's independence, the New Caledonian question has become all the more significant.

Unprompted, Chief Johnson (Anglophone) in an interview brings up the contrast with the neighboring French territory. On account of the French, he says, "the people in Caledonia are blind. If there had been a condominium in Caledonia, it would be free by now."

Liatlatmal (Francophone) is not so sure: "Religious people say, 'The Good God made us to be free. If we are not free'—meaning independent—'something is not right.' I'm okay with that but they need to be careful. They [the people of New Caledonia] should come see us often and ask us so that they not wind up on the same path as us. Before independence, everything worked fine. But once we got it, things went backward. They'll suffer more than us. You know, the Caledonians, the Kanaks, the Melanesians from there are really lazy."

Serge Vohor—who became minister of foreign affairs—put the New Caledonia question into a wider, regional one: "France has her place in the Pacific. Like the English, like the Americans, everyone has their place in the South Pacific region. . . . The future of New Caledonia belongs first of all to the Melanesian people and to the French people of Caledonia and to France to decide.... It is not for us to decide for the Melanesian Caledonians." Vohor also sees a pan-Pacific Francophonie at stake: "Caledonia must understand that if Francophonie disappears from Vanuatu, then it will be the sole Melanesian country of the region among all the Anglophone Melanesian [ones]."

Questions of New Caledonia's future are a matter not only of sovereignty but identity: that of the "Francophone Melanesian." Vohor believes that ni-Vanuatu Francophones (regardless of their stance on Kanaky's independence) are closer to the Melanesians of New Caledonia than are the pro-independence ni-Vanuatu Anglophones. "We must advise our Caledonian Melanesian brothers not to make the same mistake as us—'Independence, yes, but after? Take the reins of power, but after?'" Maxime Carlot sees the Francophone issue in larger, regional terms: "By the presence of Vanuatu, the French language becomes also the property of the South Pacific."

Undoing the Partition of the Pacific

Long after Great Britain and France had relegated much of their status as major players on the world stage, the condominium still locked New Hebrideans into an anachronistic dual international relationship with the British and French. Joining a variety of regional organizations has helped Vanuatu move away from the Anglo-French bifurcation that the condominium had long perpetrated.[32]

Vanuatu is thus an integral member of the twenty-seven-state Secretariat of the Pacific Community (formerly known as the South Pacific Commission), the sixteen-state South Pacific Forum, and the Melanesian Spearhead Group. This is one way in which it subscribes to the "Pacific Way," the postcolonial project of creating a broader, regionally focused basis of identity in Oceania. No longer dependent on largesse (competitively driven) from London and Paris, it is the beneficiary of aid from the Economic and Social Commission for Asia and the Pacific and from the Asian Development Bank. Reflective of its condocolonial heritage, Vanuatu has the rare distinction of belonging to both the Commonwealth and the Organisation Internationale de la Francophonie. It now must also entertain relations with Japan and China, much more dynamic participants in South Pacific commerce. The condocolonial skill of playing the British and French against each other[33] has been well adapted to the era of international development: some government officials seem to view offers of foreign aid as opportunities to pit new donors (e.g., Australian, New Zealander) against traditional (e.g., French) or other new ones.

Diversifying external relations and, especially, actively joining in the Pacific Way, are methods of undoing the partition of the Vanuatu people—a partition, it cannot be emphasized enough, that was ideational rather than geographical. The extent to which Pacific identity can include a French Pacific component remains to be seen, however. Until that question is resolved, the adherence of Francophone ni-Vanuatu to the Pacific Way will be problematic.

Before fully partaking in a regional Pacific project, Vanuatu must first succeed in nation building. Divisions inherited from condocolonial rule were not only Anglophone-Francophone in nature, nor Protestant vs. Catholic. Creating a single sense of nationhood from far-flung islands, many of which are themselves divided into different indigenous linguistic groups, is no small matter. Neither is the challenge of development, an aspiration that the British and French only belatedly took up as a condominial responsibility, and even then more in competition than in concert with each other ("rivalry-in-partnership.")

Due in part to its small population, from a statistical vantage Vanuatu is a middling Pacific developing nation (see Table 4). On a per capita basis, it is a relatively high regional recipient of development aid. It may be worth noting that all five former Pacific colonies for which the United Nations Human Development Report provides figures are in the "medium" human

Table 4. Material Outcomes—South Pacific

	GDP per capita (dollars, 2008)	Life expectancy (years, 2005–10)	Adult literacy (%)
Former British/ANZUS colonies			
Cook Islands[a] (20)	15,813	74.5	95.0
Fiji (844)	4,264	69.1	—
Kiribati (97)	804	64.0	—
Niue[a] (1)	5,800 (2003 est).	71.5	—
Papua New Guinea (6,577)	1,218	61.0	57.8
Samoa (179)	2,988	71.7	98.7
Solomons (511)	1,284	66.1	76.6
Tokelau[a] (1)	1,000	—	—
Tuvalu (10)	3,213	63.4	—
Former French colonies			
French Polynesia[a] (266)	17,781	74.5	98.0 (1977)
New Caledonia[a] (246)	37,678	76.3	96.2 (1996)
Wallis and Futuna[a] (15)	3,800 (2004 est.)	78.8	50 (1969 est.)
Former Anglo-French condominium			
Vanuatu (234)	2,388	70.2	78.1

Note: Number in parentheses next to country refers to population, in thousands.

[a]Nonindependent

Sources: UN Data, Country Profiles (http://data.un.org); UNDP Human Development Index 2009; (http://hdrstats.undp.org/en/indicators/89.html); CIA *World Factbook* (http://www.cia.gov); Institut National des Statistiques Economiques (http://www.insee.fr/fr/insee_regions); IRS Euro to Dollar (http://www.irs.gov).

development category, and that the one Pacific state that is in the "high" category—Tonga—was never colonized.

Projects of national development and Pacific regionalization must nevertheless contend with geocultural realities best depicted by anthropologists. Joël Bonnemaison (1984, 1986, 1994), for example, employs a tree-canoe analogy from Vanuatu's Tanna Island to get at the root of Melanesian identity. The "tree" is the individual, rooted vertically in the ground; the "canoe" is the group, crisscrossing oceanic currents to connect with others. To extend Bonnemaison's image, we may say that before the islanders of Vanuatu are to connect with the rest of the Pacific community in transnational identity, they will first have to establish meaningful relations with each other: between communities on opposite coasts of roadless islands; between peoples of different Vanuatu islands; between coastal peoples and highlanders of the same islands; and, decades after independence, between Anglophones and Francophones.

Despite threat of coup in 1988, 1995, 1996, and 2001 (Morgan 1999, 2003), Vanuatu has managed to preserve a continuously democratic (albeit oft chaotic) parliamentary system of government for over a quarter century of independence. Cleavage of the Vanua'aku Pati in 1991 may have unintentionally fostered, in the long run, postcondocolonial political reconciliation.[34] Rather than the binary Anglophone-Francophone partisan rivalry between VP and UMP that characterized the immediate postindependence period, since the 1990s and beyond politics in Vanuatu has consisted mostly of a fluid, tripartite (VP–UMP–National Unity Party) jockeying –resulting in shifting coalitional configurations.[35] Undoing the effects of colonial partition remains a national as well as regional project, even in the face of emerging postcolonial spatial, temporal, economic, legal, sexual, and racial boundaries (Miles 1998, ch. 5).

Condocolonialism and Christianity: Implications for Postcolonial Legacies

The unique nature of Anglo-French partition in Vanuatu—not geographic but rather linguistic and religious—gave rise to a peculiar type of postcolonial identity.[36] Colonial rule throughout most of the world superimposed a new sense of identity based on colonial boundary. Laying the foundation for postcolonial nation building according to their grids and borders was not the original intention of colonizers, but that is indeed what happened. After independence there was no confusion about who belonged to Laos and who to Burma, who to Niger and who to Nigeria.

In Vanuatu, however, condocolonialism created competing identities based on language and religion. The very notion of a single colony meriting independence split the population along Anglophone-Francophone lines. Many Francophones, based on their education and understanding, believed that Vanuatu was not "ready" for independence. Other Francophones joined with the Nagriamel custom movement to promote an outright secession from the new nation dominated by Anglophones. Anglophones believed that development would follow independence. Francophones believe that economic development need precede political independence in order for the state to be viable. Although Francophones eventually came around to the inevitability, if not desirability, of independence, reconciling the mindsets cloven by condocolonialism has been a major postcolonial challenge in this South Pacific setting.

As in the West Indies, Francophones in the New Hebrides perceived a choice between political independence and economic development and preferred the latter. In the Caribbean, because partition had been effected on an island-by-island basis, French West Indians could choose to remain with France indefinitely. In the New Hebrides, because partition had made Francophones a minority group among Anglophones, independence was imposed upon them, both by the British and local Anglophone politicians. That in both cases they were allergic to independence is significant, speaking to the power of French colonialism in fostering long-term identification, if not loyalty.

Overall, however, condocolonialism entailed more of a hands-off approach to European control and transformation than either French Direct or British Indirect Rule. Compared to both types of rule elsewhere in the South Pacific (e.g., New Caledonia, Fiji), outer island Vanuatu experienced relatively little transformation during the three-quarters of a century of condominium. Even among Francophones, outside Vila and Santo and immediate environs France was a remote presence, the French a foreign people. Francophonie had little to do with loyalty, or affective attachment, to France. Francophones still struggle against the Anglophone prejudice that they are not completely loyal to the Vanuatu state.[37] It is, rather, their status as a minority that they fight to protect. More practical, pragmatic reasons than Francophilia prevailed for opposing Anglophone hegemony. At the village level, there is a lack of affect—a diffidence even—in discussing British-French colonial differences, even national character differences. The contrast with the elites—and even with ordinary partitioned Africans—could not be greater. When compared with our other case of duality in inherited European languages—Mauritians—the lingering tensions between ni-Vanuatu Anglophones and Francophones are striking, indeed.

Partition in the Pacific remains a potent postcolonial legacy not only for ni-Vanuatu but for Melanesians, Polynesians, and their myriad subgroups. Whatever new relationship New Caledonia establishes with France, the Kanaks there will retain an identity quite distinct not only from the Caldoches with whom they share the "Big Island" but from their ni-Vanuatu Melanesian cousins a canoe's ride away in the Coral Sea. Christianity, too, remains another overarching colonial legacy throughout the Pacific—not only in fostering unity among the faithful but also in perpetuating distinctions according to denominations. Remember how being "Francophone" in Vanuatu means attending mass, not reciting Molière. Whereas Islam constricts it in West Africa, and secularism has made significant inroads into it in the Caribbean (especially in the French DOMs), Christianity is perhaps the most culturally transformative hallmark of colonialism in the South Pacific. On outer islands, customary religious beliefs and practices do persist (as do syncretist phenomena such as cargo cults), but the relative hegemony of the Christian religion sets the South Pacific apart from other areas of the postcolonial world where Francophone and Anglophone missionaries conducted their own quasi-colonial conquest.

If not a microcosm of the postcolonial world writ large, then, Vanuatu serves as the embodiment of British and French colonialism in the South Pacific. Both major types of colonialism cohabited, in keen rivalry, until fairly recent times. Neither power made development for the colonized a primary objective of its actions, at least until it was too late to achieve. Maybe they were not quite, as Jimmy Stephens vividly put it, "two wild dogs" tugging at the same colonized bone, but they certainly viewed their subjects through two very different pairs of colonial-era spectacles. Navigating rough seas created challenges enough for intrepid islanders daring to overcome regional barriers; overcoming colonial partitions of the ocean remains a postcolonial project for the South Pacific.

5
Soft, Sequential, and Hybridic Colonialism:
French India and the Indian Ocean

> In India... the learning of French language will continue.... Pondicherry... will continue [to be] a window of French culture.
> —Jawahralal Nehru, Speech at Pondicherry Town Hall (1955)

> Mauritius was made first and then heaven, and... heaven was copied after Mauritius.
> —Mark Twain, *Following the Equator* (1896)

> To the travel writers... the island is "a lost paradise."... To the Mauritian who cannot leave, it is a prison.
> –V. S. Naipaul, "The Overcrowded Barracoon" (1972)

The Indian Ocean—an overly ignored area, given that it comprises 14 percent of the planet's surface—is home to eight polities that clearly display the legacies of British and/or French colonialism, old and new. Like the South Pacific, it is a region of archipelagoes, the clustering of which reflects the arbitrary nature of colonial maritime partition. In terms of the interplay between colonialism and ethnicity, Indian Ocean polities combine elements of both Oceania and the Caribbean: at the time of European conquest, some islands, as in Melanesia and Polynesia, had robust indigenous cultures (e.g., Madagascar) while others, as with Barbados, had no human population whatsoever (e.g., Mauritius). On some of the Indian Ocean islands,

European enslavement of Africans for plantation work was as formative as it was throughout the West Indies.

Sovereign status runs the gamut of postcolonial possibility; there are independent republics, dependencies of Britain, and overseas possessions of France. Three are unambiguously Anglophone and four are predominantly Francophone. One island nation distinctly reflects the dual colonial legacies of both Britain and France: Mauritius.

Whereas in the South Pacific Vanuatu experienced concurrent colonization, in the Indian Ocean the islanders of Mauritius underwent consecutive, or sequential, colonialism: French, followed by British. Yet Francophonie remains stronger than British culture. Despite signs of restiveness among slave descendants, Mauritius has enjoyed relative harmony among its diverse African and South Asian populations. It has done so while maintaining a vibrant parliamentary democracy. Lacking most of the usual preconditions for democracies—including national unity—Mauritius embraces its dual colonial heritage for the purposes of managing ethnic conflict and promoting development.

This Indian Ocean people is also quite conscious of its origins in yet another great nation from which the region takes its name, and which also experienced both types of colonialism. After an overview of the Indian Ocean, a focus on Mauritius, and a comparison with Réunion, we shall take a detour to Mother India herself and examine one of the stranger legacies of colonialism from the age of French-British rivalry: Francophone Indians, and French citizens of Indian ethnicity, perpetuating French culture in southern India.

Geography and Colonial History

The origins of Indian Ocean geopolitics recall a basic pattern from the South Pacific and West Indies: European nations, in rivalry with each other, conferred distinct sovereignties upon individual islands and clusters of islands. With island nations dotting the seas from southwest of India's shores to the south-

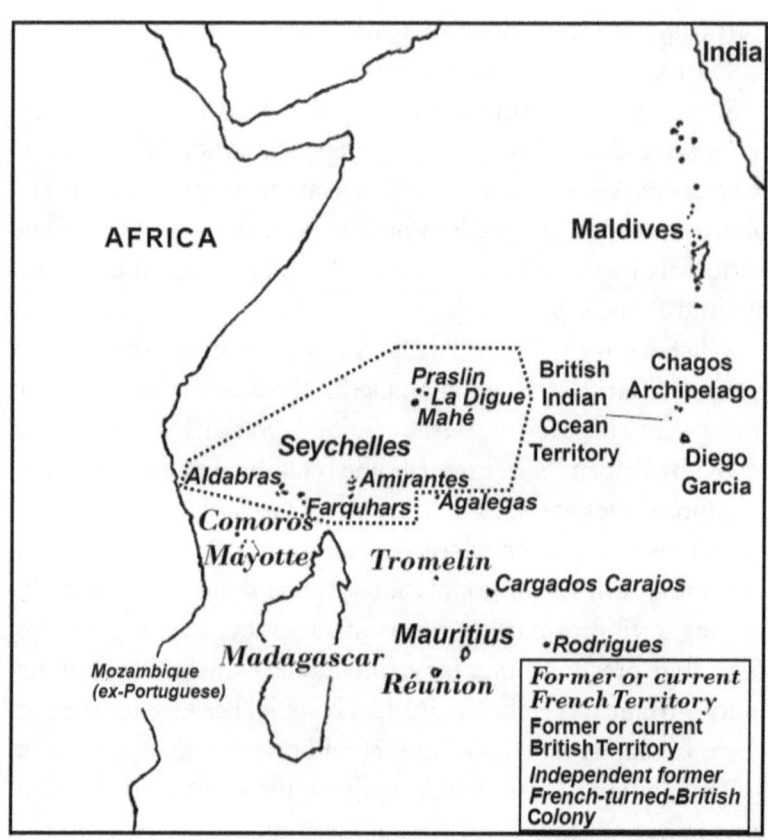

Map 13. Indian Ocean Polities

eastern coast of Africa, the region might just as easily have been called the "African Ocean." Indeed, six of the eight polities are substantially closer to the African continent than to the Subcontinent (see Map 13). Nor does India's ethnic and cultural imprint extend to even half the so-called Indian Ocean societies.

Even the Indian Ocean state geographically closest to India—the Maldives—is quite distinct from it. Governed by Muslim sultanate for centuries (Islam being introduced in the twelfth century), inhabitants of the two hundred populated islands (out of twelve hundred, clustered in twenty-seven atolls) underwent nominal Portuguese and Dutch colonialism before becoming a British protectorate in 1887. The local variation of Dhivevi—

derived from an old Sri Lankan language—reflects the Sinhalese influence upon the archipelago, one that thoroughly mixed with Dravidian (southern Indian), Australasian, Arab, and African elements. Maldivian independence came in 1965.

Also located on the continental Indian side of the Indian Ocean—but neither politically independent nor ethnically Asian—is the British Indian Ocean Territory, a controversial creation of decolonization. As a condition for acceding to Mauritian independence, in 1965 Britain insisted that the Chagos Archipelago—henceforth known as the British Indian Ocean Territory—be detached from the colonial unit from which it had been hitherto administered. No sooner had the excision been effectuated than Britain proceeded to lease one of the Chagos Islands to the United States for fifty years. That island, Diego Garcia, became a major American military base, and on account of the involuntary evacuation of its inhabitants, a long-lasting human rights issue.

On the opposite end of the so-called Indian Ocean, closest to Africa, is the three-island cluster of the Comoros. Spurred by fears of British ambitions in Madagascar, and later, by German ones emanating from East Africa, France began acquiring in the 1840s what became in 1886 the four-island "protectorate" of the Comoros. In 1914 the Comoros became a full-fledged French colony (although initially attached administratively to Madagascar). Independence came to (most of) the Comoros in 1975; however, the island of Mayotte Mahoré—the earliest of France's Comoran possessions—rejected the path of sovereignty.[1]

Réunion, like Mayotte, is also part of the French Republic, but in a much more integrated and mutually desirable manner. Like Guadeloupe, Guyane, and Martinique, Réunion was one of the "Old Colonies" (dating to the seventeenth century) that became an overseas department of France in 1946. Politically, it has tended to be more conservative than its three French West Indian counterparts. Réunionnais are of Indian and African origin but quite thoroughly assimilated into French cultural mode: Catholicism, not Hinduism, predominates.

Thanks to the considerable transfers of monies from the metropole to the Indian Ocean department, Réunion is by far the wealthiest polity in the Indian Ocean. The poorest, by far, is the region's largest island (hence its nickname, Grande Ile): Madagascar.

France faced more opposition to colonial takeover and retention in Madagascar than in any other Indian Ocean territory. Treaties and declarations of "protection" from the 1860s to 1880s set the stage for wars of resistance in 1883 and the mid-1890s. Only with the deportation of Queen Ranavalona III in 1896 could an actual colony be declared and established. Nationalist sentiment still simmered, however, and major revolt erupted in 1947. Independence came in 1960. Madagascar is also "independent" when it comes to religion. Unusual even by African standards, more than half the population adheres to non-Christian, indigenous beliefs.

With the Seychelles, we encounter the only true Indian Ocean archipelago with mixed French and British colonial heritage. Comprised of 115 islands, practically the entire population resides on only three of them—Praslin, La Digue, and Mahé. Mahé by itself is home to 90 percent of Seychellois. Southwest of these main islands are mini-archipelagic clusters: the Amirante, the Farquhar, and Aldabra, the last of which is much closer to the Comoros and Madagascar than to its own capital island of Mahé.

First claimed by France in 1756, the Seychelles switched hands several times between the French and English until it was definitively ceded to Britain in 1811. Even then, however, and beyond 1897 (when it ceased being administered as a dependency of Mauritius), the major European influence and language were French. After independence in 1976, the Seychelles became one of the only nations in the world, along with Haiti, that recognized Creole as both an official language and a language of

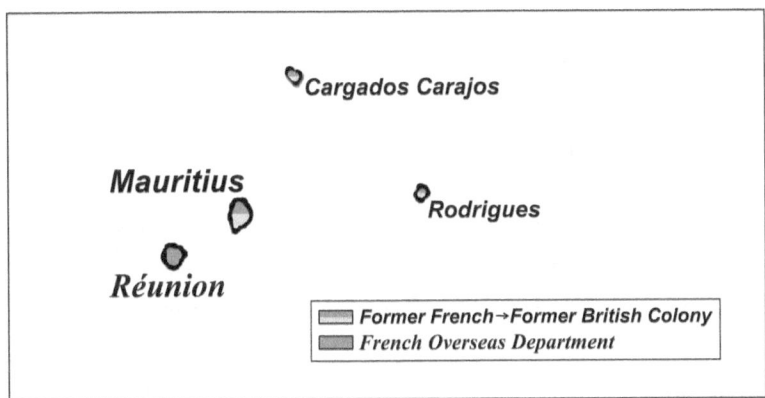

Map 14. Mascarene Islands

instruction. French also remains an official language but in postcolonial times has become subordinate to English, which is introduced earlier in the curriculum. The French colonial heritage has been more straightforward in religion: Roman Catholicism (90 percent) dominates Protestantism (8 percent).

Like the Seychelles, Mauritius—the focus of this chapter—also was officially ceded by France to Britain, in 1815. Unlike in the Seychelles (with which it shares a similar Creole), a strong Franco-Mauritian elite stamp preserved and expanded Francophonie way beyond what it ever achieved in the sprawling Seychelles. Even more distinguishing is the legacy of post-abolition Indian migrants who came to work for pay on the plantations more or less abandoned by the newly enfranchised black islanders.

Geographically, Mauritius belongs to a cluster of islands knows as the Mascarenes, which until the Napoleonic Wars Paris considered an exclusive French preserve (see Map 14). In addition to Ile Maurice, the Mascarene Islands include Réunion and Rodrigues. Rodrigues, settled by inhabitants from Mauritius, was captured by the British in 1809 and administratively reattached to Mauritius when they took it over in 1810. While officially enjoying a status of autonomy since 2002, Rodrigues is for all intents and purposes an administrative territory of Mauritius, with two seats set aside in the Mauritian Parliament for representation. The population of Rodrigues is a more ethnically homogenous reflection of an earlier era of African slave-based plantation economy; unlike Mauritius islanders, there are relatively few Rodriguans of Indian descent.

In addition to Rodrigues, the populated territory of Mauritius is also made up of the two Agalega Islands, nearly six hundred miles to the north. Physically and culturally, Agalega resembles more the Seychelles, to which it is physically closer. Uninhabited or semi-inhabited islands and islets include St. Brandon (the Cargados Carajos Archipelago). Mauritius also claims, from France, Tromelin Island, and from the United Kingdom and United States, the Chagos Archipelago, including the controversial Diego Garcia military base.

Colonized and named but eventually abandoned by the Dutch in the seventeenth and early eighteenth centuries, the island of Mauritius was claimed by France in 1715 and redubbed Ile de France. For maritime reasons the most strategically valuable of the Mascarenes, Mauritius was a major irritant to the British on account of the attacks on its ships launched from there, particularly by corsairs, privateers, or pirates.

Under British sovereignty and mercantilism, Mauritius became a world-class sugar exporter. In the 1850s it produced over 7 percent of the entire world's sugar (Bowman 1991, 19). Manpower for this labor-intensive industry might have seemed problematic in 1835 when Britain abolished slavery and former slaves seemed ill inclined to stay on as field laborers. Fortunately (from a British colonial point of view) an almost inexhaustible supply of cheap labor was available: India. By century's end, Indians and their offspring (Indo-Mauritians) greatly outnumbered the Creole-speaking progeny of African slaves. Tens of thousands of Chinese traders (Sino-Mauritians) had also established themselves in the land that, when first discovered by Europeans, had no human habitation. These demographic and cultural patterns still defined the polity by the time Mauritius obtained independence in 1968: a former British colony that sounded more French than English and felt more Francophone than Anglo-Saxon. Such was the result of sequential colonialism on an Indian Ocean island whose only "indigenous" population of note at the time of original European occupation was the dodo bird.[2]

French Colonialism and Prolonged Slavery: The Terms of Capitulation

To appreciate the Francophone stamp upon this former British colony one must examine the terms of the 1810 capitulation, and the society that those terms tended to preserve.

General Decaen, captain-general of France's Indian Ocean possession since 1802, succeeded in negotiating from the British what, to his master, Napoleon, was one of the most honorable set of terms for a vanquished adversary (Macmillan [1914] 1991, 40). In return for cessation of hostility and transfer of sovereignty, the French were guaranteed the preservation of their laws, religion, customs, and by inference, language. In this respect Mauritius was quite distinct from other French islands that came under the British flag. For instance, Grenada and Dominica (ceded to Britain in 1783) and St. Lucia (taken by the British in 1815) would retain traces of French heritage in their local language (Creole), but otherwise, by the time of independence, they had become thoroughly anglicized in jurisprudence, colonial style, religion, and language of the elite.

By 1810 Mauritius had experienced nearly a century of French settler colonialism not unlike that which we have examined in the West Indies. At first governed as a private-sector preserve (through the French East India Company from 1721), Mauritius and its dependencies were taken over by the French monarchy in 1764. Financial stringency and poor management necessitated the takeover. As in Martinique, the abolition of slavery decreed by the Jacobins was nullified by local actions: in Mauritius, island settlers in 1793 drove off the Revolutionary naval detachment dispatched to enforce emancipation.³ Shared European notions of racism and colonialism meant that for a quarter century following the capitulation—and despite the British abolition of the slave trade three years prior—the French system of slavery would continue unencumbered in Mauritius under British sovereignty.

Sugar had already been grown for export in Mauritius by the time it became a proper colony (the Dutch had first introduced the plant), but it was under French imperial rule that Mauritian sugar came to occupy a dominant role in the regional and global economy. In the eighteenth century, sugar was tantamount to slavery: sweetness for its consumers came at the expense of bitterness to its cutters.⁴

Slaves had already been brought under French East India Company rule to Mauritius from a variety of regions: India, the East Indies, West Africa. The bulk of slaves came, however, from Madagascar and Mozambique, especially during Crown rule. Conditions for enslaved Africans was as harsh in the Indian Ocean as in the West Indies, and *marronage*—slave resistance through flight (and sometimes plantation raiding)—was a recurrent problem for planters and governors. Although severely repressed, *marronage* was never completely eliminated.

As in the French West Indies, male slaveowners' sexual proclivities eventually also gave rise to a mulatto population (*gens de couleur*), many of whom were freed and several of whom themselves became slaveowners.⁵ The intermediate legal position between white slaveowners and black slaves occupied by Mauritian mulattos has carried over into a social division today that—although partially obscured by the umbrella term "Creole"—is stronger in Mauritius than in Martinique.

British Rule and Hybridic Colonialism

Continuity of Francophonie in Mauritius is due in large part to the first British governor of the island, Sir Robert Farquhar, who served from 1810 until 1823. Farquhar was no Francophobe.

He not only scrupulously respected the terms of the capitulation but also interpreted it in the most generous terms for the French settlers. Most famously, he determined that trade in slavery—which the British Parliament had otherwise abolished three years prior to the takeover of Mauritius—fell under the capitulation clause preserving the property and customs clause of the settlers. Though slavery thus prospered for another quarter century, the abolition of slavery was inevitable and irreversible. When it came in 1835, it was accompanied by a generous indemnity by the British government to the slaveowners, and a six-year phase of "apprenticeship" to supposedly ease the transition from slavery to outright freedom (but actually to force the ex-slaves to remain on the estates). "Near freedom" was intolerable, however, and disobedience of apprenticeship regulations forced its end two years earlier than originally legislated. Mass defections from the plantations, even before apprenticeship's "premature" end, created a labor shortage as former slaves quit estates for cities en masse just when sugar production was becoming the island's predominant economic activity.

The solution to the manpower loss lay across the ocean in Britain's "jewel in the crown"—India. Although the French had brought some Indians as laborers to Mauritius from Pondichéry in the first half of the eighteenth century as early as Mahé Labourdonnais' time, it was British-sponsored indentured servitude that would ultimately tip the demographic balance on the island.

Immigration was not contractually permanent for individuals, but between 1834 and 1910 almost three times as many Indians came to Mauritius as returned to India, making for a net increase of nearly three hundred thousand (Bowman 1991, 44). The Asian versus Euro-African demographic tipping point occurred between 1851 and 1861, when the share of Indians in the overall population jumped from 43 percent to 62 percent (Leclezio 1914, 142). Henceforth, the descendants of African slaves—who had outnumbered white settlers for well over the previous century—would be consigned to minority demographic status, and Mauritius would become "Little India" (Eisenlohr 2006).

Despite the social, economic, and political fissures that would emerge from the "Indianization" of Mauritius, no bipolar linguistic division actually took root along colonial language lines. Some local leaders of Indian descent, resentful of Franco-Mauritian and upper-class Creole hegemony tried to advance their cause in the middle to late nineteenth century by allying with British officialdom and enjoining their co-ethnics to embrace English against French. (So had some upwardly mobile Creoles, resentful of Franco-Mauritian prejudice and privilege). They failed. Despite hailing from India, Indo-Mauritians did not collectively become Anglophones, nor did they meld into the Afro-Mauritian, or Creole, community. Between them, the Indo-Mauritians and Creoles developed a symbiotic but parallel relationship, rarely spanned by intermarriage. A multiplicity of immigrant Indian languages (but most prominently, Bhojpuri) also meant that during most of British rule in Mauritius, there was relatively little communication across the Indo-Creole divide.

Creoles, in part to maintain their identity vis-à-vis Indo-Mauritians, identified all the more with the culture of their former masters. Slavery had effaced most memory of, or pride in, African ancestry. French and European expressions of language and culture, not Indian, Asian, or African ones, remained their model for emulation. (This was particularly so for the *gens de couleur*, or mulattos, who could claim European as well as African ancestry.) If Afro-Mauritians could not master the French language, they were satisfied with the next best thing: French Creole (Kreol), which eventually became the lingua franca for Indo-Mauritians as well. The continuing presence of Franco-Mauritians, who never lost their economic clout, also tended to reinforce the cultural Frenchness of this juridically British colony. "The British presence was often little more than a formality, a thin veneer of legality that rested uneasily atop a rigidly stratified society dominated by the Franco-Mauritian elite. For the most part the British accepted this arrangement" (Bowman 1991, 27). English language became the most neutral of languages in Mauritius, used for formal governance and upper-level jurisprudence but rarely as a medium of social intercourse. Except for the relatively small (and impermanent) community of colonial officials (including the military), few people in Mauritius were actual Anglophones.

The legal structure of British Mauritius also continued to reflect French law. The Napoleonic code was never abolished; rather, it was amalgamated within an English common law tradition and British judicial organization. The civil code, even after being amended in post-Napoleonic times, remained entirely in French; the penal code, bilingual in redaction, has continued to bear strong French legal influence. Most procedural rules were adapted to British legal practice, and laws governing corporations also were of British origin. Although one might find such a legal regime confusing, it did instill an enduring rule of law ethos: compared with classic colonies of single European dominance, Mauritius's legal structure was relatively autonomous from the colonial, and postcolonial, administration (Bridge 1997; d'Unienville 1994; Lange 2003).

Mauritius under the British was not only an Anglophone-Francophone institutional hybrid, it was also a Euro-Asian social and Islamic-Christian religious crucible. In addition to Indians, Chinese maintained distinct communities and "Indians" included Muslims as well as Hindus. Britain's restricted expansion of representation in the 1880s to Franco-Mauritians was challenged at the turn of the century by the other communities, Dr. Eugene Laurent mobilizing the upwardly mobile Creoles and Manilal Maganlall Doctor organizing Indo-Mauritian laborers. By the 1930s, political leaders of renown were the Creole Dr. Maurice Curé (founder of the Mauritius Labour Party [MLP]) and the Indo-Mauritian Seewoosagur Ramgoolam, later (also as head of MLP) the island's first prime minister.

World War II and Political Reform

The years spanning the Second World War coincided with material hardship, labor unrest, and constitutional reform. Low wages, high taxes, and employer repression that gave rise to strikes, riots, and violence in the 1930s continued, with the same colonial crackdowns, in the 1940s. Such unrest was incidental to the war, however, not a symptom of it. Although Mauritian troops did fight in the North African and Middle Eastern theaters, and were involved in a wartime mutiny in Madagascar (Simmons 1982, 71), World War II had a relatively low political impact on Mauritians, at least compared with the colonized under consideration elsewhere in this study.

Indo-Mauritians benefited most from the constitutional reforms that coincided with a general liberalization of colonial policy after the Second World War, and the "wind of change" of independence, as British prime minister Harold Macmillan characterized it. Independence from Britain was understood to be synonymous with democratization, however, and the Creole minority—not to mention the Franco-Mauritian elite—did not believe that they would benefit from majoritarian democracy. In Mauritius, the cleavage was not so much Francophone versus Anglophone as it was Francophile versus non-Francophile.

As secession was not an option (as in Vanuatu), all Mauritian groups participated fully (and fiercely) in the electoral process leading up to self-governance and sovereignty. The Creole camp was led by Gaëtan Duval under the banner of the Parti Mauricien (later the Parti Mauricien Social Démocrate). Duval lost a key 1963 election to Ramgoolam, however, who thereupon became the pre-independence premier. Creole-fomented riots in 1965 reflected that community's apprehension. At the 1967 constitutional conference, the Parti Mauricien Social Démocrate lost its bid to forestall independence by free association with Britain. Ethnic rioting (again, with fatalities) in the capital, Port Louis, marred the onset of independence six weeks later, in March 1968.

Partition as Price of Independence: Diego Garcia and the Chagossians

Negotiated independence from Britain came at some territorial cost: the administrative detachment of the sectioning off of the Chagos Archipelago and subsequent handover of part of it to the United States. Administered by the British from Mauritius, these small coral islands, twelve hundred miles to the northeast, were not given much thought by Mauritians until the question of their excision from the national territory arose. Trading in coconuts by Creole-speaking descendants of African slaves constituted the main activity there. The United States coveted one of the Chagos in particular, Diego Garica, as a naval base for Cold War strategic purposes. Resettlement evacuation of the islanders, to the Seychelles as well as to Mauritius, ensued.

Territorial excision of the budding new state, less than the involuntary displacement of its most remote islanders, outraged Mauritian politicians, particularly of the Mouvement Militant Mauricien. In the following four decades, national and international sensitivity to the cause of the exiles themselves has slowly grown. Legal action was taken in the United States in 2001 on behalf of the Chagossians, but in 2006 the U.S. Court of Appeals for the District of Columbia Circuit in Washington DC ruled that it had no authority to order compensation for the displaced islanders. That same year, however, the British courts ruled that permanent exclusion of the *îlois*, as they are also known, was "irrational and unlawful." Initially upheld by a higher court, that decision, upon appeal by the British government, was ultimately overturned by the High Court: post–September 11 security politics apparently trumped the civil rights of the deported islanders.

Chagos and Diego Garcia are relatively minor irritants with the most recent colonizer, Britain, and the postcolonial superpower, the United States. Mauritius also has a (small) bone of partition to pick with its original colonizer. France maintains a meteorological station on Tromelin Island, about three hundred miles north-northwest of Mauritius. Mauritius has claimed Tromelin since independence; France has maintained its own sovereignty over Tromelin ever since 1814, when she placed it under the jurisdiction of Réunion. Since 2007, France has grouped Tromelin within the French Southern and Antarctic Lands (TAAF).

Although France has not been averse to partitioning colonial territories on the eve of independence (the extraction of Mayotte from the Comoros is a prime example), one is hard-pressed to imagine a twentieth-century ceding or leasing of French territory to another great power, even to an ally. The transfer of Diego Garcia to the United States would have been unimaginable under the French, whether or not Mauritius was heading toward independence. Such is one of the ironic legacies of colonialism: while French settlers were encouraged to remain in Mauritius after 1810, British sovereignty led to the permanent exile of Indian Ocean islanders after 1967.

Hyper-Pluralism and Nation Building

Had France retained Mauritius, it probably would have come to resemble nearby Réunion (the erstwhile Ile Bourbon). The Creole population would have remained dominant demographically and become even more gallicized in race and frenchified in culture. Those islanders who would have still managed to immigrate from the Indian subcontinent would have assimilated more completely into the French Indian Ocean mainstream. Politically, l'Ile Maurice might very likely have been converted, as was Réunion in 1946, into an overseas department and thus become another integral unit of the French Republic. The relationship between Mauritius and Réunion would then have more resembled that between Martinique and Guadeloupe, the "sister islands" of the French Antilles, than that between a proudly independent island nation and a wealthier dependency of a remote former colonizer. As it is, given the disparities in sovereignty and prosperity, the relationship is fraught with ambivalence, providing grist for analyses ranging from a psychological to a comedian bent (Miles 1996).

Mauritius has evolved into an exceedingly pluralistic society (much more than Réunion, the Seychelles, or the Antilles), and the success of its management has taken on a number of different interpretations. The first dimension of Mauritian pluralism is ethnic. Mauritians who hail from the Indian subcontinent constitute over two-thirds of the entire population. Creoles (understood here as both the descendants of African slaves and mulatto *gens de couleur*) represent little more than one quarter of Mauritians (of whom the "coloureds" are perhaps 2 to 3 percent). Sino-Mauritians are about 2 percent. Descendants of the original European settlers (as well as those British colonial and business families who remained and mixed in with the French) make up about 1 percent: these are the Franco-Mauritians.

A strictly ethnic breakdown, however, obscures important subethnic and religious diversity. Mauritians of Indian origin, for example, need to be distinguished by religion, language, and where relevant, caste. Over 15 percent of Mauritians—mostly all descendants of the great nineteenth-century migrations from India—identify as (Sunni) Muslims. They have come to be excluded from most definitions of "Indo-Mauritian," which generally refer to Hindus of the island (about half the overall population) (Hollup 1996). But which Hindus? Just as Mother India manifests an important north-south divide, so do Indo-Mauritians cluster into communities based on ancestral region and related language. Thus the subcultures of southern Indian origin remain distinct from the much larger, Hindi- and Bhojpuri-speaking ones of northern India. The caste system has been both preserved and altered in ways different from India itself, so that "members of the higher castes sometimes joined with the middle castes to exclude lower castes from top civil service and political jobs" (Toth 1995, 114; Nave 2001, 99–100). Today, caste operates mainly (at least for Mauritian Hindus of southern Indian origin) in the realm of gender, strongly influencing marital options.

Roman Catholicism is the religion of default for the Creoles and Franco-Mauritians; a number of Sino-Mauritians also attend mass as well as the Chinese temple, so that nearly one-third of Mauritians are Christian.[6] Given its historic and ethnic associations, Catholicism is, as in Vanuatu, closely associated with Francophonie; unlike in Vanuatu, however, most Catholics are likely to understand French. The miniscule following of the Church of England underscores in Mauritius the lesser religious influence of more recent British colonialism compared to the older French one.

Beyond caste and cultural differences deriving from religion, Mauritian Hindus are theologically differentiated as well. Most are Sanatanists, following orthodox Hindu beliefs and rituals. The ubiquitous *baitkas*—Hindu community centers, especially prominent in rural areas—are a Sanatanist institution. Arya Samaj is a Hindu reform movement that came to Mauritius in the early twentieth century. Its emphasis on intercaste equality and simplified ritual appealed to *ti-nasyon* Hindus of the island and became a fulcrum for Indo-Mauritian political identity and mobilization. Even the Sunnis of Mauritius (95 percent of the Muslim community) lay claim to several subdenominations.[7]

The linguistic picture in Mauritius is as complex as the religious, caste, and ethnic configurations. Although English was the language of the colonizer for the century and a half preceding independence, it has became the mother tongue of only a tiny fraction of islanders. Over eleven times as many Mauritians invoke French, language of the older colonizer, for their primary speech (see Table 5).[8] It is the creole derived from French, however—Kreol—that serves as the lingua franca of the island—even though Kreol has no status as a subject in school or for government purposes.[9]

Next to Kreol, Bhojpuri is spoken by the greatest number of Mauritians—but it, too, except for serving informally as transitional language for the first few years of primary school, is not officially recognized.[10] Hindi, Tamil, Telugu, and Marathi, on

Table 5. Primary Home Language in Mauritius, 2000

	Number of speakers	Percentage (%)	Percentage change in total from 1990 (%)
Kreol	826,152	79.6	+9.9
Bhojpuri	142,387	13.7	−7.8
French	39,953	3.9	+0.2
Chinese[a]	8,748	0.1	−0.3
Hindi	7,250	0.1	−1.3
Tamil	3,623	—	−0.9
English	3,512	—	−0.2
Telugu	2,169	—	−0.7
Marathi	1,888	—	−0.8
Urdu	1,789	—	−0.7
Arabic[b]	—	—	—
Gujarati[c]	—	—	—
Total[d]	1,037,471		

[a]Includes Cantonese, Hakka, and Mandarin.

[b]Only listed in 2000 as a "language of forefathers" (806 such respondents); in 1990, 280 respondents claimed Arabic as a language usually spoken at home.

[c]Not listed in 2000; in 1990, 290 respondents claimed Gujarati as a primary language.

[d]Total factors out "other" languages and incomplete responses.

Sources: Compiled from data in 2000 Census, online, Table D10; *1990 Housing and Population Census of Mauritius*, vol. 2: *Demographic and Fertility Characteristics* (Government of Mauritius, Central Statistical Office, Ministry of Economic Planning and Development), tables D8 and D9, 95–97.

the other hand, are offered as language electives. So are Arabic, Urdu, and Chinese. English is the official medium of instruction, and French is a required subject.

Even if nearly 80 percent of the population claims Kreol as their primary language, most Mauritians are, at some level of proficiency, bilingual; multilingualism is also quite common. At some critical stage in Mauritian nation building, Kreol ceased being the linguistic preserve of the Creole people (and their Franco-Mauritian forebears) to become the lingua franca of the society at large. We know that the process began in the late nineteenth century, in response to British colonial ambivalence over whether to promote literacy for Indian immigrants in their various mother tongues or in English alone. This triggered "the beginning of a slide of the Indian masses towards the common use of Creole and an aspiration to knowledge of French for a better integration within Mauritian society" (Baggioni and de Robillard 1990, 32, my translation).

For the most part, the interethnic spread of Kreol was a felicitous development with respect to intergroup relations on the island. Still, Kreol's success in transcending ethnicity weakens the case that it should be treated on par with other groups' "ancestral languages" when it comes to secondary school electives and testing for ranking purposes. This was the case made by Creole activists, on behalf of Kreol, when the government decided that performance in "oriental languages" could be accorded greater weight when calculating the rank of graduating primary school. Such rankings determine the all-important entry into the island's elite secondary schools. Creole activists argued that the policy favored Indo- over Afro-Mauritians: Mauritian children of Indian origin could gain an edge by demonstrating proficiency in Hindi or Telugu, for example, but those of African ancestry had no parallel opportunity using Kreol.[11] The issue led to a 1995 landmark supreme court decision invalidating the proposal, the 1995 dissolution of government, and new parliamentary elections (in which incumbent Prime Minister Jugnauth and his Mouvement Socialiste Mauricien were routed).

Especially compared with Africa, to which it is by virtue of geographic proximity usually linked, Mauritius stands out as a beacon of intergroup harmony, though intergroup tensions do persist, and the Mauritian government recognizes the problem of what it gingerly labels "social exclusion" (Asgarally 1997).

Only on a few notable, explosive occasions have larger communal interests succeeded in overwhelming the multiple microidentities whose intertwining complexity ordinarily stymie political extremism. These violent exceptions to the rule of Mauritian social peace are linked to the one group the French brought to Mauritius in large numbers and in servitude, and whose descendants' eventual liberation would be indirectly compromised by the capitulation to the British: the Africans.

Le Malaise Creole

The disadvantaged social and economic status of the Creoles vis-à-vis Mauritians of Indian origin has long been a subject of the island's analysts, foreign and domestic (Miles 1999b). In plantation islands that remained French, the progressive sentiments of abolition eventually intersected with the egalitarian ideals of assimilationism and resulted in both citizenship and departmentalization (statehood). Descendants of slaves remained a majority, and those immigrant communities that did arrive gradually assimilated into the wider overseas French society. This does not mean that they completely abandoned their folkways. Many historians have documented East Indian survivalisms in the French West Indies. But the French settler island never developed into, as M. G. Smith (1965) classically described the British West Indies, a "plural society." Nor did any continuous French colony come to experience, as did Mauritius (and Trinidad and Fiji) an ethno-demographic tilting from French-owned African slaves (and their descendants) in favor of Indian immigrants and their offspring.

The outnumbering of Creoles in Mauritius eventually resulted in their socioeconomic marginalization vis-à-vis Indo-Mauritians. Earlier we noted how the pre-independence riot of 1965, and well as the immediate postcolonial one of 1968, were triggered by Creole fears of Indo-Mauritian domination in an independent state. In 1999 further mass violence broke out following the death, while in police custody, of a popular Creole musician, Kaya, who had been arrested during a protest against anti-Creole discrimination. No prime minister or president of Mauritius has been Creole. While some Creoles have prospered under neoliberalism (especially as laborers in export zone industries), the economic boom has left many Creoles with the sentiment that they remain second-class citizens on an island where their forebears were once slaves. However, unlike their co-islanders from the Indian subcontinent, those from the much closer African continent have a relatively dim notion of their pre-Mauritian origins. The contrast is all the more notable given that barely a decade separated the de facto end of the slave trade to Mauritius and the beginning of mass immigration from India.[12]

A Postcolonial Success Story?

Ene sel lepep—"one single people"—is the unofficial credo of the government.[13] But to what extent does Mauritius warrant the image of a harmonious, multicultural society that it self-consciously projects and that many outside analysts accept?[14] The extent of pluralist "success" would seem to depend on one's reference point. To whom should the plight of Mauritian Creoles be compared? If the reference point is purely domestic, then there is no question that with respect to Mauritians of Indian origin (northern and southern, Hindu and Muslim[15]), Creoles have legitimate grievances. If one looks to the nearby African continent, the relative plight of Creoles as an ethnic minority appears less bleak.[16] They have never been victims of deportation and/or seizure of property, as have Asians in Uganda and Lebanese in Sierra Leone. Nor have they been demonized for their ethnicity, origins, occupations, or politics, as have the Tutsi, Igbo, and Darfuri.

If we confine our regional comparison to Madagascar, the closest "African" state[17] and the origin of perhaps a majority of Afro-Mauritians, the favorable situation of Creoles still holds. Tensions between Creoles and Indo-Mauritians have never risen to the level that divided central highland Merina and coastal peoples (*côtiers*). Nor have even the worst racial riots in Mauritius approximated the victimization of Comoran immigrants in Madagascar, fourteen hundred of whom were killed in 1976 alone (Schraeder 1995, 39).

Comparison with India, although compelling on account of

superficial ethnic similarities, is a more difficult hazard (but see Hollup 1994). Are Creoles in Mauritius as badly off as *harijans* (outcastes, "untouchables") have been in India? Governments in postcolonial India have taken proactive measures ("positive discrimination") to raise the status of *harijans*, lower castes, and non-Hindu "tribal" people throughout India. Since the 1990s, governments in Mauritius have commissioned reports that explicitly acknowledge the inequalities and exclusion suffered by Creoles.[18] What is more, although periodically contested as an affront to "true democracy," Mauritius has preserved its unique system of guaranteeing parliamentary representation to all minority groups: the "best loser" system. It is an arrangement so totally antithetical to French norms of representation and citizenship that it is inconceivable that Mauritius would have adopted it were it not for British tutelage.

"Best Losers": A Most British Legacy

First adopted in 1967 for the last general elections held under colonial supervision, and retained ever since, the "best loser" system guarantees that eight seats in the seventy-member parliament be reserved for defeated candidates to ensure ethnic representativity while respecting elected party balance. For such purposes, the Mauritian Constitution categorizes the electorate into four categories: Hindu, Muslim, Chinese, and "general population." "General population" is not the generic, miscellaneous group that the term misleadingly evokes. Rather, it encompasses Creoles and Franco-Mauritians, the descendants of African slaves and the descendants of their owners. It necessarily also includes the issue of mixed sexual alliances of these two groups, *les gens de couleur*. Constitutionally, of course, there is no recognition of "coloreds" any more than there is explicit recognition of Franco-Mauritians and Creoles. By implicitly ensuring a threshold of representation for these particular ethnic minorities, the best loser system has allayed the pre-independence fear that in the postcolonial legislature, immigrant populations would completely marginalize those communities of pre-British origin. (Similarly, the system would allay the apprehensions of Muslims toward Hindus, and of Chinese toward every other group.)

The designation "general population" presents a paradox of privilege. By lumping together the Creoles and Franco-Mauritians for electoral purposes, the best loser system forces a political identity among the least and the most privileged of Mauritians. It also has induced "colored" politicians to take up the banner for the group from which it had socially distanced itself historically—islanders of unmixed African heritage. Let us recall that the French were supplanted in Mauritius as colonizers before Paris abolished slavery: abolition was never here credited to France. From a historical point of view, Creoles, coloreds, and Franco-Mauritians make unnatural political allies as common members of a "general population."

Franco-Mauritians prefer to operate in the shadows of Mauritian politics. Paul Bérenger is an exception. A founding member of the radical Mouvement Militant Mauricien and eventually a prime minister (2003–5), Bérenger has been a most prominent Franco-Mauritian politician. His native ease with the Kreol language (in addition to fluency in English and French), combined with his natural charisma, have propelled Bérenger to a political popularity belying his ancestral origins.[19]

Although criticized for its undemocratic tendency to pigeonhole each individual Mauritian according to his or her ethnic/religious group, the best loser system is generally credited with maintenance of communal harmony on the island. It encourages political parties to include members of ethnic minorities, thereby avoiding purely ethnically based political formations. Indirectly, the best loser system does, however, reinforce identification among those groups whose origins predate the British takeover and governance of the island: descendants of the French settlers, their African slaves, and their mixed offspring.

Along with Botswana, Mauritius is often cited as the only "African" example of continuously functioning democracy since

Table 6. Material Outcomes—Indian Ocean

	GDP per capita (dollars, 2008)	Life expectancy (years, 2005–10)	Adult literacy (%)
Former British colonies			
British Indian Ocean Territory[a]	—	—	—
Maldives (305)	3,916	71.2	99.3
Former French colonies			
Comoros (661)	—	65.1	84.9
Mayotte[a] (199)	—	75.8	76.0
Madagascar (1,911)	488	60.1	70.2
Reunion[a] (817)	19,417[b]	76.4	90.0
Former French turned British colonies			
Mauritius (1,028)	7,450	72.3	84.4[c]
Seychelles (84)	11,044	73.3	91.8

Note: Number in parentheses next to country refers to population, in thousands.

[a]Nonindependent

[b]In 2006

[c]In 2000

Sources: UN Data, Country Profiles (http://data.un.org); UNDP Human Development Index 2009 (http://hdrstats.undp.org/en/indicators/89.html); CIA *World Factbook* (http://www.cia.gov); Institut National des Statistiques Economiques (http://www.insee.fr/fr/insee_regions); Nations On Line (http://www.nationsonline.org).

independence (Miles 1999c). Such political accolades invariably recognize the link between democracy and development (Meisenhelder 1997; Sandbrook 2005). Granted, the luster of the Mauritian model has worn in recent years as social problems (poverty, crime, drugs, ethnic chauvinism) have surfaced as the byproduct of economic turndown (Kasenally 2011). In regional terms, however, Mauritius is still considered an "African" success story, widely touted as an "economic miracle" (a designation that rightfully pairs prosperity with independence— see Table 6). Has the sequential nature of French-British colonialism been a factor in Mauritian material prosperity?

Mauritian Economic Miracle and Its Causes

Upon independence, and for at least the first decade and a half after that, Mauritius was a poor, overcrowded, and at times economically desperate island whose plight was most evocatively portrayed by V. S. Naipaul (1972). Still a sugar-dependent monocrop country, with such high unemployment that emigration actually became government policy, Mauritius's turnaround has been so dramatic that the results are often portrayed as little short of miraculous. The pivot was a series of measures adopted in response to International Monetary Fund and World Bank structural adjustment conditionality. These included a downsizing of government and reduction of workers' salaries and benefits, devaluation of the Mauritian rupee, and a relaunching of an industrial diversification strategy. Most effective in this last regard was intensification of the island's fledgling export processing zone (EPZ) and development of tourism. Modernization of the sugar sector also assisted Mauritius to gain the title of "little tiger," an accolade correlated with high growth, earnings, exports, and employment; telecommunications and infrastructural development; and the incubation of a veritable consumer society (Bowman 1991, 122–37).

Mauritius consequently became the darling of international development advisors and political economists alike. Some observers (e.g., Darga 1996; Koop 2004) have cautioned that the very process that launched Mauritius in its miraculous performance—globalization—may in the end subvert its long-term development prospects. Still, the heretofore obscure Mauritius appeared as an economic model or foil—at least for publishing economists and political economists—with respect to a variety of developing nations of diverse colonial (and also noncolonial) provenance, including Egypt (Sandbrook and Romano 2004) and Taiwan (Bräutigam 1997).

The most econometric and technocratic of these treatments glosses over the colonial legacy as a factor in Mauritius's "miracle," or attributes its political stability to a fortuitous combination of economics and demographics (Lempert 1987). Others do recognize, at least indirectly, the importance of sequential colonialism as a condition creator for economic success. Subramanian and Roy (2003, 239) note the global linkages for trading and investment facilitated by the islands' "repository of communities (or diasporas)." The robustness of the native Chinese and Indian populations lubricated foreign direct investment from Hong Kong and India. Indian and (albeit to a lesser extent) Chinese migration, of course, was a consequence of British colonial replacement of the French.

At the same time, a continuing local French dominance in the economic sector—a result of the terms of the capitulation—planted the seeds of a postcolonial balance between those controlling the critical sugar industry (the Franco-Mauritian commercial elite) and controllers of the independent state (the Indo-Mauritian political elite). Unlike in other resource-rich nations (particularly in Africa), "Mauritius avoided . . . killing the cash cow" (Subramanian and Roy 2003, 240). In exchange for an expanded and remunerative civil service and generous welfare system (satisfying the descendants of indentured Indians), the foundation of local wealth production—the island's sugar industry—was left in the hands of the descendants of the original French settlers.

In terms of trade, the Mauritian legacy of sequential colonialism can be neatly summed up by noting the island nation's principal trading partners. For 2006, the number one destination for Mauritian exports (32 percent of the total) was the United Kingdom (with France in second place). With respect to imports, the premier supplier was France (14 percent of the total; second place was occupied by India) (Europa 2008, 786).

Mauritian democracy—which includes respect for property rights upheld by rule of law—also makes it an attractive site for foreign investment. One of the reasons that Mauritius is so democratic (and therefore so attractive) lies in the concordance established between initial opponents of independence—Franco-Mauritians and Francophone (or Francophile) Creoles—and proponents—Mauritians of Indian (and particularly Hindu) descent. Using the institutions of democracy to reassure the Franco-minorities of their place in postcolonial Mauritius had the unintended benefit of creating a hospitable investment climate down the road.

Matthew Lange (2003) also emphasizes the role of the colonial state in creating conditions for postcolonial development in Mauritius. Future broad-based development was facilitated by the embedding of the colonial state within local society. Even under the British, Lange claims, Mauritius was subject to direct rule, the colonial policy usually associated with France. Great Britain maintained the momentum of bureaucratic statism instituted under the French Revolution and perpetuated by Napoleon (403). Lange does not address whether he thinks Britain might have developed such a bureaucratic state on its own, without the structures inherited from the French. He does assert, however, that the absence of indigenous chiefs in Mauritius, whose local control of land and courts stymied development and state building elsewhere, enabled the anomaly of British direct rule. A purely British Mauritius, without French institutional antecedents (and without indigenous population), probably would have more resembled Barbados than the Anglo-French hybrid it actually became. Importantly, as Lange notes, Mauritius had no precolonial society. Colonization was concomitant with slavery. British and French colonization of Africa postdated European slavery and was all about "culture contact" between Europeans and Africans. Colonialism in the Indian Ocean more closely resembled that of the West Indies, where it grew up with slavery, often creating tabula rasa societies with no indigenous island societal input.[20] Massive British importation of Indian laborers following abolition, claims Lange, eventually led to a class of well-organized laborers who successfully pressed for social welfare programs, educational expansion, and economic development assistance (initially through agricultural credit societies). Although Lange does not tease out the extent to which sequential colonialism—especially the inherited French institutions and local elites—is responsible for the "embeddedness" of the colonial state to which he links Mauritius's economic success, his overall conclusion is compelling: "colonialism must . . . be analyzed as a historical event potentially shaping national development trajectories through institutional legacies" (418). Linguistic legacies, we would add, also play a key role in postcolonial development.

Francophonie in a Former British Colony

Legal History

British rule over Mauritius constituted "passive imperialism" (Toussaint 1969, 399). More than three decades after the British took control in 1810, British officials were still complaining that civil servants had not acquired the Queen's language (not surprising, given that serious instruction of English only began in the island's schools in 1869.) An act in 1841 officially recognized English as the primary language of government but it did not extend automatically to the judiciary, where litigation continued mostly in French. When Anglophone forces pressed the Colonial Office to fully anglicize the judicial system, London temporized by decreeing that the higher courts of the colony (but not the lower) would require the use of English as of midnight, July 15, 1847.[21] Under pressure from Franco-Mauritians and mixed-race Creoles, backpedaling on Anglicizing edicts occurred in the 1850s and 1860s. As late as 1914 French translations were used in government publications.

In more recent times, the issue of language use for court proceedings has resurfaced. In *R. v. Kramutally and anor* (1989), the court broke with precedent to allow witnesses, otherwise competent in English, to testify directly in Kreol. This was a case in which defendants—charged with attempted murder and murder—were, according to court records, "uneducated persons for whom English is a foreign language which they do not understand." Three years later, in *Kunnath v. State*, conviction for drug smuggling of a Malayalam-speaking Indian from Kerala was overturned on related grounds. Although the defendant was provided an interpreter, much of the evidence introduced was not translated for him.

Media Status

An even better indication of the overall influence of French language in Mauritian society lies in the media. Home to a vibrant newspaper culture and industry, the three dominant dailies on the island publish primarily in French: *L'Express* and *Le Mauricien* (each with a circulation of 35,000), and *Le Quotidien* (circulation 30,000). The same can be said of the lesser papers: *Le Socialiste* (circulation 7,000) and *Maurice Soir* (circulation 2,000). Articles in the highest circulation paper (70,000), the weekly *Week-End* are also mostly in French. Amazingly, for a society that had been a British colony for a century and a half prior to independence, there are two (daily) newspapers produced exclusively in Chinese but only one (a weekly) in English!

Primacy of French in the written press continues a long tradition. Outside France, the first daily newspaper in the French language (*Le Cernéen*) was published in Mauritius. This is all the more remarkable considering that it was launched twenty-two years *after* the island had come under British control (Baggioni and de Robillard 1990, 26).

Television and radio mirror this preference for French over English (with the Mauritius Broadcasting Corporation making additional allowances, particularly on radio, for Asian languages). The local news broadcast most widely viewed is in French (capped with a summary in Kreol). Challenges to French language hegemony in print and broadcast come not from Anglophone quarters, but from Kreol ones. Kreol may be the most common language in day-to-day interactions, but French is by far the dominant language of social prestige and supra-petty commerce. It was probably not hyperbole when the French cultural affairs attaché and editor of *L'Express* stated that "Mauritius is the one country in the world where French is advancing vis-à-vis English."[22]

Literature

For writers from Bernardin de Saint-Pierre in the eighteenth century to Jean-Marie Gustave Leclézio in the twentieth and twenty-first, Mauritius has been a fount for celebrated literature in French. The former is the author of the tragic romance *Paul et Virginie*; the latter, winner of the Nobel Prize in Literature in 2008. Even more notable than the renown of French authors who sojourned in Mauritius is the prolificness of Francophone Mauritian writers both through the British period of colonialism and beyond.

Role of France

From a diplomatic vantage, the fact that this onetime French colony obtained its independence from a colonizer *other* than France has actually facilitated postcolonial relations. There is none of the sensitivity to French neocolonialism that periodically erupts, for example, in Madagascar or Niger. The struggle for independence targeted Britain; France was a sympathetic bystander, a role that it exceptionally relished for a largely Francophone young nation.

France views its educational and cultural institutions operating in Mauritius as an excellent investment in linguistic diplomacy. Teacher training, research and university outreach, arts, literature, and scientific programs: all these reinforce the language links and cultural ties that a century and a half of British colonialism could not undo.

Sending Mauritians for higher education in France constitutes 90 percent of the budget of France's cultural support.[23] In 1996 approximately four hundred students were funded by the French government, seventy-six of them completely so. Happily for both countries, the experience does not lead to a brain drain of Mauritius's best and brightest Francophones to France: they return.

"Mauritius has never forgotten France," editorialized a leading Mauritian newspaper, "and France is always disposed to come to the side of Mauritius. In truth, we have never ceased to be together."²⁴ This sentiment, published in 1990, set the stage three years later for high Francophone drama in this former British colony.

Summit of La Francophonie

Hosting of the fifth Summit of Francophonie, in 1993, was a high cultural honor for Mauritius, one that inevitably strengthened its ties with France.²⁵ Numbers alone told part of the story: this relatively small island hosted twenty-four heads of state or government, four hundred journalists, and twelve hundred guests. At this pre-euro event, 26 million francs were made available by France so that the summit would be a success. The summit was an occasion to launch books (e.g., *Litteratures Francophones de l'Océan Indien*), films (e.g., *Maurice—Une Ile Pluriel*), and even stamps (see Fig. 6). The National Theatre of Cambodia performed; Life Insurance of India exhibited francophone artists; a Festival of Francophone Film screened *Les Derniers*.²⁶

Press interviews and editorials stoked the summit's image of Mauritius as an oasis of Francophonie: Shirin Aumeeruddy Cziffrin, president of the Permanent Council of Francophonie, was quoted as saying, "For the majority of Francophone speakers, native or not, French thinking is linked to democracy, human rights, sharing."²⁷ Such mainstream sentiments prompted opposition groups, such as Lalit (The Struggle) and Parti Militan Travayer (Workers Militant Party) to react in kind. In an article entitled "Francophonie without Hegemony," they were quoted thus: "Mauritians are not 'lil Frenchmen.... Mauritian language and culture are not byproducts of France."²⁸ Yet it is safe to say that even the least fluent of Francophones in Mauritius took pride in their nation's hosting of the Summit of Francophonie. On the international scene, it is as multilingual Francophones, not competent Anglophones, that Mauritians shine.

Fig. 6. Mauritius Francophone Commemorative Stamps

Linguistic Taboo?

In a self-consciously provocative vein, Baggioni and de Robillard (1990) essay to puncture the "taboo" of French language in Mauritius: its virtual exclusion in written form by officialdom despite its uncontestable oral, literary, and commercial primacy over English. Using as a springboard a bank note, as official a document as a government emits, Baggioni and de Robillard note that its writing is in English, Hindi, and Tamil. Omitted from the money, however, is French, which in reality is "massively present as a language of prestige even though this presence is not officially ratified [and is] massively rivaled in the reality of linguistic exchange by its Creole offspring symbolic," not by English (11). French is indeed massively present in Mauritius, so part of the social and cultural air that, far from being the ethno-language of exclusive power of yesteryear, it is now unconsciously, and uncontroversially, imbibed by all.[29]

But French is more than that. It is a language of "affection," according to one linguistically sensitive newspaper editor, not merely a means of communication. "The best [French-English] bilinguals"—and this, too, is a taboo, rarely stated—"are the Asians."

In Mauritius, government is conducted in English: parliamentary debate and administrative correspondence are prime symbols of the British colonial heritage. But when you call the prime minister's office, the recorded announcement, providing the different numbers of the different services, is in French.

Neofrancophonie

Baggioni and de Robillard use several terms to describe the appropriation of the French language by upwardly mobile urban Mauritians: vernaculization, de-ethnicization, neofrancophonie (1990, 162). All speak to the same phenomenon: the process by which formerly non-French-speaking communities, be they Muslim, Chinese, Hindu, or (non-elite) Creole, have gradually taken on the French language as theirs. Urbanization, education, and modernization are all factors in the delinking of the French language as ethnic markers of the Franco-Mauritian and (bourgeois) Creole communities. French becomes a language of communication among equals—equals by virtue of class and education, not race or origins.

It is important to note that neofrancophonie is not occurring at the expense of Kreol. Formality of situation and familiarity with interlocutor determine whether neofrancophones will address other Mauritians in Kreol or French. Nor is there the kind of race-linked sensitivity to the use of creolized French in Mauritius as in Martinique: a Caucasian addressing a Martinican passerby in Creole is likely to be rebuffed or redirected into French. In Mauritius, there is no equivalent stigma associated with being hailed by a white in Kreol.

If the "linguistic mobility" toward French (another felicitous Baggioni and de Robillard term) comes at the expense of any language, it is Bhojpuri. Yet even here, there are few political repercussions. As rural Indo-Mauritians move to the cities, and as the hinterland of Mauritius becomes more developed, Bhojpuri is first replaced as a vernacular by Kreol. In effect, one creolized language (linked to French) supplants another one (linked to Hindi). Kreol, more de-ethnicized than French, is not perceived as a threat to Indo-Mauritian identity and status. Bhojpuri is preserved as an in-group language; perhaps more family- and neighborhood-based than before, but no less valued. Bhojpuri speakers do not feel threatened by the expansion of Kreol and French. Rather, the function and use of Bhojpuri has shifted from de facto lingua franca in day-to-day communications to marker of membership in local community or extended family.

Anglophonie Today in the Former Ile de France

"English is no one's language." This oft-expressed sentiment refers to the fact that no ethnic or religious community in Mauritius claims English as its own. English is taught as if it is the official language of the country—which it is commonly believed to be[30]—but in practice it is used as a foreign tongue: socially by non-Mauritians; in formal exchanges by Mauritians. When English *is* used between Mauritians, it signals what we might call official "linguistic theater."

When elected officials address each other in parliamentarian session, they are performing in a game whose linguistic rules were established by colonial history. They are agreeing to share a language that is not the emotional "home" of any of them. Verbal jousting in this Mauritian theater is, in part, about showing off one's level of proficiency in this cognitively acquired language. Even when dealing with the most divisive of subjects, the "linguistic theater" takes the edge off some of the passion. As any student of foreign languages know, expressing genuine anger in a language not one's own requires a very high level of proficiency as well as a certain degree of emotional transformation. The lack of emotion in English is one reason that, as we have noted above, Mauritian literature is much more prolific in French than in English.

Outside of classrooms, the venue for ordinary Mauritians to participate in official linguistic theater is the court. Here, English is "on stage" almost every day of the week. Barristers vie with one another and with magistrates in their own country in a language that is palpably not their own. "The accused may well have been mistak*een*," intones one of the legal professional players in a court "scene," with the telltale mispronunciation and misplaced syllabic stress of a Francophone still wrestling with English. The magistrate instructs one of the barristers, "You should not flog a dead horse," in grammar that is perfect but with an intonation that bespeaks school-learned rote more than current or spontaneous English idiomatic usage.[31]

A report prepared by the Mauritius Examinations Syndicate (1992) provides a quasi-official assessment of the role of the English language within this officially Anglophone nation: "it is currently understood and written but not widely spoken.

Moreover, the increasingly predominating role of French in our everyday communication is further reducing the use of English (MES 1992, 7).

Remarkably, the only exclusively English newspaper in Mauritius—*News on Sunday*—was launched (by a Scotsman, Mike Lynch) as recently as 1996. Its fortieth issue anniversary was the occasion for a ceremony attended by diplomatic representatives of India, Australia, the United States, and Great Britain—whose British Council provided start-up assistance. Michael Bootle, the British Council director in Mauritius, later explained his support for the paper in terms of "linguistic balance," adding that "the use of English and French offers the country enormous trading advantages." Yet he is also quoted in the same article to the effect that French-language dominance "complicates the linguistic situation in Mauritius and contributes to a veritable muddle for schoolchildren."[32]

In a private interview, Bootle was less diplomatic. "In the early 1980s, the French tried to buy the [Mauritian] school system.... They bought television broadcasting, by providing free programming, state of the art equipment." Rivalry between British and French agents of culture did exist, Bootle believed, notwithstanding his newspaper's quoted remarks: there is a "policy attempt by the French to take over." Still, Bootle claimed that the use of English was understated in Mauritius, and would be reinforced as three sectors grow on the island: commerce, tourism, and computing. Whereas France promoted its language in Mauritius, he claimed, "use of English is a Mauritian matter."[33] As for the editor of a leading French-language newspaper, "*News on Sunday* is a reaction to the overly stifling presence of French."[34]

English-French Linguistic Cohabitation

The unique form of British colonialism in Mauritius fostered a linguistic climate that not only preserved French but also encouraged the development of Frenglish. Throughout British colonial rule, French in Mauritius was considered the "language of resistance." For those whose job it is to maintain and expand its superiority over English, it still may be. But for an increasing number of local users of both languages, English and French are cohabiting quite comfortably—often in the same sentences. Such "linguistic cohabitation" (Miles 1998) is not unique and is well known to those familiar with Canadian French. That it occurs in speech is not surprising; it is, after all, the familiar process of creolization, a hallmark of Mauritian language. That "Mauritian Frenglish" should also occur in the print media exemplifies a noteworthy aspect of Mauritian linguistic development.

Several categories of Frenglish in the Mauritian press can be identified. The first relates to government institutions and activities that still reflect the British colonial makeover of Mauritius. Thus, "le *Chairman* ne peut aller à l'encontre des décisions du *Board*" and "des cas pareils seront étudiés alors par le *High Powered Committee*."[35] Job descriptions similarly retain Anglophone provenance (e.g., "le *Supervising Officer* du ministère concerné"). Legal terms, even in popular newspapers, resist translation: "pour publication alléguée de *false news* le magistrat a decidé que l'affaire soit *dismissed*." Technical jargon is impervious to French translation: "aprés examen au Casualty [the patient] a été *discharged*."

Politics is rife with Frenglish: "Jugnauth est prêt pour un *come-back*"; "L'Histoire jugera s'il a suffisament de *guts* de perdre le pouvoir mais sauver à terme le pays." Feminism remains curiously Anglophone ("Qu'on homme défende les *gender issues* peut surprendre"), but beauty tips are also linguistically mixed (*News Beauté* feature: "*Do's and Don'ts* des seins.")

Mauritian journalism (in French) accordingly both sounds and looks quite different from that prevailing in nearby Réunion. Depending on the subject, conversation in Mauritian French also distinguishes itself from Réunion French by the amount of English that punctuates speech. Sequential colonialism has created in Mauritius a society that is not only comfortable with both English and French languages (albeit at starkly varying levels of proficiency), but easily interlays English vocabulary within French words. It also creates infinite possibilities for bilingual humor. Example: Is the ambivalent relationship between political rivals Bérenger and Ramgoolam one where they "agree" to disagree or just plain *aigris* (i.e., sour)?

What Kind of Sisters? Mauritius and Réunion

When the term *îles soeurs* (sister islands) is used in the context of the French West Indies, it refers to Martinique and Guadeloupe, both overseas departments of France. In the Indian Ocean, however, the same expression couples an overseas department (Réunion) with an independent republic (Mauritius).

The surface similarities between the erstwhile Ile Bourbon (Réunion) and Isle de France (Mauritius) are multiple. They are of comparable size (970 and 720 square miles, respectively), and volcanic in origin (although Réunion is more mountainous). Neither was populated prior to European settlement. Slavery and plantation economy defined both early on. Both islands are constituted by peoples originally hailing from France, India, Africa, and China, thereby giving rise to the only "indigenous" group among them: Creoles. Creolization has been much more pronounced in Réunion, however, given the continuous French colonial emphasis on assimilation.[36]

The political age of the two is worth recalling. Réunion had been a French department for twenty-two years (following three centuries of colonial status) when, in 1968, Mauritius became independent (following one century of French rule and a century and a half of British). Separated by only one hundred miles (and therefore three times closer to each other than Rodrigues is to Mauritius), Réunion and Mauritius have maintained an ambivalent relationship. These are "sisters" whose colonial "parents" have treated them quite differently.[37]

Mother France so coddled elder daughter Réunion that, upon approaching the age of adolescence, she decided to remain forever with Maman (who vastly increased her allowance, ensuring a rather comfortable lifestyle.) Younger Mauritius, hapless child of a custody dispute, found herself adopted by a rather aloof and somewhat stingy British father. When Mauritius approached maturity, her tightwad of a dad encouraged her to leave home and strike off on her own.

Living alone was rather rough during the first ten years of her independence, until Mauritius found a better way to make a living. Now somewhat well off, and relatively secure in her sense of self and self-success, Mauritius nevertheless remains the poorer of the two sisters. Réunion remains haughty: she never lost the full Mascarene attention of Maman. Both daughters identify affectively with their colonial birth mother, and are on speaking terms with each other (although Mauritius's speech is inflected by her latterly British upbringing.) But the visits are always fraught with conflicting emotions. Réunion flaunts her wealth and uninterrupted relationship with Maman; Mauritius resents the unwarranted haughtiness of her big sister, taking quiet comfort in the pride of self-reliance.

"In general, Réunionnais love France while loving less the Frenchman," notes Jean-Georges Prosper (1993). "Is it because the Réunionnais must call himself French without entirely being so?" As for his own countrymen's comparable relationships: "The Mauritian generally loves the Frenchman, while loving France less."

Commercial and communication ties between the two islands are considerable: tourism, which constitutes a significant portion of the Mauritian economy, is in significant part bolstered by visitors from Mauritius (Miles 1996). Despite two common languages (French and Creole), the actual level of knowledge about each other's society is relatively limited. "The islands of the [Indian] Ocean only exceptionally share information on television. In ordinary times, they ignore each other superbly" (Varondin 1994).

"No great history of love, but a multiplicity and diversity of relationships," is how one Mauritian newspaper summed up the Réunion-Mauritius connection.[38] A parliamentarian from Réunion is reputed to have evoked this proverb to address the same issue: "There is no marriage between carp and rabbit."[39] A leading French magazine nuanced the pat image of "sister islands" by informing readers that these are *fausse jumelles*—biological twins, perhaps, but not identical ones (Grollier 1996). In Réunion, one writer went so far as to challenge the very image of sister island by downgrading the relationship to that of cousins (Jay 1996). Some Réunionnais caricature Mauritians by borrowing the old (French) stereotype of Belgians: a naïve bumpkin with a funny accent and tendency to brag (Jay 1996). Mauritians riposte to such stereotypes in terms that conjure images of the ugly American: the Réunnionais tourist is loud, indiscreet, a show-off, and childish (Quirin 1996).

And what of the characterization of Mauritians as "Belgians"? A Mauritian living in Réunion proudly pronounced herself to carry the label of "Belgian cousin by independence" rather than being "French by dependence."[40] Such are the Indian Ocean exchanges between islanders—Francophones all—of a sovereign developing nation and those of an overseas French department. Only because they are French citizens, it is said, can Réunionnais allow themselves to mock Mauritians. They also manifest their superiority complex by systematically asking, when in Mauritius, if their sister-cousins are happy with their independence. Underlining the question are the economic implications; the oft-repeated cliché is that the unemployed Réunionnais "earns" more than the Mauritian worker.

The legacies of colonial maritime partition emerge quite visibly between Mauritius and Réunion. Despite longstanding demographic and economic interpenetrations (Wanquet 1985), official and institutional contacts between the two are relatively recent. It took a full twenty years between the independence of Mauritius—that is, forty-two years after Réunion became a département of France, before a Mauritian head of government would visit the "sister island."[41] Mauritians attribute this long delay to irrational fears: "As if we Mauritians, independent, had scabies, and they [the Réunnionais] had to avoid all contact, for fear of independentist contamination" (Cateaux 1988). At this same time, another Mauritian newspaper, while noting the mutual respect that was developing (Mauritian appreciation for infrastructure and services delivery in Réunion, Réunionnais acknowledgment of Mauritius as an economic "Little Tiger" with a distinct political culture), could not help but add: "Réunionnais, falling all over themselves with their hard cash, have tended to see Mauritians as underdeveloped. Mauritians, for their part, have looked upon Réunionnais as people without talent."[42]

Despite linguistic and cultural similarities bequeathed by history and geography, partition and psychology have given rise to significant mental and jurisprudential barriers between the one "sister" island that is a French overseas department and the other that is a member of the British Commonwealth. In numerous failed attempts to obtain the official views of the Ministry of External Relations regarding Mauritius-Réunion, I was met with this multiply revealing response in Mauritian Frenglish: "We have no relations with Réunion. Tout passe par Paris."

Regionalization, Indianization, and Globalization

Mauritius's legacy of Franco-British colonialism, upon which was added a thick layer of Indianité, has bestowed upon it an exceptionally diverse standing in the regional and international community. Through its colonial and linguistic hybridity, Mauritius is a comfortable member of both the Commonwealth and the Organisation Internationale de la Francophonie. As a founding member in 1995 of the M-7 group of maritime neighbors, Mauritius (along with India, South Africa, Australia, Oman, Singapore, and Kenya) has expanded into the eighteen-state Indian Ocean Rim Association for Regional Cooperation (IOR-ARC) founded in 1984. Except for Madagascar, it is the only IOR-ARC member with a Francophone populace.[43] Fostering trade and economic cooperation is IOR-ARC's major objective.

As a regional player, Mauritius is perhaps most invested in the Indian Ocean Commission (IOC), whose headquarters (like of the IOR-ARC) it hosts. Founded in 1984 to promote regional cooperation (especially economic development), IOC is a signature Francophone association, uniting Mauritius with the Comoros, Madagascar, the Seychelles and—so as to represent Réunion—France. (Were it not for France's membership, this would be a purely island nation club.)

Unlike Vanuatu, which also benefits from multiple regional memberships through its geographic location, Mauritius has the material means to participate fully in its respective organizations. With business and government cadres who are fully bilingual in English and French, Mauritius has positioned itself as a major offshore financial services center. Tourism—a mainstay of the Mauritian economy—also benefits from easy hosting of Francophone as well as Anglophone visitors. For the period 2004–6, with an average of about 756,000 visits per annum, 40 percent of tourists to the former French-turned-British colony hailed from France (27 percent from the mainland; 13 percent from Réunion) and 25 percent from Anglophone countries (United Kingdom, 13 percent; South Africa, 8 percent; India, 4 percent) (Europa 2008, 787). Its boom as a regional information technology provider is explained by "the bilingual nature of its workforce in providing IT services on to francophone Africa, in co-operation with Indian expertise (Europa 2008, 779–80). Bilingual colonial legacies also impart a comparative advantage to Mauritius as an up-and-coming call center.

By taking control over Mauritius from the French, the British precluded the kind of extreme assimilation policies that would characterize colonialism in nearby Réunion and in the otherwise similar Antilles. As in the West Indies, independence in Mauritius would entail a lower standard of living than would statehood in France but a higher degree of political, institutional, and cultural autonomy and distinctiveness. The forced merger of Pondicherry into independent India, on the other hand, created cultural and administrative enclaves whose relationship with both India and France remains a source of ambivalence. The conditions and terms of the transfer have also given rise to unique postcolonial variants on identity: French Indian. Still, there is a commonality between Pondichéry and Mauritius that is rather suggestive in terms of overall outcome.

Sequential and integrationist colonialism in India and the Indian Ocean have bestowed an Anglo-French legacy of hybridic colonialism. Communities of Francophones, mostly of ethnic Indian origin, operate within official institutions that are mostly of British design. And the results are generally successful. Mauritius is democratic and independent; Pondicherry is embedded within a larger democratic and independent polity. Citizens of France or not, the denizens of former French India have advantages over their co-ethnics in neighboring Indian states.

French India and the Paradox of Pondicherry

To the large numbers of Francophones of Indian origin in formerly British Mauritius should be added an even more curious colonial legacy: ethnic Indians living in India proper who hold French but not Indian citizenship. The continuity of French Indians in Britain's largest former colony presents further instances of ethnic partition based on Anglo-French rivalry, not in the Indian Ocean but in Mother India herself.

Pondichéry is the shorthand name for the enclaves scattered throughout India that France managed to hold on to beyond her eclipse by Britain and even beyond Greater India's independence in 1947. Four major ethnic groups—Bengali, Malayalam, Tamil, and Telugu—were affected by the intercolonial boundaries separating French and British zones in India. Most of those boundaries remain, grouping most of former French India into a distinct administrative unit within India—the Union Territory of Pondicherry. Within those boundaries live over ten thousand native-born Tamil and a handful of Telugus and Malayalams who are citizens not of India but of a distant France many of them have never seen. Not all can speak the language of the country whose citizenship they hold. And then there are the thousands of other Indian citizens in these same territories who are consummate Francophones but who, for reasons of quirky history and jurisprudential hazard, have less claim to French citizenship than their non-Francophone cousins.

For the first three-quarters of a century of Anglo-French rivalry in India, it was unclear which power would ultimately prevail as the dominant colonizer. François Martin's claim over the Tamil fishing village of Puducherri in 1674 on the Coromandel coast of the Bay of Bengal was followed in 1688 by the ceding of a tract of land to the French, far to the north, in the Bengali-speaking city of Chandan Nagar. These two French settlements—renamed Pondichéry and Chandernagor—initially rivaled or eclipsed their closest English counterparts, Madras and Calcutta. In fact, Madras was even captured from the British by the French in 1746.

Subsequent Anglo-French wars eventually tipped the colonial tide in India in Britain's favor. Three times the French territories were captured and held before being returned by treaty. The death knell of French military ambitions in India came with Napoleon's ill-fated dispatch of General Decaen to conquer the subcontinent in the early 1800s. The Second Treaty of Paris (1815) restored the French territories to Paris, an act that would outlive Britain's own sovereignty over India and ensure a French postcolonial legacy there. But the 1810 capitulation discussed earlier cut Pondichéry off from one of France's major Indian Ocean holdings, Mauritius.

French India was not confined to Pondichéry (capital of French India) and Chandernagor. A second possession in Tamil-speaking territory, Karikal, had been peacefully acquired in 1739. Mahé, where the Malayalam tongue prevails, was seized even earlier, in 1725. In southwest India, where the dominant ethnicity and language are Telugu, French sovereignty was recognized in Yanaon (Yanam) in 1750. French India thus entailed a par-

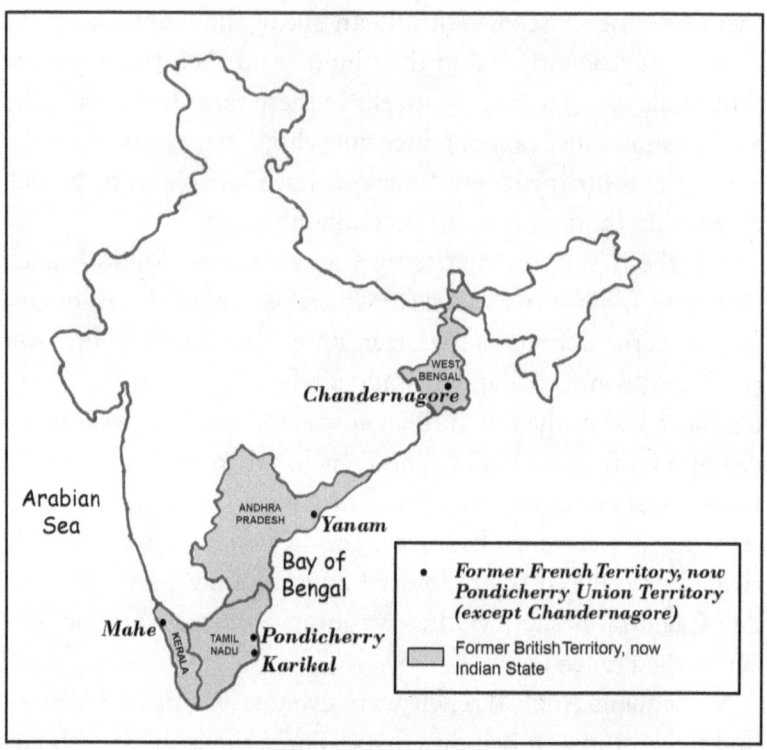

Map 15. Former Establishments of French India Located within Their Post-Merger States

tition of four ethnicities or language groups (Tamil, Bengali, Malayalam, Telugu) within five French enclaves (Pondichéry, Karikal, Chandernagor, Mahé, Yanam) adjoining British colonial administrative subregions (eventually replaced by Indian states—see Map 15).

Some of the enclaves were (and still are) subject to further internal territorial partition. Pondichéry, for example, is not only a town but a region of twelve pieces of land scattered about like a jigsaw puzzle (see Map 16).

Within two years of India's independence in 1947, France allowed the population of Chandernagor to vote on either remaining within the French Union or merging with India. The vote was overwhelmingly in favor of merger, and Chanderna-

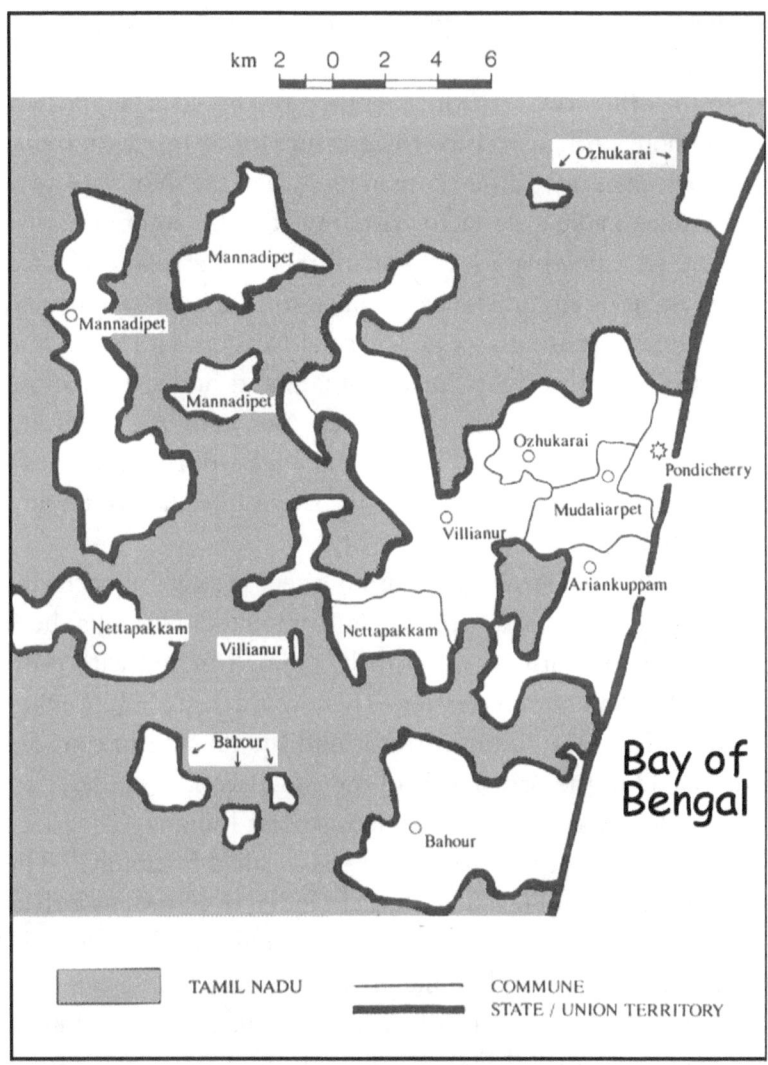

Map 16. Pondicherry Region
From *Imperial Burdens: Countercolonialism in Former French India* by William F. S. Miles (Boulder CO: Lynne Rienner Publishers, 1995), 7. Reprinted with permission.

gor eventually was incorporated into the state of West Bengal. An Indo-French Cultural Centre and Museum, and French language teachers at the ex–Collège Dupleix, valiantly strive to retain a Francophone stamp to what has become a mere suburb of metropolitan Calcutta that goes by its original name, Chandan Nagar.

In the other four territories, France and her local supporters much more strongly resisted the pressure for merger with India, with outcomes quite different than for "Chander." Not until 1954 did France make a de facto withdrawal of her administrative personnel, following a local vote of representatives conducted under dubious circumstances. France still claimed sovereignty, however, negotiating a 1956 Treaty of Cession with India that retained extensive rights for the inhabitants and special stipulations for the territories themselves. Not until 1962—fifteen years after Greater India's independence—did France ratify that treaty, marking the de jure transfer of her Indian territories to India itself.

More than a quarter of a century after "merger," French rule was still being recalled with a certain amount of nostalgia, both in comparison with nearby British colonialism and with postcolonial Indian administration. There was a degree of intimacy between European administrator and Indian subject that did not extend to the British side of the Anglo-French boundaries. As simple a matter of shaking hands with Indians—practiced by the French but not the British—is recalled favorably.[44] The diminutive size of French holdings in India, of course, as well as much more modest twentieth-century ambitions than the British had there, can explain much of the difference. So can Pondy's role as refuge for anti-British nationalists (most famously, Aurobindo Ghosh).[45] French colonialism in India was "soft" compared to that of the British, more a matter of political prestige than imperial prosperity. Yet its legacies should not be dismissed on account of its size.

One of the most significant of postcolonial legacies has been the preservation of Pondicherry, Karikal, Mahé, and Yanam as an administrative unit, distinct from neighboring Tamil Nadu, Kerala, and Andhra Pradesh. "It is better to be in a Pondicherry village today than a Tamil Nadu one," notes a denizen of the

Table 7. Material Outcomes—Former French India and Surrounding Indian States

	GDP per capita (dollars, 2006–8)	Life expectancy (years)	Adult literacy (%)
Former British colony			
Andhra Pradesh (76.2)	684	64.2	60.5
Kerala (31.8)	824	73.9	90.9
Tamil Nadu (62.4)	790	66.2	73.5
Former French colony			
Pondicherry Union Territory (0.974)	1,466	68.4	81.2

Note: Number in parentheses next to country refers to population, in millions.

Sources: Government of Andhra Pradesh (http://www.aponline.gov.in); Kerala Government—Kerala at a Glance (http://www.kerala.gov.in); Tamil Nadu Government—Tamil Nadu at a Glance (http://www.tn.gov.in); Government of Pondicherry—Puducherry at a Glance 2009 (http://statistics.puducherry.gov.in); Census of India; Profile of the Union Territory of Pondicherry, 2001–6 projections (http://ncw.nic.in/pdfReports/Gender_Profile_Pondicherry.pdf); Planning Commission of India, 2002–6 projections (http://planningcommission.nic.in/data/datatable/0904/tab_150.pdf).

region. "Salaries are higher [at least for civil servants], there is easier access to government, there are more extensive facilities provided by government. There is quicker action by government. Education is better, the police are relatively more numerous." Data tend to bear out this observation with respect to all the Indian states in which the components of former French India are physically embedded (see Table 7).

Another important legacy of former French India is the linguistic and cultural one. Both the de facto and de jure treaties bound India to retain French as an official language within the new administrative unit that would supersede the French one. Moreover, they provided for the creation of "establishments or institutions designed to prepare for degrees in French language and civilizations, in scientific research, or to promote French culture in the area of science, letters or the arts." None other than the first Indian prime minister, Jawahralal Nehru, expressed the "hope that the learning of French will continue in Pondicherry and make [it] a center in India of the French language and a window of French culture." French culture, the great Indian nationalist added, "is a great culture of the Western world."

Following from the Indo-French treaties and Nehru's Francophile sentiments, thousands[46] of young Indians pursue their education in principally in the French language. Various school systems provide this Francophone education throughout former French India: Indian government, French government, and parochial (mostly Catholic but also Muslim and ashram). Pondicherry Central University now also provides postsecondary instruction in French. Research on a wide array of topics, from Indology to irrigation, is conducted under French auspices at the Institut Français d'Indologie and the Ecole Française de l'Extême Orient. An ashram (named after Sri Aurobindo) internationalized by a Parisian (Mira Alfassa, known more popularly as "the Mother") also preserves a French flavor to Pondy. So do some charities, the Alliance Française, the St. Joseph de Cluny mission, and of course, the French consulate. The greatest postcolonial legacy, however, was the one provided by the 1956 Treaty of Cession: the option to retain French citizenship.

"French Nationals born in the territory of the Establishments and domiciled therein . . . may by means of a written declaration . . . choose to retain their nationality." No provision was made for dual nationality. Francophilia vied with fear of an unknown future, and only 6,252 persons—2 percent of eligible French Indians—took advantage of the option during the six months it was open in 1962–63. With the passage of time, however, the material advantages of French citizenship—education, pensions, welfare, migration—gave rise to greater scrutiny of another treaty stipulation: children of eligible nonresidents who became citizens of Indian, who thereby "acquired Indian nationality by reason of a decision of their parents," could, after turning eighteen, recover French nationality. More problematic was a loophole in the treaty acknowledged by French courts: offspring of French Indian mothers born just outside French Indian territory (a common practice among Hindu women from neighboring communities who returned to their parents' home for delivery) were adjudged not to be covered by the treaty. Therefore, they never lost their French citizenship. Traffic in fraudulent Tamil Nadu birth certificates allegedly ensued, a practice that the French consulate did not seriously investigate until the mid-1980s, at which point the number of Pondicherry Union Territory Indians known to be holding French citizenship was more than double (14,064 in 1984) what it had been when the option ended two decades prior. Within four years, the number decreased by seventeen hundred, largely as a result of French consular vigilance. Thousands more were struck from the rolls after a 1990 reexamination of nationality files (Gressieux 1992). Still, the existence of more than ten thousand ethnic Indians of French citizenship, residing in Pondicherry *without* Indian citizenship, is a significant postcolonial legacy (Gressieux 2005). Upwards of thirty thousand are estimated to reside in France itself. Given the intense efforts to retain French citizenship, partly as a result of French financial obligations that thereby ensue, I have proposed the paradigm of "countercolonialism" to characterize the French Indian aftermath of "soft colonialism." Countercolonialism in Pondicherry inordinately benefits French Indians vis-à-vis France, with problematic consequences for both sides.

Hybridity, Sequentialism, Countercolonialism: Implications for Postcolonial Legacies

Economically and politically, Mauritius stacks up quite favorably among the African nations with which it is, on account of its geographic proximity, more usually compared.[47]

As noted above, along with Botswana, Mauritius is often invoked as a prime example of democratic exceptionalism in the greater continent; they are the only two states with an uninterrupted record of democracy, under conditions of universal suffrage,[48] since independence. Mauritius's hyper-pluralistic society is underlain, as we have seen, with communalism, ethnoreligious favoritism, and racism; still, its structures and ethos have managed to contain these underlying tensions and to create a relatively prosperous (if not distributionally equitable) society. Along with the Seychelles (another example of sequential colonialism), Mauritius is in the high human development category of the United Nations human development index (even above Russia and Brazil). Its GDP per capita is nearly four times that of India, and more than six times that of the average for sub-Saharan Africa.

Of all the independent former French colonies examined in this book, Mauritius is by far the most materially prosperous and politically stable. Sequential and hybridic colonialism alone cannot account for Mauritian success; still, it must be incorporated as a critical factor, one that commentators on Mauritius rarely do. The flexibility of mind and language that mastering both French and English entailed has opened Mauritius to opportunities that a purely monocolonial experience would not. Sequential colonialism also created a favorable environment toward the admixture of ever more cultural and linguistic traits, as emerged with the vast migration from India. That all of this was accomplished on a colony originally based on African slaves working within a plantation economy must also be appreciated. As in the West Indies, this is a postcolonial legacy that demands continuing attention and reparation. Why legacies of slavery do not have the same psychic import in Mauritius as Martinique, for example, is a subject for further inquiry.

Colonial partition in former French India and the Indian Ocean continues to take many forms: the substate differences between the Union Territory of Pondicherry and Tamil Nadu, Andhra Pradesh and Kerala; continuance of France as a sovereign and source of national identity in Réunion, in contrast to nearby Mauritius; the unresolved fate of the Chagos Archipelago, cut off from Mauritius before independence but claimed by it afterward; and Afro-Mauritians of indeterminate ethnic origin, unrecognizable as actual Africans, who became a minority as a result of British takeover from the French. Ravi (2010) invokes literary sources to illustrate how, over time, the once permeable cultural borders in Mauritius and Pondicherry became rigid and reified.

In a world linguistically dominated by Anglicization, Mauritius is a rare counterexample of a society that freely chooses, upon a foundation of Kreol, to cultivate and innovate its own brand of Francophonie. That it thereby leapfrogs a more recent history of British colonialism, and does so absent any explicit domestic state policy, is curious. That it perpetuates French while simultaneously preserving indigenous Asian languages is especially intriguing.

Under certain conditions, postcolonial legacies are strongest when they are the least coercive. Where French colonialism encountered Hindu cultures, the scars of partition are relatively benign. Be it in the Indian Ocean or in India itself, Anglo-French division has given way to salutary, mostly Indian, blends.

6
Mainland Southeast Asia and the Conundrum of Communism

The Vietnamese plant rice, the Cambodians watch it grow, and the Laotians listen to it grow.
—Unattributed French maxim

In all of Southeast Asia, there is only one border that separates a former French colony from a former British one: the 150 miles of the Upper Mekong River dividing Laos from Burma/Myanmar (see Map 17).[1] Given the vast swaths of territory that came under French and British rule throughout all of Southeast Asia, this represents a surprisingly small colonial interface. Yet this diminutive borderland is today part of a very well known—indeed, notorious—region: the Golden Triangle, intricately and internationally implicated in drug trafficking, prostitution rings, and human trafficking. Ethnic rebellions and outright banditry also stoke incessant instability. Communist revolution in Laos and military dictatorship in Myanmar ostensibly negate French and British colonial legacies more than in any other region under our comparative consideration. Yet even here, the radical political outcomes are clearly if indirectly traceable to their respective colonial antecedents. They are also intimately (if ironically) bound up with classical paradigms of modernization and nation building (see Berger 2003). Indeed, Laos barely existed as a precolonial entity.

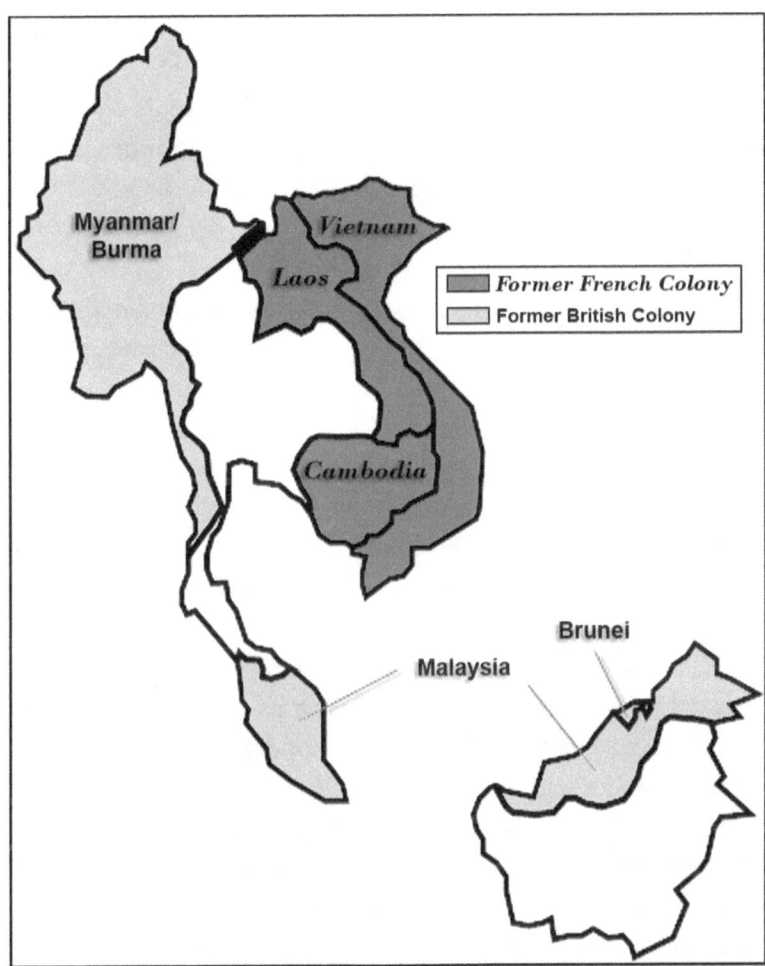

Map 17. Former French and British Colonies of Southeast Asia

Geography and History

British dominion in Southeast Asia consisted of what was then called Malaya, three parts of Borneo (including Brunei and Sarawak), and Burma (nicknamed the "Cinderella province" for its exceptionally exotic and alluring qualities). Increasingly acquired throughout the nineteenth century (including three Anglo-Burmese Wars), British-controlled territories in Southeast Asia slightly surpassed French ones in landmass; in terms of population, however, they are now only about two-thirds as large as the former French Indochina. Admittedly, distinguishing colonial Southeast Asia from South Asia is somewhat of an arbitrary academic anachronism: Burma's longstanding status as a province of colonial India, until it became a Crown Colony in 1937, created resentments, tensions, and cross-cutting loyalties that plague Myanmar to this day.

Within British Burma, the decision to expand colonial sovereignty east of the Irawaddy River also had long-term repercussions. Beyond the Irawaddy—an otherwise natural geo-cultural boundary—lay the non-Burman "hill tribes" and other ethnic minorities who distinguished themselves by their non-Burman language, non-Buddhist religions, and upper-altitude ways of life. Even combined with non-Burman ethnic minorities elsewhere in the colony, these minorities would never challenge the demographic (and political) preponderance of the Burmans (over 80 percent). But neither would they easily assimilate into the postcolonial Burmese state (population 48 million), with its Burman ethnic core.

Indochina is conveniently understood today to encompass three sovereign nations: Vietnam, Cambodia/Kampuchea, and Laos. Until France established her Southeast Asian rule in the late nineteenth century, all three were under the influence of the wider empire of Annam; imperial, pre-French Annam, for its part, was vassal to China. Prior to 1946, French Indochina was administratively divided into six territories under three juridical statuses: Cochinchina (a colony per se); Annam, Cambodia, Tonkin, and Laos (protectorates); and Kwangchowan (a leased territory) (Hall 1964). In the case of Laos, the French propped up the royal kingdom of Luang Prabang in an effort to make a case for territorial integrity, historical continuity, and political legitimacy. Kwangchowan was returned to China in 1946. Amalgamation of the "protectorates" of Annam and Tonkin, along with Cochinchina, into the Government-General of Indochina in 1887 heralded the modern nation of Vietnam. Following the anarchy that World War II unfurled, it was again subject to

Table 8. Material Outcomes—Southeast Asia

	GNI per capita (dollars, 2011)	Life expectancy (years)	Adult literacy (%)
Former British colonies			
Brunei (0.4)	45,753	78.0	92.7
Burma/Myanmar (50)	1,535	65.2	89.9
Malaysia (27.4)	13,685	74.2	88.7
Singapore (5.3)	52,569	81.1	92.5
Former French colonies			
Cambodia/Kampuchea (15)	1,848	63.1	73.6
Laos (6.3)	2,242	67.5	73.0
Vietnam (91.5)	2,805	75.2	94.0

Note: Number in parentheses next to country refers to population, in millions.

Sources: UN Data, Country Profiles (http://data.un.org); UNDP Human Development Index, 2011; CIA *World Factbook* (http://www.cia.gov).

splintering, this time along latitudinal (north–south) and ideological (Cold War) lines. Unification of Vietnam, which marked the end of U.S. military involvement in Indochina, culminated in 1974. Former French Indochina encompasses nearly 300,000 square miles and a population of 100 million.

As with Burma in British Southeast Asia, a multitude of ethnic groups characterized French Indochina writ large and Laos within it. Hmong and ethnic Chinese are only the most publicized of aggrieved minorities to uneasily coexist within their states of record. Fostering national identity has been more of a challenge in Laos than in Vietnam and Cambodia: whereas Vietnamese and Cambodians number over 90 percent in Vietnam and Cambodia, the Lao in Laos are just over 50 percent. In Laos, violence still is the fate of some settlements of Hmong, a group upon whom we shall not dwell here (for they were not partitioned into Burma) but who should nevertheless not be forgotten.

There are no archetypal nations, and the Laos-Burma comparison is no stand-in for colonialism throughout Southeast Asia writ large. French colonialism and its postcolonial aftermath was not the same in Laos as in Vietnam, any more than that Myanmar mirrors Malaya. Postcolonial material outcomes throughout the repartitioned region have been quite diverse (see Table 8).

But with respect to the delineation of boundaries and their long-term consequences, what happened here *is* quite typical. As perhaps the foremost expert on Myanmar has put it, "The European introduction of rigidly demarcated boundaries, to which power and sovereignty horizontally radiated and which was based on political and sometimes geographic circumstances, failed to consider the ethnicity or other forms of self-identification among the peoples of the region. . . . There is no country in Southeast Asia that is essentially homogeneous in ethnicity or language" (Steinberg 2001, 182).

Colonial Policy in Burma and Laos

While cognizant of shared colonial interests (primarily economic but also tactically political), most historians of Southeast Asian colonialism are members of the "difference" school. In terms of modalities of domination, structures of material extraction, and "social interference" (culture, religion, education), France and Britain pursued different policies.[2] To be sure, those policies were dynamic, reacting to circumstances as they emerged in the colonies, back in the metropoles, in the world at large. But any such reforms that accordingly crystallized were minor within the wider objective of preserving (distinct) French and British processes of control.

While Indirect Rule was explicit British policy throughout Southeast Asia, only in Malaya did it come close—for a time—to fulfilling its overall promise of local self-rule under an indigenous system of government. *Within* colonies, the British formally applied Indirect Rule to specific regions while retaining centralized control in others. Thus, five out of nine Malay states opted out of the federation that the British set up in 1896 to more uniformly and "rationally" govern them, while in Burma Indirect

Rule was officially extended only to non-ethnic Burman states and territories: those of the Chin, Kachin, Karen/ni, and most significantly, the Shan. In 1935 their special status was reaffirmed as "reserved subjects," separate from the colonial structures governing the Burman Burmese themselves: thus was the famous "dual mandate" enacted—to develop "native" peoples while protecting them. After independence, Burmese practice would mock that colonial policy. In so-called Burma proper, whose Buddhist heartland was the Irawaddy Valley, colonial policy resembled more the Direct Rule of the French than Britain's indirect one. A prime example is in 1886, when colonial rulers disestablished the monarchy. The resulting disruption of authority at both the local and central levels would have dire consequences after independence.

Still, despite the wide-ranging inconsistencies within British colonies of Southeast Asia with respect to self-rule and autonomy, as compared with the French in the region, was a distinction that did make a difference: l'Indochine was run throughout as "a highly centralized system of government without even a semblance of local autonomy." Even where traditional hierarchies and monarchies were officially retained (Annam and Tonkin in Vietnam, for instance, and Luang Prabang in Laos), it was a case of the disingenuous indigenous façade: "indirect rule was hardly different from direct rule." We need not endorse Jan Pluvier's invective that, even before the colonial war in Indochina, "French rule in Indochina represented the climax of colonial ruthlessness in South-East Asia" to accept the thesis of substantive colonial policy differences from the (not entirely consistent) British (Pluvier 1974, 11, 14, 21).[3]

Doumer's ghost assured that assimilation trumped association. Paul Doumer had been the colonial governor-general whose original template for Indochina, laid out during his 1897–1902 tenure, was *dirigiste* to the extreme, "thoroughly autocratic." Even if some higher-ranking colonials came to appreciate local culture (Evans 2002, 68), complete domination and incorporation by France within its empire remained the unwavering policy (Pluvier 1974, 19).

With respect to minority groups, the French initially dichotomized the peoples of colonial Laos into two broad racial groups: Tai (lowland Lao) and Kha (highland minorities). Kha was a "pseudo-scientific category" that came to take on self-identificational and postcolonial reality (Pholsena 2006, 27).

Colonialism Interruptus

Japanese occupation of Southeast Asia during World War II had a profound long-term effect on both French and British colonialism. In both Laos and Burma, the displacement of European overlords by Asian ones engendered nationalist aspirations that colored postwar politics. For some Burmese and Laotians, such nationalism would take on ideologically revolutionary (*qua* communist) overtones. On account of a critical difference between French and British attitudes toward their respective colonial "obligations" (the former ready to reassume, the latter prepared to jettison), postwar struggles for independence followed contrasting paths.

France's defeat in 1940 and the lengthy perpetration of a coercive, repressive Vichy government in Indochina under Admiral Jean Decoux bequeathed an indirect ally to Japan (Jennings 2001a, 2001d). It also sowed the seeds for a virulent postcolonial rebellion. Until March 1945, in exchange for titular French sovereignty Japan enjoyed territorial rights, which she used to aggrandize conquest in the region. In that final year of the war even the fig leaf of French rule was removed; in the meantime, Japan had successfully occupied Burma. Both there (where an anti-British fighting force arose, the Burmese Independence Army) and in Laos, Japan imparted unprecedented decision-making powers to local administrators. Such changes bordered on virtual independence for both these European colonies (Christie 1996, 14). The loss of French territory in Laos to Thailand in 1941 reinforced the feeling of European fragility in mainland Southeast Asia. So did local harsh Vichy treatment of European Gaullists (Jennings 2001a, 144).

The war divided the populations of Laos and Burma into pro-Western versus pro-Japanese camps. Allied resistance strategies stoked such cleavages. In Laos, the Free French suddenly viewed ethnic minorities in isolated mountain regions as potential fulcrums for guerilla warfare. So did the Anglo-American Allies in Burma. (The British military also capitalized on local ideological antipathy for the Japanese to coordinate operations with Burmese Communists.)

When the war ended, reuniting neighboring indigenous populaces that had been divided within colonies by the Japanese interregnum became a key nationalist, anticolonial objective. The Anti-Fascist Peoples Freedom League (AFPFL), founded by Aung San, was the Burmese expression of such a movement. AFPFL's aim was clear: independence for Burma. Although Britain had stoked protectionist hopes among the ethnic minorities who had fought loyally beside her against the Japanese, after the war Britain had no stomach to resist the (Burman-led) AFPFL. Even before Aung San's assassination in 1947, British administrators anticipated that the fate of the hill tribes in an independent and federal Burma would not be pretty. Yet Britain bowed to the inevitable: reasserting British colonial sovereignty over Burma was no more realistic than resisting the steamroller toward Indian independence.

Impossible n'est pas français goes a common, cocky Gallic expression. One can easily adapt the phrase and the thinking behind it to state that "The French do not accept the 'inevitable.'" In terms of postwar Indochinese French strategy, national honor demanded reassertion of colonial sovereignty. Laos as such may not have galvanized the Fourth Republic; as an extension of Vietnam, however, it was not to be abandoned.

Postwar Paths toward Decolonization

Following the Japanese interregnum, post–World War II resistance to the restoration of colonial rule was accordingly greater in Indochina than in Burma or Malaya. Even before the Viet

Minh became the famous lightening rod for anti-French resistance in Vietnam, the Lao Issara guerilla movement had garnered substantial support among anti-French and antiroyal hill peoples in Laos. Its defeat by the French would hardly be the end of anticolonial activity.

"Independence" came to Laos in varying stages: in 1949 as part of the French Union; in 1953 from a Royal Lao treaty with France; in 1954 as byproduct of the Geneva Agreements; in 1975 as the Lao People's Democratic Republic. Decolonization is better understood as a process than an event, one which, in the Laotian case, encompassed guerilla insurgency against the French (after the Lao Issara, by the Pathet Lao), Pathet Lao participation in the Vietnamese war (enduring the U.S. secret bombing campaign), forced deposition and internment of the last remaining royal family (of Luang Prabang), and consolidation of Communist Party rule. Whether to include post–Cold War economic reform as part of Laos's history of "decolonization" is an intriguing proposition. Much hinges on the weight given to the "inevitability" (a more Marxist than French concept) of decolonization in French Indochina taking a Communist form.

The strength of Laotian anti-French nationalism was surprising, given the country's overall benign neglect by the French. Pax Gallica entailed stability and peace, the likes of which the subjected peoples had not experienced in the two precolonial centuries. Beyond the basic Hobbesian benefit of the Leviathan, Laos was the backwater of French colonialism in Indochina. It hosted relatively few colonial officials, and these viewed the colony more as an opportunity for personal recreation than territorial transformation. "Laos was usually considered a dead-end colonial posting" (Evans 2002, 61). Actual administration of Laos was more often than not the province of educated Vietnamese, some of whom had even less truck with *mission civilisatrice* than the French themselves. "French rule dwelt lightly on the Lao states so that . . . they remained little exploited and therefore little developed. . . . In the twilight of French rule the country and its people were little changed from what they had been two generations earlier when the French presence was foisted upon them" (Tate 1979, 404). The ironic result—similar to what we have seen in the South Pacific for Vanuatu—is that "in failing to develop Laos for the benefit of either France or Vietnam, the French by chance preserved Laos for the Lao" (Stuart-Fox 1997, 136).

Although not simple or bloodless, in retrospect decolonization in Burma appears more linear (even if less complete in many portions of Myanmar). On January 4, 1948, as a result of the Attlee–Aung San Agreement of the previous year, Burma became independent. This followed postwar years of nationalist agitation among civil servant, police, trade union, and oilfield laborers. This agitation would abate after independence. What would not abate were pre-independence resistance movements mounted by a host of ethnic minorities, most notably the Karen, Shan, Mon, and Chin. A succession of military regimes and purges, with contradictory implications for opium cultivation and drug trafficking, would insulate Burma from democratic protesters (led by Aung San's daughter, Daw Aung San Suu Kyi). Democratic versus militaristic tensions would culminate in the 1988 coup that installed the State Law and Order Restoration Council (SLORC). A year later—invoking anticolonial etymology—the SLORC would change the country's name from Burma (a British toponym) to Myanmar (a Burman place name). (SLORC would later rebaptize itself the State Peace and Development Council, or SPDC.)

Socialist but not Communist, since independence successive governments of Myanmar/Burma have pursued internal policies of "revolutionary" change with little interference from external powers—a marked contrast with Laos, which has been strongly marked by postcolonial interference by France, the United States, Vietnam, the USSR, and China. Myanmar was the textbook example of autarchy: a regime that deliberately perpetrated its own isolation (economic as well as political) from the rest of the world. Even if some kind of reopening began in 1988 (Steinberg

2001, 16), the regime's 2008 resistance to accepting international humanitarian aid in the wake of devastating Cyclone Nargis reaffirmed its radically xenophobic stance. As much as France invests substantial resources, in the name of la Francophonie, to reestablish a place of prominence in Laos, Britain (one hesitates to employ the "great" in this context) has basically wiped its hands of its once-upon-a-colonial-time Cinderella dominion.

Allegations of lingering repression of the Hmong in Laos elicit occasional diplomatic protest, if not by the French than by the Americans. Civil conflict in Myanmar continued unabated, at least until a liberalization that began in 2011 when Daw Aung San Suu Kyi's long-stifled democracy movement, the National League of Democracy (NLD), was allowed to participate in elections and Suu Kyi herself was elected to parliament. But NLD vs. SLORC is mostly an intra-Burman conflict, resolution of which is unlikely to heal the unheroic ethnic heritage of British colonialism in Burma.

Artificial Identities

More so than Vietnam or even Cambodia, the very concept of "Laos" was tenuous, a creation of a Frenchman-gone-native, Charles Rochet. Rochet, through the written word, formal education, and public demonstrations, mobilized the population from Phong Saly in the north to Champassak in the south to think of themselves as a single people. Given previous colonial policy to turn Indochinese ricemen into Frenchmen,[4] one might think such a nationalist agenda to be contradictory, if not outright subversive. But Rochet (acting under instructions from governor-general Admiral Decoux) was actually saving Laos—for France—from an irridentist movement emanating from Thailand during World War II. He was also serving the interests of Vichy's wider colonial strategies (Jennings 2001a, 2002b). The Lao were ethnically and primordially Tai, went the pan-Thai movement, and the only natural homeland for Tai peoples, regardless of colonial boundaries, was Thailand.

Historically if not ethnically, there is a defensible foundation to the argument that Laos was an artificial European construct. Prior to France's conquest of eastern Indochina (the territories that would become Vietnam), except for those peoples acknowledging fealty to the kingdom of Luang Prabang there was little political unity, much less national identity. France coveted Laos less for what it was than for where it was—a corridor to the trading prize of China (despite expeditions that showed its impracticability) and a bulwark against British expansion from Burma. Hence, the fierceness of competition along the very lines of contact: the Mekong River in the Golden Triangle, where France could show its colonial face both to its British nemesis and to the local imperium: Siam. By wresting Lao territory from Siam (and this did entail outright warfare in 1884–85), the French unwittingly put into a motion a process that would lead to Laotian identity. This was a rather ironic outcome, given that the mid-level justification for conquering Laos was to "round out" Indochina (and then "unblock" Laos) with Vietnam as fulcrum (Stuart-Fox 1995, 119, 123). Laos was doubly subjected: to the French and to the Vietnamese.

Only toward the end of the colonial era did the French begin to address, as a matter of systematic policy, the reality of ethnic diversity. From the multiplicity of tribes and clans, numbering in the hundreds, the French constructed—and the Royal Lao regime accepted—three globalizing categories, based on ascending altitude: Lao Lum (lowlanders), Lao Theung (mountain slopers), and Lao Sung (highlanders). In a process of insurrectional jujitsu, the anti-French Pathet Lao appropriated the categories to recruit insurgents from the latter two ethnic clusters, thereby opposing not only the ethnic Europeans but also the royalist populations defending the lowlander monarchy.

Particular circumstances in each indigenous society "determined when precisely in the twentieth century the British would pull out of her Southeast Asian colonies" (Pluvier 1974, 7). In Burma, outright rebellion (the Saya San in the early 1930s and the Thakins in the late 1930s) had to be repressed. But for Britain, formal decolonization was inevitable throughout the region and she accordingly "prepared" her wards via training programs in governance and sovereignty. Britain also worked tirelessly to identify local elites with whom she could foster "collaborative relationships" (Hack 2003, 119). British decolonizers assumed that given the right successors, parliamentary democracy was the logical and preferable path to postcolonialism. They were partially right, but what was to work in Malay(si)a would not take root in Burma.

Neither Britain in Burma nor France in Laos resolved the inherited antipathy between lowlander aspirants of national power (ethnic Burmese and Lao) and the ethnic minorities (often hill peoples) under whose uneasy sovereignty they were to fall. Indeed, colonialism exacerbated these tensions. In the case of Burma, resistance from among the latter has basically gone unabated since 1948. In Laos, lines of conflict were complexified by a revolutionary ideology, embodied by the Pathet Lao, that combined Lao nationalism with an Indochinese version of Marxist-Leninist communalism. Although Laos formally became independent in 1953–54,[5] anticolonial politics continued as part of the wider war with Western powers and their proxies for another two decades. Culminating in the 1975 revolution that elevated the Communists to power (and completely dismantled the last Lao monarchy, based in Luang Prabang), the new government espoused a rhetoric of national development for all Laotians, Lao and non-Lao alike. Economic liberalization in the late 1980s brought about a kind of Indochinese *glasnost* that has laid bare some of the contradictions in this policy. Albeit in less reified form than during French colonialism, there persists in Laos an unequal power relationship between the one/majority and the other/minorities (Pholsena 2006). Market reforms notwithstanding, Myanmar and Laos have the lowest human development rankings of all former British and French Southeast Asian colonies: 131 and 135, respectively.

Colonial Convergence Point: The Golden Triangle

The expression "Golden Triangle" more commonly evokes images of lawlessness and drug-running than colonial-era boundary drawing. There is good reason for this: the cultivation and manufacture of opium, heroine, and metamphetamines has dramatic contemporary consequences on societies grappling with controlled substances coming from Southeast Asia to the United States. Yet beyond topographical factors favoring the Golden Triangle's nefarious agriculture, colonial boundary drawing also had a hand in creating an anarchic zone beyond the purview of governments. For the Golden Triangle is at the periphery of four states[6] whose borders were in large part determined by France and Great Britain.

From the middle to the late nineteenth century, the French and British vied with each other for commercial entrée into southern China at Yunnan. They also jockeyed for position, influence, and territory in those lands bordering Yunnan. Complicating their competition was the existence of a relatively strong kingdom, that of northern Siam (Thailand). Although European imperial nibbling at the outskirts of the Thai kingdom was possible, there was no question of annexing Thailand outright. Colonial rivalry here was "a mixture of African 'scramble' and central Asian 'great game'" (Keay 2005, 289).[7]

Initially, when the British had taken over the upper Burmese kingdom of Ava, military advisors recommended that the Salween River, not the Mekong, serve as Burma's eastern boundary. They were overruled for political reasons, a decision requiring the additional acquisition in 1890 of Keng Tung (Hall 1964, 653). We have both contemporary accounts of that Mekong Delta rivalry (Lefèvre [1898] 1995; Lefèvre-Pontalis [1902] 2000) as well as subsequent reconstructions (Goldman 1972; Walker 1999). Eventually, British pressure from the west through India into Burma and French expansion from the eastern edge of Indochina converged along the Mekong River and northern Thailand. Exploratory missions of French vice-consul Auguste Pavie imparted the first firm boundaries to the entity we now call Laos. Yet more important than the actual lines drawn was the concept of fixed territorial boundaries. Indigenous governance (the mandala system) allowed for two or even three overlapping suzerains over the same territory (*song fai fa* and *sam fai fa*.)

This conceptual superimposition entailed two major upshots to this tug-of-colony. First is that the Mekong itself, which had functioned both as a kind of aquatic highway and bridge for the local populations, beginning in 1893 was transformed into a demarcation of European sovereignties.[8] (This did not stop France from demanding that, where the Mekong separated it from Thailand, a twenty-five-kilometer demilitarized strip extend along the west bank. Moreover, the French invoked extraterritoriality over their indigenous subjects in this zone.) Stuart-Fox writes that, for the Lao in particular, the Mekong had been "the central artery of their political space." Now it was their territorial end point.

The second upshot was the creation of the only border in all of Southeast Asia that separated a British colony, Burma, from a French one, Laos.[9] As with most superimposed colonial boundaries from this era, decolonization reified the partition rather than transcending it.

Prior to European French colonization, the Mekong-as-Later-Boundary flowed through the indigenous polities of Nan (a major northern Siamese center), Keng Tung (within the Shan territories), and Muang Sing (which by the time of European colonialism had become tributary to Keng Tung) (see Map 18). The history of Muang Sing evokes the arbitrary indigenous outcome of the use of the Mekong as partition.

Originally founded on the east bank of the Mekong in the fourteenth century by a Lue (Lü) royal from Sip Song Panna, Muang Sing was moved in the mid-1800s to the west side of the river. Had it remained there, the French either would have

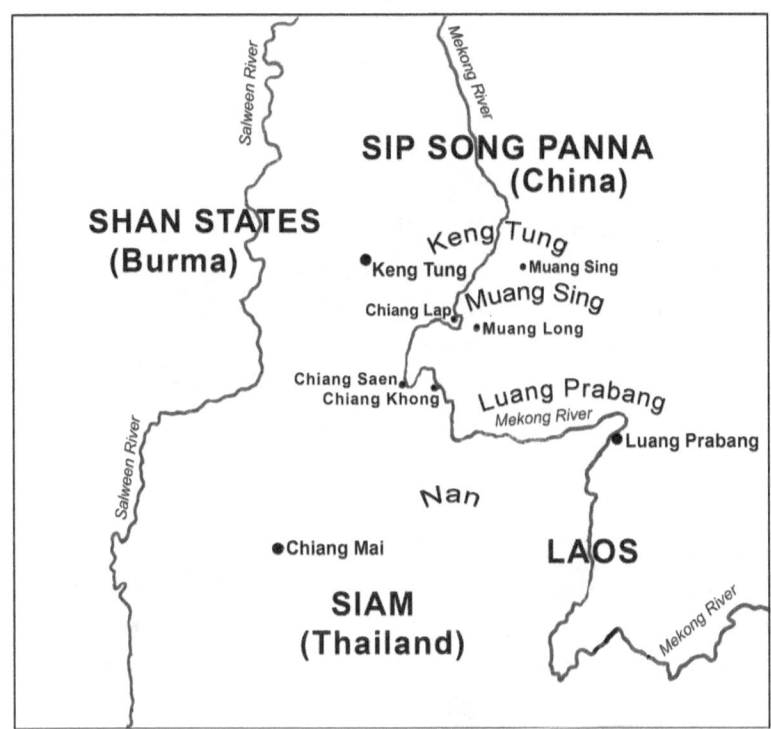

Map 18. Precolonial Mekong Polities

argued that the Mekong was an insufficient frontier or would have been frustrated with an even more diminished northwestern Indochina frontier. But in 1885, under the Cao Fa (King) Silinor, the Muang Sing capital moved yet again across the Mekong, this time nearly forty miles inland.

Beyond Muang Sing, Shan-Siamese warfare in the first half of the nineteenth century had resulted in the depopulation of much of the jungle territory. Following the Battle of Vientiane in 1828, Siam specifically evicted indigenous Lao dwellers east of the Mekong. This demographic vacuum was partially filled by upland Lahu and particularly, on both sides of Mekong, lowland Shan. For northern Laos, the most important caravan route was the overland path between Muang Sing and Chiang Lap (Keng Lap), along the Mekong.

In today's language, we might say that precolonial sovereignty over Muang Sing was "outsourced" to three local polities (Keng Tung, Nan, and Chiang Mai) by their own respective contractors: Burma (subcontracting to Keng Tung) and Siam. In local parlance, Muang Sing was a *muang sam fai fa*, "a principality under three overlords" (Cohen 1998, 50). (So was Luang Prabang, subject to Hue, Bangkok, and Beijing.) Which one of these indigenous overlords had "owned" Muang Sing would become a source of contention for the colonial powers jockeying to extend their own imperial rule. *Sam fai fa* was incomprehensible to the European colonial mind more used to a spatial "this side, that side" conception of sovereignty than a notion of multiple overrule.

Silinor's own home *muang* was to fall, just a few years after his cross-Mekong resettlement, under the British as part of Burma. He could not have foreseen this imperial outcome; however, he probably would not have regretted his capital move. When it came to participating in the contest between French and British, he weighed in on the side of the latter. Inasmuch as there are ample accounts from European protagonists and their historical chroniclers of this episode (cf., for example, Le Boulanger 1931; Jeshurun 1977; Grabowsky 1999), it is worth the space to provide a local account of how partition played itself out in this locality. It was related to me in 2005 via translator by sixty-two-year-old three-time former mayor of Muang Sing, Khamkeo, based on his own Lao transcription from Touathari. Invocations of the *cao fa* (king) of the time refer to Oun Kham, who in 1884 moved with his people from west of the Mekong to Muang Sing. But in July 1895, "Ankit [England] came and told Muang Sing, 'Those who came from Myanmar[10] ought to return.' One-hundred-fifty British soldiers came to back up the demand. The Cao Fa of Muang Sing disliked Ankit, so in 1896 he asked the Farong [French] into his territory. Farong said to Ankit: 'I come by invitation of the Cao Fa.' Ankit responded: 'I came here before you. I am not returning home.'"

The ruler strategized about an open meeting he had scheduled to gauge the (supposed) will of the people; representatives of both European powers would be present. "If I ask, 'Do you want Ankit?' then remain silent. If I ask, 'Do you want Farang,' you should raise your hands. After the meeting, Ankit and Farong conferred with each other. Ankit insisted, 'I arrived before you. So we must divide Lao country.' And that is what they did."

This local account interestingly plays up the indigenous input into the colonial line drawing. The partitioned do not see themselves as completely passive subjects of European boundary markers. (Another informant in Muang Sing, in his own oral account, inversed the usual European-dominant narrative this way: "Ankit said, 'Because the Cao Fao won't allow me to colonize Laos, then I'll colonize Burma.'" In spite, "Ankit burned down the Cao Fa's palace.")

Note that there is no mention of the Mekong River, however: sovereignty here is constructed as a matter of affinity for one colonizer over another, and colonial counterclaims over given communities, not fixed territorial lines per se. Nor is ethnicity invoked, either as a basis for resistance to the foreigner or an argument for maintaining contiguity of co-ethnics.

Local preference (or at least elite preference) for the French is not static, however. More than a century after the deed, the fickleness of political alliances (then and now!) is well appreciated.

> Of the twenty-five provinces, Ankit took thirteen, leaving Farong and Cao Fa twelve. But Cao Fa was not informed of this arrangement, and he instructed his people to borrow food and money from the English side. Ankit prevented this, saying "No borrowing here of money and food. The people here are mine."
>
> So Cao Fa asked Farong: "Why did you divide Lao country and give some to Ankit? Why did you not ask me first? I am very sore about this." To which Farong replied: "I cannot reunite Laos." From then on, Cao Fa disliked Farong and wished him badly. He even devised a plan to kill him.[11]

One would expect such resistance to colonialism to be lauded. But the account hardly idealizes the precursors to later anti-French resistance. In the oral rendition to which I was treated, a certain amount of mockery was conveyed.

> The Cao Fa invited Farong to dinner, instructing his men to hide with their swords under the dinner table to behead the French. "When I wink three times," he told them, "that is when you should kill them." But instead of arriving with just three soldiers, as had been agreed, Farong arrived with twelve additional guards—with guns. And so when Cao Fa winked, his men balked.
>
> Farong suspected something when he noticed all this winking by the Cao Fa and he queried him. Cao Fa replied that he was just not feeling well. "If you are unwell," Farong berated him, "then why do you invite us to such a banquet?" Cao Fa pretended to faint. So Farong left. Three days later, he invited the Cao Fa for dinner at the Frenchman's place. But Cao Fa knew this was a plan to assassinate him. In the middle of the night, he fled to Myanmar, and then to Sip Song Panna.

This personalized account of partition then turns tragic. It even foreshadows the demise of royalty in Laos. The possibility of French colonial remorse is evoked, even as it intimates imperial treachery.

> During his four-year exile in Sip Song Panna, Cao lamented the loss of his provinces. The King of Sip Song Panna urged him to fight Farong, and Cao Fa indeed instructed his people to do so. But Farong found out and threatened to conquer Sip Song Panna. The King ceased his support, and so Cao Fa had no one to help him. His melancholy was such that he no longer ate and no longer slept. And so he died.
>
> Farong apologized to Cao Fa's widow and invited her to return to Muang Sing. She did so, and Farong even gave money to send the late Cao Fa's son to school in Luang Prabang. But after three years, he fell sick and died there. It was suspected that he had been poisoned. After that, his mother in Muang Sing died, too. One by

one, all the relatives of the Cao Fa died off. That was the end of the Cao Fa [dynasty of Muang Sing].

Conventional scholarship, in contrast to this indigenous version, frames the Muang Sing story within the larger picture of intramural European competition (British Burma versus French Indochina) with an indigenous imperial backdrop (Sip Song Panna–China; Nan–Siam).

Shortly before European colonization, Muang Sing had exerted its anti-indigenous colonial muscle by spinning off as a vassal of Keng Tung. Well placed to take advantage of salt and caravan commerce, it began to develop into an important trading center. Muang Sing's leader even fought with Keng Tung, unsuccessfully, for control of Keng Lap. In 1895 the British would invoke Oun Kham's predecessor's fealty to the Shan and Keng Tung (which had fallen to Britain five years earlier) and lay claim to his fiefdom. The French counterclaimed that Muang Sing had properly belonged to Nan, and therefore, through a recently concluded treaty with Siam, now belonged to France.

Sachchidanand Sahai (2005) has most perceptively analyzed the changing meaning of the Mekong as a space for the populations who defined themselves in relation to it. Prior to colonialism, the operational notion was altitudinal: less important than which side of the river people lived was how high up the mountains from its banks they dwelled. Indeed, the Mekong "had never served as a political or administrative frontier for the indigenous states in the valley. Far from acting as a natural frontier, the Mekong represented a means of linkage and exchange for the communities on both its banks" (Sahai 2005, 156). Colonizing the Mekong, moreover, was more a French preoccupation than a British one: whereas the French (despite the reservations of explorer extraordinaire Auguste Pavie[12]) invested in the Mekong as a demarcational reality, the British merely acceded to it (at least with respect to Burma) out of diplomatic compromise.

Resolution of Anglo-French conflict over Muang Sing not only resulted in the market town coming under French sovereignty. It also ratified the principle (pushed by the French) that in its upper reaches, the river become the boundary. But had the leaders of Muang Sing not, for their own purposes, returned to the east-bank side of the Mekong, would the French have made the case that the river constituted a natural boundary? Had the Mekong indeed become the boundary without Muang Sing on the French side, then in all likelihood it would have reverted to a British version of *song fai fai*: ultimately under the British crown but for local administrative purposes beholden to its recent (co-)master, Keng Tung. On the other hand, it would then have been spared the violence (and resulting depopulation) incurred by the war between communists and royalists and the consequent bombing from U.S. involvement in the widened Vietnam conflict.[13]

The Mekong as Postcolonial Boundary

Historical revisionism aside, geographic resolution of the Anglo-French showdown at Muang Sing is 238 kilometers of Mekong serving as boundary between Myanmar and the Lao People's Democratic Republic.[14] It also serves as international landmark for the two countries within the Golden Triangle that were never formal colonies, China and Thailand. At its southern tip, Sop Ruak in Thailand fashions itself (being the convergence point of Myanmar, Lao, and Thailand) as the very heart of the Golden Triangle.[15] On the west bank of the Mekong lies Burma (and its casino), and on the east bank, Laos (with its tourist-fabricated market village—see Map 19).

As it meanders in a northeasterly direction from Sop Ruak, Thailand, the Mekong separates Shan State in Myanmar from the provinces of Bokeo and then Luang Nam Tha in Laos. Halfway upstream lies the Lao settlement of Xiang Kok (population 400), which has grown exponentially from its origins as a small Lue village a little ways from the river. In 1986 New Xiang

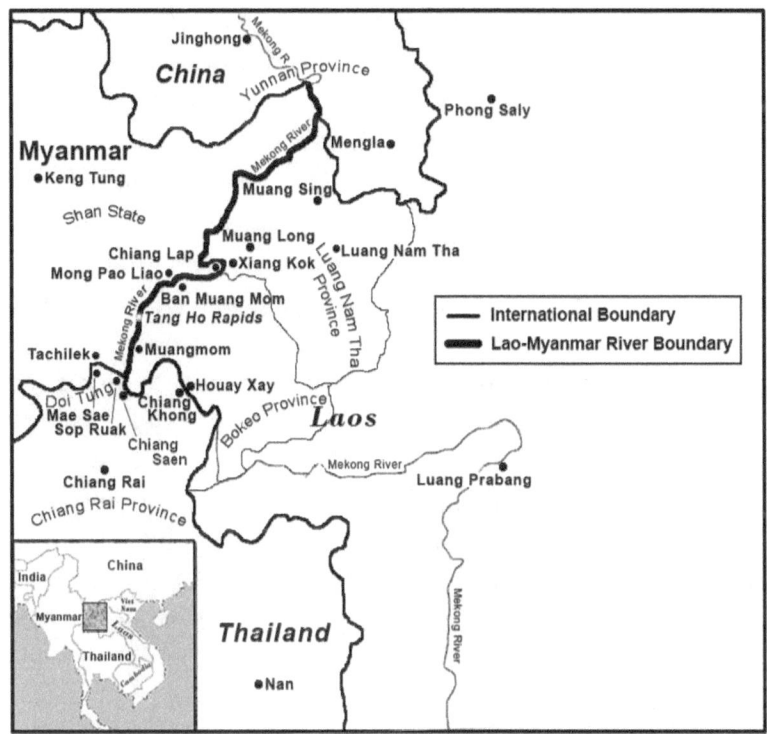

Map 19. Golden Triangle—Mekong as Lao-Burmese Borderland

Kok was designated as an official border station for goods transiting off and on cargo boats, and modest port facilities were built. Less official is Xiang Kok's trade in drugs and women. A World Bank loan in 1996 for east-bank road construction has had major health and migratory impacts, as well as challenging the Mekong as the sole "highway" of commerce linking China to Thailand (Lyttleton et al. 2004).

Another Lao control point along the Mekong has been established at Ban Muang Mom, about halfway to Xiang Kok. Across the river, in Burma, is the Mong Pao Liao temple complex. The largest Mekong settlement on the Myanmar side is Chiang Lap, scene of periodic government-rebel conflict. Xuay Kum is the Lahu village across the river from Chiang Lap in Laos. Cross-river traffic for indigenes continues but is hazardous and subject to increasing government control, including customs payments on both sides. Unauthorized crossing over into Myanmar to cut wood (an activity for which authorization can be obtained in Chiang Lap) has gotten Lao riverside villagers arrested and detained. When a Lao-side village headman needs to make the otherwise short dugout ride to the other side of the Mekong, he must first walk four hours to the closest official police post to obtain permission (and repeat the process for his return).[16]

Apart from the above-mentioned, settlements along the Mekong are relatively few and sparse: in the early 1990s, twenty on the Lao side and eighteen on the Burmese, most of them between Sop Ruak and Xiengkok, with a heavy concentration toward the Thai-Lao-Myanmar convergence point—Tachilek municipality in Myanmar, Muang Ton Pheung and Muang Long districts in Laos. (This and the following paragraph rely heavily on Gay and Phommachack 1990, 11.) On the Lao side the villages along the Mekong are mixed Lue and Lahu (sometimes shared with Akha); on the Burmese, Tai Lu (similar to Lue), Tainoi, and Lahu. Nearby the river in Laos, Kui are also present. Impermanence characterizes most settlements along the Mekong, however. Villages disappear and reappear, published maps rarely keeping up with the dynamics of Mekong settlement mobility.

In 1990 the governments of Laos and Myanmar agreed to undertake a joint border delimitation mission and to draft a border treaty in the interests of modernizing and clarifying the colonial boundary legacy. (Establishing a common anti-drug-trafficking policy was also one of the objectives of this diplomatic offensive.) On account of the strong Mekong currents, rather than floating water buoys, in 1991–92, eighty-six pairs of land posts were placed at fixed distances from the axis of the river's thalweg every three kilometers on each bank (see Fig. 7).

There is no notable settlement where the Laos frontier ends and Sip Song Panna, China, begins at its northeastern apex.

Fig. 7. Mekong Boundary Marker

Twenty miles farther on, the Mekong enters Chinese territory entirely, the (land) border with Myanmar/Burma then taking a southwesterly turn. Jinghong is the major Chinese port on this stretch of the Mekong. Between it and Chiang Saen in Thailand (about ten miles south of Sop Ruak) ply large cargo ships.[17]

Inland on the Lao side of the Mekong as international boundary, beyond the town of Muang Sing itself, the district of Muang Sing (population 24,000) is home mostly to Akha and Lue villages (68 and 26, respectively), with small numbers of Neua, Dam, Yao, and Hmong (14 villages combined). Increasing numbers of Chinese are also reported to be settling. In recent years the Akha of Muang Sing have been the targets of strong government and international attempts to transform their highland dry rice and opium cultivation patterns to a drugless and paddy lifestyle. Opium addiction nevertheless remains a major social problem among them, particularly given the increased mortality (human and livestock) that they have experienced from their "lower" way of life (Cohen 2000). Yet even opium is vulnerable to the disruptive effects of "modernizing," "developmental," "capitalistic" change: in nearby districts, synthetic amphetamine-type stimulants (ATS) are taking the place of "traditional" opium among Akha (cf. Lyttleton 2004).

Colonial Opium and Other Postcolonial Habits

Contemporary Western stigmatization of the Golden Triangle for its role in the global drug trade is ironic: within a Buddhist cultural zone that frowned upon the use of mentally distracting narcotics, the British and French encouraged the production and business of opium in their Southeast Asian colonies. "From almost as soon as the French annexed Laos in 1893, the colonial government promoted the opium trade" (Renard 1997, 314). As for the British, who had notoriously fought an Opium War decades before to make China safe for narcotics, Burma was initially viewed as a consumers' center for its Indian export drug.

Even as Euro-American attitudes toward narcotics changed from benign to nefarious, administrators on the ground were reluctant to outlaw it. Opium, after all, "represented a way to finance empire. Because of the high level of usage in French Indochina and British Burma, the income generated by opium monopolies constituted a substantial portion of the government's budget, a situation that officials were loathe to change" (Renard 1997, 319).

When the British did begin to suppress the trade, they did not outlaw poppy cultivation west of the Salween River—where most of it was grown. Keng Tung became a center of Burmese opium commerce, even as it went underground. Colonial borders and narcotics trafficking went hand in hand, inasmuch as the regions for growing opium were in the most remote of areas (Renard 1997, 317). Initially, the French sold opium imported from India and therefore tried to ban its growing in Laos. The Hmong, growing opium since the 1820s, sold mostly to annual Yunnanese pony caravans. Colonial boundaries, in short, were paired with drug criminality. The trend continued well into the postcolonial era, during which time human trafficking joined drug trafficking as a major Golden Triangle activity.

In the early twenty-first century, the Laotian government finally came to embrace Western anti-opiate norms. On the formerly French side of the Mekong, policies of opium suppression, financed by internationally sponsored crop substitution projects, have been surprisingly successful (even if home-use cultivation persists). The same cannot be said for the formerly British side of the river, where continuing contestations over sovereignty have been good for opium. (Open warfare among competing actors in the drug trade imparts another dimension to "sovereignty struggle" in Burma.) Shan opium traders continue to provide the raw material for processing that is exported along the Mekong. Eastern Myanmar, moreover, has more recently become a major production center for ATS pills, the "modern" drug of choice in the Golden Triangle and elsewhere (Lyttleton 2004). In Xieng Kok, where Laotian and Burmese territory come closest to each other—far away from the prying eyes of drug suppressors dispatched from Bangkok and Vientiane—ATS trade flourishes.

Walker (1999) argues that despite the reification of boundaries, French colonial rule only slightly disrupted ongoing commercial activity of the indigenous polities. In particular, the French never succeeded in economically assimilating northwest Laos into Vietnam. His main thesis is that the Upper Mekong borderlands that once separated France and Britain from Siam (and from each other) are today characterized by a contradictory mix of both greater liberalization *and* regulation. Yes, the institutional heirs to the colonies continue to micromanage the border passage of persons and goods and to take the lead in erecting borderland infrastructure. But these state activities are inextricably enmeshed with private sector actors, especially the well-organized syndicate of trans-Mekong boat operators and Laotian female *commerçants*. An entire economic regime and intertwined social structure has arisen at the interstices of the colonial borders. That which had essentially been an indigenous north–south riverine avenue has become, as a result of European colonization, an east–west borderland. To understand today's cross-border activity, one must appreciate the "regulated interconnections of the past" and the "subtle and complex realities of borderlands history" (Walker 1999, 63).

War and Migration

Even if the physical border between France and Britain in Southeast Asia has remained juridically stable since the colonial era, the populations contiguous to it have been repeatedly displaced as a result of international and civil wars. Late in World War II, after the French in Indochina finally broke with Vichy (and therefore Japan), they were forced to evacuate Muang Sing and Luang Nam Tha. These provinces were taken over and plundered by the Chinese Kuomintang, until finally retaken (but not before the final opium crop was harvested) by the French in 1946. In 1953–54, during the anti-French struggle, Vietnamese fighters took over swaths of these areas, with the Pathet Lao encroaching in the countryside. In 1962 a military post in Muang Sing was captured by combined North Vietnamese and Pathet Lao forces. Heavy bombing from U.S. forces in the 1960s resulted in another large-scale evacuation. With the Communist takeover of 1975, remaining Lue populations fled, and Lao People's Democratic Republic cadres encouraged their allied upland peoples (principally the Akha) to take over the abandoned land. When these Lue eventually returned with government encouragement, the Akha had to be accommodated elsewhere. In the meantime, other Lue emigrated from Sip Song Panna, mostly in response to forced land collectivization. Although not directly related to war, a road link built by the victorious Communists from Mengla in China to Luang Nam Tha in Laos (begun in 1962 but interrupted until the late 1980s) has bypassed Muang Sing, "ending its position as a regional trading centre"—and presumably its draw for population (Walker 1999, 55).

Internal conflict on the Burmese side of the border has been more constant, even if of lower intensity than in postcolonial Laos. Instability in eastern Myanmar periodically spikes as a result of Shan rebel offensives, Myanmar military counteroffensives, drug lord fallouts, and various narco-political permutations of the above. Along the Mekong itself, on the west bank (Burma), Wa insurgents combine their dislike of Burman hegemony and penchant for drug running into stop-and-go control of the area. Local populations are accordingly disrupted and displaced—many permanently—as interviews with elder Akha, Lahu, and Shan in Thailand attest:

> I would like to return to "the place where my placenta and umbilical cord are buried" (*fang hok, fang henh*; that is, hometown). But the Burmese government has moved the Shan from [my village] to the town, and Burmans have come to settle in their place. They take what they want—farms, land, homes. —Sunanta Jonglang, seventy-eight-year-old Shan in Mae Ai, Thailand, originally from Meung Pan, Myanmar.

> When I was about sixteen, my family migrated [to Thailand] on account of fighting between the Burmese and Chinese (KMT). Now I don't even know if my home village still exists. The Burmese, Shan, Chinese, Wa—all are fighting. The situation is all so complicated, unclear, in Myanmar. The government is itself divided. It is difficult to communicate, to know what is going on, to know who is in control. —Jaka, sixty-six-year-old Akha in Payang village, Thailand, originally from Basa, Myanmar.

> I moved to Thailand when I was forty, because of forced labor by the Burmese military. They made me be a porter for them, carrying weapons and food. Here, I have grown all of the crops I did there—rice, maize, corn, sugar cane, pumpkin and cucumber—all except for opium. I have never returned. I don't want to be captured and go to jail. . . . *Nobody* wants to return to Myanmar. —Atu, ninety-year-old Akha in Doi Tung, Thailand, originally from Hu Loka, Myanmar.

The informants quoted above are beneficiaries of the Doi Tung Development Project, founded and sponsored by the late queen mother of Thailand. Begun as a reforestation project, the physical boundary is graphic: where Myanmar and Thailand touch, there is a tree line on the eastern (Thai) side but denuded mountain slope on the western (Burmese) side.

Shan insurgency resulted in the 1995 closing of the crossing between Tachilek, Myanmar, and Mae Sae, Thailand. As a result, much easier relations prevailed between Laos and Thailand, but not Burma, although Lao traders did bring their tobacco and alcohol products, obtained in Houay Xay (Laos) all the way to northeast Burma for sale. Accounts of the open border between Houay Xay and Chiang Khong (Thailand) resemble that of the early 1970s between El Paso, Texas, and Ciudad Juarez, Mexico.[18] "It was like one village": Thai borderlanders frequented the French-built hospital in Houay Xay for health services, patronized its cinema for entertainment, and visited its women for companionship (Walker 1999, 57). Those halcyon days ended when the Lao-Thai border was effectively shut from 1976 to 1988.

To this day, there are no official border crossing stations between Myanmar and Laos, such as those prevailing between Myanmar and Thailand (e.g., Tachilek and Mae Sae) or between Laos and Thailand (e.g., Huay Say and Chiang Khong). Nor are there Thai immigration facilities in Sop Ruak (or nearby Chiang Saen) that will issue exit stamps, for either Thai or foreign nationals, valid for disembarkation northward along either Laotian or Burmese banks of the Mekong River. Golden Triangle visitors arriving from Thailand can legally travel upriver along the Mekong only by securing permission from Lao immigration authorities in Houay Xay. Where local river became colonial boundary, one-and-a-half centuries later strange principles of sovereignty and international riverine law apply.

Postcolonial Reification: Muang Sing and Keng Tung Unbound

Colonial partition, we have seen above, eventually placed Muang Sing under French sovereignty and Keng Tung under British.

In 1914 Muang Sing revolted. From exile in Sip Song Panna (China), its leader (Oun Kham) mobilized the Lue against the French. It took three tries before the colonial military squelched the rebellion. From then, "reduced from a principality to a *meuang* under direct [colonial] administration" (Stuart-Fox 1997, 38), Muang Sing remained firmly entrenched in a French Indochinese saga that included diffidence to Laotian development, World War II evacuation, nationalist resistance to recolonization, communist revolt and civil war,[19] internment of royalists and other so-called counter-revolutionaries, and a gradual opening up to the outside world via backpackers and international development experts.

The French particularly appreciated Muang Sing as a viable competitor to Siamese (Thai), not British, trade. Walker (1999, 23–24) notes that commerce across the Mekong between northwest Laos (whose major center is Muang Sing) and Keng Tung town in Burma used to be significant, but it is no longer so. Authorities are counting that the completion of a new covered market on the outskirts of town will both alleviate vehicular congestion on market days and rejuvenate overall economic activity.

More than as a commercial hub, it is from an ethnic point of view that Muang Sing perhaps retains its greatest significance. "[U]nder French colonial rule and subsequent royalist and communist governments of independent Laos, [it] has preserved a strong sense of local autonomy and identity as 'the secret capital of the Lue in Laos'" (Cohen 1998, 50, citing an unpublished manuscript of Grabowsky and Kaspar-Sickermann). Khun (an ethnicity not found in Laos) are also well represented here.

Random interviews in Keng Tung evince more benevolent and less traumatic memories of colonialism and its aftermath. "The British are a good people. They don't interfere. They didn't rule directly, but asked the *sawbwa* [traditional chief] to govern for them."[20]

Unlike the other cases we have examined, there is a strongly perceived policy contrast between pre- and post-independence rulers. Not only did postcolonial Burmese depose the Sawbwa of Keng Tung, but in later years they razed the royal palace, even though Keng Tung is one of the few northeast centers to which the Myanmar government encourages visitors with foreign currency. Myanmar's military government has succeeded in establishing Rangoon writ in the town (if not in all the surrounding countryside), including the pervasive system of domestic spies.[21]

On the French side of the border, evacuation and displacement during the Indochina War of the 1960s and 1970s so disrupted the population of Muang Sing that there are no elders who can recall the French colonial period.[22] A French-era fort and French-language sign outside the post office are scanty remains of a half-century effort to create a permanent outpost for France in this would-be rival to Keng Tung.

Bilateral relations between the Laotian and Myanmar governments have been consistently "amicable" (Liang 1990, 125). Yet despite their shared boundary, most official interaction occurs at the multilateral level, far from their line of actual contact. It is therefore not surprising that in a very comprehensive book on Myanmar politics, Laos does not merit mention in the chapter on foreign affairs (Steinberg 2001). By finally joining the Association of Southeast Asian States (ASEAN) in the late 1990s, both countries at least entered an ongoing institutional framework that would overcome the geopolitical anomaly of decreased postcolonial interaction along their superimposed frontier. But Burma would not join the Mekong River Commission in 1995 (successor to the mostly moribund Mekong Committee from the 1950s) and is not an official partner to the Economic Quadrangle Joint Development Corporation (EQJDC), either.

Established in the mid-1990s as a joint venture between the Lao government and private Thai business interests, by its very name EQJDC wishes to geometrically change the connotation of a drug-ridden triangle to an economically promising quadrangle. Its arithmetic act of $n + 1$ acknowledges the incontrovertible role that China plays in a region otherwise obscured by the triadic Thai-Lao-Burma appellation. Increased Myanmar participation in regional trading and commercial organizations will be an inevitable consequence of growing Chinese dominance, as China literally changes the shape, size, and flow of Burma's river border with Laos. Downstream consequences of Chinese blasting and damming of the Mekong go well beyond the boundary per se, however.

In the 1890s, Britain and France feuded over the inter-fiefdom fealty affecting Keng Tung and Muang Sing. The result was the Mekong-as-Later-Boundary, with Keng Tung falling under the British crown and Muang Sing governed by la République Française. More than a century later, this "Mother of Rivers" remains an international border, the two Upper Mekong sister settlements still lying under separate national jurisdictions based in Rangoon and Vientiane. Yet we are witnessing a gradual reversion to the precolonial system of *sam fai fa*, subordination to multiple rulers. Even as Keng Tung and Muang Sing remain formally unbound from each other as a result of colonial partition, they are simultaneously incorporated into the same postcolonial *sam fai fa*, subject to China's expanding economic influence and ensuing political power. Yes, the superimposed colonial boundary lines remain, but the operative colonialism, at least in the Upper Mekong, is no longer European.

Partitioned Ethnicity and Minorities in the Golden Triangle

Coincidentally, Laos and Burma have virtually the same number of ethnic minorities (see below). More than numbers, when one considers the long-term impact of colonial partition on indigenous peoples in Southeast Asia and particularly the Golden Triangle, one must distinguish between dominant and minoritarian ethnic groups. The distinction is tied to geography: lowlanders who can claim a sovereign home (e.g., the Lao in Laos, the Tai in Thailand, the Burmese and even Shan in the Shan states of Burma/Myanmar) have in general had an easier postcolonial experience than the hill peoples who have found themselves split into two or more independent states without any natural affinity for any of them. To a great extent, these are the consequences of the European partition:

> [T]he choice of natural boundaries such as rivers . . . which are the natural roads and thoroughfares of the region, has proven a major impediment to the development of peoples suddenly cut off on either side of international frontiers. Many of Burma's minorities are today divided across such international borders. The once free-roving Akha and Lahu of the Shan State, for instance, instead find themselves increasingly isolated in small pockets between the modern borders of Burma [and] Laos. . . . The origins of the hill-tribe Hmong and Mien rebellions which have broken out across . . . Laos . . . over the last 40 years can be traced to very similar causes. (Smith 1991, 41)

According to Kunstadter's comparative ethnic table (1967, 87–88) there are only two ethnic groups in Burma—the Akha and the Lue—who also reside in Laos. Both groups are more numerous in Yunnan (China) than in Myanmar and Lao People's Republic but supposedly less numerous there than they are in Thailand. Yet according to LeBar, Hickey, and Musgrave's (1964) incomparable ethnic map, there are two other groups who ought to be spanning the Mekong, that arbitrary delineation of former European sovereignty in the Golden Triangle (see Map 20).

Akha

The Akha, a one-thousand-meter-altitude people belonging to the Tibeto-Burman branch of the Sino-Tibetan language family (LeBar, Hickey, and Musgrave 1964; Schliesinger 2003; Tribal Museum 2004; Young 1961). Akha lore has it that they are descended from seven brothers in Sip Song Panna of southern Yunnan (China),[23] and that they have accordingly preserved seven distinguishable sets of customs (known as Akhazang, or "the Akha Way") and speech patterns. The Akha have not,

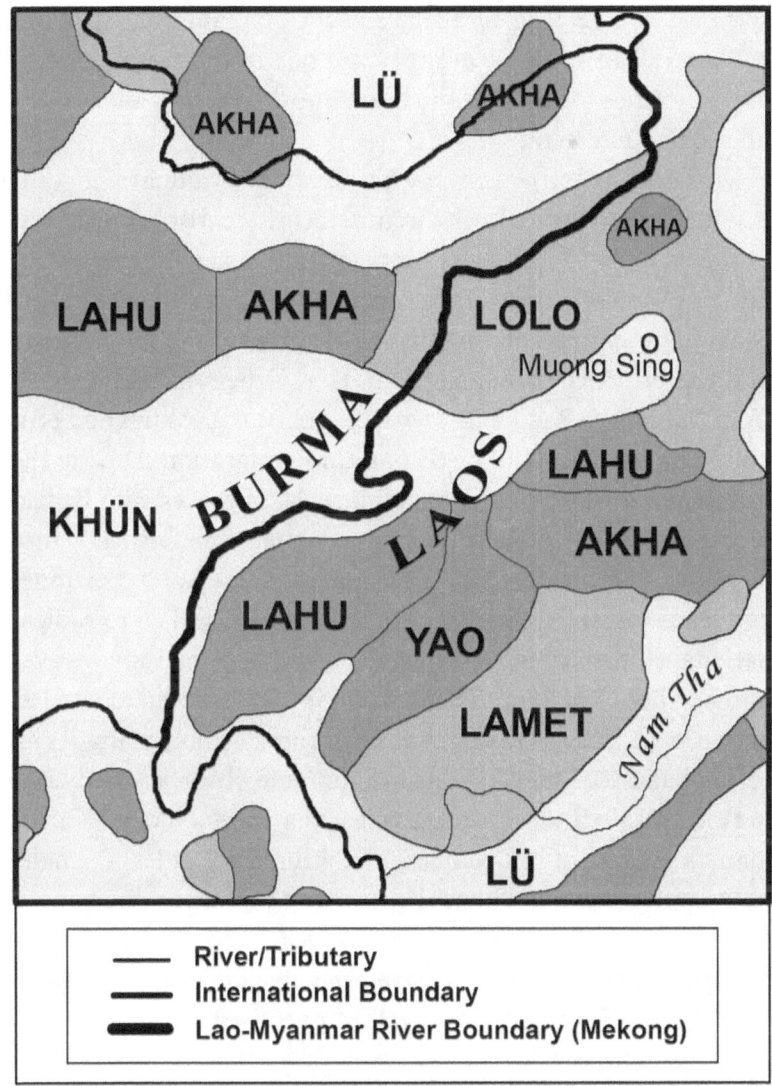

Map 20. Partitioned Ethnicities of Lao-Burmese Borderlands

however, aspired to political autonomy or undertaken any of the classical actions of nationalism or irredentism. This is true of most of the partitioned hill peoples under discussion. In Burma, however, where they number over two hundred thousand, some of them have joined with Shan, Kachin, Wa, Lahu, and Lisu insurgents under the Burmese Communist Party (Bunge 1983, 232). In Laos, where they are one of the largest of ethnic minorities (66,000 in the mid-1990s), they are much more politically quiescent.

While Akha settlement in what became Myanmar and Laos began in the first half of the nineteenth century, most of it occurred (coincidentally, by all accounts) during the early colonial era. Burma was the first destination, but substantial numbers of Akha migrants kept moving eastward into French territory and the province of Luang Nam Tha. Others moved directly from Yunnan to Phongsaly Province. Political pressures and economic hardship encouraged continuing migration. During the terminal period of colonialism, more Akha moved into British territory in eastern Keng Tung and under French sovereignty in Phong Saly in northern and northwestern Laos. Postindependence instability in both former colonies, linked to radical nationalist ideologies, has triggered secondary migratory waves into northern Thailand. There, they are now believed to number between 50,000 and 100,000. Born there or not, many Akha in Thailand face virtually insurmountable obstacles in obtaining citizenship. Indeed, statelessness is a common condition of many members of hill peoples inhabiting the Golden Triangle.

Despite educated Akhas' belief that they suffer discrimination in Thailand, compared with political conditions prevailing in Myanmar and Laos they have been able (at least since 1989, with Thai government approval) to exercise the freedom necessary to achieve their highest levels of formal organization. In this respect, Thailand is said to be "sweet cake" for the Akha. There are no Laotian or Burmese equivalents, for example, of the Association for Education and Culture in Thailand (AFECT), which works to improve the culture, health, and environment of Akha women, men, youth, and elders. In Laos—officially a multiethnic state that promotes collective group equality—the Akha are but one of forty-seven recognized ethnic groups, and are hardly encouraged to mobilize into any special interest groups. The same can be said for the Akha of Myanmar, where there are 135 listed "races," several of them agents of revolt and targets of repression.

From Thailand, AFECT maintains some informal cultural exchange with Akha in Myanmar, despite resistance from the Burmese government. Guerilla warfare there has forced Akha down from their traditional mountain homelands. In Laos, many Akha villages are also "coming down," but not as a result of overt violence so much as from government resettlement policies (Cohen 2000).[24]

In terms of Akha association, the traditional seven brothers' separation is less important today than the vertical one dividing those Akha closer to northern Yunnam culture (Hani) from those influenced by southern (Tai) inflected society. Different Akha associations, even in Thailand, reflect this split and compete among each other accordingly. Von Geusau (2003) identifies six of them. Colonial partition is not the only influence that undermines this hill tribe's (as well as others') potential unity.[25]

Lue/Lü

Like the Akha, the Lue (or Lü) of former French Laos and former British Burma (especially Keng Tung) also trace their ancestry to Sip Song Panna. Unlike the Akha, the Lue are a lowland people with much greater ethnic and linguistic affinity to the Tai who numerically predominate in the Quadrangle. Also unlike the Akha, they are more numerous outside their ancestral home of Sip Song Panna than inside. In Laos alone, they number over 120,000. As with the Akha, southern migration over the last century accounts for much of their extra-Yunnan redistribution. Colonial-era line drawing (to France's Lue numerical advantage) is also partially responsible.[26]

In many contexts Lue expect (and receive) homage from the Akha and other mountain peoples. The Laotian government pressure we have noted above to make Akha villagers resettle from the mountains has afforded Lue with cheap wage labor—

especially by opium addicts—for paddy field clearing and ditch digging (Cohen 2000).

Once again, we know more about the postcolonial state-inflected specificity of Lue as they have evolved in distinction between Laos and Thailand, not Laos and Burma; indeed, even the numbers of Lue in Myanmar are not easily known. Paul Cohen, following Keyes, confirms that the Lue there exhibit "localized ethnic identity"; that is, a sense of a collective self autonomous from the national (i.e., Laotian) culture that surrounds it. By contrast, in Nan province (Thailand), Lue culture is evolving in response to deliberate socioeconomic and cultural intervention by the Thai state. Far from wishing to suppress or force assimilation of Lue specificity, Thai policy is to preserve it. However, state preservation of minority culture, within the context of overall national development, has resulted in a (nationally) specific kind of cultural transformation.

For the Lue of Muang Sing, a chronically underdeveloped Lao state has lessened the culturally transformative impact of the state. Even through communism and socialism, Muang Sing retains its territorial and administrative identity and is administered by agents chosen from among the local populace. In Muang Sing, the Lue define themselves predominantly in relation to their (sacralized) physical surroundings and worship guardian spirits of Muang Sing proper. This privileging of locality reinforces their sense of privilege over the "inferior" hill peoples of their sacralized environs.

Lahu

The Lahu reputation for fierceness explains only in part their willingness to create an insurgent military force, the Lahu State Army. During the 1980s the Lahu State Army resisted Burmese government forces by joining the National Democratic Front (NDF, a loosely organized umbrella group that linked the Lahu to four other ethnically based rebel groups on Burma's side of the Golden Triangle). Less powerful and ideological than the other major resistance movement in the northeast—the Burmese Communist Party—the NDF had at its formation prodemocracy pretenses. Yet the Lahu themselves were less concerned with political modernity than preservation of tradition. Among all the hill peoples whose prowess in hunting is legendary, the Lahu stand out (hence, their outgroup name, Mussur, or "hunter").

The Lahu range from Yunnan to Thailand, in addition to Myanmar (Kengtu state) and Laos (Luang Nam Tha province). Like the Akha, they are a hill people speaking a Tibeto-Burman language and sharing similar territory. The Lahu distinguish themselves according to communal origins and customs: the so-called Black Lahu, based in northeastern Myanmar and southwest Yunnan (from where they migrated to the Laotian side of the Mekong); the Red Lahu and Shehleh Lahu, the strongest in Thailand; and the Yellow Lahu, also most numerous in Burma and China.

Lahu are thus partitioned by postcolonial borders into several countries, and even within countries, they are dispersed. Accordingly, "this people can claim no particular stretch of country as being exclusively 'Lahuland'" (Walker 1974–75, 330). The same can be said of the other hill peoples. Postcolonial politics in both former British and French territories of the Golden Triangle have been hurtful to the Lahu. Along the Mekong, the headman of Pung Lo reports that five years prior, the government commanded the entire village to relocate from the interior to the riverside, so that the inhabitants would be more accessible to the government.[27] Asylum represented by (noncolonized) Thailand has beckoned, and they have migrated accordingly. It is not an orderly migration, however, and is most destructive to the weakest: females and children, whose statelessness makes them all the more vulnerable to human trafficking. "Poverty, warfare, forced labour, and repression bring . . . upland minority peoples . . . across the Myanmar border, and make entry into the sex industry a rational (if dangerous) choice" (Feingold 2000). One visible response to this phenomenon, the Development and Education Programme for Daughters and Communities Centre, has been established not far from the Burmese border in Mae Sae, Thailand, to save the dignity, memory, and health of homeless, orphaned, and broken-family girls.[28]

With respect to induced migration and its unfortunate consequences, the otherwise underpopulated Lahu are also representative of the other doubly partitioned hill peoples: "In Burma and Laos internal political unrest has caused great hardship to Lahu and other hill peoples who have been caught up in the conflicts between government armies and 'liberation' forces" (Walker 1974–75, 342). Partition of ethnic groups nevertheless has had longer and greater implications for those peoples of the Golden Triangle who found themselves on the British side of the line. "The perception of oppression, and thus of minority-consciousness, has been promoted partly by the threat state penetration has posed to the *peripheral communities' links with co-ethnics across the state borders*. The Burmans are the only major ethnic group not divided by the Burmese state boundaries" (Brown 1994, 51–52, emphasis added).

The Lao, not normally thought of as a minority people, were partitioned in ways that affected their long-term prospects as a nation-state.[29] France could have sued for all the ethnic Lao to come under their wing in the Laotian sector of Indochina. This is what the territorially voracious Gallic Auguste Pavie would have preferred. But they did not, leaving a good four-fifths of the Lao people in Siam. The remaining one-fifth, in Laos proper, constituted but one-half of the entire colony's population. It did not prove to be a politically healthy demographic.

This outcome was not because France was constrained to draw the line so close to its Indochinese chest; in the *rapport des forces*, France could have prevailed over Siam for this part of its territory (if not over the kingdom in toto.) Indirectly, partition of the Lao between Laos and Thailand was a result of Franco-British relations as constructed from the Quai d'Orsay. Despite a dynamic of competition on colonial ground, rapprochement with *les Anglais* was then the *mot d'ordre* for a Europe defined by Entente Cordiale. Dilution of Lao power thus resulted as a diplomatic concession to Britain, not from any Siamese strategic fait accompli. Future management of "minority" groups by a Lao elite, which is itself a bare majority, is one of the ambivalent colonial legacies of ethnic partition. Similarly, European rivalry also indirectly affected Indochinese partition of the Lue between France and China, the former keen to achieve an entrée to the latter rivaling that of the British. "The imposition of artificial borders between Laos and China had divided the ancient [Lue] polity and created political instability in the parts annexed to Laos" (Stuart-Fox 1997, 37). Thus, while the Lao wound up with (an albeit truncated) nation-state that the Lue did not, both Lao and Lue share the dubious distinction of experiencing an indigenous partition (with Siam and China) prompted by European colonial rivalry (between Britain and France).

Other Austro-Thai Groups

In addition to the Lao and Lue, there are other Austro-Thai groups that are disproportionately represented on both sides of the Lao-Burma boundary: Tai Khoen (100,000 in Myanmar, 600 in Laos); Tai Yai (better known as Shan, of whom there are millions in Myanmar but only hundreds in Laos, though they did at one time trade down the Mekong); and, perhaps, N(e)ua (Northern) Thai (except that the "Tai Nua of . . . Laos are not identical with the . . . Tai Neua of . . . Burma" [Schliesinger 2003, 231]). Numerous ethnic groups in Laos, Austro-Thai as well as Sino-Tibetan-speaking, have roots, recent or ancient, in Burma. Mobility is a hallmark of peoples from the Upper Mekong region, a phenomenon that highlights the local novelty of fixed territorial boundaries as introduced by the colonial powers.

Differential Ethnicization

To a certain extent, both colonial regimes reified ethnicity. But in the Golden Triangle, the impact and consequences have been more disruptive and violent for those who came under British sovereignty in Burma. Previously, fluidity and porous ethnic boundaries had characterized relations between majorities and minorities. Upland versus lowland, Buddhist versus non-Buddhist, monarchical versus acephalous: these, not ethnicity, were the shifting foundations of social and political hierarchy. Patron-client relationships also inflected communal differences. British colonialism created an "institutional separation" between "Burma proper" (that is, Burma of the Burmese) and that of the hill peoples and other Golden Triangle minorities. Being Burman became associated with proximity to the levers of postcolonial power. Rejection—perceived and actual—of and by the Shan and Karen minorities has been the most enduring of this ethnicized politics, but members of other minorities—ones who have otherwise accommodated themselves to the postcolonial state in Laos—have also been in constant opposition to the postcolonial state in Myanmar.

British colonialism set in motion its own brand of postcolonial assimilationism (through administrative centralization, educational policy, linguistic Burmanization) in the name of a modernized Burmese ethnic state. From there, postcolonial Burma has teetered into outright objectification and oppression of minority groups. Taking a page from antiquated colonial anthropology, the SLORC/SPDC regime, David Steinberg notes, has classified all citizens into one of eight major "races" (the overwhelmingly dominant one being Burman); these "races" are further subdivided into an unwieldy 135 ethnic groups (which the government on occasion also calls "races.") These "categories that all postcolonial governments have used for the major populations outside of the core area of Burma Proper have taken on a life of their own" (Steinberg 2006, 24). Such sociological complexity justifies, according to the military regime's internal logic, a strong, unifying government (Steinberg 2006, 23). The defensive backlash of non-Burman minorities, led by otherwise disenfranchised local leaders, has largely defined postindependence Myanmar. Brown (1994, 64) summarizes the argument thus: "It was the [British] colonial impact upon the authority structure of the majority [Burman] community which generated the ethnocratic state tendency, and it was the ethnocratic character of the weak state which caused state penetration to take on an assimilationist form which provoked the disruption of communal authority structures amongst the peripheral communities. The outcome was the emergence of minority consciousness and the translation of this by displaced élites into ethnic nationalist rebellion against the state."

In contrast, "in spite of the varying social, cultural and economic conditions of the different ethnic groups, ethnic conflicts are comparatively rare in [Laos] as a whole" (Ovesen 2004, 237). Indeed, Laotian officials disdain their Burmese counterparts for so overtly maintaining ethnically divisive policies (Goudineau 2000, 18, 20–22, 25, 29). Having displaced French sovereignty, Laotian revolutionaries retained Jacobin ideas about national unity "with the official policy of rapid consolidation of all the inhabitants of Laos into a single indivisible state entity" (Kossikov 2000, 229). One method has been to reduce the total possible universe of distinct ethnic groups in Laos from 820 to 210 to 60 to (a more manageable) 47. As several ethnologists of Laos point out, however, such categorization smacks more of political desirability than sociological reality, "the ultimate objective being the formation of a homogenous national culture out of real heterogeneity" (Pholsena 2002, 194). On the ground, it is more common for citizens of Laos to identify themselves ethnically using the French colonial triad, based on altitude of origin (lowlanders, mountain slopers, and highlanders). One identity, of course, does not preclude another; citizenship and locality are also importance dimensions of self-description.

This is not to argue that the postcolonial Laotian government has been altogether beneficent vis-à-vis the minorities partitioned on its side of the boundary. Despite constitutional provisions that recognize Laos as a polyethnic state, in reality the Lao People's Democratic Republic has been pursuing a policy of Laoicization. Inheriting from the colonial carving, we have seen, a demography that put more Lao people *outside* of Laos than within it, and *within* Laos barely one-half of a Lao population, this is perhaps understandable. Given the government's communist ideology, preoccupation with ethnic integrity of the state is perhaps ironic; in any event, Ovesen (2004) argues that assertion of superiority (cultural as well as political) among the Lao is implicit in the way that the government perpetuates, even in its heralding of them, the triad of ethnic categories (Lao Lum, Lao Theung, and Lao Sung). As we have seen above, this triad has its roots in the late colonial era. But it harks back to an even older dichotomy embedded in colonialism that the French themselves eventually repudiated: *évolué* (read Francophone) versus *rétrograde* (read indigenous). Only now, the colonial master—even at its most patronizing—is not ethnic Gaul but lowland Lao. An indigenous (re-)colonization is reproducing itself in former French Indochina, perhaps not to the extent as Mbembe's postcolony but still noticeably. While one could argue that a similar process of Burman chauvinism is at work across the border, there its takes a relatively crude (indeed, brutal) form, absent the ideological baggage of French ideals of *assimilation*.

With respect to Golden Triangle minorities, the most controversial Laotian government policy—one whose very raison d'être lies in colonial-era beliefs about *montagnard* ravishing of virgin forests—is the relocation of highland ethnicities to the lowlands (see Baird and Shoemaker 2005; Cohen 2000; Evraud and Goudineau 2004). Touted by the government as voluntary, resettlement is undertaken under conditions of systemic duress.[30] While the rationale for resettlement has some basis in developmental and ecological logic (reducing environmentally harmful slash-and-burn agriculture, improving service delivery access, eradicating opium, monitoring groups suspected of subversion, fostering cultural integration and nation building), the outcomes have been dire. These include lower rice yields in lowland paddy as compared with upland production; higher rates of hunger, disease, and infant mortality; and failed adaptation to ecological niche. The Akha have been particularly affected by Laotian internal relocation.

In a single paragraph, Evans (2002, 283) well summarizes the colonially inflected differences in ethnic relations in modern-day Myanmar vis-à-vis Laos. By artificially elevating the status of traditional authorities over ethnic minorities, and by administering the Shan states separately (as protectorates) from the rest of what would become Myanmar, the

> British helped prepare the ground for the post-colonial ethnic revolts and separatist nationalist movements which have continued in Burma to this day. . . . In Indo-China . . . French colonialism supported the upland Tai. . . . In contrast to Burma, and because of the historical peculiarities of the development of nationalism and communism, separatist nationalism [in Laos] failed. . . . In further contrast to Burma, none of the other upland groups . . . became politically mobilized. [The Hmong are an exception.] Thus [in Laos] we do not find . . . strong political movements which can give expression to localized feelings of ethnic identity.

While focusing on indigenous ethnicities partitioned between former British Burma and former French Laos, we should not ignore other approaches. Martin Stuart-Fox (1997) emphasizes the political culture of the Pathet Lao, which was inherently more inclusive than that of the Royal Lao government. Geography, too, is critical: the Burmese Communist Party never penetrated Karen, Kachin, or Shan territory to the extent that the Pathet Lao did throughout Laos.

Turton (2000) stresses the commonality of these peoples "of peripheries and borderlands" within a transcendent, transnational, political domain of Tai-speaking peoples. These include those groups whose language are related to Tai (e.g., Lao, Lue) as well as non-Tai minorities whose communal lives are nevertheless encapsulated within a Tai universe (e.g., Akha, Lahu). "They may form new nuclei in newly (re)configured transnational regions, for example in the 'Golden Triangle' [or] the 'Mekong Quadrangle'" (Turton 2000, 9, 10). Whether Tai-hood will live up to its promise as an indigenous third way in distinction to post-French, post-British cultural models—especially for those peoples divided at the cusps of imperial partition—remains to be seen.

Noncolonized Neighbors and Violent Revolution: Implications for Postcolonial Legacies

Noncolonized Neighbors

More than any other continental case, the Anglo-French boundary and partition in Southeast Asia was affected and conditioned by indirect interface with other nations' borders. While themselves subject to colonial pressures, both Thailand and China functioned as quasi-sovereign states, and Britain and France had to deal with them accordingly.[31] Those colonial-created realities are ones with which Laotian and Burmese policy makers and borderlanders have to deal today.

Creation of the Anglo-French boundary between Burma and Laos intertwined with the need for the British to establish Burmese borderlines, and for the French to establish Laotian ones, with Thailand. Those lines are ultimately responsible for the economies, livelihoods, and life prospects of communities on both sides of the Mekong. They are also responsible for the slow maturation of a modern Laotian nation (Brocheux and Hémery 1995, 369). Much more than paper nationality is at stake: political freedom, material opportunity, and ethnolinguistic identity present very different options depending on the side of the river to which one belongs. Differences in everyday life are more obvious and dramatic in the urban settlements than the rural ones: inhabitants of Houay Xay, in the Lao People's Democratic Republic, display much more limited choices and opportunities vis-à-vis their counterparts in the more freewheeling Thai territory of Chiang Khong than do their rural compatriots vis-à-vis Thai *bans*. But improved transportation linkages, in Laos as well as Thailand, are rapidly reducing even these rural-urban dichotomies.

Differences in material conditions are more dramatic between Laos and Thailand than they are between Laos and Myanmar. Regional (and especially borderland) differentials are not taken into account by aggregate human development index figures. But it is still significant that Houay Xay townsfolk inhabit a nation with human development index ranking of 135, in which nearly three-quarters of their compatriots survive at under two dollars a day, and struggle through with a life expectancy of fifty-four years (including a 28 percent probability at birth of not surviving to forty years). Across the river, residents of Chiang Khong belong to a country with a human development index of 74 (just under oil-rich Saudi Arabia!), in which fewer than one-third of the population fall under the two dollars a day threshold, and where the people can expect to live fifteen years longer on average. Probability at birth of surviving to forty years is about three times greater than in Laos. It is incalculable how many Laotians today are thus disadvantaged because of where the French and the British drew their lines of demarcation with Thailand; and *those* lines, to reiterate, were drawn in large part as a result of intense Anglo-French competition in the Upper Mekong region of Southeast Asia.

Concessions to the non-Western borderline mentality, it must be admitted, are made. There is, for instance, a five-kilometer zone inside Thailand along the Mae Sae River border with Myanmar where expatriates from Burma are allowed to live and work. It is an informal concession, however, and periodically the migrants are pushed back across the border.

Thailand's political status as a functioning constitutional monarchy today (in contrast with a relatively dysfunctional British monarchy) is also significant. Despite both British and French desires to preserve some semblance of traditional authority (the latter more heavy-handed about it than the former), both Myanmar and Laos dispensed—and rather violently—with their respective *sawbwa* and *cao fa*. As such they stand in stark contrast to a Thai neighbor that, as evidenced by the outpouring of popular sentiment on the occasion of the sixtieth anniversary in 2006 of the king's reign, both revels in and reveres its indigenous method of governance. This is a monarchy that is not only constitutional but also developmentalist, raising implicit questions about the socioeconomic costs, for Laos as well as Myanmar, of wholesale eradication of traditional systems of rule. In the domain of chieftaincy, the contrast between Laos and Myanmar on the one hand, and Niger and Nigeria on the other, could not be starker.

China is the other non–former colony that both informed original French and British policy in the region and continues to loom over life there. The British and the French so coveted, respectively, Burma and Indochina as a gateway to Yunnan, that it was on account of the desire of European powers to clearly delineate their own boundaries that Yunnan was formally incorporated into China. Today, it is of little exaggeration to say that Beijing has eclipsed London and Paris as the dominant neocolonial power. Chinese economic influence in Myanmar and Laos is an incrementally evolving indication.

Revolution and Insurgency

Violent revolution and incessant ethnic insurgency also differentiate Southeast Asia from the other cases of colonial partition's aftermath. World War II had disruptive and triggering implications throughout the imperial world (Benda 1956). Only here, however, was there outright occupation by a foreign power. Japanese conquest of Burma and Nippon-Vichy authority in Laos, however temporary, set into motion nationalist and revolutionary reactions that define both countries today. Not until 1975 did Communists succeed in taking over government in Laos; however, that revolutionary outcome (with indispensable Vietnamese help) was inextricably linked to anti-Axis agitation more than three decades before. Anticommunist insurgency (even if now more imagined than real) continues to fuel Lao repression of the Hmong. A decade and a half of anti-Western and especially anti-

French policies created a "lost generation" of would-be French speakers and a former French colony in which Francophonie, despite the best efforts of the French government, is still struggling to restore itself.

Myanmar possesses the dubious record of longest continuous ethnic insurgency in the post–World War II era. All ethnic groups inside Myanmar's angle of the Golden Triangle have been dramatically affected by the ethnic unrest. That unrest, it bears repeating, is a function not only of artificial colonial boundaries but long-term responses to arbitrary colonial policies.

At first blush, Myanmar and Laos represent consummate renunciations of their former colonial "masters." At independence Burma refused membership in the Commonwealth; until recently, it subsequently (and vociferously) rejected democracy, Westminster-style or otherwise. It makes a mockery of the idea of local government. Laos for its part not only renounced French hopes for postcolonial constitutionalism within a capitalistic framework but primacy of the French language itself. Myanmar-style socialism and Laotian-type communism seemingly negate the comparative template that otherwise undergirds our model of colonial legacies.

Yet even as ostensible outliers within the comparative postcolonial universe, our Southeast Asian pair of neighboring former French and British colonies do reflect, if perversely, their superimposed pre-independence paths. Most fundamentally, Laos exists—even in the shadow of Thailand and Vietnam—an enduring creature of French colonial buffer making. France surely did not desire a Communist Laos any more than she did a Communist Vietnam; direct rule, nevertheless, endures. Not many Laotians may actually speak French today, and young ones want to learn English, but la Francophonie in Laos is alive—and internationally, People's Republic or not, Laos is a member of the organization dedicated to its promotion.

Myanmar/Burma shows what happens when a colonial power does not follow its own rules or colonizes carelessly. Many of Burma's problems began when, from the outset, Britain attached her to India—hardly a decision reflective or respectful of indigenous governance. Thereupon followed an inappropriate and ill-adapted reorganization of traditional rulership (Steinberg 1982, 36–37). "Burma proper," unlike the Frontier Areas, was subject to that most un-British method of colonial governance, direct rule. Ethnic minorities outside the Irawaddy Valley, and particularly east of the Salween, were administered separately, and less tightly, in more classic indirect style. They have not looked back, ill-brooking any postcolonial subservience to a basically Burman ethnic elite.

In terms of aggregate material outcomes, life in formerly British Burma and formerly French Laos do not appear so different. Only four places differentiate Myanmar from Laos on the human development index. There is a recorded life expectancy difference of only three years (to Myanmar's ostensible advantage), and whereas Laos can boast a GDP per capita income of six hundred dollars more than Myanmar, its adult literacy rate is 20 percent less.[32] When Stuart-Fox (1995, 121) writes that European partition had the effect of "permanently . . . divid[ing] the Lao territories, and . . . relegat[ing] French Laos to the status of a remote colonial backwater, landlocked, underpopulated and underdeveloped," he retrospectively forecast Laos's fate well into the future.

With respect to life along on the Mekong River border, insurgency, banditry, and overall instability have incontestably been much more intense and longstanding in Myanmar than Laos. Rangoon has never come close to establishing its authority over the Shan states as Vientiane has, even with loose implementational control, for Bokeo and Luang Nam Tha provinces. From the perspective of peace and security, better to be a Laotian peasant of any ethnicity on the east bank than a Burmese one on the west. One can of course counterargue that *wherever* the French and British had decided to draw their colonial line would have become a fulcrum for smuggling and other transboundary behavior. Be that as it may, turn-of-the-century strategists succeeded in turning a natural phenomenon—a river—into an unnatural one—a political boundary. Postcolonial official contact between the Laotian and Burmese states has been minimal. Border markets such as Muangmom in Laos (a magnet for Thai traders from 1978 to 1986 during the Thai-Lao border closure) continue to thrive in apparent obliviousness to their respective national governments. The Mekong stretch attaching Myanmar to Laos is one of the rare borderlands in the world where there are no official immigration posts serving neighboring nations. Informally, convergence of high-stake Laotian and Burmese commercial activity along the Mekong boundary—as in Xieng Kok, a major drug offload site—highlights the instrumental use of political boundaries in unpoliced areas.

Individuals belonging to indigenous groups at the point of convergence—in the Golden Triangle, and particularly along the Mekong River—reflect less awareness of their respective colonial histories (and actual colonial rulers) than elsewhere in the Anglo-French border world. Neither the French in Laos nor the British in Burma ventured much out into their contiguous peripheries; certainly not like in West Africa or in any of the other frontiers we examine in this study. Ironically, however, it is here, in Southeast Asia, that indigenous groups have been subjected to worse fates than partitioned Africans, Indians, Melanesians, and Caribbeans. Their misery takes distinct forms, depending on which side of the Mekong boundary colonial history and postcolonial politics have placed them. On one side, where the French once held sway, hill peoples are actively induced by the government to leave their mountain homelands, exposing them to disease, mortality, and psychosocial pressures to switch from opium to methamphetamines. On the other side, the government of Myanmar has no equivalent "development policy." Instead, it has a repressive military force that conscripts, impresses, confiscates, and otherwise terrorizes its hill peoples and minorities into rebelling or fleeing. The most vulnerable subgroups on both sides of the boundary—women and young girls—migrate to territories of prostitution. Bisecting the Golden Triangle is an inherited colonial line with exceedingly grievous consequences.

7

Scars of Partition in Postcolonial Borderlands and Beyond

[P]hysical distance from the centres of sovereignty is no measure of the power [that border peoples] may hold in locality and nation.
—Hastings Donnan and Thomas Wilson, *Borders: Frontiers of Identity, Nation and State* (1996)

The colonial state was probably never intended to bear the burden of modern statehood that was thrust upon it. These were, after all, conquest states, their external boundaries defined by international rivalry.
—Martin Shipway, *Decolonization and Its Impact* (2008)

It is no use decrying in the twenty-first century the arbitrary boundaries by which Britain and France carved up a good part of the world in the seventeenth through early twentieth centuries. These lines will not be undone, certainly not on the basis of redressing historical injustice. They have taken on a reality of their own, particularly since decolonization has brought forth national structures recognized and protected by the international community under the rubric of sovereignty. What *is* worthwhile is to acknowledge (1) the multiple nature of colonial partition and (2) the differential ethnic dimensions of it. That is the pathway for previously colonized and partitioned peoples to recover their rightful place in the retrospective telling of the colonial story and its aftermath. With no umbrage intended to the inheritors of Belgian, Dutch, Italian, Portuguese, and Spanish colonialism, I believe that the borderlanders inhabiting the space between former French and British colonies have much to tell us.

Multiple Nature of Colonial Partition

Throughout this book I have argued that the classical image of partition—far-off European powers drawing arbitrary lines in the sand or through the jungle—is only part of the colonial story of territorial demarcation. Yes, this is how Britain and France did carve up most of their adjoining spaces in continental Africa: Hausaland is but the most elaborated upon of the many examples we have considered. But water, no less than land, has also served as demarcator: rivers separating Burma from Laos in Southeast Asia or defining Gambia vis-à-vis Senegal, or nautical miles, within which France and Britain claimed nearby islands in the Indian Ocean, South Pacific, and Caribbean Sea. Today, colonial Anglo-French maritime partition culturally and linguistically separates Haitians from Jamaicans, New Caledonians from Solomon Islanders. At the same time, Francophonie (an important legacy of Anglo versus French colonialism) joins Haitians with New Caledonians with Comorans with Réunion Islanders—all otherwise insular peoples.

I have also argued, perhaps more unconventionally, that legacies of Anglo-French partition also constitute psychological and cultural borders between previously colonized subjects of France and Britain who have come to inhabit the same space. Postcolonial New Hebrideans—the ni-Vanuatu—inheriting institutional and linguistic legacies of an Anglo-French condominium are the prime example of a people (Melanesian) having to overcome mental boundaries, not geographical ones, of a colonial making. To a lesser extent (on account of the sequential nature of French and British colonialism) are the continuing social and psychological divides between Afro-Mauritians (Creoles) and Indo-Mauritians. For sure, substantial differences grounded in the ancestral origins of each of these groups count for much, but the fact that Afro-Mauritians first arose as a collectivity out of the early French colonial crucible, and Indo-Mauritians emerged from a later British colonial fount, must also be invoked in explaining the continuing social divide between these two communities on the same island. Furthermore, I have tried to show that the dispersal of various African ethnicities as slaves to plantation islands (East African to Mauritius, Seychelles, Réunion, etc.; West African to Barbados, Guadeloupe, Haiti, etc.) is a kind of double partition: colonially driven separation from continental homeland followed by additional cleavage into British and French colonies. This leads us to the ethnic dimension of colonial partition.

Differential Ethnic Implications of Colonial Partition

Even where postcolonial peoples cross freely between former French and British territories, even when they move among kinsmen, they bring with them the basic mental construct bequeathed by colonialism: national appurtenance. For sure, those borderlanders who have been more socialized by colonial legacy institutions and communication patterns (essentially, education and European language) carry more of the colonial imprint with them than do their less postcolonially socialized brethren. But even the most rustic of borderlanders hold on to their national identity cards with the due care reflective of the importance that agents of the postcolonial regimes attach to them.

Regardless of degree of education, it is among the borderlanders split by Anglo-French partition that the legacies of colonialism are most poignant. Whether they travel overland without constraint between Ghana and Togo (as do the Ewe) or risk traversing the Mekong at their peril (as do the Akha between Myanmar and Laos), borderlanders know quite well to which country they belong and to which government they are subject. Even where the boundary demarcation is invisible to the naked eye, they will know where "their" country ends and the next one begins.[1] They may get off their Dominican fishing boats in

Guadeloupe speaking a locally understood Creole but those maritime West Indian borderlanders know, even before encountering any patrolling gendarmes, that they are not *chez-eux*. They may cross not a single official border in their walk from a Francophone to an Anglophone village on the island of Efate, but ni-Vanuatu will feel (especially on Sundays!) the colonial missionizing difference between the two communities. Individual memory of the colonial era may fade, but the legacies of partition are embedded in the borderlanders. As Donnan and Wilson infer at the beginning of this chapter, the significance of the border peoples' experience may well transcend the borderlands themselves.

Despite nuances in colonial status and policy (see Table 9), with one exception Francophone influence remains significant in all the former French colonies we have considered in the previous chapters. This holds true whether the colony was integrated fully within France (Martinique), was merged into another country entirely (Pondicherry), or became completely independent from *la mère patrie* (Niger, Vanuatu, Mauritius). The exception—worth further reflection—is Laos.

Revolution in Southeast Asia sets that region apart from all five others we have considered (West Africa, West Indies, South Pacific, South Asia, and Indian Ocean).[2] Communism in the long run may not have succeeded, but the extirpation of manifestly colonial structures, institutions, and language was almost total. (Only the arguably Jacobin nature of the people's war, I have asserted, links this part of Indochina with its French antecedents.)

Yet even without communist ideology, anticolonial revolution in next-door Burma was also quite thorough: while former British colonies have in general deviated more from British models of governance and education than their Francophone counterparts have from France, Myanmar remains a particular outlier in rejecting British colonial influences and institutions. Even while acknowledging the important differences between Burman and Lao cultures (not to mention the minority ethnic

Table 9. Cross-Regional Typology of Franco-British Partitioned Regions and Outcomes

Geocultural context	West Africa	West Indies	South Pacific	South Asia	Indian Ocean	Southeast Asia
Exemplar(s)	Hausaland	Martinique; Barbados	Vanuatu	Pondicherry	Mauritius	Laos; Burma/Myanmar
Colonial status	Partitioned into French and British colonies (1904)	"Old Colony" (1635); "Old Representative System" (1639)	Anglo-French condominium (1914)	French Indian enclaves (1635) within British India	French (1715), then British (1810) sovereignty	Partitioned into French and British colonies (1893)
Colonial policy	Direct rule; indirect rule	Assimilation; "saxonization"	Condocolonialism, dual government	Soft colonialism	Hybridic colonialism	Direct rule; dual mandate
Postcolonial regime	Parallel independence for Niger and Nigeria (1960)	Statehood in France (1946); outright independence from United Kingdom (1968)	Independence (1980), though contested (by Francophones)	Merger with Greater India (1962)	Independence (1968), though contested (by Creoles)	Anticolonial war with France; independence (1948–54) from United Kingdom, though contested (by ethnic minorities)

Status of European language(s)	French sole official language in Niger; English sole official language in Nigeria	French sole official language in Martinique; English sole official language in Barbados	Anglophones numerically dominant (60%); endangered Francophonie	French is nominal, marginalized; English for administrative use, privileged	French is language of prestige; English is language of commerce and government; bilingualism	French marginalized in Laos, English marginalized in Burma
Partitioned ethnicities and/or language groups	Hausa, Fulani, Kanuri	Ashanti, Dahomey, Ewe, Fulani, Hausa, Igbo, Nupe, Yoruba+	100+ Melanesian ethnolinguistic groups	Tamil, Malayalam, Telugu	Bhojpuri, Chinese, Creole, French, Hindi, Marathi, Tamil, Urdu+	Akha, Lahu, Lolo, Lue, various Tai groups

groups that have been at odds with central government in both postcolonial polities), the possibility that mainland Southeast Asian culture—in contrast with West African, Caribbean, Melanesian, and East Indian varieties—allows for exceptionally totalistic transformation ought to be considered.

Moreover, the extent to which a postcolonial culture, or ethnicity, has been influenced by its colonial imprint must be recognized. With rare exceptions, there are no abstract cultures that exist independently from their colonially defined national identities. One can no longer comprehensively describe life in Yorubaland without specifying if the Yoruba so described live in Nigeria or Benin, if their children are schooled in English or in French. Is it meaningful to say "Melanesian" if we don't know if the Melanesian in question is the Catholic Kanak of New Caledonia or the Protestant Papuan of New Guinea?

Toward a Summing Up

Despite the basic distinctions between French and British colonial philosophies that I outlined in chapter 1, we have seen how intervening variables have significantly inflected actual policies on both sides of the European enterprise. It is worth considering those variables here, as encapsulated in Table 9.

Ethnicity, History, and Variability in Colonial Policy

Whether or not an ethnic group or groups already inhabited the colonial territory greatly affected the extent to which British and French colonialism would leave its postcolonial mark. Unlike in West Africa, the South Pacific, South Asia, and Southeast Asia, several West Indian and Indian Ocean islands were unpopulated at the time of colonial occupation. Barbados under the British and Mauritius under the French were *tabulae rasae*, with no indigenous populace to contend with. Significantly, colonization of the West Indies and Indian Ocean occurred during the first of the colonial eras, the seventeenth and eighteenth centuries, when neither colonizer recognized the fundamental right to life, liberty, or due process for non-European, non-Christian peoples. Thus, hitherto empty island groups (the Seychelles, the Caymans) could be populated by African slaves, creating new Creolized cultures from scratch. Indigenous populations that did inhabit colonially claimed islands were ruthlessly dispensed with through disease, enslavement, exile, or genocide. Amerindians throughout the Windward and Leeward Islands were thus supplanted by the same types of dispersed African ethnicities brought to work on the uninhabited islands. Mascarenes and Antilles, though antipodes apart, were similarly reconstituted as African-based slave plantation societies. The long-term logic of abolition (1835 for Britain, 1848 for France) differed, as did the consequences: British emancipation meant that the descendants of slaves, who were individually freed from their masters, would achieve collective liberty as individual nations; French emancipation implied an extension of freedom within la République, into which the slave descendants would merge as French citizens. Their territories, too, would be "assimilated" into Greater France. From Réunion in the Indian Ocean to French Guiana on the northeast coast of South America, decolonization of these "Old Colonies" has translated into full integration within the French Republic. This is quite unlike the postcolonial pathway of that other Indian Ocean polity, the independent Republic of the Seychelles; or in South America, British Guiana—now the Cooperative Republic of Guyana. As for the Indian Ocean Republic of Mauritius, known as l'Ile Maurice under the French, it also began as a *tabula rasa* island with an initial trajectory similar to that of the French Antilles (Guadeloupe, Martinique) and the other French Mascarenes (Réunion and Rodrigues): population by ethnic African slaves under French colonists and slaveowners. Conquest by Britain, followed by massive immigration from British India, changed both the ethnic complexion of the island as well as colonial policy away from assimilation.

Assimilationist logic drove French attempts to decolonize after World War II without the rupture implied by outright independence. But neither formal creation of the French Union (1946) nor the French Community (1958) managed to prevent the overwhelming majority of the non-Creolized colonies from becoming fully independent. Where indigenous African and Asian populations retained, despite colonization, a strong social and cultural autonomy predating the French, they eventually opted for complete political separation. Except for Indochina, however, independence from France did not mean postcolonial rejection of French institutions, educational and linguistic models, and bureaucratic mentalities.

New Caledonia and French Polynesia present important challenges to these general conclusions and therefore demand attention. Both are former colonies populated by indigenous non-Creole peoples, and do persist as constituent parts of the French Republic, their inhabitants full-French citizens with voting rights and economic benefits. They also represent stark differences with respect to assimilationist attitudes vis-à-vis France. Due to its long heritage as a settler colony, and erstwhile open immigration from other South Pacific islands, the indigenous islanders—the Kanaks—do not constitute a majority of the population. Defying electoral reality, they have agitated (sometimes violently) for juridical change. New Caledonia, already with a special juridical status, and developing its own flag, hymn, motto, and currency, may very well vote for out-and-out independence by 2019. If it does so, it will logically (however belatedly) join those former French colonies whose indigenous non-Creole populations opted for independence decades before.

French Polynesia represents a conundrum. Here we do have a strong indigenous culture and a population originally colonized in the same era as were New Caledonia, Indochina, and West Africa. Yet French Polynesians, even as they have evolved toward more administrative autonomy as part of an overseas "collectivity" rather "territory," have in general been much more accepting of an indefinite (if not eternal) future within the bosom of France. Should we not consider the possibility that Polynesian and Indochinese cultures represent antipodes on a spectrum mapping accommodation to French postcolonial assimilationism?

Counterpart colonies in the British West Indies, West Africa, and South Asia initially carried on with British models of governance and elite training but have gradually succumbed to the less doctrinal, but no less powerful, assimilationist influences of American culture, language, and politics. Mauritius, an unusual but informative case of hybridic colonialism, demonstrates the relative success that derives from an amalgamation of dual (but sequential) colonial imprints with clearly defined parameters (French: media, culture, mobility; English: governance, judiciary, commerce) eagerly absorbed by an immigrant culture with continuing economic and cultural ties to their ancestral home (India). Vanuatu, on the other hand, serves as a more cautionary tale when dual colonial powers vie simultaneously for influence over an already diverse indigenous population (namely Melanesian) over the same territory, deploying uneven economic resources (French greater than British) and politico-religious incentives (Protestant liberation theology for Anglophone nationalists, Catholic educational support for Francophiles). Where a similar kind of colonial rivalry for political loyalty among indigenous peoples or language groups prevails (as it did in India), it surely helps that there are clear territorial divisions (unlike in condocolonialism) whose existence may be maintained, in some administrative fashion, in the postcolonial era (e.g., the Union Territory of Pondicherry). It surely helps postcolonial Pondicherrians, too, that France practiced what I have called a "soft colonialism" in French India.

Postcolonial Regimes

Local resistance to independence among Francophones and Francophiles can be invoked in many ways, from opposition by Mauritian Creoles in the late 1960s to separatism in parts of the New Hebrides in 1980 to Martinican rejection of even mild proposals for administrative change in the first decade of the twenty-first century. How a direct, popular vote on the merger with Greater India would have come out in Pondichéry will never be known—diehard Francophiles insist that India's refusal to allow a direct vote in 1954 is itself evidence of more popular antimerger sentiment. In contrast, there are few instances of active opposition to independence from Britain—Anguilla's desire to remain British separate from independent St. Kitts–Nevis being "the exception that proved unruly" (Hintjens 1995, 39). Hill tribe resistance to independence in Burma, as we have seen, was motivated less by love of the Queen than fear of lowland Burman oppression; as in so many domains we have examined, Southeast Asia (represented by Myanmar and Laos) presents postcolonial exceptions.

Out of the six borderland cases we have focused on, eight independent nations have emerged. Four of those countries are former British colonies (Barbados, Burma, India, Nigeria) and two of them are former French ones (Laos, Niger). Vanuatu was at the same time French and British, while Mauritius was French and then British. In addition, two of the polities have been integrated into much larger nations: Martinique as part of France, and Pondicherry as part of India. What can their geoculturally specific experience tell us about the wider phenomenon of partition and postcolonialism? How have their respective populations fared? Do these borderlanders have a common message?

Regional and Geocultural Extrapolations

Considered in light of the wider West African experience of British and French colonialism and its aftermath, we have seen how the partition of Hausaland into Nigeria and Niger serves as classic example of ethnic separation into separate postcolonial polities. Beyond that, however, it reminds us of the arbitrary imbalance of partition's eventual national outcomes: some postcolonial states are much larger or wealthier or more powerful than their neighbors, and their borderlanders therefore inherit disproportionate postcolonial opportunity. Niger is larger in territory, but Nigérien Hausa must subsist in the nation consistently ranked by the United Nations as the least developed in the world: Nigérien uranium hardly rivals Nigerian petroleum in its trickle-down effect (however skewed and distorted that petro-naira trickle-down may be).

Similarly, while the Lao People's Democratic Republic is no socialist haven, the Lahu, Lolo, and Lue there, not to mention the Akha and Tai, lead a more peaceable and secure existence than their cousins over the border in Myanmar. Burma may have more people and greater natural resources, advantages that may one day redound to its borderlands, but until that time, and notwithstanding the Indochinese War and its Hmong resistance legacies, the Mekong as postcolonial boundary remains a demarcator of imbalanced suffering.

It is in South Asia that British-French colonial line drawing most lopsidedly divided an ethnic group. In India, the overwhelming majority of Tamils would experience British colonialism while a tiny fraction would be Frenchified. Yet the smaller the colonial unit, the French Indian experience suggests, the greater the possibility for colonial transformation: Madras never resembled London the way that Pondicherry evoked Paris. The "softness" of colonialism in French India, compared both to the British raj next door and to French varieties farther away, must also be partly attributed to the partition's demographic imbalance. How else to account for Chandernagor becoming a haven for the revolutionary Aurobindo Ghosh?

From a spatial perspective, island colonies are particularly subject to intensive colonization, with one caveat: archipelagoes present complications for sovereignty. In addition to the nexus between Creole society and colonialism that we have discussed above, the geographical fact that Barbados, Martinique, and Mauritius were also mono-island colonies rendered their societies much more susceptible to British and French colonialism than any of the continental colonies—and much more so than the sprawling archipelago of the New Hebrides (Vanuatu).

We must refrain from the temptation to draw sweeping cultural conclusions as we reconsider the six geocultural cases of British versus French colonialism. At a macro level, it is tempting to contrast Sanskritization—the cultural absorption, incorporation, and transcending of imperial overlords by militarily conquered Indian civilizations—with the Southeast Asian proclivity to confront colonial domination by violent resistance, be it nationalist (e.g., Burman) or communist (Laotian and Burmese) in inspiration. The problem emerges when we disaggregate, as we must, the overarching cultural regions. A Hmong from Laos will emphatically remind you that he is not a Lao; it is on the basis of not being Burman that Karen and Shan of Burma have risked their lives for decades in organized resistance to the Burmese government.

Can we so easily contrast the "Pacific Polynesians," who assume their citizenship as French citizens more easily than the "militant Melanesians" of New Caledonia, on the basis of culture? The Melanesians of the New Hebrides were hardly united in their opposition to condocolonial rule, and we have seen how the supposedly unifying indigenous principle of *kastom* (traditional Melanesian practices, norms, and beliefs) itself became politicized and thereby divisive.

And what generalization could we possibly make of the more than fifty African ethnolinguistic groups partitioned into former French and British colonies in West Africa? What cultural similarity—other than some familiarity with French—do the Ewe of Togo really have with the Wolof of Senegal? Diversity in Africanity precludes generalization, be it with respect to response to colonialism or other historical adaptations: Tuareg militancy culture is the antithesis of Igbo mercantilism. Perhaps the best generalization with respect to the cultural dimension is the paradoxical invocation of specificity: partitioned peoples in individual borderlands must be queried about their own colonial and postcolonial experiences and beliefs.

Material and Political Outcomes

Within both postcolonial camps, French and British, political outcomes have varied wildly among our ten polities. On the mono-Anglophone side, we have both the oldest continuously functioning legislature in the Western world (Barbados) and until recently one of the most repressive (not to say bizarre) military dictatorships in modern history (Myanmar). In between, we have the fitful and flawed but continuously aspiring democracy in Africa's most populous nation (Nigeria). And although we have not examined it at length, the "world's largest democracy" (India) is one beset with major political challenges in the realm of human rights, judicial impartiality, and in several locales, local government gangsterism.

On the monocolonial French side, we have both a robust democratic system that is quite competitive notwithstanding its lack of sovereignty (Martinique) and a "people's republic" that makes little pretense of democracy (Laos). In between, we have an African state whose political pathway seesaws between constitution and coup d'état (Niger).

The three mixed Anglophone-Francophone polities present a slightly better prospect for generalizability. Merger into a former British colony of a French one (Pondicherry) has extended to the inhabitants of former French India the expectations and habits of Western democracy and rule of law. This has been tempered, however, by periodic bouts of presidential rule from Delhi as party coalitions fissure and the central government dissolves the local legislature. Had Pondicherry been merged into the state of Tamil Nadu, Delhi would have no such prerogative, but Pondicherry is a Union Territory.

Independence following coextensive and simultaneous British-French rule (Vanuatu) has also been characterized by democratic governance, but not without serious problems. Putting aside the rebellion that initially opposed independent rule under an "Anglophone" government, serious challenges to postcondominial democracy have been posed by sustained corruption at the ministerial level, pressures exercised on the judiciary, an uneasy relationship between equal rights and customary law, discontent within the paramilitary defense forces, and lingering suspicions between Anglophones and Francophones.

Sequential (French, then British) and hybridic (Indo-Sino-Anglo-Franco) colonialism has netted an oft-envied political outcome (Mauritius). Independence-eve unrest has been followed by overwhelming acceptance of a political system in which parliament is practically the sole English-only-speaking institution in a French Creole and East Indian society. With its "best loser" system (guaranteeing representation for otherwise excluded ethnic minorities), Mauritian democracy may be inimitable, though the best loser system is not universally hailed in postmillennial Mauritius. Persistent marginalization of the Afro-Mauritian (Creole) community remains a major challenge. Still, this is one mixed Anglophone-Francophone system where postcolonial politics are, from a democratic standpoint, quite healthy.

The range in postcolonial outcomes among former French, British, and mixed colonial polities belies simple generalization. Colonial legacy is not a singly determinative factor in political outcomes. Still, it is no coincidence that a persistent centralization of political authority remains most pronounced in the former French colonial sphere, despite much ballyhooed decentralizing reforms in several of them: Sahelians and Saharans of Niger are still beholden to Niamey; East Mekong riverine peoples and hilltop Laotians remain firmly subject to Vientiane; and Martinique, for all its local government, still answers to Paris. One cannot say in like manner that Abuja controls Nigeria, or that Naypyidaw rules all Myanmar, or that Bridgetown defines Barbados.

Consumerism, too, should be viewed as a differential outcome factor in certain configurations of postcolonial partition. Writing in the context of France's nonindependent postcolonies (overseas departments and territories) in the early 1990s,

Aldrich and Connell already noted that "[c]hanges in the last twenty years, including the advent of consumer society, have increased gaps between the DOM-TOMS and their neighbours and made acceptance of a fall in living standards less likely" (1992, 297).[3] Money to Mayotte, for example, militates against reunification with Comoros, on account of a widening wealth gap between the two. Economics is most apparent as a legacy of colonial partition where decolonization occurred without sovereignty (Miles 2005a).

Status of European and Indigenous Languages

Perhaps the strongest generalization can be made in the realm of language. Concerted efforts to preserve and defend the erstwhile colonial language exist in former French colonies in ways without equivalent in the former British colonies that border them.[4] As a language of international prestige and diplomacy, French has declined substantially from the days of decolonization, not to mention from the epochs of partition. In contrast, defense of the "British" language is not necessary or even logical. As English increasingly becomes the global lingua franca, its instruction and acquisition becomes the communicatory default for developing nations.

Francophone leaders are acutely aware of their minority linguistic status, particularly in places like Pondicherry and Vanuatu. Speaking only French (or French Creole) in the West Indies makes that region even more of a Francophone holdout than West Africa, where the two most populous countries are Anglophone: Nigeria and Ghana. Among our case studies, only in Mauritius is French flourishing in a nondefensive context—this, in a highly multilingual context where English is the language of government and law, no less.

It is disconcerting that official dealings between ethnically similar representatives of bordering nations must often be intermediated by interpreters, because only the official—that is, colonial—languages are permitted by diplomatic convention.

Such is the case when the prime minister of St. Lucia visits the general council of Guadeloupe, for example, or a Kanak representative from New Caledonia meets with an Anglophone legislator of Vanuatu. Although both may speak Hausa, a Nigerian statesman and his Nigérien counterpart may be bound by protocol to address each other, via translation, in English and French.

Of course, they may very well not share a language after all. When prime minister of Barbados Tom Adams happened to drop by the government documentation office in Martinique when I was doing research there, I was the only one in the room (besides the official interpreter) who could speak to him directly. Linguistic divisions remain among the most scarring legacies of colonial partition.

In a postcolonial turnaround, the movement of la Francophonie—itself a very postcolonial phenomenon—fashions itself as a defender of endangered indigenous languages. Given that French colonial policy tacitly and overtly denigrated the "native" languages of the peoples it colonized (especially in its educational endeavors), this is quite an irony. But themselves challenged by English as the quasi-omnipotent tongue of the postcolonial world, promoters of the French language (among whom France is a major, albeit far from exclusive, actor) now join forces with other minority-language speakers to preserve the invented right not to have to Anglophonize. As seen by the disappeared African languages in the West Indian diaspora, the disappearing Asian languages in the Indian Ocean islands, and the endangered Melanesian languages in the South Pacific, resisting linguicide in the postcolonial world is an uphill battle. Ironically, indigenous languages seem to be healthiest in the poorest countries with the least degree of globalization: Laos, Myanmar.

Toward a Common Borderlander Message?

There is no overarching multinational organization for borderland or partitioned peoples writ large. By definition and postcolonial practice, they are among the most marginalized casualties of colonial line drawing, the least likely to connect on the base of shared demarcation. One can only posit what common message borderlanders would have, and wonder if they would align, within such an organization, into interest groups of Anglophone and Francophone postcolonies.

Due to education, language, and in some cases military experience, one can infer commonalities among Nigérien, Martinican, and Pondicherrian elites that they do not share vis-à-vis their Nigerian, Barbadian, and Indian counterparts. A sense of Francophone cultural superiority despite global Anglophone linguistic besiegement would be one of them. With respect to the humble, probably poorer, borderlanders of their respective postcolonies, along with those of Southeast Asia and the South Pacific, it is more difficult to imagine how they would articulate their common identity. Most likely it would center on the distance between them and their superimposed political centers, the originally artificial but increasingly real divisions between them and their juridically foreign co-ethnics, and above all, the lack of attention paid to them by their own governments and the world at large. Inattention to, and neglect of, the lands and peoples partitioned between French and British colonies have been a common thread of postcolonial politics, one to which borderlanders as a group wish to see redressed.

Communism and Colonialism, Scars and Healing

The sudden shift from a bipolar Cold War paradigm of superpowers evokes irrepressible echoes from a not-so-distant time when European colonialism (as embodied by two erstwhile superpowers) also quickly dissipated. Even as the formal system (colonialism on the one hand, communism on the other) ends, its legacies live on in the realms of politics, economy, culture, and language. Decades of institutional habits and psychological patterns are not easily shed. Understanding those legacies helps guard against the dangers of postconflict forgetfulness and triumphalism.

I shall resist the temptation, in these concluding lines, to dwell on the long-term implications of ideological expansion and imperial breakdown within the Soviet orbit. Readers are free to invoke their own parallels, either in Eurasia or wherever sudden "liberation from tyranny" fails to deliver promised freedom and prosperity. Raymond Betts (2004) and M. E. Chamberlain (1999) included in the second editions of their identically main-titled books *Decolonization* new portions reflecting the collapse of the Soviet empire. If I have succeeded in demonstrating how, after a much longer period of formal decolonization, British and French policies, mentalities, and institutions *still* differentially shape and condition life possibilities in their former colonies in Africa, Asia, Oceania, and the Caribbean, then I shall have achieved my goal. If these findings can be applied elsewhere where promises from "regime change" falter, so much the better.

My concern with the scars I have probed throughout these pages lies less with the lines on the map than with the people cut by them—distinct and distinctive ethnic peoples, severed in the borderlands by a combination of British and French competition, complicity, and compromise, and then mostly forgotten by the colonial powers and their postcolonial chroniclers. Kanuri or Creole, Melanesian or Malayalam, it is they—and not their erstwhile European overlords—who ought rightfully to capture the imagination of those grappling with the legacies of colonialism. It is with them, in the borderlands of colonialism, that the scars of partition must first begin to heal.

NOTES

1. Anglo-French Partition

1. Full introspective honesty inclines me to acknowledge psychology as an additional possible framework for exploring the "compulsion" of border crossing (see Babineu 1972).

2. For a working definition of borderlands, we may defer to eminent political scientist William Zartman (2010, 2), who in his global project to understand life in them, writes: "Borderlands are inhabited territories located on the margins of a power center, or between power centers, with *power* understood in the civilizational as well as the politico-economic sense." For a comparative history of borderlands, see Baud and van Schendel (1997).

3. My allergy to this trendier framework of "coloniality" is shared by Frederick Cooper (2002). By stressing the effects of partition (one of the less mutable of colonial phenomena), I believe I am also less vulnerable to the fallacies he identifies in other scholars of colonial studies: story-plucking, leapfrogging, and time flattening. The collection by Forsdick and Murphy (2003) provides a good mix of perspectives. Mbembe's early (1992) contribution was also quite useful.

4. Studies of French colonialism have a time-honored place in the scholarly literature (Aldrich 1995; Betts 1961; Conklin 1997; Deschamps 1953; Lewis 1961–62; Quinn 2000), Vichy's aggravating role receiving particular attention (Cantier and Jennings 2004; Ginio 2006; Jennings 2001e). They serve as building blocks for general treatments of decolonization (Betts 1991; Davidson 1992; Dixon and Hefferman 1991; Gifford and Louis 1988; Von Albertini 1982) and race-based colonialism (Peabody and Stovall 2003). Ongoing French influence in the postcolonial era has also been the subject of excellent academic work (Aldrich and Connell 1992, 1998; Hintjens 1995). Closest to the project at hand are those works that explicitly contrast French with British modes of colonialism and decolonization (Asiwaju 2001; Dimier 2002; Fry 1997; Hargreaves 1993; Hawkins 1996; Morris-Jones and Fisher 1980; Smith 1978; Whiteman 1993).

5. Early exemplars of the position minimizing the long-term import of colonialism, and by implication the nuances among colonial systems, were J. F. A. Ajayi (1969) and A. G. Hopkins (1973).

6. Under the apparent influence of Braudel's *longue durée* and persuaded by overall colonial superficiality, Betts writes that "French domination was not so deep-rooted in most colonial territories, was not so structurally fixed"; it was mostly an urban affair, "rather easily removed and with little lasting monuments or desires." Yet two pages later he concedes that "in the immediate, in the decades after decolonisation, the French colonial influence has remained strong" (Betts 1991, 130, 132).

7. "[C]olonialism . . . marks a clear watershed in the history of the continent, and Africa's subsequent development is bound to be very much determined by some of its legacies. . . . The British bequeathed a far better trained and numerically stronger civil service to its former colonies than the French" (Boahen 1987, 111, 98).

8. L'*Organisation de la Francophonie* (OIF), as the multinational Francophone association is currently known, annually spends ten times as much money per inhabitant of its member country as the Commonwealth (Auplat 2003, 64).

9. Britain and France jointly ruled these islands as a condominium.

10. Not that this is a purely colonial phenomenon: Peter Sahlins (1989) applies a similar framework in tracing the development of national societies in the borderlands of France and Spain.

11. Even along the Mekong, my case where the borderline has least mental effect, the Laotian fugitive on Thai territory is acutely aware of the reality of the boundary.

12. Fredrik Barth (1969), from an anthropologist's perspective, conveys the seemingly trivial ways in which otherwise similar ethnic groups construct social boundaries to differentiate one another. Sigmund Freud, as a psychologist, wrote famously (and mockingly?) of the "narcissism of small differences," connoting the striving by peoples to maintain their unique identities. Neither was invoking actual juridical borders, but even arbitrarily superimposed boundaries are convenient tools for such internal differentiation.

13. This is why, although I have compiled regional tables of "material outcomes" between former French and British colonies in the chapters, I have not created averages of their constitutive data or otherwise rank ordered them in any quantitative way. While cognizant of the fine work of Acemoglu, Johnson, and Robinson (2001) and Lange (2005), I have resisted the temptation to follow them down the quantitative path to explain postcolonial developmental outcomes. Two sobering postcolonial statistics do nevertheless need to be singled out: in Africa between 1960 and 1990, for every 10,000 inhabitants the number of "victims of repression or massacres" was 35 in former French colonies as opposed to 790 in former British ones. Over the same period,

the number of overall victims of political violence was 40,000 in the former versus 2 million in the latter (Glaser and Smith 2005, 84; Smith 2013, 167).

14. This circumstance enabled me to interview many more participants in the lead-up to, and immediate aftermath of, independence than for the other cases. The chapter on the South Pacific thus contains much more in the way of primary-source oral history than the other chapters.

2. West Africa

1. Specialists of the partition are keen to point out that local politics and political structures *were* in fact taken into account by colonial line drawers more than is commonly supposed. See, for example, Prescott (1987, citing Gann and Duignan 1969 and Touval 1972), Nugent (2002, citing Anene 1970), and Thom (1975).

2. For otherwise overlooked peoples, even an accent mark reinforces identity.

3. In her comparative Francophone-Anglophone analysis (see below), Widner (1994, 77n12) does not count Cameroon as being either Francophone or Anglophone. If anything, I would argue, its unique colonial legacies means it should be considered both. For an early treatment of the dual postcolonial legacy in Cameroon, see Ardener (1967).

4. Nigeria also borders Chad, which the French administered as part of French Equatorial Africa. Lake Chad, through which Nigeria's northeast boundary with the similarly named state passes, has since shriveled to the point of turning a maritime border into a terrestrial one.

5. "Intact" qualifies the otherwise longer border between Nigeria and Cameroon. In 1961 the inhabitants of northern Cameroon voted to join Nigeria, while those of southern Cameroon opted for amalgamation with Cameroon proper. Southerners impart to Cameroon its Anglophone (albeit minoritarian) flavor within an officially bilingual state.

6. Examples in the former category are Benin and Nigeria; Niger and Nigeria; and Togo and Benin. Instances of the latter case are Cameroon and Nigeria, and Benin and Burkina Faso.

7. I am including here among the Anglophone independent states Liberia, which was not a British colony but an asylum state, established in 1847 for freed American slaves.

8. Gobir, Rano, Daura, Garun Gabas, Zaria, Kano, Katsina.

9. As noted in chapter 1, scholars of the similarity school challenge the reality of British hands-off overrule. For Northern Nigeria, Ikime (1968) was an early dissident on substantive colonial differences; two decades later, Peter Tibenderana (1988, 1989) resurrected the argument in his focus on Sokoto.

10. Sir Frederick Lugard (1858–1945), the embodiment of Indirect Rule, was the first high commissioner of Northern Nigeria (1900–1906) before becoming governor of Hong Kong (1907–1912). He then returned to Nige-

ria, where he served until 1919, the last five years of which were as governor general.

11. Although more difficult, there were also a trans-Saharan route moving downward from the Mediterranean coast in the Maghreb.

12. The rest of this section summarizes primary research first published in Miles (1993) and expanded in Miles (1994b, 99–115).

13. "Sardauna" is a traditional royal title for chief political advisor to the sultan.

14. Vernacular terms for the white man, also reflective of different racial world views, also persist. In Nigeria, he (or she) is referred to as "Bature," European; in Niger, "Anasara," or Christian. In a Muslim context, use of the latter accentuates the distancing between black and white.

15. United Nations Development Programme, *Human Development Report* 2013. Niger's ranking has consistently been last in overall human development out of the (now) 187 countries so included. It should be noted, however, that with an indicator 55 years, life expectancy in Niger is higher than in Nigeria.

16. Elsewhere (Miles 1994b, 234–35) I have described the threats, insults, and beatings I witnessed during a school visit.

17. But see Clarke (1979) regarding initial resistance to Universal Primary Education on the part of the Qur'an schoolteachers in northern Nigeria.

18. "Shehu" is both a Fulani proper name and a traditional royal title.

19. The dominance of the sultanate of Sokoto in overall Nigerian politics (military as well as civilian) from independence until 1986 is argued in *Africa Confidential* 27 (July 2): 14 ("Nigeria: Breaking with Tradition"). Alhaji Muhammadu Maccido's appointment as sultan of Sokoto in 1996, and that of distinguished army officer Sa'adu Abubakar in 2006, may be viewed as a restoration of the influence of Hausa/Hausa-Fulani chieftaincy, as embodied in its paramount sultanate.

20. See Callaway (1984,1987a, 1987b, 1991), Coles (1991), Frishman (1991), Imam (1991, 1994), Mack (1991), Pellow (1991), Pitten (1983, 1984, 1991), Schildkrout (1983), Sule and Starratt (1991), and Yusuf (1991). Barkow (1972) and Longhurst (1982) have focused on Hausa women in rural Nigeria.

21. See Beik (1991), Dunbar (1991), Echard (1991), Stephens (1991).

22. The first use of microwave radio technology telephonically linked the nearby cities of Maradi (Niger) and Katsina (Nigeria).

23. Dispute with Cameroon over the oil-rich Bakassi Peninsula has been especially tendentious, resulting in military clashes, international arbitration, and the eventual cession of about 250 villages previously claimed by Nigeria.

24. Note the continuing descriptor of Nigeria by its indigenized "English" colonial name, *Ingilishi*.

25. *Faransi*—meaning France or French—remains the borderland name for Niger.

3. West Indies

1. There does persist on the island of Dominica a reserve for Carib Indians whose ancestors were granted a kind of asylum from further decimation: many were expelled there from neighboring islands. Although they retain communal property rights, the language of these Caribs is Creole, their religion, Christian. Although retaining some ethnic features of their precolonial forebears, beyond producing handicrafts (mainly for a tourist clientele) they do not preserve Carib culture in any meaningful sense.

2. But see Chambers (1997), who discusses an initial "Igboization" of, for instance, Jamaica, the Bahamas, and St. Domingue. Igbo cultural residues have also been identified in Virginia and Barbados.

3. Probably the most detailed account of the fate of Hausa in the New World comes from the French consul in Bahia, Brazil, in the 1840s, Francis de Castelnau. Hausa were at the head of plans to mount a slave rebellion. See Reis (2003).

4. Girard (2000) cautions that the independentists, concerned more with cultural identity than electoral democracy, could very well threaten ethnic equilibrium and local freedom should they ever gain power.

5. Still, Mervyn Alleyne (2002, 171) is correct to note that French West Indians, when referring to the Anglophones from the Leeward and Windward Islands, employ the construction *les Caribéens*: "note the implication that Martinique is not part of the Caribbean but part of France." Alleyne contrasts Martinicans primarily with Jamaicans, particularly in terms of the former's rejection of Africanity and blackness ("distanciation").

6. Berrian (2000) and Guilbault (1993) interpret the French West Indian musical scene differently.

7. Bacchus (1996) shows that the education of ex-slaves was much greater in Barbados than other British colonial governments. As capital of the French West Indies, Martinique's public school system developed earlier than that of Guadeloupe and French Guiana.

8. The others are nature of colonization, tradition of representative government, early provision of education, small size, and "economic luck."

9. A legendary if apocryphal telegram was dispatched from Barbados to London at the outbreak of war (Boer? First World?): "Go ahead, England," it reputedly encouraged. "Little England [or Barbados] is behind you."

10. More than one-third of Barbados' own population.

11. The closest Martinican equivalent to the Red Leg, the *béké goyave* (guava), did not form part of a discrete community in a similar way.

12. It is nevertheless worth quoting from the extraordinary autobiography of the well-traveled Igbo slave Olaudah Equiano. Equiano, who was owned by a series of Englishmen, visited much of the West Indies, including Barbados and Martinique. Of the latter he wrote, "In general . . . slaves were better treated, had more holidays, and looked better than those in the English islands" (Equiano [1789] 1995, 136).

13. Linden Lewis (2001, 154) lambastes the article as being "stunningly unsophisticated and incredibly sexist."

14. Meyerson, Hornbeck, and Haggerty (1989) report 90 percent black; 5 percent mulatto; 5 percent white.

15. "Intermarriage across ethnic boundaries was taboo, and Barbados . . . came into the twentieth century with a very small mixed-race population and a minimally diluted African gene pool" (Beckles 2004, 170).

16. Hilary Beckles (2004, 2006) is the foremost Barbadian historian to challenge, from an "Afro-Barbadian" perspective, this English social model. Beckles advances a more radical interpretation of Barbadian political culture and democratization rooted in a protracted and "sophisticated grassroots struggle" (2004, xii) on the part of plantation and working-class islanders. The "crisis of black intellectuals" today is that they have done little "to liberate . . . society from this plantation 'cocoon' that incubates a mind of submissiveness to the legacy of the English mercantile model of socioeconomic exploitation" (154).

17. Duncan (1994, 90) criticizes political parties in Barbados for their "dilettantism and personality cultism."

18. The accuracy of this sentiment may be challenged on generational grounds. George Lamming claimed that "Barbados has always been ruled by fear. There was no black man of my generation, irrespective of class or occupation, who was not afraid of white people. There was no black boss who did not see it as his role to intimidate his black subordinates: and to do so on behalf of white power. This legacy of fear, created and nourished by an ideology of racism, has never been overcome to this day" (quoted in Lewis 2001, 144). But even Linden Lewis (2001, 152) acknowledges that "[i]n Barbados, perhaps given the absence of frequent overt conflict, research on race is largely undeveloped."

19. Gmelch and Gmelch (1997, 156–59) do, on the other hand, note a general loosening of religiosity. They attribute it to modernization.

20. For the 2003 referendum, see Miles 2006; for 2010, see Miles 2012.

21. In this camp may be included such personalities as Alfred Almont, Michel Chalono, the late Max Elizé, Miguel Laventure, André Lesueur, Roger Lise, the late Emile Maurice, Yann Monplaisir, Pierre Petit, and the late Michel Renard.

22. Hilary Beckles, Anthony Layne, Linden Lewis, and Hilbourne Watson.

23. Over 20 percent of annual revenues goes to schooling in Barbados, an impressive allocation even for developed countries.

24. Not much, at least for Anglophone Caribbeanists. Carlene Edie's (1994) edited volume, for example, has fourteen chapters (including ones on Cuba and Puerto Rico) that explore *Democracy in the Caribbean* but not one essay on the FSA. An even more comprehensive volume, tantalizingly entitled *Living at the Borderlines: Issues in Caribbean Sovereignty and Devel-*

opment contains twenty-four chapters, but again none on the French islands (Barrow-Giles and Marshall 2003).

Colonial legacies redound upon Anglophone academics of the Caribbean, many of whom dismiss, overlook, exclude, or ignore the FSA as not really belonging to their region. I am reminded of my experience as a graduate student in the Widener Library at Harvard University, when I suggested that the periodicals collection subscribe to *Info Caraïbe*, the sole news compendium on the French Caribbean then in existence. The acquisitions librarian for Latin America referred my request to colleagues collecting serials on France, who themselves believed the matter was best covered by . . . the periodical collectors for Latin America!

25. Haiti's earthquake in 2010 tragically revealed, for those who did not already appreciate it, the infrastructural, governmental, and emergency response insufficiencies of this otherwise independent West Indian state.

4. The South Pacific

1. North of the equator lies Micronesia ("small islands") which, coming under Japanese and U.S. influence, escaped the British-French rivalries and partitions of Polynesia and Melanesia.

2. Samoa, formerly known as Western Samoa, should not be confused with American Samoa. As the names imply, the partition of the Samoans was not a British-French affair matter, but an Anglo-Anglo one: Kiwi vs. Yankee.

3. Administration over the New Hebrides was officially tripartite. While the condominium per se was responsible for joint services (e.g., courts for Melanesians, transportation, communications, agriculture, livestock), Britain and France each still retained independent responsibilities (e.g., police, health, education, courts for their respective nationals and for non-Melanesian "optants").

4. The best (or most notorious) example was dubbed "Tanna Law" on the island by that name, established by an Irish Presbyterian missionary and strictly enforced by local adepts.

5. For sure there was some crossover: the Free Evangelical church, first established in New Caledonia, has created a hybrid category of Protestant Francophones.

6. Classic maritime partition also defines postcolonial Vanuatu: the most northern island of Hiu and the most southern one of Aneityum are closer, respectively, to the Solomon Islands and New Caledonia than they are to each other.

7. Scottish Presbyterian John Paton led the missionary lobby, four decades after Williams's death, for British annexation.

8. A rare Indochinese inference on comparative racism emerges in this context through the memoir of one Sy Hua Dong, who is noted as claiming that the "French colonists [are] . . . of the worst kind, behaving like kings

and given to 'displays of the most basic racism, and the nastiest forms of racial contempt'" (Dong, cited in Meyerhoff 2002, 50).

9. Reminiscences of Jean-Jacques Robert, the highest official representing France in the New Hebrides at the run-up to independence, deny this but are conflicted by accounts of tape recordings in Robert's meetings with rebels. See Bresnihan and Woodward (2002, 434–35, 504).

10. Of course, one could argue that the West Indies provides a contemporary, ongoing case. But inasmuch as the independence of the French West Indies is far from certain, a postcolonial assessment of it, even in comparison with the already independent Anglophone islands, is premature. Most of the interviews summarized here were conducted eleven years after independence.

11. Interview by author, in Bislama, March 27, 1991.

12. John Peter, interview by author, in Bislama, 1991. John Peter was born in 1925 and volunteered that he was circumcised in 1932.

13. Interview by author, in French, August 3, 1991.

14. Interview by author, in English, August 9, 1992. The most extensive collection in the genre of recollections (one that prominently features former district agents) may be found in Bresnihan and Woodward (2002). For the perspective of French settlers, see Delpech and Bellaïche (1987). Only one of the interviewees here appears in those other works.

15. Interview by author, in Bislama, August 18, 1991, shortly after Stephens's release from prison. In the interview he insisted that he had no problems with Lini personally; it was the latter's ministers who pushed him toward prosecution.

16. Interview by author, in English, July 1991.

17. Some ni-Vanuatu Francophones are more dismissive of Bislama: "Any small kid can speak it," jeers the principal of a Catholic school on Ambae Island. That the national language would become the object of derision of such a significant portion of the population—educated Francophones—is one of the most problematic legacies of Anglo-French partition in the South Pacific.

18. Interview by author, in Bislama, June 4, 1991.

19. When high school students at the Lycée de Bougainville went on strike, the French educational advisor spoke admiringly of them. "Resisting the system" and rebelling were, for him, a sign of successful French acculturation (*ésprit critique, ésprit contestataire*). Among Anglophone students, in contrast, the notion of a student strike was alien.

20. Among ni-Vanuatu, there is a virtually uniform congruence in thought between politics as a process and partisan political activities. In all my interviewing, only Jimmy Stephens conceived of politics in a broader, precolonial context: "Before the white man came, we had politics—not voting, not parties . . . If a chief fights another chief's country—that's the politics of the black man. . . . Politics for me is not talk—it's work. It is my food." Stephens's broader notion of politics was also compatible with custom: "Kas-

tom is about fixing problems.... My politics is work—feeding pigs, many women, lots of everything."

21. Interview by author, in French, June 7, 1991.

22. Interview by author, in French, at the Vanuatu Parliament building, April 20, 1991.

23. Interview by author, March 25, 1991. Quotations are literal translations from the Bislama.

24. Note that in the West Indies slaves were also barred from, and punished for practicing, these group-affirming activities.

25. Pierre Paul Tariala, interview by author, in French, June 3, 1991.

26. "Ambae/Maweo Tua: PM I risivim bigfala welkam!" *Vanuatu Weekly Hebdomadaire* 432, March 13, 1993, 1.

27. I deliberately echo Hobsbawm and Ranger's (1983) felicitous expression "invention of tradition." For treatments of the politics of *kastom*, see the works of Joan Larcom, Lamont Lindstrom, Robert Norton, Jean-Marc Philibert, William Rodman, Christopher Tilley, and Roger Tonkinson.

28. Liatlatmal's French culinary sophistication ought to be juxtaposed with the dietary traditions of his father's generation:

I.L.: There used to be tribal wars up in the mountains. You killed someone, you carried him away, you ate him. That was the rule of nature here. [Laughter.] It wasn't all that long ago.

W.F.S.M.: And your ... your father?

I.L.: My father, to use a crude expression, did "chug down" some flesh [*en parlant en mot nègre, disons, mon père a "bouffé" de l'homme*].

W.F.S.M.: Your own father?

I.L.: *Oui*! Why not? [Laughter.] According to the old guys, it's a meat just like any other, you see!

29. There had been a campaign on the part of certain fundamentalist Protestant churches, reported in the press, to denounce the arts festival as un-Christian. Charges included its opening on a Sunday, its alleged propagation of "black magic," and the ceremonial killing of a pig by the president of the republic.

30. Transcribed from radio broadcast.

31. Expatriate priests still play a role, and bring their own perspective to the interplay between religion, health, and law and order. Expatriate Catholic priest John Cecil stresses the need for pastoral, medical, and security elite to work together: "The police locks 'em up, the priest gets 'em out. The doctor cuts 'em up, the priest buries 'em." Interview by author, June 4, 1991.

32. In the 1980s, as part of their revolutionary image as a newly decolonized state, some of Vanuatu's leaders toyed briefly with establishing relations with Cuba and Libya.

33. Elsewhere I refer to this as the strategy of "divide though conquered" (Miles 1998, 191–92).

34. The immediate impact of the schism, however, was personally chilling. At the end of my fieldwork in August 1991—coinciding by chance with the VP-NUP split—my offer to present a comparative perspective on the condominium at the local university was declined on the grounds that "the condominium is still too sensitive a topic—especially with what's happening now. . . . You may talk about your research elsewhere, but not in Vanuatu." I eventually did speak, at the Vanuatu Centre for International Relations.

35. Francophones have not evinced that much more unity in national politics. Splintering of the UMP, for example, led to the formation of the Vanuatu Republican Party. A host of other parties, including the Melanesian Progressive Party, also add to the coalitional mix.

36. Condocolonialism also mitigated against comprehensive development (why invest so that the rival colonizer would also benefit?), which in turn permitted relative cultural autonomy and another kind of boundary: "The isolated village culture, the hallmark of a traditional anthropology in search of native simplicities, has become, like everywhere else in the world, a kind of borderland" (Tilley 1997, 74).

37. A humorous but revealing slip of the tongue reminds one of the sensitivity of the Francophone position. During a discussion with two Francophone headmasters on the island of Epi, one of them accidentally referred to Vanuatu's day of independence as July 14 (that is, Bastille Day) rather than July 30. After recovering from embarrassed laughter, he at first requested (before stating that he didn't give a damn [*je m'en fous*]), "Don't tell this to the people in Vila" (the capital).

5. French India and the Indian Ocean

1. As the oldest, and most French, of the Comoro Islands, Mahoré's eagerness to remain French even as the rest of the Comoros opted for independence was welcome in France. In fact, the Mayotte option served as hypothetical model for the French in the Vanuatu: perhaps the island of Santo could successfully extract itself from the rest of the New Hebrides, either in association with France or at least in Francophone separation from an Anglophone-dominated government in Vila. In practicality, it was not a scenario that traveled well.

2. For all its negative connotations and use as a mild insult in the West, the dodo claims pride of place in Mauritius, where it is a national mascot and appears on the currency. The guileless bird was consumed en masse by the Dutch dwellers, to the point that it had already been extinct by the time the French era of colonization had begun.

3. In 1848 France had a second opportunity, as we have seen, to follow through in its emancipatory impulse, in the West Indies. But not in Mauritius: abolition there would be a British initiative, not one inspired from Paris.

4. Hence the main title of Vijaya Teelock's treatment of nineteenth-century Mauritius: *Bitter Sugar.*

5. According to Bowman (1991, 16), by the 1790s so-called free coloreds possessed 13 percent of the slaves and 7 percent of the land in Mauritius.

6. According to the 2000 census, Roman Catholics make up 73 percent of the Christian population in Mauritius.

7. In addition to the majoritarian Hanafites, there are Gujarati Meimons (further divided into those hailing from Kutch and Kathiwar) and Suratis. Outside Sunni Islam, Muslims in Mauritius follow Ali (Shiites) or the Aga Khan or Ghulam Ahmad. A Mauritian Muslim group calling itself Hezbollah arose in the 1990s, but with little connection to the more widely recognized Lebanese-based movement by that name.

8. Between 1990 and 2000, English made incremental gains in the absolute number of primary speakers (1,272). Francophones registered a gain of 5,498. (Except for Chinese, all other Asian languages lost considerable ground. By far, Kreol made the most progress, both in absolute and proportional terms.)

9. "Government purposes" here excludes testimony in court, which rulings in the 1990s permit where necessary.

10. In an interview with the author, S. Ramchurn of the primary inspection division of the Mauritian ministry of education, refers to this function of Kreol and Bhojpuri as *languages de soutien,* an expression that highlights both their utility for learning and their subordination to English and French.

11. It was never proposed that an African language be offered in Mauritian schools. Nor is there an Afro-Mauritian equivalent of the *baitka,* by which local Creole communities would undertake their own private education. Such is the distance in ancestral cultural preservation between the descendants of African slaves and those of indentured Indian laborers. The Nelson Mandela Africa Centre (founded in 1986 as the African Cultural Centre) is the sole institution dedicated to preserving and promoting African and Creole arts and culture in Mauritius.

12. The provisions of the 1807 act outlawing the British slave trade are usually thought to have taken effect in 1822 for Mauritius, although Teelock (1998) suggests that the slave trade continued even beyond then. Bowman (1991), recalculating earlier data, uses 1834–40 as the first-time entry for arrivals from India.

13. The full expression, "Ene sel lepe, ène sel nasyon," was originally the slogan of the Mouvement Militant Mauricien.

14. Given its size, the number of countries to which Mauritius has been compared, with respect to its multiculturalism alone, is impressive. "On account of its similarity as an island immigrant society with a significant Indian-origin population, Carroll (1994) has compared Mauritius with *Fiji.* For similar reasons, Eriksen (1991) has contrasted Mauritius with *Trini-*

dad. Impressive economic development and stable democratic systems link Mauritius to *Botswana* (Carroll and Carroll 1997) and *Taiwan* (Bräutigam 1997). An inquiry into responses to globalization favorably casts Mauritius vis-à-vis *Egypt* (Sandbrook and Romano 2004). . . . As a multiracial, democratic, immigrant society, Mauritius has even been compared with the *United States* (Crystal 1996)" (Miles 2008). For a comparison of Mauritian and Afro-American Muslims, see Toorawa 2003.

Rosabelle Laville (2000)/Boswell (2005) is perhaps the harshest critique of an ersatz "harmonious Mauritius" (my expression), taking to task those scholars, like Srebrnik (2000), who view the overall picture so favorably as to minimize the plight of the Creoles. Prabhu (2005) similarly criticizes the national lack of historical consciousness about slavery.

15. Yet Muslims, too, have grievances as a Mauritian minority. They are also more easily organized, both on domestic and global levels. See Hollup 1996.

16. Some may object to comparison with Africa on the grounds that, as a relatively small and immigrant society predominated by Indians, Mauritius is incomparable with the African continent. Notwithstanding these real differences, by convention Mauritius *is* usually grouped together with the rest of Africa, and it accepts this designation for purposes of international and regional organization membership.

17. Madagascar, of course, is not part of the African land mass either and has many unique sociological and ecological features that distinguish it from Africa writ large. But there is much less dispute about Madagascar's status as a "truly" African country than Mauritius's.

18. See, for example, Asgarally 1997.

19. Bérenger's forceful promotion, in the 1980s, of Kreol as an official language for Mauritius is often reported as having precipitated his temporary downfall from governance authority. In an interview with the author (Port Louis, May 22, 1997), however, he claims that the Kreol controversy was not the primary cause of the breakup of the coalition. Anerood Jugnauth, prime minister (1982–95) and president (from 2003), has never viewed Kreol as requiring official status (interview with author, Port Louis, December 19, 1996).

20. One needs to acknowledge the difference between a Barbados, which like Mauritius was unpopulated at the time of British colonialism, and a Martinique, whose indigenous population was wiped out by the French. Such genocide problematizes the issue of antecedent identity today. In terms of colonial administration, however, the eradication of indigenous islanders rendered Martinique more similar to Barbados—and certainly to Mauritius—than any of these three were to colonies on the African (or American) mainland.

21. The symbolism of having such an order take effect immediately at the end of Bastille Day can be parsed. Be that as it may, the ardent Franco-

phone lawyer Célicourt Antelme prolonged his last address to the Court of Appeal, in French, up to the stroke of midnight, concluding with an emotional farewell to the French language (Toussaint 1969, 411n1).

22. Jean-Claude de l'Estrac, interview by author, in French, October 8, 1996.

23. Mr. Sabatier, director of the French Cultural Center, interview by author, in French , Port Louis, September 1996.

24. "Dossiers la Française," *L'Express*, June 13, 1990.

25. The Summit of Francophonie has become a biennial event. The fourteenth one took place in Kinshasa in 2012.

26. For a summary of the eight-month program, see "Les activités dans le cadre de ce sommet ont ainsi été arrêtées," *Week-End*, March 21, 1993.

27. "La Pertinence d'Une Pensée," *Le Mauricien*, October 9, 1993.

28. "Francophonie san l'hégemonie." *5-Plus Dimanche*, October 19, 1993.

29. One statistic reported in the press during the Sommet de la Francophonie was that for their personal letters and book reading, 75 percent of Mauritians use French.

30. Although the mandating of government correspondence by government officials is dated to 1841, according to magistrate Rex Stefan, "no text says that the official language of Mauritius is English." Interview by author, September 20, 1996. Magistrate Stefan favors increasing use of Kreol in the Mauritian court system: "A country must have its own language for itself."

31. Port Louis, September 16, 1996. As an observer to this high court session (and having donned a tie for the occasion), I violated protocol by leaning on the writing table in front of me. A court officer rebuked me—in French: *Assez-vous convenablement* ("Sit properly").

There are of course many nonlinguistic aspects of court "theater." In the district court of Curepipe (and presumably in other jurisdictions), during trial the defendant stands behinds gray bars that are pointed on the top. This is not a security measure but rather pure symbolism. The bars do not confine, being open on every other side.

32. "News on Sunday 'Here to Stay,'" *News on Sunday*, February 23, 1997, 2.

33. Michael Bootle, interview by author, November 4, 1996.

34. De l'Estrac, interview by author.

35. Emphases for these and all succeeding quotes are in the original. Examples were culled over a nine month period in 1996–97 from the dailies *L'Express* and *Le Mauricien* and the weeklies *Le Défi* and *Week-End*.

36. Both islands were occupied by British naval forces during the Napoleonic wars. Whereas l'Ile Bourbon was restored to France, British sovereignty over the Isle of France was officialized.

37. The family analogy is inspired by Hintjens (1992).

38. *Le Mauricien*, November 11, 1980.

39. The politician in question is V. P. Virapoulle of the French center-right party Union de la Démocratie Française.

40. "Défonce du lecteur; Mauriciens, Belges de l'Océan Indien: Question de Degré...," *Visu*, November 1996.

41. Sir Anerood Jugnaud in 1988.

42. "Editorial: Entre îles-Soeurs," *The Sun*, December 9, 1988.

43. The Seychelles—like Mauritius, a colony of France that became British but retained French culture and language—withdrew in 2003.

44. More enigmatic is the oft-repeated observation that greater respect for the dead is still practiced in Pondicherry than in nearby non-Francophone parts of India. "Even passing rickshaw wallas will stop and make a sign of respect" if they come across a corpse. But even just outside Pondy, people won't bother with "just another dead body." (Group interview with author at Annalamali University, Annamalainagar, December 1987.)

45. But see Edwards's (2010) nuancing of Pondicherry's image as a site of anti-British resistance.

46. Over three thousand in 1987–88 (Miles 1995, 122, 154, 157).

47. Inclusion of Mauritius within the African Union, and more broadly within the idea of Africa, should be contested more than it is.

48. This caveat excludes South Africa, whose parliamentary institutions functioned quite regularly during the apartheid years but which restricted voting eligibility according to race.

6. Southeast Asia

1. More than for any other country, academic specialists duel over which name to employ in describing this former British colony. For some, acceptance of "Myanmar" implicitly endorses the legitimacy of the military regime that renamed the nation and remains in power. Not invested personally in the issue (for better or for worse), I shall practice nomenclature agnosticism and use Burma and Myanmar interchangeably.

2. Pluvier (1974) also examines Dutch and U.S. colonialism (in, respectively, Indonesia and the Philippines). Dutch colonialism was marginal in the other regions covered in our study (notwithstanding two Caribbean examples of Dutch-French partition [Saint Maarten–St. Martin and Suriname-Guyane] and one Dutch-British one [Suriname-Guyana].)

3. Lea Williams (1976, 149) is more phlegmatic: "[T]here would be no point in seeking to rank colonial powers in terms of beneficence toward subject peoples.... However, it is not particularly difficult to conclude that the record of the French in Indochina is not one to inspire admiration."

4. The paraphrasing refers to Weber (1976), "Peasants into Frenchman." Evans (2002, 42–43) explicitly invokes the late nineteenth-century parallels that existed between urban-rural and colonializing-colonized France.

5. Laos's declared independence in 1945 was contested and initially nullified by French recolonization.

6. It is for this reason (and a desire to rehabilitate the region's reputation) that more technocratically minded developers and their analysts prefer the term "economic quadrangle"—as in Economic Quadrangle Joint Development Corporation (EQJDC)—to "golden triangle."

7. An intriguing novel that captures the ambience of the colonial rivalry, at least from the British side, is Daniel Mason's *The Piano Tuner* (2002).

8. Pavie himself, it should be noted, understood the arbitrariness of such usage, eschewing the Mekong as a natural frontier (Evans 2002, 40).

9. Here as elsewhere in this chapter, I use "colony" in the generic sense. Juridically, France considered Laos a "protectorate."

10. Use of Myanmar in this context may sound anachronistic and throughout this account is profoundly revealing of the SLORC's ability to influence language and political identity in contemporary Burma.

11. At this point, the story interlaces with that of the widely reported, ill-fated revolt of Oun Kham. More conventional accounts of the "Affair of Muang Sing" can be found in Le Boulanger 1931; E. Lefèvre [1898] 1995.

12. Auguste Pavie (1847–1925) extended French influence in Laos by undertaking the first European expeditions up the Mekong River, whose left bank he led a campaign for Siam to renounce. He served as France's diplomatic agent in Bangkok.

13. Where there was a significant Chinese presence in northern Laos (mostly from road building), the United States did not bomb. Dr. Martin Stuart-Fox, personal communication with author, October 25, 2006.

14. The 150-mile figure mentioned at the beginning of the chapter represents a slight rounding up. See St. John 1998.

15. Moniker of "Capital of the Golden Triangle" is also claimed by Keng Tung, Myanmar.

16. Interviews with author: Nai Ban (headman), Pung Lo, Laos, June 25, 2007; Maihun Paw, Cheng Dao, Laos, June 29, 2007.

17. According to Walker (1999, 81) there was little upstream traffic along this stretch of the Mekong, on account of various natural impediments. Muangmom was the final destination of most crafts from Laos that did hazard the river; from there, goods were offloaded for sale in Myanmar. A few reached into China for livestock transport. More recent rapids blasting and dam building by China are quickly changing the ecology and trading patterns along the river.

18. "We would have our [University of Texas] departmental meetings, over lunch, in Ciudad Juarez. The restaurants were better, the food cheaper, and we could easily get back in time for our afternoon classes." All that changed with the erection of a much tighter border infrastructure on the U.S. side of the border. Prof. Anthony Kruszewski, personal communication with author, March 2006.

19. One elderly Muang Sing resident, Caokwoi Phyphya (b. 1934), who attended a mountain school and regrets that he can no longer speak French, insists that from 1962 until 1975 Muang Sing was basically empty during daylight hours. Even now, he regrets, there are much fewer people than before.

20. Myanmar's formidable network of secret police made itself menacingly apparent during my visit to Keng Tung, and I am thus reluctant to identify informants.

21. This became apparent within a few minutes of an interview I began conducting with an elder in a Buddhist temple. A man in civilian clothes unceremoniously sidled up, and though not offering any identification, baldly interrupted to interrogate me (albeit with forced smile) about my identity, origin, motives, etc. (Unbeknownst to the inquisitor, the tape recorder in the interviewee's pocket was still winding away, documenting the intrusion.)

22. In 2005 I was informed that the last Francophone in Muang Sing had died the year before.

23. Anthropologists trace their prehistoric origins to Tibet.

24. Military dictatorship and jungle fighting also inhibit research—not only among the Akha but among all hill tribes in the Myanmar. To a lesser extent, the same phenomenon has prevailed for Laos. As a result, virtually all cross-border research about the hill tribes of the Golden Triangle is Thai or Chinese based. My literature searches have uncovered not a single example of research that explicitly investigates an ethnic group or hill tribe from the perspective of Laos-Myanmar.

25. Only among some Akha subgroups in northern Laos is there any record of a chieftaincy claiming to speak on behalf of "the Akha." See LeBar, Hickey, and Musgrave 1964, 37.

26. Ethnic boundaries, as Fredrik Barth (1969) has shown, are rarely neatly delimited. This is especially the case in Southeast Asia, and for the Lue in particular it has been well problematized by Moerman 1965.

27. Nai Ban (headman), interview by author, June 25, 2007.

28. My thanks to Sompop Jantraka, founding director of the DEPDCC, for introducing me to his center. Human trafficking having become a regional problem, DEPDCC hosts girls from Vietnam and Cambodia, in addition to Laos and Myanmar, for education and training.

29. The Lao are not, like the other ethnic groups discussed in this chapter, represented in Myanmar; they did not experience Anglo-French partition. Given their importance in the region, however, it is worthwhile to recognize their status as an important trans-Thai-Laotian ethnicity.

30. Evraud and Goudineau (2004, 939), pointing out that this policy is not official, prefer the expression "resettlement-induced forms of mobility."

31. "Thailand only really emerged from the shadow of 'informal British dominance,' presumably something a shade less intimidating than 'informal imperialism,' in the 1920s to 1930s" (Hack 2003, 113).

32. There is one intriguing (if doubt-provoking) statistic: the percentage of undernourished people, as recorded by the UN Development Program, is four times higher in Laos (at 24 percent) than in Myanmar.

7. Scars of Partition

1. I am referring, of course, to borderlanders between former French and former British colonies. As Peter Chilson (1997) evocatively illustrates, the international borders that now separate formerly administrative divisions *within* the French African empire are subject to a much higher degree of uncertainty, dispute, and contestation.

2. Mention should at least be made of Algeria and Kenya, instances of widespread, organized, and violent resistance to French and British colonialism, respectively. Neither the Maghreb nor East Africa has been included in this study, mostly for reasons of symmetry: in North Africa, no country, whether previously under French colonial rule (the more common case) or British control (Egypt, 1914–1936), borders a country formerly under the other colonial power. In East Africa, the only people separated by a British-French colonial border are the Somali, partitioned between Djibouti (former French Somaliland) and Somalia proper.

3. Prior to constitutional change in 2003, most French possessions that were not *départements* were *territoires d'outre-mer* (TOM), or overseas territories.

4. Again, Southeast Asia represents an exception: not only was French jettisoned as a mandatory language of study by revolutionary, anticolonial governments in Laos, but even English has been marginalized by the notoriously autarkic, nationalistic, and ethnically chauvinist Burman leaders of Myanmar.

BIBLIOGRAPHY

Abba, Souleymane. 1990. "La chefferie traditionnelle en question." *Politique Africaine: Le Niger* 38:51–60.
Aborisade, Oladimeji, ed. 1985. *Local Government and the Traditional Rulers in Nigeria*. Ile-Ife: University of Ife Press.
———. 1986. *Readings in Nigerian Local Government*. Ile-Ife: Obafemi Awolowo University Press.Acemoglu, Daron, Simon Johnson, and James A. Robinson. 2001. "The Colonial Origins of Comparative Development: An Empirical Investigation." *American Economic Review* 91:1369–1401.
Abuja Daily Trust. 2007. "Nigeria; Dole—One Village, Two Countries." June 3 (LexisNexis Academic).
ACSS (Africa Center for Strategic Studies). 2003. *North and West Africa Counter-Terrorism. Topical Seminar, Program Highlights*. Bamako, Mali: National Defense University.
ADM (Archives Départementales de la Martinique). 2001. *L'Eglise martiniquaise et la piété populaire. XVII–XX siècles*. Fort-de-France.
Adnan, Alhaji Muhtar. 1993. "The Role of Traditional Institutions and Cultural Values in Fostering Transborder Co-operation: The Case of Nigeria-Niger Border." In Asiwaju and Barkindo 1993, 100–107.
Affergan, Francis. 1989. "Eléments pour une anthropologie du magico-religieux à la Martinique." *Cahiers Internationaux de sociologie* 87:265–81.
Africa Confidential. 2007. "The New Man in Abuja." January 8.
Africa News. 2001. "Abuja, Niamey Re-Demarcate Common Border." November 6 (LexisNexis Academic).
———. 2006. "Nigeria Relocates 13 Villages." October 2 (LexisNexis Academic).
Ajayi, J. F. A. 1969. "Colonialism: An Episode in African History." In *Colonialism in Africa*, edited by L. H. Gann and P. Duignan, 1:497–509. Cambridge: Cambridge University Press.

Aldrich, Robert. 1995. *Greater France: A History of French Overseas Expansion.* New York: St. Martin's.
Aldrich, Robert, and John Connell. 1992. *France's Overseas Frontier: Les Départements et Territoires d'Outre-Mer.* Cambridge: Cambridge University Press.
——. 1998. *The Last Colonies.* Cambridge: Cambridge University Press.
Alexis, Gerson. 1976. *Vodou et Quimbois: Essai sur les avatars du vodou à la Martinique.* Port-au-Prince: Les Éditions Fardin.
Alidou, Hassana, and Ingrid Jung. 2002. "Education Language Policies in Francophone Africa: What Have We Learned from Field Experiences?" In *Language Policy: Lessons from Global Models*, edited by Steven J. Baker, 59–73. Monterey: Monterey Institute for International Studies.
Alidou, Ousseina D. 2000. "Popular Hausa Drama in Niger and the Politics of Its Appropriation." In *African Visions. Literary Images, Political Change, and Social Struggle in Contemporary Africa*, edited by Cheryl B. Mwaria, Silvia Federici, and Joseph McLaren, 193–208. Westport CT: Greenwood Press.
——. 2005. *Engaging Modernity: Muslim Women and the Politics of Agency in Postcolonial Niger.* Madison: University of Wisconsin Press.
Alleyne, Mervyn C. 2002. *The Construction and Representation of Race and Ethnicity in the Caribbean and the World.* Barbados: University of the West Indies Press.
Allsopp, Richard. 1972. "The Question of Barbadian Culture." *Bajan Booklet No. 1. Bajan Magazine.*
Anene, J. C. 1970. *The International Boundaries of Nigeria, 1885–1960.* London: Longman.
ARB (*Africa Research Bulletin*). 2004. "Nigeria: 'Taliban'-Style Revolt." Vol. 41 (January 1–31): 15610–612.
Ardener, Edwin. 1967. "The Nature of the Reunification of Cameroon." In *African Integration and Disintegration: Case Studies Economic and Political Union*, edited by Arthur Hazlewood, 285–337. London: Oxford University Press.
Asgarally, Issa, ed. 1997. *Etude pluridisciplinaire sur l'exclusion à Maurice.* Réduit: State House.
Asiwaju, A. I. 1970. "The Alaketu of Ketu and the Onimedu of Meko: The Changing Status of Two Yoruba Rulers Under French and British Rule." In *West African Chiefs: Their Changing Status Under Colonial Rule and Independence*, edited by Michael Crowder and Obaro Ikime, 134–60. New York: Africana.
——. 1976. *Western Yorubaland under European Rule, 1889–1945: A Comparative Analysis of French and British Colonialism.* London: Longman.
——, ed. 1985. *Partitioned Africans: Ethnic Relations across Africa's*

    International Boundaries, 1884–1984. Lagos and New York: University of Lagos Press and St. Martin's Press.

———. 1989. "Borderlands: Policy Implications of Definition for Nigeria's 'Gateway' State Administrations and Local Governments." In Asiwaju and Adeniyi 1989, 63–84.

———. 1996. "Transborder Cooperation Policy Promotion at the Local Level: West African Experience Focusing on Nigeria and Adjacent Countries." *Regional Development Dialogue* 17:156–72.

———. 2001. *West African Transformations: Comparative Impact of French and British Colonialism*. Ikeja: Malthouse Press.

———. 2005. "Transfrontier Regionalism: The European Union Perspective on Postcolonial Africa, with Special Reference to Borgu." In *Holding the Line: Borders in a Global World*, edited by Heather N. Nicol and Ian Townsend-Gault, 119–41. Vancouver: UBC Press.

Asiwaju, A. I., and P. O. Adeniyi, eds. 1989. *Borderlands in Africa: A Multidisciplinary and Comparative Focus on Nigeria and West Africa*. Lagos: University of Lagos Press.

Asiwaju, A. I., and Barkindo M. Barkindo, eds. 1993. *The Nigeria-Niger Transborder Co-operation*. Lagos: National Boundary Commission.

Asiwaju, A. I., and O. J. Igué, eds. 1994. *The Nigerian-Benin Transborder Cooperation*. Lagos: University of Lagos Press.

Auplat, Claire. 2003. "The Commonwealth, the Francophonie, and NGOs." *Round Table* 368:53–66.

Ayeni, Victor. 1985. "Traditional Rulers as Ombudsmen: In Search of a Role for Natural Rulers in Contemporary Nigeria. *Indian Journal of Public Administration* 31:1318–30.

Babineu, G. Raymond. 1972. "The Compulsive Border Crosser." *Psychiatry* 35:281–90.

Bacchus, M. K. 1996. "Consensus and Conflict over the Provision of Elementary Education." In *Caribbean Freedom: Economy and Society from Emancipation to the Present*, edited by Hilary Beckles and V. Shepherd, 296–313. Princeton NJ: Markus Weiner.

Bach, Daniel C. 2003. "Application et Implications de la Charia: Fin de Partie au Nigéria." *Pouvoirs* 104:117–27.

Baggioni, Daniel, and Didier de Robillard. 1990. *Ile Maurice: Une Francophonie Paradoxale*. Paris: L'Harmattan.

Baird, Ian G., and Bruce Shoemaker. 2005. *Aiding or Abetting? Internal Resettlement and International Aid Agencies in the Lao PDR*. Toronto: Probe International.

Bako, Commandant Nouhou. 1993. "Discours du Préfet de Zinder." In Asiwaju and Barkindo 1993, 313–17.

Barkindo, Bawuro M. 1985. "The Mandara Astride the Nigeria-Cameroon Boundary." In Asiwaju 1985, 29–49.

———. 1993. "General Editor's Note." In Asiwaju and Barkindo 1993, xvii–xix.

Barkow, Jerome H. 1972. "Hausa Women and Islam." *Canadian Journal of African Studies* 6:317–28.

Barrow-Giles, Cynthia, and Don D. Marshall, eds. 2003. *Living at the Borderlines: Issues in Caribbean Sovereignty and Development*. Kingston, Jamaica: Ian Randle Publishers.

Barth, Fredrik. 1969. *Ethnic Groups and Boundaries*. Boston: Little, Brown.

Baud, Michiel, and Willem van Schendel. 1997. "Toward a Comparative History of Borderlands." *Journal of World History* 8:211–42.

BBC (British Broadcasting Corporation). 1991. BBC Summary of World Broadcasts. June 27 (LexisNexis Academic).

———. 2001. BBC Monitoring Africa—Political. June 9 (LexisNexis Academic).

Beckles, Hilary McD. 2004. *Chattel House Blues: Making of a Democratic Society in Barbados*. Kingston, Jamaica: Ian Randle Publishers.

———. 2006. *A History of Barbados: From Amerindian Settlement to Caribbean Single Market*. 2nd ed. Cambridge: Cambridge University Press.

Beik, Janet. 1984. "National Development as Theme in Current Hausa Drama in Niger." *Research in African Literatures* 15:1–23.

———. 1991. "Women's Role in the Contemporary Hausa Theater of Niger." In Coles and Mack 1991, 232–43.

Beissinger, Mark R., and Crawford Young. 2002. "Introduction: Comparing State Crises Across Two Continents." In *Beyond State Crisis? Postcolonial Africa and Post-Soviet Eurasia in Comparative Perspective*, edited by Mark Beissinger and Crawford Young, 3–18. Washington DC: Woodrow Wilson Center Press.

Benda, Harry J. 1956. "Communism in Southeast Asia." *Yale Review* 45:417–29.

Benmessaoud Tredano, Abdelmoughit. 1989. *Intangibilité des Frontières Coloniales et Espace Etatique en Afrique*. Paris: Librairie Générale de Droit et de Jurisprudence.

Berger, Mark T. 2003. "Decolonisation, Modernisation, and Nation-Building: Political Development Theory and the Appeal of Communism in Southeast Asia, 1945–1975." *Journal of Southeast Asian Studies* 34:421–48.

Bernabé, Jean, Patrick Chamoiseau, and Raphaël Confiant. 1993. *Éloge de la Créolité / In Praise of Creoleness*. Paris and Baltimore: Gallimard and Johns Hopkins University Press.

Berrian, Brenda. 2000. *Awakening Spaces: French Caribbean Popular Songs, Music, and Culture*. Chicago: University of Chicago Press.

Betts, Raymond F. 1961. *Assimilation and Association in French Colonial Theory*. New York: Columbia University Press.

———. 1991. *France and Decolonisation, 1900–1960*. New York: St. Martin's.

———. 2004. *Decolonization*. 2nd ed. New York: Routledge.

Blackman, Courtney N. 1998. "The Barbados Model." *Caribbean Affairs* 8:61–68.

Boahen, A. Adu. 1987. *African Perspectives on Colonialism*. Baltimore: Johns Hopkins University Press.

Bolton, Lissant. 1998. "Chief Willie Bongmatur Maldo and the Role of Chiefs in Vanuatu." *Journal of Pacific History* 33:179–95.

Bonnemaison, Joël. 1984. "The Tree and the Canoe: Roots and Mobility in Vanuatu Societies." *Pacific Viewpoint* 25:117–51.

———. 1986. *La Dernière Ile*. Paris: Arléa/Orstom.

———. 1994. "The Metaphor of the Tree and the Canoe." *Pacific Arts*, July, 21–24. Translated by Peter Crowe.

Boswell, Rosabelle. 2005. "Unravelling *Le Malaise Créole*: Hybridity and Marginalisation in Mauritius." *Identities: Global Studies in Culture and Power* 12:195–221.

Bougerol, Christiane. 1991. *Une ethnographie des conflits aux Antilles: Jalousie, commérages, sorcellerie*. Paris: Presses Universitaires de France.

Bowman, Larry. 1991. *Mauritius: Democracy and Development in the Indian Ocean*. Boulder CO: Westview Press.

Boyd, J. Barron. 1979. "African Boundary Conflict: An Empirical Study." *African Studies Review* 22:1–14.

Bräutigam, Deborah. 1997. "What Did Mauritius Learn from Taiwan?" In *Rethinking Development in East Asia and Latin America*, edited by James McGuire, 133–38. Los Angeles: Pacific Council on International Policy.

Bresnihan, Brian, and Keith Woodward, eds. 2002. *Tufala Gavman: Reminiscences from the Anglo-French Condominium of the New Hebrides*. Suva: University of the South Pacific.

Bridge, John W. 1997. "Judicial Review in Mauritius and the Continuing Influence of English Law." *International and Comparative Law Quarterly* 46:787–811.

Brocheux, Pierre, and Daniel Hémery. 1995. *Indochine: La colonisation ambigüe*. Paris: Éditions La Découverte.

Brown, David. 1994. "Burma: The Ethnocratic State and Ethnic Separatism in Burma." In *The State and Ethnic Politics in Southeast Asia*, edited by David Brown, 23–46. London: Routledge.

Brunet-Jailly, Emmanuel. 2005. "Theorizing Borders: An Interdisciplinary Perspective." *Geopolitics* 10:633–49.

Buddan, Robert. 2001. "Political History: Patterns of Colonialism and the 'Barbados Model.'" In *Foundations of Caribbean Politics*, edited by Robert Buddan, 26–35. Kingston, Jamaica: Arawak Publications.

Bunge, Frederica, ed. 1983. *Burma: A Country Study.* Washington DC: U.S. Government Printing Office.

Burton, Richard D. E. 1992. "Towards 1992: Political-Cultural Assimilation and Opposition in Contemporary Martinique." *French Cultural Studies* 3:61–86.

———. 1993a. "*Ki Moun Nou Ye*? The Idea of Difference in Contemporary French West Indian Thought." *New West Indian Guide* 67:5–32.

———. 1993b. "'Maman-France Doudou': Family Images in French West Indian Colonial Discourse." *Diacritics* 23:69–90.

Callaway, Barbara J. 1984. "Ambiguous Consequences of the Socialisation and Seclusion of Hausa Women." *Journal of Modern African Studies* 22:429–50.

———. 1987a. *Muslim Hausa Women in Nigeria: Tradition and Change.* Syracuse NY: Syracuse University Press.

———. 1987b. "Women and Political Participation in Kano City." *Comparative Politics* 19:349–93.

———. 1991. "The Role of Women in Kano City Politics." In Coles and Mack 1991, 145–59.

Campbell, I. C. 1989. *A History of the Pacific Islands.* Berkeley: University of California Press.

Cantier, Jacques, and Eric Jennings, eds. 2004. *L'Empire Colonial Sous Vichy.* Paris: Odile Jacob.

Carroll, Terrance. 1994. "Owners, Immigrants and Ethnic Conflict in Fiji and Mauritius." *Ethnic and Racial Studies* 17:301–24.

Carroll, Barbara-Wake, and Terrance Carroll. 1997. "State and Ethnicity in Botswana and Mauritius: A Democratic Route to Development?" *Journal of Development Studies* 33:464–86.

Cateaux, Gérard. 1988. "Maurice/Réunion: Malgré les contours de l'Histoire." *Week-End* [Maurice], December 4.

Césaire, Aimé. (1939) 1971. *Cahier d'un retour au pays natal* [Return to my native land]. Paris: Présence Africaine.

Chamberlain, M. E. 1999. *Decolonization: The Fall of the European Empires.* 2nd ed. Malden MA: Blackwell.

Chambers, Douglas B. 1997. "'My Own Nation': Igbo Exiles in the Diaspora." In *Routes to Slavery: Direction, Ethnicity, and Mortality in the Atlantic Slave Trade*, edited by David Eltis and David Richardson, 72–97. London: Frank Cass.

Charlick, Robert B. 1972. "Participatory Development and Rural Modernization in Hausa Niger." *African Review* 2:499–524.

———. 1991. *Niger: Personal Rule and Survival in the Sahel.* Boulder CO: Westview Press.

———. 2007. "Niger: Islamist Identity and the Politics of Globalization." In *Political Islam in West Africa. State-Society Relations Trans-*

formed, William F. S. Miles, 19–42. Boulder CO: Lynne Rienner Publishers.

Chilson, Peter. 1997. "The Border." *The Smart Set*, http://www.thesmartset.com/article/article11300702.aspx.

Christelow, Allan. 1985. "Religious Protest and Dissent in Northern Nigeria: From Mahdisim to Qur'anic Integralism." *Journal Institute of Muslim Minority Affairs* 6:375–93.

Christie, Clive J. 1996. *A Modern History of Southeast Asia: Decolonization, Nationalism, and Separatism*. London: I. B. Taurus.

Clapham, Christopher. 1999. "Boundaries and States in the New African Order." In *Regionalisation in Africa: Integration and Disintegration*, edited by Daniel C. Bach, 53–66. Oxford: James Currey.

Clarke, Peter. 1979. "The Religious Factor in the Development Process in Nigeria: A Socio-Historical Analysis." *Genève-Afrique* 17:46–63.

———. 1982. *West Africa and Islam: A Study of Religious Development from the 8th to the 20th Century*. London: Edward Arnold.

Cohen, Paul T. 1998. "Lue Ethnicity in National Context: A Comparative Study of Tai Lue Communities in Thailand and Laos." *Journal of the Siam Society* 86:49–61.

———. 2000. "Resettlement, Opium, and Labour Dependence: Akha-Tai Relations in Northern Laos." *Development and Change* 31:179–200.

Coleman, James. 1958. *Nigeria: Background to Nationalism*. Berkeley: University of California Press.

Coles, Catherine. 1991. "Hausa Women's Work in a Declining Urban Economy: Kaduna, Nigeria, 1980–1985." In Coles and Mack 1991, 163–91.

Coles, Catherine, and Beverly Mack, eds. 1991. *Hausa Women in the Twentieth Century*. Madison: University of Wisconsin Press.

Collins, John D. 1976. "The Clandestine Movement of Groundnuts across the Niger-Nigeria Boundary." *Canadian Journal of African Studies* 10:259–78.

———. 1985. "Partitioned Culture Areas and Smuggling: The Hausa and the Groundnut Trade across the Nigeria-Niger Border from the Mid-1930s to the Mid-1970s." In Asiwaju 1985, 195–221.

Conklin, Alice. 1997. *A Mission to Civilize: The Republican Idea of Empire in France and West Africa, 1895–1930*. Stanford CA: Stanford University Press.

Cooper, Barbara M. 1998. "Gender and Religion in Hausaland." In *Women in Muslim Societies: Diversity within Unity*, edited by Herbert Bodman and Nayereh Tohidi, 21–37. Boulder CO: Lynne Rienner Publishers.

Cooper, Frederick. 2002. "Decolonizing Situations: The Rise, Fall, and Rise of Colonial Studies, 1951–2001." *French Politics, Culture, and Society* 20:47–76.

Crowder, Michael. 1968. *West Africa under Colonial Rule*. Evanston IL: Northwestern University Press.

Crystal, Susan R., ed. 1996. *U.S.A.-Mauritius. 200 Years: Trade, History, Culture.* Moka: Mahatma Gandhi Institute.

Darga, Amédée. 1996. "Autonomous Economic and Social Development in Democracy: An Appreciation of the Mauritian 'Miracle.'" *Africa Development* 21:79–88.

Davidson, Basil. 1992. *The Black Man's Burden: Africa and the Curse of the Nation-State.* New York: Random House.

Davies, A. E. 1990. "The Fluctuating Fortunes of Traditional Rulers in Nigeria." *Plural Societies* 19:133–44.

Dawisha, Karen, and Bruce Parrott, eds. 1997. *The End of Empire? The Transformation of the USSR in Comparative Perspective.* Armonk NY: M. E. Sharpe.

Degoul, Franck. 2000a. *Le Commerce Diabolique.* Petit-Bourg: Ibis.

——. 2000b. "Le Diable, Les Deux Indiens et le Chabin: Une illustration en récit de l'imaginaire du pacte diabolique en Martinique." In *Au visiteur lumineux: Des îles créoles aux sociétés plurielles,* edited by Jean Bernabé et al., 437–50. Petit Bourg, Guadeloupe: Ibis Rouge Éditions.

Delawarde, J.-B. 1983. *La sorcellerie à la Martinique et dans les îles voisines: Ses Positions et ses réactions dans ses rapports avec le culte chrétien ambiant.* Paris: Téqi.

Delpech, Christiane, and Félix Bellaïche. 1987. *Hier les Nouvelles-Hébrides.* Arles, France: Imprimerie Perrin.

Deng, F. M. 1993. "Africa after the Cold War: Rethinking Colonial Borders." *Current,* September, 35–38.

Deschamps, Hubert. 1953. *Méthodes et doctrines coloniales de la France.* Paris: Armand Colin.

De Vassoigne, Christiane. 1994. "Implantation et dynamisme des congrégations religieuses d'origine nord-américaine en Martinique." In *Guadeloupe, Martinique et Guyane dans le monde américain,* edited by Maurice Burac, 213–26. Paris: Karthala.

Dimier, Véronique. 2002. "Direct or Indirect Rule: Propaganda around a Scientific Controversy. " In *Promoting the Colonial Idea: Propaganda and Visions of Empire in France,* edited by Tony Chafer and Amanda Sackur, 163–83. London: Palgrave.

——. 2004. *Le gouvernement des colonies, regards croisés franco-britanniques.* Brussels: Université de Bruxelles.

Dixon, Chris, and Michael Heffernan, eds. 1991. *Colonialism and Development in the Contemporary World.* London: Mansell Publishing.

Djimba, Ali. 1997. "Land-Locked Niger and Its Alternative Seaport Access." *Geopolitics and International Boundaries* 2:40–55.

Djité, Paulin G. 1990. "The Place of African Languages in the Revival of the Francophonie Movement." *International Journal of the Sociology of Language* 86:87–102.

Donnan, Hastings, and Thomas M. Wilson, eds. 1999. *Borders: Frontiers of Identity, Nation, and State*. Oxford: Berg.

Dottridge, Mike. 2002. "Trafficking in Children in West and Central Africa." *Gender and Development* 10:38–42.

Duluq, Sophie, Jean-François Klein, and Benjamin Stora, eds. 2008. *Les mots de la colonisation*. Toulouse: Press Universitaires du Mirail.

Dunbar, Roberta Ann. 1991. "Islamic Values, the State, and 'the Development of Women': The Case of Niger." In Coles and Mack 1991, 69–89.

Duncan, Neville. 1994. "Barbados: Democracy at the Crossroads." In Edie 1994, 75–91.

d'Unienville, Raymond. 1994. *L'Evolution du Droit Civil à l'Ile Maurice*. Port Louis: Best Graphics.

Early, Robert. 1999. "Double Trouble, and Three is a Crowd: Languages in Education and Official Languages in Vanuatu." *Journal of Multilingual and Multicultural Development* 20:13–33.

Easterly, William. 2006. *The White Man's Burden: Why the West's Efforts to Aid the Rest Have Done So Much Ill and So Little Good*. New York: Penguin Press.

Echard, Nicole. 1991. "Gender Relationships and Religion: Women in the Hausa *Bori* of Ader, Niger." In Coles and Mack 1991, 207–20.

Edie, Carlene J., ed. 1994. *Democracy in the Caribbean: Myths and Realities*. Westport CT: Praeger.

Edouard, Bertrand. 1972. *Les Antilles en Question*. Fort-de-France: Imprimerie St. Paul.

Edwards, Penny. 2010. "A Strategic Sanctuary: Reading *l'Inde française* through the Colonial Archive." *Interventions: International Journal of Postcolonial Studies* 12:356–67.

Eisenlohr, Patrick. 2006. *Little India: Diaspora, Time, and Ethnolinguistic Belonging in Hindu Mauritius*. Berkeley: University of California Press.

Eltis, David, and David Richardson. 1997. "The 'Numbers Game' and Routes to Slavery." In *Routes to Slavery: Direction, Ethnicity, and Mortality in the Atlantic Slave Trade*, edited by David Eltis and David Richardson, 1–15. London: Frank Cass.

Englebert, Pierre, Stacy Tarango, and Matthew Carter. 2002. "Dismemberment and Suffocation: A Contribution to the Debate on African Boundaries." *Comparative Political Studies* 35:1093–1118.

Equiano, Olaudah. (1789) 1995. *The Interesting Narrative of the Life of Olaudah Equiano, Written by Himself*. New York: St. Martin's Press.

Eriksen, Thomas Hylland. 1992. *Us and Them in Modern Societies: Ethnicity and Nationalism in Mauritius, Trinidad, and Beyond*. Oslo: Scandinavian University Press.

Europa Publications. 2008. "Mauritius." *Africa South of the Sahara 2007*. London: Routledge.

Evans, Grant. 2002. *A Short History of Laos: The Land In-Between*. London: George Allen and Unwin.
Evraud, Olivier, and Yves Goudineau. 2004. "Planned Resettlement, Unexpected Migrations and Cultural Trauma in Laos." *Development and Change* 35:937–62.
Fanon, Frantz. (1952) 1967. *Black Skin, White Masks*. Translated by Charles Lam Markmann. New York: Grove Press.
Feingold, David A. 2000. "The Hell of Good Intentions: Some Preliminary Thoughts on Opium in the Political Ecology of the Trade in Girls and Women." In *Where China Meets Southeast Asia: Social and Cultural Change in the Border Regions*, edited by Grant Evans, 183–203. New York: St. Martin's Press.
Firmin-Sellers, Kathryn. 2001. "The Reconstruction of Society: Understanding the Indigenous Response to French and British Rule in Cameroun." *Comparative Politics* 34:43–62.
Fischer, Steven Roger. 2002. *A History of the Pacific Islands*. Basingstoke: Palgrave.
Forsdick, Charles, and David Murphy, eds. 2003. *Francophone Postcolonial Studies: A Critical Introduction*. London: Arnold.
Förster, Stig, Wolfgang J. Mommsen, and Ronald Robinson, eds. 1988. *Bismarck, Europe, and Africa: The Berlin Africa Conference, 1884–1885, and the Onset of Partition*. Oxford: Oxford University Press.
Foucher, Michel. 1991. *Fronts et frontières: Un tour du monde géopolitique*. Paris: Fayard.
Frère, Marie-Soleil. 1999. "Démocratie au Bénin et au Niger." *Mots* 59:89–105.
Frishman, Alan. 1991. "Hausa Women in the Urban Economy of Kano." In Coles and Mack 1991, 192–203.
Fry, Michael Graham. 1997. "Decolonization: Britain, France, and the Cold War." In Dawisha and Parrott 1997, 121–54.
Fuglestad, Finn. 1983. *A History of Niger, 1850–1960*. Cambridge: Cambridge University Press.
Gaffarel, Paul. 1880. *Les Colonies françaises*. Paris: Baillière.
Gann, L. H., and P. Duignan. 1969. "Reflections on Imperialism and the Scramble for Africa." In *Colonialism in Africa, 1870–1960*, vol. 1: *The History and Politics of Colonialism, 1870–1914*, edited by L. H. Gann and P. Duignan, 101–31. Cambridge: Cambridge University Press.
Ganster, Paul, and David E. Lorey, eds. 2005. *Borders and Border Politics in a Globalizing World*. Latham MD: SR Books.
Gay, Berhard, and Ouan Phommachack, eds. 1990. *La Nouvelle Frontière Lao-Myanmar: Les Accords de 1993–1995*. Paris: L'Harmattan.
Gervais, Myriam. 1997. "Niger: Regime Change, Economic Crisis, and Perpetuation of Privilege." In *Political Reform in Francophone Africa*,

    edited by John F. Clark and David E. Gardinier, 86–109. Boulder CO: Westview Press.

Gifford, Prosser, and William Roger Louis, eds. 1988. *Decolonization and African Independence: The Transfers of Power, 1960–1980.* New Haven CT: Yale University Press.

Ginio, Ruth. 2006. *French Colonialism Unmasked: The Vichy Years in French West Africa.* Lincoln: University of Nebraska Press.

Giraud, Michel. 2000. "Après la colonie, la nation? Le devenir politique des départements français d'Amérique en question." *Pouvoirs dans la Caraïbe* (PDLC) 12:79–109.

Glaser, Antoine, and Stephen Smith. 2005. *Comment la France a perdu l'Afrique.* Paris: Calmann-Lévy.

Glissant, Edouard. 1981. *Le Discours Antillais.* Paris: Éditions du Seuil.

Gmelch, George, and Sharon Bohn Gmelch. 1997. *The Parish Behind God's Back: The Changing Culture of Rural Barbados.* Ann Arbor: University of Michigan Press.

Goldman, Minton. 1972. "Franco-British Rivalry over Siam, 1896–1904." *Journal of Southeast Asian Studies* 3:210–28.

Goudineau, Yves. 2000. "Ethnicité et déterritorialisation dans la péninsule indochinoise: Considérations à partir du Laos." *Autrepart* 14:17–31.

Grabowsky, Volker. 1999. "Introduction to the History of Muang Sing (Laos) Prior to French Rule: The Fate of a Lu Principality." *Bulletin de l'Ecole Française d'Extrême-Orient* 86:233–91.

Graf, William. 1986. "Nigerian 'Grassroots' Politics: Local Government, Traditional Rule, and Class Domination." *Journal of Commonwealth and Comparative Politics* 24:99–130.

Greenfield, Sidney. 1966. *English Rustics in Black Skin: A Study of Modern Family Forms in a Pre-Industrialized Society.* New Haven CT: College and University Press.

Grégoire, Emmanuel. (1986) 1992. *The Alhazai of Maradi: Traditional Hausa Merchants in a Changing Sahelian City*, translated by Benjamin Hardy. Boulder: Lynne Rienner Publishers.

———. 1993. "Islam and the Identity of Merchants in Maradi (Niger)." In *Muslim Identity and Social Change in Sub-Saharan Africa*, edited by Louis Brenner, 106–16. Bloomington: Indiana University Press.

Gressieux, Douglas. 1992. "La France et ses anciens comptoirs des Indes." *Mondes et Cultures* 52:22–45.

———. 2005. *Cinquantenaire du Transfert des Comptoirs à l'Inde (1954–2004).* Coulommiers: Édition Dualpha.

Grier, Robin M. 1997. "The Effect of Religion on Economic Development: A Cross-National Study of 63 Former Colonies." *Kyklos* 50 (1): 47–62.

———. 1999. "Colonial Legacies and Economic Growth." *Public Choice* 98:317–35.

Griffiths, I. 1996. "Permeable Boundaries in Africa." In *African Boundaries*, edited by Paul Nugent and A. I. Asiwaju, 68–73. London: Pinter.

Grollier, Bernard. 1996. "Réunion-Maurice: Les fausses jumelles." *Le Point* 1226 (March 16).

Guilbault, Jocelyn. 1993. *Zouk: World Music in the West Indies*. Chicago: University of Chicago Press.

Guillemin, Jacques. 1983. "Chefferie traditionnelle et administration publique au Niger." *Le Mois en Afrique* 213–14:115–24.

Hack, Karl. 2003. "Theories and Approaches to British Decolonization in Southeast Asia." In *The Transformation of Southeast Asia: International Perspectives on Decolonization*, edited by Marc Frey, Ronald Pruessen, and Tan Tai Yong, 105–127. Armonk NY: M. E. Sharpe.

Hall, D. G. E. 1964. *A History of South-East Asia*. London: Macmillan.

Hargreaves, John D. 1985. *West Africa Partitioned*, vol. 2: *The Elephants and the Grass*. Madison: University of Wisconsin Press.

———. 1993. "La décolonisation, styles français et britanniques." In *Etats et Sociétés en Afrique Francophone*, edited by Daniel Bach and Anthony Kirk-Greene, 11–24. Paris: Economica.

Harrison, Lawrence E. 1985. "Barbados and Haiti." In *Underdevelopment Is a State of Mind: The Latin American Case*. Cambridge MA: Harvard University Press.

Hart, Jonathan. 2003. *Comparing Empires: European Colonialism from Portuguese Expansion to the Spanish-American War*. New York: Palgrave Macmillan.

Hart, Richard. 1998. *From Occupation to Independence*. London: Pluto Press.

Hawkins, Peter. 1996. "Esquisse d'Une Comparaison des Mondes Anglophone et Francophone." In *Le Français dans l'Espace Francophone*, edited by Didier de Robillard and Michel Beniamino, 835–45. Paris: Honoré Champion Éditeur.

Haynes, Jeff. 1994. *Religion in Third World Politics*. Boulder CO: Lynne Rienner Publishers.

Hearne, John. 1967. "What the Barbadian Means to Me." *New World Quarterly* 3:6–9.

Henry-Valmore, Simone. 1983. "Une figure de l'Imaginaire Antillais: le Quimboiseur." *Les Temps Modernes* 441–42:2090–2107.

———. 1989. "Magie des Espoirs: L'auberge espagnole des croyances et des religions." *Autrement* 41:166–69.

Herbst, Jeffrey. 1989. "The Creation and Maintenance of National Boundaries in Africa." *International Organization* 43:673–92.

———. 1992. "Challenges to Africa's Boundaries in the New World Order." *Journal of International Affairs* 46:17–30.

Herskovitz, Melville. 1937. *Life in a Haitian Valley*. New York: Alfred A. Knopf.

Hintjens, Helen. 1992. "France's Love Children? The French Overseas Departments." In *The Political Economy of Small, Tropical Islands*, edited by Helen Hintjens and M. Newitt, 64–75. Exeter: Exeter University Press.

———. 1995. *Alternatives to Independence: Explorations in Post-Colonial Relations*. Avesbury: Dartmouth.

Hiskett, Mervyn. 1984. *The Development of Islam in West Africa*. London: Longman.

———. 1987. "The Maitatsine Riots in Kano, 1980: An Assessment." *Journal of Religion in Africa* 17:209–23.

Hobsbawm, Eric, and Terence Ranger, eds. 1983. *The Invention of Tradition*. Cambridge: Cambridge University Press.

Hollup, Oddvar. 1994. "The Disintegration of Caste and Changing Concepts of Indian Ethnic Identity in Mauritius." *Ethnology* 4:297–316.

———. 1996. "Islamic Revivalism and Political Opposition among Minority Muslims in Mauritius." *Ethnology* 35:285–300.

Hopkins, A. G. 1973. *An Economic History of West Africa*. London: Longman.

Horowitz, Michael M., et al. 1983. *Niger: A Social and Institutional Profile*. Binghamton NY: Institute for Development Anthropology.

Hurbon, Laënnec. 1989. "Les nouveaux Mouvements Religieux dans la Caraïbe." In *Le Phénomène Religieux dans la Caraïbe: Guadeloupe-Martinique-Guyane-Haïti*, 309–54. Montréal: Les Éditions du CIDIHCA.

Hutchison, John, and Michel Nguessan, eds. 1995. *The Language Question in Francophone Africa*. West Newbury MA: Mother Tongue Editions.

Hyden, Gorden. 2006. *African Politics in Comparative Perspective*. Cambridge: Cambridge University Press.

Ibrahim, Jibrin. 1991. "Religion and Political Turbulence in Nigeria." *Journal of Modern African Studies* 29:115–36.

———. 1994. "Political Exclusion, Democratization and Dynamics of Ethnicity in Niger." *Africa Today* 41:15–39.

Ibrahim, Jibrin, and Niandou Souley. 1998. "The Rise to Power of an Opposition Party: The MNSD in Niger Republic." In *The Politics of Opposition in Contemporary Africa*, edited by Adebayo O. Olukoshi, 144–70. Uppsala: Nordiska Afrikainstitutet.

Ikime, Obaro. 1968. "Reconsidering Indirect Rule: The Nigerian Example." *Journal of the Historical Society of Nigeria* 4:421–38.

Imam, Ayesha. 1991. "Ideology, the Mass Media, and Women: A Study from Radio Kaduna, Nigeria." In Coles and Mack 1991, 244–52.

———. 1994. "Politics, Islam, and Women in Kano, Northern Nigeria." In *Identity Politics and Women: Cultural Reassertions and Feminisms in International Perspective*, edited by Valentine M. Moghadam, 123–44. Boulder CO: Westview.

Imbert-Vier, Simon. 2011. *Tracer des frontières à Djibouti: Des territoires et des hommes aux xixe et xxe siècles*. Paris: Éditions Karthala.

Jalabert, Laurent. 2004. "Les Antilles de L'Amiral Robert." In *L'Empire Colonial Sous Vichy*, edited by Jacques Cantier and Eric Jennings, 51–68. Paris: Odile Jacob.

Jardel, Jean-Pierre. 2000. "Représentations des cultes afro-caribéens et des pratiques magico-religieuses aux antilles: une approche du préjugé racial dans la littérature para-anthropologique." In *Au visiteur lumineux: Des îles créoles aux sociétés plurielles*, edited by Jean Bernabé et al., 451–63. Petit Bourg, Guadeloupe: Ibis Rouge Éditions.

Jay, Philippe. 1996. "De nos relations de voisinage avec les Mauriciens . . . Les 'cousins' terribles de l'Océan Indien." *Visu* [Réunion] 651 (October).

Jennings, Eric T. 2001a. "Adapting the National Revolution to Indochina." In Jennings 2001e, 130–61.

———. 2001b. "Guadeloupean Society under Vichy." In Jennings 2001e, 105–29.

———. 2001c. "Suppressing the Republic in Guadeloupe." In Jennings 2001e, 79–104.

———. 2001d. "Toward a New Indochina." In Jennings 2001e, 162–98.

———, ed. 2001e. *Vichy in the Tropics: Pétain's National Revolution in Madagascar, Guadeloupe, and Indochina, 1940–1944*. Stanford CA: Stanford University Press.

Jeshurun, Chandran. 1977. *The Contest for Siam, 1889–1902: A Study in Diplomatic Rivalry*. Kuala Lumpur: Penerbit Universiti Kebangsaan Malaysia.

Kane, Ousmane. 1990. "Les Mouvements Religieux et le Champ Politique au Nigéria Septentrional: Le Cas de Réformisme Musulman à Kano." *Islam et sociétés au sud du Sahara* 4:7–24.

———. 1994. "Izala: The Rise of Muslim Reformism in Northern Nigeria." In *Accounting for Fundamentalisms: The Dynamic Character of Movements*, edited by Martin E. Marty and R. Scott Appleby, 490–512. Chicago: University of Chicago Press.

———. 2003. *Muslim Modernity in Postcolonial Nigeria: A Study of the Society for the Removal of Innovation and Reinstatement of Tradition*. Leiden: Brill.

Kasensally, Roukaya. 2011. "Mauritius: Paradise Reconsidered." *Journal of Democracy* 22:160–69.

Kastfelt, Niels. 1989. "Rumours of Maitatsine: A Note on Political Culture in Northern Nigeria." *African Affairs* 88:83–90.

Keay, John. 2005. "The Mekong Exploration Commission, 1866–68: Anglo-French Rivalry in South East Asia." *Asian Affairs* 36 (3): 289–311.

Kirk-Greene, A. H. M. 1965. "Bureaucratic Cadres in a Traditional Milieu." In *Education and Development*, edited by James Coleman, 372–407. Princeton NJ: Princeton University Press.

Kirwin, Matthew. 2005. "The Political and Economic Effects of Nigerian

Shari'a on Southern Niger." *Review of African Political Economy* 104/5 (Summer): 407–14.

Knight, Franklin W., and Colin A. Palmer. 1989. "The Caribbean: A Regional Overview." In *The Modern Caribbean*, edited by Franklin W. Knight and Colin A. Palmer, 1–20. Chapel Hill: University of North Carolina Press.

Koop, Kirsten. 2004. "L'Ile Maurice à l'ère de la mondialisation: Un modèle d'un développement de rattrapage?" *Autrepart* 31:109–32.

Kossikov, Igor. 2000. "Nationalities Policy in Modern Laos." In *Civility and Savagery: Social Identity in Tai States*, edited by Andrew Turton, 227–44. Richmond, Surrey: Curzon Press.

Kunstadter, Peter, ed. 1967. *Southeast Asian Tribes, Minorities, and Nations.* Princeton NJ: Princeton University Press.

Labo, Abdullahi. 2000. "The Motivation and Integration of Immigrants in the Nigeria-Niger Border Area: A Study of Magama-Jibia." In *Trans-Border Studies*. Occasional Publication no. 13. Ibadan: Institut Français de Recherche en Afrique.

La Guerre, John. 1986. "The Social and Political Thought of Aimé Césaire and C. L. R. James: Comparisons." In *Dual Legacies in the Contemporary Caribbean: Continuing Aspects of British and French Dominion*, edited by Paul Sutton, 201–22. London: Frank Cass.

Laitin, David. 1982. "The *Shari'a* Debate and the Origins of Nigeria's Second Republic." *Journal of Modern African Studies* 20:411–30.

Lange, Matthew. 2003. "Embedding the Colonial State. A Comparative-Historical Analysis of State Building and Broad-Based Development in Mauritius." *Social Science History* 27:397–423.

Lanne, Bernard. 1983. "Régime militaire et société de développement au Niger (1974–1983)." *Afrique Contemporaine* 125:38–44.

Larémont, Ricardo René. 2005. "Borders, States, and Nationalism." In *Borders, Nationalism, and the African State*, edited by Ricardo René Larémont, 1–32. Boulder CO: Lynne Rienner Publishers.

Last, Murray. 2000. "La Charia Dans le Nord-Nigeria." *Politique Africaine* 79:141–52.

Laville, Rosabelle. 2000. "In the Politics of the Rainbow: Creoles and Civil Society in Mauritius." *Journal of Contemporary African Studies* 18:277–94.

LeBar, Frank, Gerald Hickey, and John Musgrave. 1964. *Ethnic Groups of Mainland Southeast Asia*. New Haven CT: Human Relations Area Files Press.

Le Boulanger, Paul. 1931. *Histoire du Laos Français: Essai d'Une Etude Chronologique des Principautés Laotiennes*. Paris: Librarie Plon.

Leclézio, Henri. (1914) 1991. "People and Politics." In *Mauritius Illustrated: Historical and Descriptive, Commercial and Industrial Facts, Figures, and Resources*, edited by Allister Macmillan, 137–42. London: Les Éditions du Pacifique.

Lefèvre, E. (1898) 1995. *Travels in Laos: The Fate of the Sip Song Pana and Muong Sing (1894–1896)*. Bangkok: White Lotus.

Lefèvre-Pontalis, Pierre. (1902) 2000. *Travels in Upper Laos and on the Borders of Yunnan and Burma*. Bangkok: White Lotus Press.

Lempert, David. 1987. "A Demographic-Economic Explanation of Political Stability: Mauritius as a Microcosm." *Eastern Africa Economic Review* 3:77–90.

Leti, Geneviève. 2000. *L'univers magico-religieux antillais*. Paris: L'Harmattan.

Lewis, Gordon. 1967. "British Colonialism in the West Indies: The Political Legacy." *Caribbean Studies* 7:3–22.

———. 1985. "The Contemporary Caribbean: A General Overview." In *Caribbean Contours*, edited by Sidney W. Mintz and Sally Price, 219–50. Baltimore: Johns Hopkins University Press.

Lewis, Linden. 2001. "The Contestation of Race in Barbadian Society and the Camouflage of Conservatism." In *New Caribbean Thought: A Reader*, edited by Brian Meeks and Folke Lindahl, 144–55. Kingston, Jamaica: University of the West Indies Press.

Lewis, Martin Dening. 1961–62. "One Hundred Million Frenchmen: The 'Assimilation' Theory in French Colonial Policy." *Comparative Studies in Society and History* 4:129–53.

Liang, Chi Shad. 1990. *Burma's Foreign Relations: Neutralism in Theory and Practice*. New York: Praeger.

Loimeier, Roman. 1997. *Islamic Reform and Political Change in Northern Nigeria*. Evanston IL: Northwestern University Press.

———. 2007. "Nigeria: The Quest for a Viable Religious Option." In *Political Islam in West Africa: State-Society Relations Transformed*, edited by William F. S. Miles, 43–72. Boulder CO: Lynne Rienner Publishers.

Longhurst, Richard. 1982. "Resource Allocation and the Sexual Division of Labor: A Case Study of a Moslem Hausa Village in Northern Nigeria." In *Women and Development: The Sexual Division of Labor in Societies*, edited by Lourdes Benerias, 95–117. New York: Praeger.

Lowenthal, David. 1972. *West Indian Societies*. New York: Oxford University Press.

Lubeck, Paul. 1985. "Islamic Protest under Semi-industrial Capitalism: 'Yan Tatsine Explained." *Africa* 55:369–87.

Lucrèce, André. 2000. *Souffrance et jouissance aux Antilles*. Tartane, Martinique: Gondwana Éditions.

Lund, Christian, and Gerti Hesseling. 1999. "Traditional Chiefs and Modern Land Tenure Law in Niger." In *African Chieftaincy in a New Socio-*

Political Landscape, edited by E. Adriaan B. van Rouveroy van Nieuwaal and Rijk van Dijk, 135–54. Leiden: LIT Verlag.

Lyttleton, Chris. 2004. "Relative Pleasures: Drugs, Development, and Modern Dependencies in Asia's Golden Triangle." *Development and Change* 35: 909–33.

Lyttleton, Chris, Paul Cohen, Houmphanh Rattanavong, Bouakham Thongkhamhane, and Souriyanh Sisaengrat. 2004. "Watermelons, Bars, and Trucks: Dangerous Intersections in Northwest Lao PDR: An Ethnographic Study of Social Change and Health Vulnerability along the Road through Muang Sing and Muang Long." Institute for Cultural Research of Lao and Macquarie University.

Mack, Beverly. 1991. "Royal Wives in Kano." In Coles and Mack 1991, 109–29.

Macmillan, Allister, ed. (1914) 1991. *Mauritius Illustrated: Historical and Descriptive, Commercial and Industrial Facts, Figures, and Resources.* London: Les Éditions du Pacifique.

Maingot, Anthony P. 1989. "Caribbean International Relations." In *The Modern Caribbean*, edited by Franklin W. Knight and Colin A. Palmer, 259–92. Chapel Hill: University of North Carolina Press.

Mamdani, Mahmood. 1996. *Citizen and Subject: Contemporary Africa and the Legacy of Late Colonialism.* Princeton NJ: Princeton University Press.

Massé, Raymond. 1978a. "Les Adventistes du Septième Jour aux Antilles françaises: anthropologie d'une espérance." *Revue canadienne de sociologie et anthropologie* 15:452–65.

———. 1978b. *Les Adventistes du septième jour aux antilles françaises: anthropologie d'une espérance millénariste.* Publications du Centre de Recherches Caraïbes, Université de Montréal.

Massé, Raymond, and Véronique Poulin. 2000. "La Place des Eglises Fondamentalistes dans la Société et Dans la Culture Martiniquaise." In *Au visiteur lumineux: Des îles créoles aux sociétés plurielles*, edited by Jean Bernabé et al., 403–15. Petit Bourg, Guadeloupe: Ibis Rouge Éditions.

Mauritius Examinations Syndicate (MES). 1992. *Learning Competencies for All.* Port Louis: Ministry of Education.

Mbembe, Achille. 1992. "Provisional Notes on the Postcolony." *Africa* 62:3–37

———. 2002. "At the Edge of the World: Boundaries, Territoriality, and Sovereignty in Africa." In Beissinger and Young 2002, 53–80.

Mead, Walter Russell. 2007. "Entente Infernale: How 300 Years of Anglo-French Rivalry Shaped the World" (Review Essay). *Foreign Affairs* 86:147–52.

Meeks, Brian. 2001. "On the Bump of a Revival." In *New Caribbean Thought: A Reader*, edited by Brian Meeks and Foke Lindahl, viii–xx. Kingston, Jamaica: University of West Indies Press.

Meisenhelder, Thomas. 1997. "The Developmental State in Mauritius." *Journal of Modern African Studies* 35:279–97.

Metz, Helen C., ed. 1995. *Indian Ocean: Five Island Countries*. Area Handbook Series. Washington DC: Federal Research Division, Library of Congress.

Meunier, Olivier. 1997. *Dynamique de l'enseignement islamique au Niger: Le cas de la ville de Maradi*. Paris: L'Harmattan.

———. 2000. *Bilan d'un siècle de politiques éducatives au Niger*. Paris: L'Harmattan.

Meyerson, Beatrice Berle, John F. Hornbeck, and Richard A. Haggerty. 1989. "Barbados." In *Islands of the Commonwealth Caribbean: A Regional Study*, edited by Sandra W. Meditz and Dennis M. Hanratty. Washington DC: U.S. Government Printing Office.

Meyerhoff, Miriam. 2002. "A Vanishing Act: Tonkinese Migrant Labour in Vanuatu in the Early 20th Century." *Journal of Pacific History* 37:45–56.

Miles, William F. S. 1987. "Partitioned Royalty: The Evolution of Hausa Chiefs in Nigeria and Niger." *Journal of Modern African Studies* 25:233–58.

———. 1993. "Colonial Hausa Idioms: Toward a West African Ethno-Ethnohistory." *African Studies Review* 36:11–30.

———. 1994a. "Francophonie in Post-Colonial Vanuatu." *Journal of Pacific History* 29: 49–65.

———. 1994b. *Hausaland Divided: Colonialism and Independence in Nigeria and Niger*. Ithaca NY: Cornell University Press.

———. 1994c. "Retour au Paradis? France and Vanuatu in the South Pacific." *French Politics and Society* 12:58–71.

———. 1995. *Imperial Burdens: Countercolonialism in Former French India*. Boulder CO: Lynne Rienner Publishers.

———. 1996. "Relations étrangères dans le cadre d'un département d'outre-mer: les rapports Réunion-Maurice." Intervention de colloque, 1946: La Réunion, Département. Université de la Réunion.

———. 1998. *Bridging Mental Boundaries in a Postcolonial Microcosm: Identity and Development in Vanuatu*. Honolulu: University of Hawai'i Press.

———. 1999a. "Abolition, Independence, and Soccer: Premillennial Dilemmas of Martinican Identity." *French Politics and Society* 17:23–33.

———. 1999b. "The Creole Malaise in Mauritius." *African Affairs* 98:211–28.

———. 1999c. "The Mauritius Enigma." *Journal of Democracy* 10:91–104.

———. 2003a. "Contradictions in the Caribbean: Martinique and the 2002 French National Elections." *French Politics, Culture, and Society* 21 (3): 107–26.

———. 2003b. "A Horse, a Chief, and a Political Anthropologist: Indigenous Politics, Conflict Resolution, and Globalization in Niger." In *Indigenous Political Structures and Governance in Africa*, edited by Olufemi Vaughan, 291–321. Ibadan, Nigeria: Sefer Books.

———. 2003c. "The Irrelevance of Independence: Martinique and the French Presidential Elections of 2002." *New West Indian Guide* 77 (3–4): 221–52.

———. 2003d. "Shari'a as De-Africanization: Evidence from Hausaland." *Africa Today* 50:50–75.

———. 2005a. "Democracy without Sovereignty: France's Post-Colonial Paradox." *Brown Journal of World Affairs* 11 (2): 223–34.

———. 2005b. "Development, Not Division: Local versus External Perceptions of the Niger-Nigeria Boundary. *Journal of Modern African Studies* 43:297–320.

———. 2006. "When Is a Nation 'a Nation'? Identity-Formation within a French West Indian People (Martinique)." *Nations and Nationalism* 12 (4): 631–52.

———. 2007. "Once Again, from a Distance: Martinique and the French Presidential Elections of 2007." *French Politics, Culture, and Society* 25 (3): 102–22.

———. 2008. "Britain, France, and the Dual Colonial Inheritance of Mauritius: Mauritian Decolonization in Comparative Perspective." Toorawa Trust Occasional Paper, 8. [Port Louis, Mauritius]: William F. S. Miles and Hassam Toorawa Trust.

———. 2009. "'Metaphysical Considerations Can Come Later, but the People Have Children to Feed': An Interview with Aimé Césaire." *French Politics, Culture, and Society* 27:63–75.

———. 2012. "Schizophrenic Islands, Fifty Years after Fanon: Martinique, the Pent-Up 'Paradise.'" *International Journal of Francophone Studies* 15:9–33.

Miles, William F. S., and David A. Rochefort. 1991. "Nationalism versus Ethnic Identity in Sub-Saharan Africa." *American Political Science Review* 85:393–403.

Moerman, Michael. 1965. "Ethnic Identification in a Complex Civilization: Who Are the Lue?" *American Anthropologist* 67:1215–30.

Morgan, Michael. 1999. "Political Chronicles: Vanuatu, 1995–1998." *Journal of Pacific History* 33:287–93.

———. 2003. "Converging on the Arc of Instability? The Fall of Barak Sope and the Spectre of a Coup in Vanuatu." In *'Arc of Instability'? Melanesia in the Early 2000s*, edited by R. J. May, 41–54. Canberra and Christchurch: Australian National University and University of Canterbury.

Morgan, Philip D. 1997. "The Cultural Implications of the Atlantic Slave Trade: African Regional Origins, American Destinations, and New World Developments." *Slavery and Abolition* 18:122–45.

Morris-Jones, W. H., and Georges Fisher. 1980. *Decolonisation and After: The British and French Experience.* London: Frank Cass.

Murch, Arvin. 1971. *Black Frenchmen: The Political Integration of the French Antilles.* Cambridge MA: Schenkman Publishing.

Naipaul, V. S. 1972. "The Overcrowded Barracoon." *Sunday Times Magazine* (London), July 16.

Nave, Ari. 2001. "Nested Identities: Ethnicity, Community, and the Nature of Group Conflict in Mauritius." In *Community, Empire, and Migration: South Asians in Diaspora*, edited by Crispin Bates, 87–108. London: Palgrave.

Niandou-Souley, Abdoulaye, and Gado Alzouma. 1996. "Islamic Renewal in Niger: From Monolith to Plurality." *Social Compass* 43:49–265.

Nugent, Paul. 2002. *Smugglers, Secessionists, and Loyal Citizens on the Ghana-Togo Frontier: The Lie of the Borderlands since 1914*. Athens: Ohio University Press.

Nugent, Paul, and A. I. Asiwaju. 1996a. "Introduction: The Paradox of African Boundaries." In *African Boundaries*, edited by Paul Nugent and A. I. Asiwaju, 1–14. London: Pinter.

———. 1996b. "Conclusion: The Future of African Boundaries." In *African Boundaries*, edited by Paul Nugent and A.I. Asiwaju, 266–72. London: Pinter.

Nwaka, Geoffrey I. 1999. "Traditional Rulers and the Development Agenda in Nigeria." *African Administrative Studies* 54:133–46.

Oliver, Roland, and Anthony Atmore. 1972. *Africa since 1800*. Cambridge: Cambridge University Press.

Olivier de Sardan, Jean-Pierre. 1999. "L'Espace public introuvable: Chefs et Projets dans les Villages Nigériens." *Revue Tiers Monde* 40:139–67.

Onishi, Norimitsu. 2001. "Winds of Militant Islam Disrupt Fragile Frontiers." *New York Times*, February 2.

Onoja, Colonel Lawrence Anebi. 1993. "Problems of Local Administration and the Imperative of Transborder Co-operation: The Experience of Katsina State." In Asiwaju and Barkindo 1993, 306–12.

Orewa, G. O. 1978. "The Role of Traditional Rulers in Administration." *Quarterly Journal of Administration* 12:151–65.

Ovesen, Jan. 2004. "All Lao? Minorities in the Lao People's Democratic Republic." In *Civilizing the Margins: Southeast Asian Government Policies for the Development of Minorities*, edited by Christopher Duncan, 215–40. Ithaca NY: Cornell University Press.

Paden, John. 1973. *Religion and Political Culture in Kano*. Berkeley: University of California Press.

Parker, Gabrielle. 1996. "French Language Policy in sub-Saharan Africa." *Modern and Contemporary France*, n.s., 4:471–81.

Payne, Anthony, and Paul Sutton. 1993. "Introduction: The Contours of Modern Caribbean Politics." In *Modern Caribbean Politics*, edited by Anthony Payne and Paul Sutton, 1–27. Baltimore: Johns Hopkins University Press.

Peabody, Sue, and Tyler Stovall, eds. 2003. *The Color of Liberty: Histories of Race in France*. Durham NC: Duke University Press.

Périna, Mickaëlla. 2003. "Martinique." In *African Caribbeans: A Refer-

ence Guide, edited by Alan West-Durán, 229–41. Westport CT: Greenwood Press.

Pellow, Deborah. 1991. "From Accra to Kano: One Woman's Experience." In Coles and Mack 1991, 50–68.

Pholsena, Vatthana. 2002. "Nation/Representation: Ethnic Classification and Mapping Nationhood in Contemporary Laos." *Asian Ethnicity* 3 (2): 175–97.

———. 2006. *Post-War Laos: The Politics of Culture, History, and Identity*. Ithaca NY: Cornell University Press.

Pitten, Renée. 1983. "Houses of Women: A Focus on Alternative Life-Styles in Katsina City." In *Female and Male in Africa*, edited by Christine Oppong, 291–302. London: George Allen and Unwin.

———. 1984. "Migration of Women in Nigeria: The Hausa Case." *International Migration Review* 18:1293–1313.

———. 1991. "Women, Work, and Ideology in Nigeria." *Review of African Political Economy* 52:38–52.

Pluvier, Jan. 1974. *South-East Asia from Colonialism to Independence*. Kuala Lumpur: Oxford University Press.

Polgreen, Lydia. 2007. "Nigeria Turns from Harsher Side of Islamic Law." *New York Times*, December 1, A1, A6.

Prabhu, Anjali. 2005. "Representation in Mauritian Politics: Who Speaks for African Pasts?" *International Journal of Francophone Studies* 8:183–97.

Pred, Allan, and Michael John Watts. 1992. "The Shock of Modernity: Petroleum, Protest, and Fast Capitalism in an Industrializing Society." In *Reworking Modernity: Capitalisms and Symbolic Discontent*, edited by Allan Pred and Michael John Watts, 21–64. New Brunswick NJ: Rutgers University Press.

Prescott, J. R. V. 1987. *Political Frontiers and Boundaries*. London: George Allen and Unwin.

Prosper, Jean-Georges. 1993. *L'Ile Maurice au sommet de la vague économique francophone*. Paris: L'Harmattan.

Quinn, Frederick. 2000. *The French Overseas Empire*. Westport CT: Praeger.

Quirin, Sabrina. 1996. "Quand les Réunionnais nous traitent de 'Belges de l'océan Indien.'" *Week-End/Scope* [Maurice], November 8–14.

Ramutsindela, Maano. 1999. "African Boundaries and Their Interpreters." *Geopolitics* 4:180–98.

Ravenhill, John. 1988. "Redrawing the Map of Africa?" In *The Precarious Balance: State and Society in Africa*, edited by Donald Rothchild and Naomi Chazan, 282–303. Boulder CO: Westview.

Ravi, Srilata. 2010. "Border Zones in Colonial Spaces: Imagining Pondicherry, Mauritius, and Lucknow." *Interventions: International Journal of Postcolonial Studies* 12:383–95.

Reilly, Ben. 2000. "The Africanisation of the South Pacific." *Australian Journal of International Affairs* 54:261–66.

Reinhardt, Catherine A. 2006. *Claims to Memory: Beyond Slavery and Emancipation in the French Caribbean.* New York: Berghan Books.

Reis, João José. 2003. "Ethnic Politics among Africans in Bahia." In *Trans-Atlantic Dimensions of Ethnicity in the African Diaspora*, edited by Paul E. Lovejoy and David V. Trotman, 240–64. London: Continuum.

Renard, Ronald D. 1997. "The Making of a Problem: Narcotics in Mainland Southeast Asia." In *Development or Domestication? Indigenous Peoples of Southeast Asia*, edited by Don N. McCaskill, 307–28. Chiang Mai: Silkworm Books.

Reno, Fred. 1989. "Types d'Etats et Contestation Politique Dans la Caraïbe: Essai d'Analyse Comparative de la Question Nationalitaire à la Barbade et à la Martinique." *Les Cahiers de l'Administration Outre-Mer* 2:15–41.

République du Niger. 1993. *Journal Officiel*, Special Number 13, July 1.

Richardson, Bonham C. 1989. "Caribbean Migrations, 1838–1935." In *The Modern Caribbean*, edited by Franklin W. Knight and Colin A. Palmer, 203–28. Chapel Hill: University of North Carolina Press.

Robinson, Pearl. 1983. "Traditional Clientage and Political Change in a Hausa Community." In *Transformation and Resiliency in Africa as Seen by Afro-American Scholars*, edited by Pearl T. Robinson and Elliott Skinner, 105–28. Washington DC: Howard University Press.

———. 1991. "Niger: Anatomy of a Neotraditional Corporatist State." *Comparative Politics* 23:1–20.

———. 1994. "The National Conference Phenomenon in Africa." *Comparative Studies in Society and History* 36:575–610.

Rodman, Margaret C. 1998. "Creating Historic Sites in Vanuatu." *Social Analysis* 42:117–34.

Rotberg, Robert. 1997. "Peripheral Successor States and the Legacy of Empire: Succeeding the British and French Empires." In Dawisha and Parrott 1997, 198–217.

Ryan, Selwyn. 1994. "Problems and Prospects for Survival of Liberal Democracy in the Caribbean." In *Democracy in the Caribbean*, edited by Carlene Edie, 233–50. New York: Praeger.

Sablé, Victor. 1955. *La Transformation des Isles d'Amérique en départements français.* Paris: Éditions Larose.

———. 1972. *Les Antilles sans complexes—une expérience de décolonisation.* Paris: Éditions G. P. Maisonneuve et Larose.

Sabra, Roland. 2007. "Serge Letchimy: Soldat de la cause martiniquaise face à l'Etat français . . . l'attente commence." *Le Naïf* 142 (June/July): 18.

Sahai, Sachchidanand. 2005. *The Mekong River: Space and Social Theory.* Delhi: B. R. Publishing.

Sahlins, Peter. 1989. *Boundaries: The Making of France and Spain in the Pyrenees*. Berkeley: University of California Press.

Sandbrook, Richard. 2005. "Origins of the Democratic Developmental State: Interrogating Mauritius." *Canadian Journal of African Studies/Revue Canadienne des Études Africaines* 39:549–81.

Sandbrook, Richard, and David Romano. 2004. "Globalisation, Extremism, and Violence in Poor Countries." *Third World Quarterly* 25:1007–30.

Sanusi, H. U. 1993. "Imperatives of Nigeria-Niger Transborder Co-operation." In Asiwaju and Barkindo 1993, 21–32.

Schildkrout, Enid. 1983. "Dependence and Autonomy: The Economic Activities of Secluded Hausa Women in Kano." In *Female and Male in West Africa*, edited by Christine Oppong, 107–26. London: George Allen and Unwin.

Schliesinger, Joachim. 2003. *Ethnic Groups of Laos*, vol. 1: *Introduction and Overview*. Bangkok: White Lotus Press.

Schraeder, Peter. 1995. "Madagascar." In Metz 1995, 1–87.

Shepard, Todd. 2006. *The Invention of Decolonization: The Algerian War and the Remaking of France*. Ithaca NY: Cornell University Press.

Sidikou, Amirou Garba, and Sarki Mahamane Djika. 2000. *Association des Chefs Traditionnels du Niger: Présentation, Structuration, Couverture géographique*. Niamey: Nouvelle Imprimerie du Niger.

Simmons, Adele S. 1982. *Modern Mauritius: The Politics of Decolonization*. Bloomington: Indiana University Press.

Simmons, Peter. 1976. "'Red Legs': Class and Color Contradictions in Barbados." *Studies in Comparative International Development* 11:3–24.

Sleeman, Michael. 1986. "Sugar in Barbados and Martinique: A Socio-Economic Comparison." In *Dual Legacies in the Contemporary Caribbean: Continuing Aspects of British and French Dominion*, edited by Paul Sutton, 62–88. London: Frank Cass.

Smith, M. G. 1965. *The Plural Society in the British West Indies*. Berkeley: University of California Press.

Smith, Stephen W. 2013. "France in Africa: A New Chapter?" *Current History* 112 (May): 754.

Smith, Tony. 1978. "A Comparative Study of French and British Decolonization." *Comparative Studies in Society and History* 20:70–102.

Soulas de Russel, Dominique. 1998. "Niveaux et degrés d'intégration des 'modernités' chez les chefs traditionnels: l'exemple du Niger." *Afrika Spectrum* 33:99–116.

Srebrnik, Henry. 2000. "Can an Ethnically-Based Civil Society Succeed? The Case of Mauritius." *Journal of Contemporary African Studies* 18:7–20.

Steinberg, David I. 1982. *Burma: A Socialist Nation of Southeast Asia*. Boulder CO: Westview Press.

———. 2001. *Burma: The State of Myanmar*. Washington DC: Georgetown University Press.

———. 2006. *Turmoil in Burma: Contested Legitimacies in Myanmar.* London: Routledge.

Stephens, Connie. 1991. "Marriage in the Hausa *Tatsuniya* Tradition: A Cultural and Cosmic Balance." In Coles and Mack 1991, 221–31.

St. John, Ronald Bruce. 1998. *The Land Boundaries of Indochina: Cambodia, Laos, and Vietnam.* Boundary and Territory Briefing 2, no. 6. Durham: International Boundaries Research Unit.

Stuart-Fox, Martin. 1995. "The French in Laos, 1887–1945." *Modern Asian Studies* 29 (1): 111–13.

———. 1997. *A History of Laos.* Cambridge: Cambridge University Press.

Subramanian, Arvind, and Devesh Roy. 2003. "Who Can Explain the Mauritian Miracle? Meade, Romer, Sachs, or Rodrik?" In *In Search of Prosperity: Analytic Narratives on Economic Growth*, edited by Dani Rodrik, 205–43. Princeton NJ: Princeton University Press.

Sule, Balaraba B. M., and Priscilla E. Starratt. 1991. "Islamic Leadership Positions for Women in Contemporary Kano Society." In Coles and Mack 1991, 29–49.

Sutton, Paul, ed. 1986. *Dual Legacies in the Contemporary Caribbean: Continuing Aspects of British and French Dominion.* London: Frank Cass.

Tate, D. J. M. 1979. *The Making of Modern South-East Asia*, vol. 2: *The Western Impact: Economic and Social Change.* Kuala Lumpur: Oxford University Press.

Teelock, Vijaya. 1998. *Bitter Sugar: Sugar and Slavery in 19th Century Mauritius.* Moka: Mahatma Gandhi Institute.

Thom, Derrick J. 1970. "The Niger-Nigeria Borderlands: A Politico-Geographic Analysis of Boundary Influence upon the Hausa." PhD dissertation, Michigan State University.

———. 1975. *The Niger-Nigeria Boundary, 1890–1906: A Study of Ethnic Frontiers and a Colonial Boundary.* Papers in International Studies, Africa Series no. 23. Athens: Ohio University Center for International Studies, Africa Program.

Thorndike, Tony. 1991. "Politics and Society in the South-Eastern Caribbean." In *Society and Politics in the Caribbean*, edited by Colin Clarke, 110–30. New York: St. Martin's Press.

Tibenderana, Peter. 1988. "The Irony of Indirect Rule in Sokoto Emirate, Nigeria, 1903–1944." *African Studies Review* 31:67–92.

———. 1989. "British Administration and the Decline of the Patronage-Clientage System in Northwestern Nigeria, 1900–1934." *African Studies Review* 32:71–95.

Tilley, Christopher. 1997. "Performing Culture in the Global Village." *Critique of Anthropology* 17:67–89.

Toorawa, Shawkat. M. 2003. "'We Were Here First': The Rhetoric of Identity and Anteriority among African-American Muslims and Muslims in Mauritius." *Journal of Islamic Law and Culture* 8:2–39.

Toth, Anthony. 1995. "Mauritius." In Metz 1995, 91–135.

Toussaint, Auguste. 1969. "La langue française à l'Ile Maurice." *Revue française d'Histoire d'Outre-Mer* 56:398–427.

Touval, Saadia. 1972. *Boundary Politics of Independent Africa*. Cambridge: Harvard University Press.

Tribal Museum. 2004. *The Hill Tribes of Thailand*. Chiang Mai: Technical Service Club.

Triaud, Jean-Louis. 1981. "L'Islam et l'état en République du Niger." *Le Mois en Afrique* 192–93:9–26.

Turton, Andrew, ed. 2000. *Civility and Savagery: Social Identity in Tai States*. Richmond, Surrey: Curzon Pres.

Uzoigwe, G. N. 1985. "European Partition and Conquest of Africa: An Overview." In *General History of Africa VII: Africa under Colonial Domination, 1880–1935*, edited by A. Adu Boahen, 19–62. Paris and London: UNESCO and Heinemann.

Varondin, Joseph. 1994. "Kakalizié et trachome." *Week-End*, April 17.

Vaughan, Olufemi. 1991. "Chieftaincy Politics and Social Relations in Nigeria." *Journal of Commonwealth and Comparative Politics* 29:308–26.

Villalon, Leonardo. 2003. "The Moral and the Political in African Democratization: The *Code de La Famille* in Niger's Troubled Transition." *Democratization* 3:41–68.

Virelala, Jean-Paul. 1995. "To Be a Francophone in Vanuatu." In *Melanesian Politics: Stael Blong Vanuatu*, edited by Howard Van Trease, 403–6. Christchurch and Suva: University of Canterbury and University of the South Pacific.

Von Albertini, Rudolf. 1982. *Decolonization*. New York: Holmes and Meier.

Von Geusau, Leo A. 2003. "Protecting the Cultural Heritage of Minority Groups in the Mekong Quadrangle Area." In *Laos and Ethnic Minority Cultures: Promoting Heritage*, edited by Yves Goudineau, 239–43. Paris: UNESCO Publishing.

Walker, Andrew. 1999. *The Legend of the Golden Boat: Regulation, Trade, and Traders in the Borderlands of Laos, Thailand, China, and Burma*. Honolulu: University of Hawai'i Press.

Walker, Anthony. 1974–75. "The Lahu of the Yunnan-Indochina Borderlands: An Introduction" *Folk* 16–17:329–44.

Wanquet, Claude. 1985. "Les Fondements Historiques de la Coopération Régionale." In *Annuaire des Pays de l'Océan Indien 1982–3*, vol. 9. Université Paul Cézanne Aix-Marseille III.

Warner-Lewis, Maureen. 1999. "Cultural Reconfigurations in the African Caribbean." In *The African Diaspora: African Origins and New World*

Identities, edited by Isidore Okpewho, Carole Boyce Davies, and Ali A. Mazrui, 19–27. Bloomington: Indiana University Press.
Watt, Albert. 1995. "Vanuatu Independent Francophone." In *Melanesian Politics: Stael Blong Vanuatu*, edited by Howard Van Trease, 235–37. Christchurch and Suva: University of Canterbury and University of the South Pacific.
Watts, Michael. 1996. "Islamic Modernities? Citizenship, Civil Society, and Islamism in a Nigerian City." *Public Culture* 8:251–89.
Weber, Eugen. 1976. *Peasants into Frenchmen: The Modernization of Rural France, 1870–1914*. Stanford CA: Stanford University Press.
Welch, L. V. Pedro. 2003. "Barbados." In *African Caribbeans: A Reference Guide*, edited by Alan West-Durán, 29–41. Westport CT: Greenwood Press.
Wesseling, H. L. 1996. *Divide and Rule: The Partition of Africa, 1880–1914*, translated by Arnold J. Pomerans. Westport CT: Praeger.
Whiteman, Kaye. 1993. "Francophonie et anglophonie: regards portés sur 'l'autre'. In *Etats et Sociétés en Afrique Francophone*, edited by Daniel Bach and Anthony Kirk-Greene, 291–304. Paris: Economica.
Widner, Jennifer A. 1994. "Political Reform in Anglophone and Francophone African Countries." In *Economic Change and Political Liberalization in Sub-Saharan Africa*, edited by Jennifer A. Widner, 49–79. Baltimore: Johns Hopkins University Press.
Will, Marvin. 1972. "Political Development in the Mini-State Caribbean: A Focus on Barbados." PhD dissertation, University of Missouri.
Williams, Lea E. 1976. *Southeast Asia: A History*. New York: Oxford University Press.
Yerro, Philippe Alain. 2000. "A partir du mouvement rastafari de Martinique: système discursif, ethnicité et retour du refoulé." In *Au visiteur lumineux: Des îles créoles aux sociétés plurielles*, edited by Jean Bernabé et al., 115–35. Petit Bourg, Guadeloupe: Ibis Rouge Éditions.
Young, Crawford. 1994. *The African Colonial State in Comparative Perspective*. New Haven CT: Yale University Press.
———. 2012. *The Postcolonial State in Africa: Fifty Years of Independence, 1960–2010*. Madison: University of Wisconsin.
Yusuf, Bilkisu. 1991. "Hausa-Fulani Women: The State of the Struggle." In Coles and Mack 1991, 90–106.
Zartman, I. William, ed. 2010. *Understanding Life in the Borderlands: Boundaries in Depth and in Motion*. Athens: University of Georgia Press.

INDEX

Africa: chiefs and chieftaincy in, 30, 36–37; colonial legacies in, 72–74; comparative study of, 5–6; culture of, 298, 302; decolonization of, 297–98; economy of, 72–73; ethnicity in, 292, 297, 300; French Equatorial, 22, 311n4; identity in, 131; languages in, 302, 306; postcolonial violence in, 6, 48, 64, 68, 69, 71, 73, 310–11n13; slavery in, 16–17, 81–82, 292; and South Pacific, 136, 141, 142, 143–144. *See also* East Africa; Maghreb; West Africa

African Borderlands Research Network (ABORNE), xvi

"African Ocean," 189–90

Afro-Saxonism, 115–17, 132

Agadez, 31, 35

Akha (Akhas), 273 map 20, 301, 324n25

Aldrich, Robert, 304–5

Algeria, 10, 11, 325n2

Americanization, 42, 94, 105, 152–53, 299

American Samoa. *See* Samoa

Amerindians, 78, 81, 297

Anguilla, 78, 93, 107, 300

Andhra Pradesh, 234–35, 238

Antigua, 77, 93, 99, 103 table 3

Antilles, 297, 305

Arabic, 50, 51, 52, 205

Arawaks, 80

Ashanti, 84

Asiwaju, A. I., 52, 62, 71–72

assimilation, 9, 29–30, 75, 80, 112, 116, 282, 297–300. *See also* France: colonial policy of

Australia, 136, 143, 145; and Indian Ocean, 228; and New Caledonia, 139; and Papua New Guinea, 141–42, 146; and Vanuatu, 149–51, 164, 176, 182

Bach, Daniel, 69

Bahamas, 77, 93, 103 table 3, 313n1

Bakassi, 312n23

Barbados: colonization of, 107; creolization of, 117, 126, 131; democracy in, 125, 303; dependency of, 120; development in, 108; economy of, 107, 108, 121; education in, 108, 110, 313n7, 314n23; English influence in, 109, 114, 115–17, 314n16; geography of, 77, 79 map 9, 109–11, 301; Igboization in, 313n1; independence of, 108, 126–27; language of, 110; legal system of, 125, 126; and Martinique, 107–33, 313n12; and Mauritius, 320n20; migration from, 11; national identity in, 109, 118, political culture of, 111, 117–19, 120, 124, 314n17; political parties of, 19; population of, 111; race and racism in, 114, 314nn14–15, 314n18; radicals in, 128–29; Red Legs of, 107, 113; religion in, 121–22, 314n19; slave legacy of, 112; slavery in, 84, 107, 113, 117, 313n12;

Barbados (*cont.*)
  slaves freed in, 110; as *tabula rasa* colony, 296; voting in, 131
Barbuda, 77, 93, 103 table 3
Barth, Fredrik, 310n12, 324n26
Beckles, Hilary, 314n16
Beissinger, Mark, 6
Belize, 76, 77, 103 table 3
Bengali, 230, 231–32
Benin, 25, 47 table 2, 72, 311n6
Bérenger, Paul, 210, 320n19
Bermuda, 78
Betts, Raymond, 12, 14, 308, 309n4, 310n6
Bhojpuri, 198, 203, 204, 205 table 5, 221, 319n10
Bislama, 168, 173–75, 316n17
Boahen, Adu, 12, 310n7
Bonaparte, Napoleon. *See* Napoleon
borderlands: defined, 309n2; Lao-Burmese, 18, 265–66, 267–68, 270, 271, 284–85, 288–89, 301; marginalization of, 306–8; Mexican-U.S., 268, 323n18; Nigerian-Nigérien, 16, 32–33, 46–50, 59–70, 300–301; South Pacific, 136 map 11, 140; study of, xvi, 3–4, 8, 14–15, 19, 37, 70–71, 265–66; of Thailand, 268, 270–72; and urban areas, 15; village as, 318n36
"borderline" and "borderliners," 2, 14, 65, 285, 290, 292, 307, 310n11; renamed, 24
border markets, 69, 259, 260, 265, 268, 269, 289
border security, 57, 63, 64, 65, 68, 69, 71, 288
Borgu, 84
Borno State, 64
Bornu, 31
Botswana, 211, 237, 320n14
boundaries: arbitrary and artificial, 2, 12, 14, 33, 70, 244, 290, 291; and borderlanders, 292; colonial, 2–3; Burmese-Lao, 253–55, 259–263, 268, 284–85, 289; demarcation of, 63–64, 262; ethnic, 4, 7, 13–15, 280, 290, 310n12, 324n26; as fixed lines, 7, 253–54, 257, 279; and identity, 292–93; Lao-Thai, 268, 284–85; maritime, 13, 14, 15, 104, 133; mental, 13–14, 74, 149, 291; porousness of, 6, 65; 280; riverine, 104, 265, 268, 272, 288. *See also* partition; psychology
Britain: colonial policy of, 8–13, 36, 311n9; decolonization by, 11, 297. *See also* British Overseas Territories; Commonwealth; Crown Colonies; Indirect Rule
British Guiana. *See* Guyana
British Honduras. *See* Belize
British Indian Ocean Territory, 211 table 6
British Overseas Territories (BOT), 77–78, 93
British Virgin Islands, 78, 93
British West Indies, 77–78, 87–90, 92–95, 102–4
Brunei, 241, 243 table 8
Burkina Faso, 25, 26, 47 table 2, 311n6
Burma: anti-British resistance in, 247, 287; autarchy in, 249, 250; boundaries of, 244; chiefs and chieftaincy in, 253, 269–70, 285; colonial policy in, 242, 244–45; colonization of, 242–45; communism and communists in, 246, 247, 173–74, 276–77; democratization in, 250; development of, 243 table 8, 252; dictatorship in, 249, 303; ethnic groups and ethnicity in, 242, 247, 249, 274–75, 279, 280–81, 283, 287; as ethnocratic state, 281; hill tribes of, 242, 247, 300, 301; independence of, 249, 293; and India, 242, 247, 253, 264, 287–88; and Japan, 246–47; languages of, 242, 244, 271–79, 283, 325n4; and Laos, 240, 260–64, 268, 270–71, 283, 287–89, 325n32; name of, 249; population of, 242; religion in, 242, 245, 264, 280; sex trafficking from, 324n28; surveillance in, 324nn20–21; violence in, 250, 266–67, 279–80, 288; and World War II, 246–47. *See also* Burmans; Burmese; Mekong River

Burmans, 242, 245, 278
Burmese, 280

Caldoches, 140, 146, 186
Cambodia, 243 table 8, 324n28
Cameroon, 5–6, 24–25, 28, 47 table 2, 63, 64, 311n3
Canada, 94, 111
Caribbean: culture, 99–102, 105–7; democracy in, 95–99; economy of, 102–5; geography of, 76–78; as identity marker, 89, 100, 102; and Oceania, 134–35. *See also* Commonwealth Caribbean; West Indies
Caribs, 80, 81, 313n1
Cayman Islands, 78, 93, 103 table 3, 297
centralization, 42, 304. *See also* Direct Rule
Césaire, Aimé, 91–92, 97, 99, 100–102
Chad, 29, 63, 64, 311n4
Chagos Islands, 191, 194, 201–2, 238
Chamberlain, M. E., 308
Chandan Nagar. *See* Chandernagor (Chandernagore)
Chandernagor (Chandernagore), 231–34, 301
Charlick, Robert, 36–37, 41, 48, 52, 67, 68
chiefs and chieftaincy: in Africa 13, 30, 36–37, 39, 52–57, 62, 192, 312n13, 312nn18–19; in Britain, 10, 30, 95, 107, 128, 260, 271, 300; and development, 56–57; in France, 107, 195; in Southeast Asia, 242, 245, 251, 252, 253–54, 256, 258, 268, 269–70, 278, 285–86, 324n25; in South Pacific, 137–38, 140, 142, 143, 151–52, 155, 177, 178, 316n20
China: in Indochina, 242, 251, 253, 259, 268, 270–71, 284; in Laos, 243, 266, 323n13; and Mekong, 260–61, 271, 3n17; in Mauritius, 194, 199, 204, 209, 210, 211, 213; in Southeast Asia, 261, 270–71, 284, 323n13, 17; and South Pacific, 182, 225. *See also* Yunnan
Chinese language, 205, 216, 319n8
Ciudad Juarez, 268, 323n18
Cold War, 5–6, 19, 146–47, 201, 242–43, 307–8

colonialism: British vs. French, 8–12, 18–19, 296–99; and communism, 5–6, 307–8; comparative, 5, 15–16, 18, 19–20, 37, 291–92, 296–99; concurrent, 17, 189; hybridic, 17, 59, 237–39, 299, 304; legacies of, 2–13, 19–20, 74, 204, 292–96, 304, 307–8, 310nn5–7; resistance to, 37, 40, 80, 110, 143, 151–52, 152–53, 182, 196, 247–49, 325n2; sequential, 17, 189, 237–39, 304; soft, 299, 301; *tabula rasa*, 80, 214, 296–97. *See also* condocolonialism; education; language and languages; partition; psychology; slavery: legacies of
COM. *See* France: overseas administrative units of
Commonwealth, 12, 125, 136, 182, 228, 287, 310n8
Commonwealth Caribbean, 93–99, 102, 104, 113–14
communism and communists, 6, 72–73, 302, 307–8; in Burma, 246, 247, 273–74, 276–77; and colonialism, 5–6, 307–8; in France, 41; in French West Indies, 90, 92, 96, 96, 101; in Laos, 240, 246, 248, 252, 266, 282–83, 286, 287, 293. *See also* Soviet Union
Comoros (Comoran Islands), 191, 192, 202, 208, 211 table 6, 229, 291, 305, 318n1
condocolonialism, 13, 147–55, 184–87, 299, 318n33, 318n36. *See also* New Hebrides
condominium, 141, 147–48, 150–52, 153, 155, 174, 181, 185, 291, 315n3, 318n34; oral history of, 156–62. *See also* New Hebrides; Vanuatu
Conference of Berlin, 22, 88
Conklin, Alice, 9, 36
Connell, John, 304–5
Cook Islands, 137–38, 145, 183 table 4
Côte d'Ivoire. *See* Ivory Coast
Creole identity: in West Indies, 84, 88, 100, 109–10, 117, 134–35; in Mauritius, 196, 198–210, 213, 215, 221, 225, 299, 301. *See also* Mauritians: Afro-

Creole language: in Mauritius, 195, 206, 220, 226; in West Indies, 77, 80, 86, 129, 192,195. *See also* Kreol
creolization, 100, 297
cricket, 102
cross-border movement: Southeast Asian, 260–61, 265–68, 274, 277, 285, 289; South Indian, 236–37; South Pacific, 298; West African, 26, 59–60, 62
Crowder, Michael, 50
Crown Colonies, 89, 124–25, 242
Cuba, 76, 317n32

Dahomey. *See* Benin
Damagaram. *See* Zinder
decolonization, 1–2, 4–5, 11, 297–98, 308, 309n4; "chaotic," 6; as harlot, 1
de Gaulle, Charles, 91, 96–97, 144
democracy and democratization, 53–54, 72, 86–88, 91, 95–99, 137, 249–50, 303
departmentalization. *See* France: overseas administrative units of
diaspora, 76, 96, 213, 306, 313n1
Diego Garcia, 191, 194, 201–2
Direct Rule, 8, 11; in Mauritius, 214; in Niger, 36–38: in Southeast Asia, 244–45, 287–88; in West Indies, 122. *See also* France: colonial policy of
Djibouti, 325 n2
Dominica and Dominicans, 76, 77, 79 map 9, 85, 86, 88, 90, 93, 99, 103 table 3, 107, 110, 195, 313n1
Dominican Republic, 76, 82
DOM. *See* France: overseas administrative units of
Donnan, Hastings: quoted, 290, 293
Doumer, Paul, 245
drugs and drug trafficking, 260, 263–66, 267, 289

East Africa, 31, 325n2
Easterly, William, 6–7
East Indians, 78, 82, 193, 197–98
economy: colonial, 82–83, 102–5, 120–21, 196; postcolonial, 12, 72, 73, 94, 105, 133, 226, 229, 238, 310n13

ECOWAS, 61–62
education, 13, 292, 293, 307, 312n17: in Barbados, 108, 110, 313n7, 314n23; in Hausaland, 50–52, 312nn16–17; in Martinique, 108, 129, 313n7; in Mauritius, 204–6, 215, 223, 319nn10–11; in New Hebrides, 150, 152–53, 154, 158, 163–64, 172; in Pondicherry, 236; in South Pacific, 144; in Vanuatu, 162–63, 165–68, 299, 316n19
Egypt, 320n14, 325 n2
El Paso, 268, 323n18
English language, 305–6, 307, 325n4; in Mauritius, 199, 204, 205, 221–23, 304; in Vanuatu, 148, 162, 163–68, 173–75
environment, 132–33, 315n25
Equiano, Olaudah, 313n12
ethnic groups and ethnicity, 292, 296–99, 308, 310n12
European Union, 128, 130
Ewe, 26, 83, 84

Fanon, Frantz: quoted, 75, 112, 116
Farquhar, Robert, 192, 197–97
Fashoda, 32
Fiji and Fijians, 140, 141, 142, 146, 183 table 4, 207, 319n14
Fodio, Usman dan, 29, 35
France: colonial policy of, 8–13, 36, 297–98, 304, 309n4, 316n9; communism and communists in, 241; decolonization by, 11, 17, 297–98; First Colonial Empire of, 9, 296–97; Second Empire of, 87; Second Republic of, 87; Third Republic of, 36, 88; Fourth Republic of, 247, 298; Fifth Republic of, 96; "Old Colonies" of, 91, 124, 191, 297; overseas administrative units of, 79–80, 297–300, 304–5, 325n3; and Treaty of Paris (Napoleonic rule), 85, 193, 195, 214, 321n36; Vichy, 25, 40, 246, 309n4. *See also* Direct Rule; French Community; French Revolution; French Union
Francophonie: in Laos, 250, 270, 286–87, 293, 324n22; 325n4; in Mauritius, 204–5, 215–21, 223–25, 238,

319nn10–11; minority status of, 305; in Niger, 50–52, 58, 73; Organization of, 182, 228, 310n8; in Pondicherry, 188, 230–31, 235–36; Summits of, 218, 321n25; as unifier, 293; in Vanuatu, 159, 162–63, 165–68, 170, 175, 176, 180–81, 182, 186, 316n17, 316n19, 318n34, 318n37
French Community, 298
French Guiana, 76, 78,93, 103 table 3, 297
French India, 230–36. *See also* Pondicherry; Pondichéry
French language, 75, 305. *See also* Francophonie
French Polynesia, 136–37, 142, 143, 144, 146, 155, 183 table 4, 298–99
French Revolution, 72–73, 85, 195. *See also* Jacobins
French Southern and Antarctic Lands, 202
French States of America (FSA). *See* France: overseas administrative units of
French Union, 146, 232, 248, 298
French West Africa, 22, 25, 325n1; popular view of, 23 map 2
French West Indies, 78–79; communism and communists in, 90, 92, 96, 96, 101; economy of, 104–5; identity in, 98, independence movement in, 99, 316n10; language of, 86; music of, 313n6; political parties of, 97; slavery in, 84–85; slaves freed in, 86–87; view of Haiti in, 315n25; views of Anglophone Caribbeans in, 313n5; voting in, 87–88, 95–99, 124
Freud, Sigmund, 310n12
Frum, John, 152–53
Fulani, 29–31, 33, 35 map 5, 36, 84, 312nn18–19

Gambia, 25, 26, 47 table 2
gender. *See* women
genocide, 80, 81, 297, 320n20
Germany, 24–25, 137, 141, 143, 191
Ghana and Ghanaians, 25, 26, 47 table 2, 48, 50, 73
Ghosh, Sri Aurobindo, 234, 236, 301

globalization, 13, 19, 132, 306
Gold Coast. *See* Ghana
Golden Triangle, 253–84; alternative name for, 323n6; British-French rivalry in, 251, 253–55, 278–79, 285, 286; boundaries of, 253, 260–63; boundary marker in, 263 fig. 7; capital of, 323n15; Chinese influence in, 286; ethnic groups of, 271–9; hill tribes of, 300, 324n24; oral history of, 256–58, 267, 269, 311n14; statelessness in, 274
Gordon, Arthur, 142
Great Britain. *See* Britain
Grenada, 96, 103 table 3
Grenadine Islands, 78, 103 table 3
Guadeloupe: colonization of, 191–92, 297; culture of, 99–100; East Indians in, 89; as French overseas state, 79–80; French Revolution in, 85–86; geography of, 79, 84, 103 table 3; and Haiti, 129; and Martinique, 112, 202; slavery in, 84
Guinea, 25, 26, 29, 47 table 2, 73
Gujarat and Gujarati, 205 table 5
Guyana, 76, 77, 103 table 3, 297

Hack, Karl: quoted, 1, 252
Haiti, 80; and Barbados, 129–30; development, 80, 103 table 3; earthquake, 315n25; French West Indian view of, 80, 129; geography of, 76; identity in, 80
Harrison, Lawrence, 129–30
Hausa (Hausas), 26, 29–31, in Brazil, 313n1; colonial memories by, 31, 37–39; identity in, 34, 36, 44–45, 46–48; and Islam, 46–47; and Nigerian politics, 42–44; and Nigérien politics, 41–42, 43; political culture of, 44; slaves, 84. *See also* Hausa-Fulani; Hausaland; Hausa language
Hausa-Fulani, 29–30, 33, 39, 44
Hausaland: boundary markers in, 32 fig. 3, 61 fig. 4, 63; and education, 50–52, 312nn16–17; geography of, 35 map 5, 45 map 6; oral history of, 31, 37–39, 44; precolonial, 29–30, 34; rural, 50; women in, 57–59, 312n20

Hausa language, 36, 38, 39, 50–51
Herskovits, Melville, 83–84
Hindi, 203, 205, 206, 220, 221
Hispaniola, 76
Hmong, 243, 250, 263, 264, 272, 283, 286, 301
Holland. *See* Netherlands
Hollande, François, 99
human trafficking, 6, 277–78, 324n28

identity, African, 131, 319n11; black, 91–92, 117, 119; and boundaries, 14; and colonialism, 1–2, 33, 36, 116–17, 296; ethnic; 44–48, 50, 85–86, 276, 283; Melanesian, 302; national, 47–48, 80, 85, 114, 117–18, 149, 243, 292; Pacific, 181; postcolonial, xiii–xiv, xvii, 20, 59, 308; randomness of, xiii–xiv; Tai, 250, 283–84. *See also* assimilationism
Igbo (Igbos, Igboization), 34 map 4, 39, 42–43, 84, 313n1, 313n12
India: Anglo-French rivalry in, 17; and Burma, 242, 247, 253, 264, 287–88; democracy in, 303; migration from, 17, 297; precolonial, 302
Indian Ocean, 294–95 table 9; colonization of, 189–95; geography of, 189–95; and Pondicherry, 238; regional organizations in, 228–30; and West Indies, 188–90, 191, 196, 207, 214, 225, 229
indigenous cultures and peoples: colonial legacies of, 3, 4, 12, 291; partition of, 290–91, 300–301, 311n1. *See also under individual group names*; oral history
Indirect Rule, 8, 11, 30, 170, 311n10–11; in Burma, 244–45, 288; in Indochina, 245; in Northern Nigeria, 30, 37, 39, 53; in Southeast Asia, 244
Indochina, 242–43; anti-French resistance and sentiment in, 298, 322n3; ethnicity in, 243; colonial rule in, 242–43, 245–46; geography of, 242–43; population of, 243; precolonial, 242, 245; U.S. involvement in, 243; and World War II, 242–43

Indochinese: in New Hebrides, 315–16n8
Iraq, xiv
Irawaddy River (Irawaddy Valley), 242, 245, 288
irredentism, 247, 273
Islam: in West Africa, 28–29, 36, 39, 44, 51–52, 57–58, 65–70. *See also* Muslims; sharia
Ivory Coast and Ivorians, 25, 26, 27 table 1, 28, 47 table 2, 48, 50

Jacobins, 85, 195, 281, 293
Jamaica and Jamaicans, 77, 78, 103 table 3, 313n1, 313n5
James, C. L. R., 100–102
Japan and Japanese: and Micronesia, 315n1; and World War II, 246–47
jihad, 29, 35–36
Jordan, xiv

Kampuchea. *See* Cambodia
Kanak (Kanaks, Kanaky), 140, 142–43, 147, 181, 186, 298
Kanuri, 33, 35 map 5, 36, 42
Karen, 245, 249, 280, 283, 302
Karikal, 231, 232, 234
kastom. *See* Vanuatu: custom movement in
Keng Tung, 253, 254–56, 259–260, 264, 268–71, 274, 323n15
Kenya, 11, 325n2
Kerala, 235 table 7, 238
Kiribati, 183 table 4
Kreol, 198, 204, 319nn8–10, 320n19, 321n30

La Guerre, John, 100–101
Lahu, 301
Lake Chad, 34 map 4, 35 map 5; 36, 49 map 7, 62, 311n4; Basin Commission, 61–63
Lamming, George, 99, 100, 314n18
language and languages: and colonialism,75, 292, 305–6; in Africa, 302, 306; in Barbados, 110; in Burma, 242, 244, 271–79, 283, 325n4; in French West Indies, 86; indigenous, 306, 325n4; in Laos, 271–79, 283, 287; in Martinique, 110; in Mauritius, 198,

204–6, 304, 319n8, 320n19; and nationalism, 305–6; in Niger, 33, 35, 36, 58; in Nigeria, 33, 44; in Pondicherry, 235–36; in Pondichéry, 230–2; in West Indies, 75, 86, 115

Lao: as minority group, 278–79, 324n29; percentage in Laos, 243

Laos: chiefs and chieftaincy in, 253–59, 285; colonial status of, 245–46, 323n9; colonization of, 242; communism and communists in, 240, 246, 248, 252, 266, 282–83, 286, 287, 293; development of, 243 table 8, 252, 285, 288; dictatorship in, 303, 324n24; ethnic groups and ethnicity in, 243, 246, 250, 252, 274, 281–84; 301; Francophonie in, 250, 270, 286–87, 324n22; French colonial rule in, 245–46, 251; independence of, 248–50, 252, 323n5; in Indochina, 242–43, 247, 248, 272, 278; languages in, 271–79, 283, 287; migration in, 266, 289; and Myanmar, 240, 260–64, 268, 270–71, 283, 287–89, 325n32; national identity in, 250–53; resettlement in, 282, 324n30; resistance to France in, 248, 287; sex trafficking from, 324n28; and Thailand, 246, 250; and Vietnam or Vietnamese, 247, 248, 249, 251, 265, 286–87; and World War II, 246–47

Last, Murray, 70

League of Nations, 25

Lebanon, xiv

Leeward Islands. *See* Lesser Antilles

legal systems: in Barbados, 125, 126; in Martinique, 123–24; in Mauritius, 199, 320–21n21, 321nn30–31; in Niger, 66–70; in Nigeria, 66–70; in Pondicherry, 236–37

Lesser Antilles, 76, 77 map 8, 79 map 9, 81; and Vanuatu, 134, 135 map 10

liberation theology, 172, 292

Liberia, 311n7

Libya, 317n32

Lini, Walter, 155, 159, 161–62, 172, 177–79, 316n15

Lue, 262, 266, 269, 275–76, 283, 301, 324n26

Lugard, Frederick, 11, 30, 311–12, n10

Macmillan, Harold, 200

Madagascar, 200, 208, 211 table 6, 217, 228–29, 320n17

Maghreb, 325n2

Maguzawa, 36, 46

Mahé (Indian Ocean), 192

Mahé (Pondicherry), 231, 232

Malaya and Malaysia, 241, 241 map 17, 243 table 8, 244

Malayalam, 230, 232

Malaysia, 5, 243 table 8

Maldive Islands, 190–91, 211 table 6

Mali, 25, 28, 29, 47 table 2

Mamdani, Mahmood, 12

Marathi, 205

Marie-Galante, 79

marronage. *See* slavery: escape from

Marshall, A. J.: quote, 134

Martinique: and Barbados, 107–29; 313n12, 320n20; *békés* of, 107, 313n11; colonization of, 85, 107, 109; democracy in, 303; dependency of, 120, 121, 123; development of, 103 table 3, 112; economy of, 107, 108, 305; education, 108, 129, 313n7, 313n7; emigration from, 111; in European Union, 128; French identity of, 108, 109–10, 115–16, 117–18, 313n5; as French overseas state, 108, 124, 127–28; geography of, 78, 79 map 9, 107, 108–10, 301; and Guadeloupe, 202, 225; independence movement in, 128, 313n4; language of, 110; legal system of, 123–24; and Mauritius, 196, 221, 238, 297, 320n20; music of, 100, 313n6; political culture of, 118, 123–24, 126; population of, 107, 111; race and racism in, 112, 113, 114, 116, 129; religion in, 121, 122–23; secularism in, 121; slave legacies of, 112–13, 114–15; slavery in, 84, 110, 313n12; slaves freed in, 115, 195–96; voting in, 95–99, 299–300

Marxism and Marxists, 96, 101, 119, 248, 252. *See also* communism and communists

Mascarene Islands, 297

Mauritania, 25, 29, 47 table 2

Mauritians: Afro-, 193, 194, 197, 198, 203, 206, 207–8, 299, 304, 319n11, 320n14; Catholic, 204, 319n6; Franco-, 193, 198–99, 203; free colored, 319n5; Hindu, 203, 204; Indo-, 193, 194, 198, 299, 319n12; Muslim, 203, 204, 319n7, 320n15; Sino-, 194, 203, 213

Mauritius, 294–95 table 9; as "African" country, 208, 320n16, 322n47; and Barbados, 320n20; and Botswana, 320n14; British colonialism and conquest of, 196–99, 201, 202, 321n36; capitulation by France to Britain in, 193, 195–96, 197; caste in, 203–4; democracy in, 200, 209–11, 237, 304; development of, 211 table 6, 212–15; economy of, 194, 196; education in, 204–6, 215, 223, 319nn10–11; and Egypt, 320n14; emigration from, 212; English language in, 199, 204, 205, 221–23, 304; ethnicity in, 194–95, 197–98, 203, 304; and Fiji, 319n14; and France, 201–2, 229; Francophonie in, 193, 195, 196, 204, 215–21, 216 fig. 6, 239, 305, 319n8, 320–21n21, 321n25; French colonial rule in, 194–96; "Frenglish" in, 223–25; geography of, 193–94, 301; and globalization, 212–13, 229–30; hybridic colonialism in, 196–99, 230, 299, 304; and India, 194, 197–98, 203, 208–9, 213, 228–29; immigration to, 193; independence of, 195, 200, 304; language of, 198, 204–6, 304, 319n8, 320n19; legal system of, 199, 320–21n21, 321nn30–31; and Madagascar, 208, 320n17; and Martinique, 195, 203, 320n20; migration in, 193, 197–98, 208, 213; national identity in, 189, 201; pluralism in, 202–7; political culture of, 206–9; political parties in, 199, 200, 201, 319n13; and Pondicherry, 229–30; and Pondichéry, 197, 229–30; regional memberships in, 228–29; religion in, 199, 203–204; and Réunion, 202, 203, 224, 225–28, 229, 321n36; rivalries in, 194; sequential colonialism in, 230; and Seychelles, 203, 322n43; slavery in, 193, 195–96, 197, 319n5, 320n14; slaves freed in, 193, 195, 197, 318–19n2, 319n12; and South Africa, 229, 322n48; as *tabula rasa* colony, 195, 296; and Taiwan, 320n14; trade in, 213, 228; and Trinidad, 319–20n14; and United States, 201; 320n14; and Vanuatu, 186, 204, 229; and West Indies, 229; and World War II, 200. *See also* Chagos Islands; Diego Garcia; Mauritians

Mayotte, 211 table 6, 305, 318n1

Mbembe, Achille, 4, 11–12, 71

Mead, Walter Russell, 4

Mekong River: as boundary, 13, 181, 289, 301, 240, 254, 259–63, 271, 272, 288, 301, 310n11, 323n8; Chinese blasting of, 271, 323n17; Commission, 270; European explorations of, 253–54, 259; lawlessness along, 267, 288; Quadrangle, 283–84; settlements on, 277; trade on, 265–66, 269, 279, 323n17

Melanesia and Melanesians, 138–42, 306, 315n1

Mexico, 268, 323n18

Micronesia, 315n1

Middle East, xiv, 5

military rule: in Southeast Asia, 240, 249, 270, 280, 289, 32n1; in South Pacific, 140–41; in West Africa, 40–43, 55, 72

miscegenation, 83, 196

mission civilisatrice, 9, 248. *See also* assimilation; France: colonial policy of

Montserrat, 78

Moyne Report, 90, 102–3

Muang Sing, 254–60, 263, 266, 268–70, 276, 323n11, 324n22

music, 68, 69, 100, 116, 174, 313n6

Muslims: in Mauritius, 319n7, 320nn14–15; in Niger-Nigeria, 39; in West Africa, 28–29. *See also* Islam
Myanmar, as opposed to "Burma," 322n1

Nagriamel, 154–55, 159, 185
Naipaul, V. S., quoted: 75, 188
Napoleon, 85, 214, 231
Napoleonic Code, 124, 150, 199
Napoleonic Wars, 321n36
nationalism: in Indian Ocean, 191–92, 201–2; in Southeast Asia, 246, 248, 252, 283; in South Pacific, 141, 145–47, 153–54, 172; in West Africa, 39–41; in West Indies, 94–95, 124, 127–29
Nazism, 91, 96
négritude, 91–92, 117. *See also* Césaire, Aimé
Nehru, Jawaharlal: quoted, 188
Netherlands, 76, 79, 80, 134, 141, 190–91, 194, 196, 322n1
Nevis, 78
New Caledonia, 139–40, 146–47, 186, 298; and Australia, 149; anti-French sentiment in, 143–44; development of, 183 table 4; religion in, 315n5; and Vanuatu, 155, 164, 180–81, 185, 315n6
New Guinea. *See* Papua New Guinea
New Hebrides: administration of, 147–48, 315n3; and Africa, 148, 149, 174; Anglo-French rivalries in, 148–49, 150, 157, 160, 299; anti-settler movements in, 151–52; British policy in, 149–50, 153, 155; cannibalism in, 149–50, 171, 172, 317n28; cargo cults in, 152–53; chieftaincy in, 155; colonization of, 147–50; concurrent colonialism in, 17, 189; custom movement in, 154, 302; economy of, 150, 151; education in, 150, 152–53, 154, 158, 163–64, 172; French policy in, 149, 153, 154–55; independence movement in, 153–55; land issues in, 150, 151, 154; legal system of, 150–51; missionaries in, 148–49, 150, 152, 315n4, 315n7; oral history of, 156–73, 175–76, 311n14, 316n14; political parties in, 154–55; religion in, 148–49, 154; secessionism in, 155, 299, 302, 303; and World War II, 152–53. *See also* condocolonialism; condominium; Vanuatu
New Zealand, 136, 137, 138, 142, 143
Niger: boundary disputes in, 311n6; chiefs and chieftaincy in, 36–37, 38, 52–57; colonization of, 32–33; democracy in, 41–42, 56, 73, 303; development of, 21, 47 table 2, 48, 301, 312n15; French colonial rule in, 31–38; geography of, 21, 35–36; governance in, 54–57; independence of, 33; languages of, 33, 35, 36, 50, 58; legal system of, 66–70; military in, 40–41, 48; nationalism in, 40–41; political parties of, 41, 42; population of, 21; religion in, 36, 46, 57–58, 65–70; school violence in, 312n16; women in, 67; and World War II, 40–41. *See also* Hausa (Hausas); Hausaland; Tuareg; Zarma
Nigeria: boundary disputes of, 311n6; 312n23; British colonial rule in, 24, 29–31; chiefs and chieftaincy in, 30, 39, 53–57, 312n13, 312nn18–19; colonization of, 24, 30; countries bordering, 25–26, 311n4; democracy in, 42, 48, 73, 105; development of, 21, 43, 47 table 2, 301; geography of, 21; governance of, 53–55; independence of, 25, 33; languages of, 33, 44, 50; legal system of, 66–70; military in, 54; nationalism in, 39–41; political parties of, 39–40; population of, 21; religion in, 29, 35, 44, 46, 57–58, 65–70, 311n17, 312n17; women in, 67, 312n20; and World War II, 39–41. *See also* Hausa (Hausas); Hausa-Fulani; Hausaland, Fulani; Kanuri
Niger River, 21
Niue, 183 table 4
Nkrumah, Kwame, 131
North Africa. *See* Maghreb
Nupe, 29, 84

Oceania, 138, 153–54, 181, 188; and Caribbean, 134–35. *See also* South Pacific

"Old Colonies." *See* France

opium. *See* drugs and drug trafficking

oral history: importance of, 3, 5, 12, 13, 290, 308; instances of, 31, 37–39, 44, 155–73, 175–81, 234, 256–58, 267, 269, 311n14

Organization of African Unity, 27

Oyo, 84

Palestine, xiv

pan-Africanism, 39, 131

Papua New Guinea, 183 table 4

partition: of Africa, 24, 27, 88; archipelagic, 15, 188, 134, 301; and democracy, 7, 303; differential impacts of, 6–7, 12, 19, 46, 48, 284, 289, 292–96, 300–302; "double," 83–84, 292; ethnic, 7, 14–15, 83–84, 271–84, 290–92, 300–301, 311n1; of Golden Triangle, 253–60, 268–70; and identity, 14, 16–17, 33–35, 64–65, 74, 292; in India, 231–32, 232, 232 map 15, 233 map 16; in Indian Ocean, 189–94; indigenous perspectives of, 3, 33–34, 44, 290–91, 302, 308; of land, 143, 151; linguistic, 86, 302, 306; maritime, 104, 291, 315n6; multiple types of, 13–15, 26, 83–86, 135, 290, 291–92; reification of people by, 3; slave-based, 75–76, 83–84; of Southeast Asia, 240, 242, 268–71, 284; of South Pacific, 136–41, 186; "triple," 86; of West Indies, 75–80, 85–86; of West Africa, 22–29. *See also* borderlands; boundaries; Vanuatu: condocolonialism

Pathet Lao, 248, 251–52, 266, 283

Pavie, Auguste, 323n8, 323n12

plantation economy, 80–83, 105, 110, 112–23, 140, 142, 151, 188–89, 225, 238, 292, 297, 314n16

political culture, 117, 118; in Barbados, 44, 111, 115, 117–19, 131, 314n16; in Caribbean, 95, 105–7; in Laos, 283; in Martinique, 118, 123–24, 126, 131;
in Mauritius, 206–9, 228; in Vanuatu, 316–17n20

Polynesia and Polynesians, 136–38, 315n1

POM. *See* France: overseas administrative units of

Pondicherry: citizenship in, 230, 236–37, 322n46; colonization of, 231; countercolonialism in, 237, 239; development of, 294–95 table 9; education in, 236; Francophonie in, 12, 231, 233–34, 235–36, 305, 306; geography of, 232 map 15; languages in, 235–36; legal system of, 236–37; and Mauritius, 197, 229–30, 231; oral history of, 234; partition of, 231–32; religion in, 236; respect for dead in, 322n44; and Tamil Nadu, 234–35; Union Territory of, 230, 234. *See also* Pondichéry

Pondichéry, 230–37; anti-British asylum in, 322n45; ethnicity in, 230, 231–32; geography of, 232 map 15; languages of, 230–32; and merger with India, 234, 300, 303; migration from, 197; "soft colonialism" in, 299, 301, voting in, 232–33. *See also* Pondicherry

Portugal, 190–91

postcolonialism, 1, 4, 8, 18, 19, 299–300, 303–5, 309n3; study of, 72

postcolony, 4, 290

precolonial polities: Southeast Asian, 242, 251, 252, 253–60, 268–69; in South Pacific, 142, 143; West African, 23–24, 29–30, 31, 33, 34 map 4

psychology, 9, 13, 75, 112–13, 291, 292, 293, 307, 309n1, 310n12. *See also* dependency

Puerto Rico, 76, 79

race and racism, 25, 81, 83, 312n14, 315–16n8

Rastafarianism and Rastafarians, 116, 122

Rawls, John, 18

religion: 13; in Barbados, 121–22, 314n19; in Burma, 242, 245, 264, 280; in Martinique, 121, 122–23; in Mauritius, 199, 203–4; in New Hebrides, 148–49, 152–53, 154; in Niger,

36, 46, 57–58, 65–70; in Nigeria, 29, 35, 44, 46, 57–58, 65–70, 311n17, 312n17; in Pondicherry, 236; in South Pacific, 186; in Vanuatu, 153, 170–73, 177–78, 293, 299, 315n5, 317n29, 317n31; in West Africa, 28–29. *See also* liberation theology

Réunion, 191–92: British occupation of, 321n36; development of, 211 table 6; as French overseas state, 91, 238, 297; geography of, 193; and Mauritius, 202, 203, 224, 225–28, 229, 321n36

revolution, 18, 286–87, 293–94. *See also* French Revolution

Robinson, Pearl, 72

Rodrigues, 193–94, 225, 297

ROM. *See* France: overseas administrative units of

Rotberg, Robert, 74

Sahara, 21, 23–24, 28, 312n11

Sahel, 22, 23–24, 28, 29, 46, 64, 65

Saints Islands, 79

Salween River, 264, 288

Samoa, 137–38, 145, 183 table 4, 315n1

Sanskritization, 302

Santo, 150, 151–52, 177–78, 318n1

Sarkozy, Nicolas, 98–99

Schoelcher, Victor, 87

Senegal, 25, 26, 29, 44, 47 table 2

Senghor, Léopold, 92

September 11, 2001, 65

Seychelles, 211 table 6, 297, 322n43

Shagari, Shehu, 43, 53–54

Shan, 244–45

sharia, 66–70

Shephard, Tom, 11

Shipway, Martin: quoted, 290

Siam, 251, 253, 255–56. *See also* Thailand

Sierra Leone, 25, 26, 47 table 2

Singapore, 243 table 8

Sip Song Panna, 254, 258–59, 262, 266, 269, 272, 275

slavery: abolition of, 86–87, 194, 297, 318–19n3, 319n12; and colonialism, 16–17, 75, 297; and creolization, 297; cultural affirmation in, 317n24; escape from, 40, 110, 111, 196; in Indian Ocean, 189–90, 194, 195–97, 214, 225; legacies of, 16–17, 74, 75, 84, 87, 105, 112–15, 132, 198, 207–8, 238, 292; restored, 85; trade in, 76, 81–82, 84, 107, 197, 319n12; in West Africa, 31; in West Indies, 75–76, 78, 80–86, 109–10, 114–16, 117, 129–30, 134–35; psychological results of, 75, 105–6, 112–15, 238

smuggling, 6, 59, 288. *See also* drugs and drug trafficking; human trafficking

soccer, 102

Sokoto, 29; empire of, 31, 34 map 4; sardauna of, 40; sultan of, 30, 53, 311n19

Solomon Islands, 183 table 4, 315n6

Somalia, 325n2

Songhay, 33, 34 map 4

South Africa, 180, 228, 229, 322n48

South Asia, 242, 294–95 table 9, 299, 301

Southeast Asia, 294–95 table 9; boundaries of, 240, 244; British colonial policy in, 241–42, 244–45, 251–52; culture of, 296; decolonization of, 247–50, 295–96; ethnicity in, 244; exceptionalism of, 245, 298, 300, 325n4; geography of, 241–44; migration in, 266–8; partition of, 284; population of, 241–42; regional organizations in, 270–71; and South Asia, 242; violence in, 302; and World War II, 246–47. *See also* Indochina

South Pacific, 294–95 table 9; and Africa, 136, 141, 142, 143–44; British colonial rule in, 142, 143–44; and cargo cults, 144–45, 146, 186; colonization of, 135–42; decolonization of, 145–47; education in, 144; French colonial rule in, 142–43, 144; geography of, 135–141, 294–95 table 9; migration in, 298; nuclear testing in, 146, 147, 155; partition of, 134, 136–41, 186; regional organizations in, 181–82; religion in, 186; and West Indies, 134–35; and World War II, 144–45

Soviet Union, 5–6, 308
Spain, 76, 151, 80, 82, 89, 90, 310n10
sport, 102
St. Barthélemy, 79–80
St. Domingue, 84, 313n1. *See also* Haiti
Stephens, Jimmy, 154, 159–60, 172–73, 316n15, 316–17n20
St. Kitts, 77, 103 table 3, 300
St. Lucia, 76, 77, 79 map 9, 85, 86, 88, 90, 93, 103 table 3, 107, 195
St. Martin, 76, 79, 322n2
St. Pierre and Miquelon, 80
St. Vincent, 77, 103 table 3
sugar, 82, 102, 107, 109, 111, 113, 126, 140, 142, 194, 196, 197, 212–13
Suriname, 76, 322n2
Syria, xiv

tabula rasa colonies, 80, 81, 195
Tahiti and Tahitians, 136, 142, 143
Tai, 301
Taiwan, 320n14
Tamil and Tamils, 230, 231–32, 301
Tamil Nadu, 232 map 15, 234–35, 237, 238, 303
Telugu, 205, 230–32
Thailand: Anglo-French rivalry in, 253, 323n7; asylum in, 277, 285; British influence over, 284, 324n31; development in, 266–67, 274, 277–78, 285, 286; French influence over, 254; monarchy in, 285–86; nationalism in, 250
Tibet, 324n23
Togo (Togoland), 25, 26, 47 table 2, 311n6
Tokelau, 183 table 4
Tonga, 137, 182
transborder institutions: of Mekong, 270–71, 323n6; of Niger-Nigeria, 27, 59–64
transborder violence, 64, 71, 240, 253, 266–70, 312n23
Trinidad and Tobago, 77, 78, 82, 96, 103 table 3, 319–20n14
Tromelin Island, 201–2
Tuareg (Tuaregs), 31, 34, 35, 36, 41
Turks and Caicos Islands, 78, 103 table 3
Tuvalu, 183 table 4
Twain, Mark: quoted, 188

United States: and Caribbean, 79, 94, 96, 105–6, 111, 120; and Indian Ocean, 191, 194, 202; in Indochina, 243, 248, 249, 253, 260, 266, 323n13; and Mauritius, 194, 201, 202, 320n14; and Micronesia, 315n1; in New Hebrides, 152–53, 154–55, 315n1; overseas states of, 79; and West Africa, 65, 105; and World War II, 91, 144–45, 152–53, 247. *See also* Cold War
Upper Volta. *See* Burkina Faso
Urdu, 205

Vanuatu: and Africa, 186; Anglophone-Francophone tensions in, 154–55, 159, 161–62, 166–67, 170, 304; chiefs and chieftaincy in, 151, 155–58, 162, 165, 170–72, 177, 178, 180; and Cuba, 317n32; custom movement in, 170–73, 178–79, 302, 316–17n20, 317n27, 317n29; democracy in, 303–4; development in, 182, 183 table 4; education in, 162–63, 165–68, 299, 316n19; English language in, 148, 162, 163–68, 173–75; and Fiji, 185; foreign aid to, 182; Francophonie in, 159, 162–63, 165–67, 170, 175–76, 180–81, 182, 305, 316n19; geography of, 134, 135 map 10, 301, 315n6; independence of, 141, 148–49, 154–55, 176, 316n9; jealousy in, 172; languages of, 162, 168, 173–75, 316n17; and Lesser Antilles, 135 map 10, 185, 297; and Libya, 317n32; and Mauritius, 186; and Mayotte, 318n1; as microcosm of colonialism, 147–48, 187; national identity in, 149, 184–86; and New Caledonia, 155, 164, 180–81, 185, 315n6; political culture of, 165, 316–17n20; political parties in, 154, 176, 318n35; religion in, 153, 170–73, 177–78, 293, 299, 315n5, 317n29, 317n31; rural-urban differences in, 162–69. *See also* condo-colonialism; New Hebrides
Vichy, 25, 40, 246, 266, 309n4
Vietnam: chiefs and chieftaincy in, 245; creation of, 242–43; development of, 243 table 8; and Laos, 247, 248, 249,

251, 265–66, 286–87 265; partition of, 242–43
Vietnamese: in Thailand, 324n28
Virginia, 313n1
Virgin Islands, 79

Wa, 267, 273–74
Wallis and Futuna, 137, 138, 144, 183 table 4
Weber, Eugen, 322n4
West Africa, 294–95 table 9; borders within former French, 25, 325n1; British colonial rule in; 24–25; colonial legacies in, 72–74, 299; colonization of, 22–25, 31–33; decolonization of, 25; ethnic groups and ethnicity in, 26–27, 28; French colonial rule in, 22–24, 25; geography of, 22–24, 28; languages of, 28, 29, 33; migration in, 26; partition of, 22–26, 31–33; partition continuing in, 27–28, 63–64; population of, 29; regional organizations in, 62–63; religion in, 28; and slavery, 31, 292; and World War I, 24; and World War II, 25
West Bengal, 233
Western Samoa. *See* Samoa
West Indies, 294–95 table 9; British colonial rule in, 76–78; decolonization of, 91–95; economy of, 82–83; French colonial rule in, 78–79; and French West Indies, 314–15n24; and Indian Ocean, 188–90, 191, 196, 207, 214, 225, 229; languages of, 75, 86, 115; and South Pacific, 134–35. *See also* British West Indies; Caribbean; slavery
Widner, Jennifer, 12, 73–74, 311n3
Wilberforce, William, 87
Wilson, Thomas: quoted, 290, 293
Windward Islands. *See* Lesser Antilles
women: in Caribbean, 99; in Golden Triangle, 204, 260, 265, 277, 289, 324n28; in Hausaland, 35, 57–59, 67, 312n20
World War II, 25, 39–41, 91, 144–45, 242–43, 246–47, 266

Yanam, 231, 232, 234
Yoruba and Yorubaland, 26, 34 map 4, 39, 52, 83, 84, 296
Young, Crawford, 3–4, 5–6, 16, 72–73
Yunnan, 253, 264, 272, 274, 275, 277, 286

Zarma, 35, 36, 40, 42
Zartman, William: quoted, 309n2
Zimbabwe, 156
Zinder, 31, 34 map 4, 40

www.ingramcontent.com/pod-product-compliance
Lightning Source LLC
Chambersburg PA
CBHW030603230426
43661CB00053B/1819